LECTURES IN THE
PHILOSOPHY OF EDUCATION:
➛➛➛ 1899 ⬅⬅⬅
BY
JOHN DEWEY

LECTURES IN THE PHILOSOPHY OF EDUCATION:

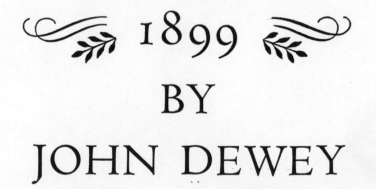 1899

BY

JOHN DEWEY

EDITED AND WITH AN INTRODUCTION

BY

REGINALD D. ARCHAMBAULT

RANDOM HOUSE NEW YORK

370.1
D

ACKNOWLEDGMENTS

The preparation of this manuscript was facilitated by the encouragement and assistance of many people. Mrs. John Dewey gave generously of her time and knowledge in effecting the publication of the work. James H. Stauss, Dean of Grinnell College, was most helpful in providing conditions under which the manuscript could be prepared. Frederick Eby and Dr. W. W. Charters aided greatly in the authentication of the manuscript. Hilmar Sieving, Librarian at the School of Education of the University of Chicago, provided considerable assistance, as did M. Halsey Thomas, Dewey's bibliographer. The staff of the Burling Library of Grinnell College, and especially Richard Ryan, were more than generous in their efforts to procure needed material.

A special note of thanks is due Judith Roberts, of Grinnell College, whose assistance in gathering and validating bibliographical material proved to be indispensable in the editing of this volume.

R. D. A.

PREFACE

I came across this collection of lectures in the Grinnell College library in 1963, while engaged in research for another book on John Dewey. The original document is a hectographed copy of a verbatim stenographic report, by an unknown student, of Dewey's lectures in Pedagogy I B 19 given at the University of Chicago in the winter term of 1898–99. The pages of the original document are brittle, and green print is dim on the yellowing pages, but still clearly legible. The volume was given to Grinnell College by Professor James Simmons who was, in 1899, Professor of Philosophy and Pedagogics there. He had attended the University of Chicago part-time during the years in which Dewey taught there, but he had not attended this particular course. Dr. W. W. Charters explains the existence of the manuscript in this way:

When I went to the Univ. of Chicago in May, 1901, it was already an established custom for some student in Dr. Dewey's classes to take copious notes (in shorthand, always, I think) on the lectures, which was the method Dr. Dewey used in his classes. This student then had his notes duplicated, hectographed, in every case while I was there, and given to each of us who paid a small sum for this service to which we subscribed at the beginning of the course. So far as I know, every lecture course was thus supplied to any student who subscribed. I am sure Dr. Dewey would always have been consulted by the student who wanted to earn the small sums he would realize, probably Dr. Dewey might even select a reliable student to take care of this. Dr. Dewey's lecture method was slow enough for any of us to take complete notes in our own abbreviated style, but we subscribed to the copies, too, to check or supplement our notebooks.[1]

Frederick Eby, another student of Dewey's at the time, maintains that Dewey had the practice of distributing materials to his classes. Sometimes lectures were distributed in condensed form, as in the course which Eby took with Dewey in 1896. He holds a copy of this condensation.[2] The Swen Franklin Parson Library of Northern Illinois University has a duplicate of the stenographic report which serves as the basis for these edited lectures, together with a ten-page summary of the same. There are undoubtedly many other copies of reports of Dewey's lectures still in existence. Grinnell College has, for example, a copy of his lectures in *Social Ethics* delivered at Chicago in the spring quarter of 1898.

There can be little doubt that this document is a faithful report of Dewey's actual lectures. The rhetorical style is obviously Dewey's, with its long and involved sentences, its extended use of modifying phrases and clauses for the sake of avoiding misunderstanding, its tendency toward repetition, and its final logical clarity. In content it is clearly the work of Dewey, completely consistent with his contemporaneous publications and precursive of his later published work. Key treatments, such as that of the reflex arc principle, the theory of habit, and the critique of the culture epoch theory are completely consistent in content and form with accounts published elsewhere.[3] Finally, there is an obvious correlation between the lectures and the syllabus for the course,[4] which was published by the University of Chicago Press, with Dewey as author, and distributed to the students in the course and others.

There are three forms of organization that are involved in the lectures. The first is the organization of the syllabus itself, serving, as it does, as the *intended* form of organization of the course, as it is envisaged in its logical totality. There is, as we have noted, a significant consistency between the course as logically outlined and as actually given. However, the consistency is not complete, and this is due to two factors. The first is that which becomes evident to all university teachers

1 Personal letter to the editor, April 10, 1965.
2 Personal letter to the editor.
3 See Introduction, pp. xv-xxxv.
4 The syllabus is reprinted on pp. 3-11.

at one time or another: the inexorable pressure of time. Dewey simply ran short of time. He was aware of this pressure, making constant references to the plan of the syllabus and finally giving a nod to its "authority" by a hurried critical exposition of Herbart's steps in the last lecture. The second reason for the difference between the development of the final lectures and their planned execution is, of course, allied with the first: Dewey seized upon several topics (*manual training* is particularly worthy of note) that were seen to demand more attention than he had originally decided to give to them.

This discrepancy between syllabus and lectures is interesting and instructive for several reasons. It reflects, first of all, Dewey's concern, often expressed but seldom acknowledged, for the need for clearly delineated aims. The failure to adhere to the program outlined in the syllabus is significant, too, because it is an example of Dewey's insistence upon a flexible procedure in implementing aims, and a reflection of his belief in the reciprocity of ends and means.

In this connection there is one further point that should be particularly noted: the course, as finally given, has a logical coherence of its own. Shifting emphases are woven into a different, but equally coherent whole, so that the end product is an integrated pattern that has unity. This is all the more remarkable when we consider that Dewey used few, if any notes, and that his lectures were largely improvisations.

In addition to these two forms of organization (the planned syllabus and the actual pattern of the completed course) there is a third natural unit, the individual lectures themselves. It is clear that in this course at least, Dewey did not consider the lecture periods, with their obvious limitations of time, as significant units in themselves. He was working from a much broader plan which had a larger unity, and there is little attempt here at giving the individual lectures a unified structure. This too is significant, for it indicates how little regard Dewey paid to teaching as performance. Threads of previous lectures are picked up and quickly woven into the larger pattern that is being developed; major units are introduced in the middle or toward the end of a given lecture. Continuity between lectures is much more important, then, than logical unity within them.

In the editing I have attempted to take these three modes of

organization into account. The first is indicated by an exact
reprinting of the original syllabus of the course. This indicates
the general direction of the course as planned, and the divisions and subdivisions of topics and their treatment as Dewey
envisaged them in outline form. The second form of organization, that of the material as actually presented, is indicated
by the outline of topics treated (the "Abstracted Contents")
which I have constructed after analyzing the entire volume.
As I have said, this treatment is generally similar to, but in
some instances distinctly different from the course as planned.
Thirdly, the lectures, as they were given on separate dates,
are maintained as individual units.

Prior to the text of the lectures, pertinent ancillary material
has been supplied for the purpose of facilitating the analysis
of the lectures. There is first the syllabus with its numbered
headings. These are correlated to the individual lectures as
total units by designations at the head of each lecture indicating those sections of the original syllabus that are treated
within the lecture under consideration.

Following this designation is a brief précis of the general
content of the particular lecture which follows it, indicating
its general subject matter. Both of these are printed as part
of the general outlines prefatory to the lectures, entitled "Contents of the Individual Lectures."

Also supplied is the Abstracted Contents referred to above,
which provides an abstract of topics. This is correlated to the
text at appropriate points within the body of the work. Numerical and alphabetical designations are intended to provide the
reader at each point with appropriate indications of the way in
which any specific section relates to broader phases of the organization of Dewey's ideas. To orient the reader a full designation is supplied at the beginning of each lecture. Thereafter
abbreviated designations are given to indicate the organization
of the ideas presented within the lecture.

Finally an index of names appears at the end of the volume,
to aid the reader in following the treatment of specific figures
and key ideas throughout the text.

Appendices are included in order to assist scholars in interpreting the various aspects of the work. By far the most
important of these is the Amplified Bibliography (Appendix I),

which supplies the bibliographical data for the works that Dewey cited in the original syllabus. It is of major value because it demonstrates the breadth of Dewey's reading in the field, the types of writing that commanded his attention, and the nature of the emphasis that he placed on such writing. The bibliography, as printed in the syllabus, is skeletal. Considerable effort has been expended in finding full and complete citations for the works noted in his bibliography. This has also been done for references within the text itself.

Two shorter bibliographies are included. One is a brief listing of the more important items written about Dewey and his connection with the University of Chicago (Appendix III). The other is a bibliography of writings by Dewey relevant to the lectures (Appendix II). These include writings that are contemporaneous with his tenure at the University and that treat topics discussed directly or indirectly in the lectures. They are provided as a starting place for those scholars who would like to examine treatments of topics in the lectures herewith as compared with those in other of his published works.

Finally, two other appendices are included. One is a reprinting of Dewey's plan for the Department of Pedagogy which he sent to President William Rainey Harper in 1897 (Appendix V). This describes in considerable detail his views of the total function of the department. The other (Appendix IV) is a reprinting, from the Register of the University, of the rationale, course descriptions, personnel, and calendar of the Department of Pedagogy for the year 1898–99.

As to the text itself, there has been very little editing. Infrequently it has been necessary to correct obvious misspellings and obvious mistakes in punctuation, but these instances are rare. In most cases the original punctuation of the stenographer is maintained. The one major exception is the editing of paragraph units which was obviously necessary after a careful logical analysis of the entire work. The stenographer, operating within the context of the individual lectures and under great pressure of time, did not make proper or sufficient paragraph divisions. I have maintained the original paragraph divisions, with only rare exceptions, but I have also added many more that seemed obvious and appropriate.

None of the footnotes in the text are Dewey's. They are all

supplied by me in order to clarify more fully for the reader the references made by Dewey within the text.

It is hoped that this volume, as edited, will serve as an aid in the clarification and interpretation of the canon of Dewey's work on education.

R. D. A.

CONTENTS

INTRODUCTION

1899—Dewey's Milieu

In 1899 John Dewey published a pamphlet through the University of Chicago Press entitled *The School and Society.*[1] This is an important volume, not only because of its popularity (it became something of an immediate "best seller" and was subsequently translated into many foreign languages), but because it is emblematic of many essential aspects of Dewey's approach to education. Its format was significant, for it consisted of three lectures which had been given to interested laymen wherein Dewey had indicated not only the typical practice of schooling prevalent at the time but also the theory of pedagogy that underlay it. The lectures illustrated his view of the relation between theory and practice by drawing out that relationship in the last essay, "Three Years of the University Elementary School." Significantly, Dewey himself was teaching educational theory in the university classrooms and directing the Laboratory School during the same period. In its content the book emphasized the principle encapsulated in its title: that the school, and indeed the intellectual community in general, must be inseparable from the social milieu in which it functions. This principle is applicable to the intellectual contributions of Dewey himself, for he found the genesis of his ideas a result of a need for a "reconstruction of philosophy" forced by the inadequacies of traditional views to account for and cope with new and ever changing realities. It is for this reason that Dewey's educational thought must be seen in the context of the intellectual, social, and specifically educational milieu in which he found himself at the turn of the century. Dewey saw educational theory as a synthesis of philosophy, sociology, and psychology, and formed his own theory in

[1] Chicago: University of Chicago Press, 1899.

considerable part by criticizing the dominant views in these disciplines that were prevalent at that time.

In philosophy Dewey found several major strands of thought which had been inherited from the past and held great sway in his contemporary scene. The major influence of Greek philosophy was still present, not only in philosophy *per se,* but in ancillary areas that stemmed from it and influenced educational policy. Hence in these lectures we see a great deal of attention given to the Greek concept of education, to Plato's psychology of learning, to Aristotle's view of habit, as well as to the "dualisms" of Greek philosophy that Dewey saw as the central and the most dangerous influence in contemporary philosophical thought. For Dewey, stasis, dichotomy, oversimplification and overclassification, and escape from reality were characteristic of this mode of thought and preventive of progress in philosophy or public policy.

But by this time Dewey had mounted his attack on the three major current theories that held sway in departments of philosophy: idealism, empiricism, and Scottish common sense. He had already broken away from the influence of George Sylvester Morris, who was a major proponent of Hegelian idealism and Dewey's mentor at the Johns Hopkins University while Dewey was a Ph.D. candidate from 1882–84. Later he had absorbed and then critically rejected the Kantian idealism of T. H. Green and Edward Caird.[2] These strands of idealism were a dominant force in academic philosophy at the turn of the century, and the general influence of idealism, as well as the incipient attack on it of pragmatism, is symbolized by the presence of the idealist Josiah Royce and the radical pragmatist William James serving together on the philosophy faculty at Harvard at that time. Dewey was later to share James's view that this "noisy and nauseating idealism is an expression of the emotions which would cover and disguise a mixed situation." Dewey soon saw Royce's philosophy of "Loyalty" as an escape from the pressing problems of the real world. Although he would retain the strong Hegelian tendency toward unification and the reconciliation of apparent opposites, its idealistic base was rejected completely.[3]

---

[2] For an excellent discussion of the influences on Dewey's early philosophy, see Morton G. White, *The Origins of Dewey's Instrumentalism* (New York: Columbia University Press, 1943.)
[3] Dewey gives an interesting and lively account of his early career in

Scottish common-sense philosophy was taught to Dewey at Vermont by H.A.P. Torrey. It was a conservative philosophy that helped to reinforce traditional religious beliefs, perhaps because of its heavy emphasis on intuition as a direct means of perception of an objective order. Its main feature was a belief in dualism: of subject and object, body and soul, man and God. Dewey soon rejected this mode of philosophy as he came under the wing of Morris, and in his rejection of it began to build a philosophy of his own which would substitute inquiry for intuition and relatedness for dualism.

Psychology was not yet a fully developed science. G. Stanley Hall, under whom Dewey studied at Chicago, was an early experimental psychologist who would produce many influential followers, and William James had set forth his functional psychology. However, the dominant psychology was empiricistic, atomistic, and analytic. It did not account for, indeed was not even concerned with, the social, which Dewey was coming more and more to believe was crucial to an adequate description of psychological experience. This dominant psychology of the time was non-physiological and non-experimental. It emphasized mental faculties which were said to be strengthened through exercise. It nurtured, Dewey felt, the mind-body dualism.

Social theory and social psychology were equally wanting, in Dewey's view. Herbert Spencer's influence had been pervasive and had culminated in a wide acceptance of Social Darwinism, a theory propagated by William Graham Sumner and emphasizing an extreme laissez-faire theory of government together with a pseudo-revolutionary view that maintained that perfection was inevitable as a result of the "survival of the fittest." In it Dewey found another example of what he considered to be an odious automaticity which, combined with contemporary religion, helped to perpetuate an idea of experience as undergoing, as passive. For Dewey experience consisted in an active process of reconstruction which mediated between the individual and the environment, both physical and social.

These major intellectual influences had made an enormous

"From Absolutism to Experimentalism," in G. P. Adams and W. P. Montague, eds., *Contemporary American Philosophy* (New York: The Macmillan Company, 1930).

impact on educational theory, both directly and indirectly. The Pestalozzian influence had been intermittently effective throughout the century, but its major emphasis on love and on the needs and interests of the child had made inroads into all educational thought. It became most manifest in the popular "child study" movement to which Dewey would pay so much attention in these lectures. In the Pestalozzian doctrine (for that is what Dewey felt it had become in the hands of his followers) he saw an over-sentimentality regarding the child, together with further evidence of the widespread tendency to break down the subject-object relation.

Many of the gains of Pestalozzian theory had been absorbed by Herbartianism. The enormous influence of this doctrine is evidenced not only by its hold on pedagogical theory and its consequent rigid formalization in schools of education, but by the existence and importance of the Herbart Society (later to be named "The Society for the Study of Education"), to which Dewey contributed some of his most important early pieces on pedagogy. He was also a member of its original Executive Council, a body of nine directors. The enormous amount of attention in these lectures to the principles of Herbartianism is evidence of its importance in general, and its influence on Dewey in particular. Again, rigidity of interpretation, atomistic psychology, neglect of the social, and naïve interpretation of certain key points in the original theory (such as the culture epoch) led Dewey to reject much of this popular movement.

However, to speak of Pestalozzianism and Herbartianism as significant movements is to mention the most sophisticated of contemporary educational theory. Dewey's conception of the shortcomings of these views is mild indeed when compared with the relatively uncodified but nevertheless real and influential thinking that actually shaped educational practice at the time. He saw this riddled with erroneous Lockian psychological theory that emphasized drill and routine; the social aspect of learning, he felt, was almost totally neglected; separation of students and curricula gave evidence of a perpetuation of artificial class differences; the entire period of schooling, he felt, was finally artificial.

Dewey found ample evidence in educational practice of the gross inadequacies he found in its theory. In fact, he felt that a true theory of education was virtually nonexistent, and he set out to build a conception of what educational theory might be, not as a separate and complete disciplined study, but as a truly scientific attempt to employ the gains in knowledge and techniques of inquiry from the major scientific disciplines in solving practical problems of educational import.

Dewey's Intellectual Background

His early training had equipped him well for this task. We have seen that the major intellectual trends of the latter nineteenth century had touched him directly through his teachers. The religious background which he described as a "conventionally evangelical atmosphere of the more 'liberal' sort"[4] was sustained by his work at the University of Vermont, where philosophy and theology were inseparable. Here he was influenced by the dominant academic philosophy of the time. His experience as a teacher immediately after graduation had given him a first-hand acquaintance with the actual curricula and methods of secondary education. We have already noted the influence of George Sylvester Morris at Johns Hopkins, but the general experience as a Ph.D. candidate must have had a total impact on his views. For there he met not only Morris, but also William T. Harris, who was to have such a pervasive effect on psychology, and Charles Sanders Peirce, whose philosophy of pragmatism, with its central focus on doubt and inquiry, was to prove of crucial significance in Dewey's development.

After receiving his degree from Johns Hopkins in 1884, Dewey became an Instructor in Philosophy at the University of Michigan. This was his permanent position (except for a brief stint at Minnesota) until his appointment to the University of Chicago in 1894. It was at Michigan that he held a chair in Philosophy and Education, a situation symbolic of his belief in the intimate relation between the two. It was there too that he met George Herbert Mead, whose seminal views on social psychology proved to be so instrumental in developing his own theory of education. Again, the isolation of the individual from his environment characterized descriptions of mental activity. From Mead, Dewey took over the idea of the essential importance of the environment in its organic relation to the de-

4 *Ibid.*

velopment of the individual, a stress which begins in practically his first utterance in these lectures and remains a basic leitmotif throughout them.

It was at Michigan, too, that Dewey's tendency toward merging the theoretical and practical became clearly manifest. There was a close relation between the University and the state school system and he participated in meetings, conventions, and institutes devoted to the improvement of public education.

The Chicago Experience

We see, then, that Dewey, by the time he arrived at Chicago, had already formed a firm basis for his philosophy of experimentalism with its merging of the logical, psychological, and social. What emerged was a view that was highly critical of the strains of thought dominant at the time, and highly receptive to the new psychology of James and Harris, the social significance in the thought of Mead, and the logic of pragmatism of Peirce. But it was not merely eclectic. It also manifested a truly inventive quality of its own which was due in great part to Dewey's truly pragmatic temper, which enabled him to reconcile and synthesize the several strands of modern thought that were emerging at the time. Education served as a prime focus in this regard.

This development of those unique features of his thought which would allow him to arrive at a consistent and synthetic philosophy based on a pragmatic temper, an experimentalist approach, and a sociological framework are evident in the progress and the variety of his writings from 1882–94. His early work is strikingly conservative in some respects, particularly with regard to his sympathy with idealism and his concomitant acceptance of conventional religious thought. But characteristic innovations are common, even in the early years. In "The New Psychology" (1884)[5] we find an early attack on empiricism and a proposal for a biological framework that would be basic to functional psychology. Between 1887 and 1889 Dewey published three books, *Psychology*,[6] *Leibniz's New*

5 *Andover Review*, II, September, 1884, pp. 278–289.
6 New York: Harper and Brothers, 1887.

Essays,[7] and *Applied Psychology* (with J. A. McLellan)[8] all of which constituted an attack on dualism and formalism. In his "Logic of Verification" (1890)[9] he attempts to sytematically merge "idea" and "fact," maintaining that theories and facts are reciprocal. In 1894 he published *The Study of Ethics*[10] in which he describes valuing in terms of mediation between native impulses and social consequences. He had not yet begun a systematic application of these principles to education, but his continuing interest in education is evidenced by his intermittent articles on school practice.

Dewey joined the faculty at the University of Chicago in 1894. His daughter Jane Dewey tells us that "One of the factors leading to [the offer's] acceptance was the inclusion of Pedagogy in the department with Philosophy and Psychology."[11] It was at Chicago that he would have an opportunity to demonstrate the reciprocal relationship between theory and practice by founding the "Laboratory School," which he headed from 1896 until 1904, when he left Chicago for Columbia University. It was during the Chicago years that the essential outlines of his philosophy became fully formed. Morton White marks the publication in 1903 of Dewey's *Studies in Logical Theory*[12] as the point of Dewey's final and complete break with idealism and as the first full statement of his instrumentalism.[13] The change, of course, was gradual. Dewey himself says, "I drifted away from Hegelianism in the next fifteen years [after his initial contact with Morris in 1884]; the word 'drifting' expresses the slow and, for a long time, imperceptible character of the movement, though it does not convey the impression that there was an adequate cause for the change."[14]

7 *Leibniz's New Essays Concerning the Human Understanding* (Chicago: S. C. Griggs and Co., 1888).
8 Boston: Educational Publishing Co., 1889.
9 *Open Court*, IV, April 24, 1890, pp. 225–228.
10 *The Study of Ethics: A Syllabus* (Ann Arbor: Register Publishing Co., 1894).
11 Jane Dewey, "Biography of John Dewey," in P. A. Schilpp, ed., *The Philosophy of John Dewey* (Evanston: Northwestern University Press, 1939), p. 27. This is an authorized biography by Dewey's daughter, checked and approved by him.
12 (Chicago-University of Chicago Press, 1903).
13 White, *op. cit.*, Chapter Ten.
14 "From Absolutism to Experimentalism," in Adams and Montague, pp. 20 f.

This would suggest that at the time of these lectures Dewey had reached a climactic point in the development of his basic view of philosophy. In 1895 he had taken a major step in his publication, with James McLellan, of *The Psychology of Number*,[15] significant because of its seeking into the origins of a formal concept through the evolutionary method. In 1896 his epoch-making critique of contemporary psychology appeared in "The Reflex Arc Concept in Psychology,"[16] wherein he stressed the intimate relation between environment and individual as a basis for correlation.

But the interesting thing to note is that in 1894 there is a significant shift in emphasis in Dewey's writing. He becomes preoccupied by educational theory, and in fact uses the educational context as a means of working out his basic philosophical ideas. Given the course which his philosophical development was taking, this seemed to him to be a natural thing to do. In his autobiography he later explained the significance of his interest in educational theory:

> While I cannot write an account of intellectual development without giving it the semblance of a continuity that it does not in fact own, there are four special points that seem to stand out. One is the importance that the practice and theory of education have had for me: especially the education of the young, for I have never been able to feel much optimism regarding the possibilities of "higher" education when it is built upon warped and weak foundations. This interest fused with and brought together what might otherwise have been separate interests—that in psychology and that in social institutions and social life. I can recall but one critic who has suggested that my thinking has been too much permeated by interest in education.[17]

The Psychology of Number deals in great part with problems of pedagogy, beginning with a general statement concerning the ways in which psychology can be helpful to the teacher. In the "Reflex Arc" we find the chief examples of the principle

15 J. A. McLellan and John Dewey, *The Psychology of Number and Its Applications to the Methods of Teaching Arithmetic* (New York: D. Appleton and Co., 1895).
16 "The Reflex Arc Concept in Psychology," *University of Chicago Contributions to Philosophy*, I, 1896, pp. 39–52.
17 "From Absolutism to Experimentalism," in Adams and Montague, p. 22.

of learning as co-ordination or reconstruction culled from problems of early child training. These are the critical years in the development of Dewey's theory of education and they are marked by the publication of articles of central importance: "Interest as Related to the Training of the Will"[18] and "Interpretation of the Culture Epoch Theory,"[19] (1896); "Ethical Principles Underlying Education"[20] and "My Pedagogic Creed"[21] (1897); and, in 1899, the key statement, *The School and Society*. It is through these works that Dewey was developing an approach to central problems: the importance of the merging of habit and purposive activity through an analysis of moral instruction; the relation between the individual and the social through an analysis of the dual function of education; the merging of subject and object through the interpretation of learning as reconstructive adaptation. This, then, was a period in which old views were being overturned through critical analysis, recent formulations were being consolidated, and new directions in Dewey's thought were being forged. All of these facets of Dewey's development are in evidence in these lectures.

Dewey's appointment at Chicago was as head of the Department of Philosophy, Psychology, and Pedagogy, an appointment symbolic of the range and interrelatedness of his interests. He was to distribute his time along the continuum of theory and practice ranging from instruction in graduate seminars in epistemology through classes in the philosophy of education to courses in the methods of instruction and finally to the directorship of the experimental school. Hence this reciprocity between theory and practice is evident in the very rhythm of his professional work. He was drawn to Chicago not only by the promise of a laboratory school, but also by the attraction of advanced classes, stimulating colleagues, and a vital university atmosphere. President Gilman seems to have taken some effort to provide him with conditions that would stimulate and satisfy him, even to the extent of allowing his wife to be the principal of the Laboratory School. His colleagues in

[18] National Herbart Society, *Second Supplement to the Herbart Yearbook for 1895* (Bloomington, Illinois, 1896), pp. 209–255.
[19] *Second Yearbook of the National Herbart Society* (Bloomington, Illinois, 1896), pp. 89–95.
[20] *Third Yearbook of the National Herbart Society* (Chicago: 1897), pp. 7–34.
[21] New York: E. L. Kellogg and Co., 1897.

the philosophy department would serve as source of nourish-
ment for him. George Herbert Mead had left Michigan to join
the staff at Chicago. In 1899, when these lectures were given,
he had, in addition to Mead, as colleagues in the Department of
Philosophy, James H. Tufts, with whom he collaborated on
the *Ethics*,[22] James R. Angell, a major proponent of functional
psychology, and Addison Moore, a radical pragmatist. These
men were to prove to be positive influences on his development.
In the Department of Pedagogy the influences were not so positive. Throughout these lectures we find critical references to
Wilbur S. Jackman, the most noted of his pedagogical colleagues. These criticisms are typical of Dewey's attitude toward most of his contemporary educationist colleagues.
However, another colleague was Ella Flagg Young, who taught
pedagogy and helped to direct the Laboratory School. Jane
Dewey tells us that "He regards Mrs. Young as the wisest person in school matters with whom he has come into contact in
any way."[23] Outside the University there were other stimulating
people, including Jane Addams, who ran Hull House, and
Francis W. Parker, who was principal of the Cook County
Normal School and director of its influential practice school.
These influences, both positive and negative, weave themselves
through these lectures.[24]

The Department of Pedagogy was not without plan. The
Register of the University describes the general aims of the department and emphasizes that there is no discipline of "abstract
pedagogy" and that educational theory can only be studied in
relation to, and after a thorough grounding in, the "parent disciplines" of philosophy and psychology, since educational issues are related to problems of epistemology, psychology,
ethics, and their backgrounds in history.[25] Hence we see the reflection of Dewey's emphasis on the need for the nurture of
educational theory by the established disciplines. For the bal-
ancing emphasis we must look to his "Plan for Organization of
Work in a Fully Equipped Department of Pedagogy."[26] After
outlining the importance of the parent disciplines and the

22 New York: Henry Holt and Co., 1908.
23 Jane Dewey, in Schilpp, p. 29.
24 For reference to background material relevant to Dewey's years at the
University of Chicago, see Appendix III.
25 See Appendix IV.
26 See Appendix V.

scientific approach to pedagogy, he calls for the "speedy inauguration" of two further phases: a manual training school, and a director of supervision for a planned program of practice teaching in the Laboratory School. In these proposals we see again the Deweyan emphasis on the practical context for the application of educational theory. The theory, then, is a midpoint between abstract scientific investigation on the one hand, and practical application on the other, and the reciprocity between the two gives educational theory its validity. The focus on manual training is worthy of note, since Dewey gives such strong emphasis to it in these lectures. It is stressed because for Dewey it symbolizes the merging of the theoretical and practical, the individual and the social, the intellectual and the manual; and it stresses the importance of knowing how—of translating knowing into doing.

It is in this setting that the lectures must be read and understood.

The Lectures As a Critique

The above account, necessarily condensed and impressionistic, of the milieu in which these lectures were given will perhaps help to indicate some of the reasons for the emphases that we find within the lectures. Dewey found many of the theories that were prevalent in his day grossly deficient; we could not hope to discuss all of them in detail: Bain's conception of a narrow science of education; G. Stanley Hall's preoccupation with child study; Spencer's narrow view of evolution; Harris's artificial basis for co-ordinating studies; and there are many more. Each receives its attention here and serves as an irritant to move Dewey to his own interpretations. But these are merely individual instances and examples of the more general deficiencies in viewpoint that Dewey found to be characteristic of contemporary educational theory. They can be briefly noted.

Dewey's antagonism toward dualisms has already been mentioned and that between theory and practice has been underscored. But in these lectures the split between the individual and social is considered of central importance. The reciprocal relation between the two would, of course, serve as one of the key levers of Dewey's philosophy throughout his life, but here it is given intensive emphasis in every facet of the lectures, serving as a theme for the entire course. This was, after all, the age of reform, and Dewey's statements at this time were polemical. He was interested not only in the statement of philosophic truth, but also in the betterment of society, and he saw education as the chief vehicle for social improvement. Hence his conception of the social side of education is translated into indictments of class divisions and their perpetuation through the medium of education itself. And the notion worked its way into his more detailed analyses of specific educational issues: the management of the curriculum, the organization of learning, the growth and maturation of the student.

A second focal point was Dewey's conception of the inadequacies of the scientific bases of contemporary educational theory. His sustained attack on Herbartianism can best be seen as a critique of merely rationalistic science. The center of scientific thought, he says, is to be found in its method, and this method should aim at breaking down rigid classification, going beyond mere surface phenomena, and formulating new and flexible modes of generalization. In educational theory, science was being treated in only a superficial sense. Observations of culture "epochs" were translated grossly into phases of child development; observations of occupations led to an immediate inference regarding corollary games. The examples could be and are multiplied many times. But the most important example is the use of psychology itself. Contemporary psychology is seen as dualistic, separating mind and body, or individual and environment, and hence able to give no true account of "mental" phenomena. Its scope is limited, and this limitation leads to the bifurcation of the world which science ought ideally to unify. The result is a plethora of artificial, rigid, and hence inapplicable principles of education.

The third general emphasis in the lectures is on the contemporary divorce of subject matter and method. Dewey saw typical educational theory and practice as presenting the whole paraphernalia of instruction as external factors to be somehow absorbed by the child. Principles were invoked to facilitate this process of absorption. Indeed, subject matter and method were commonly conceived to be components of the *teacher's* repertoire of activities representing the logical and psychological aspects of instruction, which was in turn equated with education. For Dewey, subject matter was seen as properly representing the content of social life, and method the capacities of the child. Now the two components, considered individually, were to be redefined. Subject matter was not to be considered an arbitrarily selected body of data or principles merely abstracted on logical grounds, but rather as a distillation of the social life of the race generated in conflict and struggle. And method was to be properly seen as the means by which the child actively experienced this content by merging impulse and desire with the problems that social life set forth.

Now we see that we have come full circle, for we are back to the attack on the separation between the individual and social. Properly so. For we can see the organic relationship between even the most basic of principles.

Positive Emphases in the Lectures

The lectures are not concerned exclusively with negative criticisms of educational practice or even with rebuttals of the more sophisticated views of others. They are a vehicle for building Dewey's own views. And just as the primary focus for attack is philosophic dualism, the chief basis on which the positive theory is built is unity, organism, or balance. Here Dewey describes education as an ideal balance of conditions, a merging of the apparently divergent aspects of experience. This notion was to govern Dewey's thinking for the remainder of his career.

We have mentioned some of Dewey's publications in the years prior to or contemporaneous with these lectures. They certainly represent a foreshadowing and a supplement to the views that he expresses here, and it will be seen that there is a basic consistency between his views as expressed here and those in his current publications. However, there are emphases here that are more explicit than those found in other publications.[27]

There is here an informality of tone and a more impressionistic approach to material, and with these a tendency to deal in practical applications of principle. In this document we have a far more explicit statement of Dewey's views on the specific subjects in the curriculum than we find elsewhere in his

[27] For an annotated list of selected contemporary writings by Dewey relevant to these lectures, see Appendix II.

published work. There are exhaustive analyses of the place of literature, science, and history at every level of instruction. And there are detailed prescriptions of all sorts, dealing with the provision for individual differences, procedures for grading and promotion, and the place of play and games. Dewey's philosophical inclination was toward the practical, and this was reinforced by the implementation of his views in the Laboratory School. Yet we can see that there was a great deal of reciprocity between this practical aspect and the theory of education that he was developing in his course work, for the practical implications of his position are illustrated at every turn.

This is related, in turn, to another major emphasis—the preoccupation with method. For Dewey, method represented the manner of study and learning of the individual pupil, whom Dewey considered to be the forgotten personage in the educational enterprise. The entire repertoire of theory and policy, he felt, had been turned against the student, so that even theories which aimed to be child-centered neglected the individual in their quest for formal organization. For Dewey, method is the child's way of doing, of reacting, of reconstructing experience, of grappling with his environment. Teaching methodology, properly conceived, is the facilitation of the student's inquiry, the catalyzing of his interest, the stimulus toward the co-ordination of his impulses and aims. So we have a wealth of suggestions with a great cache of examples to illustrate how this basic theoretical concept can be translated into specific phases of classroom methodology.

Dewey's theory of method is, of course, directly related to his notions of educational psychology. Just as method represents the treatment of the individual as seen in his relation to the social, so psychology must serve as the theoretical basis for this aspect of the educational process. Hence we find a heavy emphasis on the psychological, but again in a very practical context. Psychological discussions are often couched in pedagogical terms: direct and indirect suggestion, expression, construction, modes of generalizing material. What is being developed here in great and specific detail are the principles that later are set forth in a more general way in his major treatise on educational method, *How We Think*.[28] The central focus of interest in his general psychological treatment is, as

28 Boston: D.C. Heath and Co., 1910.

we have noted, his theory of co-ordination, expressed in terms of his criticism of the reflex arc. It is here that he sets the essential learning situation as a biological-evolutionary one and finally abandons all vestiges of idealism as a philosophical-psychological explanatory construct. This is seen not only in the principle of co-ordination itself; it is reflected in Dewey's treatment of habit and his treatment of imagery. In Gordon Allport's discussion of Dewey's psychology in the retrospective Schilpp volume, he says:

> Dissatisfied with the reflex-arc, Dewey felt his way toward a unit that might better express the circuit character of all behavior. Twenty-six years after his attack upon the reflex-arc he finally proposed habit as the unit most suitable for psychology to employ. . . . When between 1917 and 1922 he decided to dispense with instincts, the need for a dynamic unit, one that should be "assertive, insistent, self-penetrating" became all the more urgent.[29]

Allport then goes on to quote a crucial passage from page 41 of *Human Nature and Conduct,* which he uses to characterize Dewey's "finally formed" theory of habit and his attack on the notion of habit as routine.[30] Yet a careful reading of Dewey's treatment of habit in these lectures reveals not only that his essential approach to habit was formed by 1899, but also that the very wording of his treatment here is strikingly similar to that in the later work. (See particularly sections IV. B. 4. and I. B. 3.) This is but one example, as we shall see, of many foreshadowings of later treatments of key concepts that are to be found here.

The treatment of imagery here is especially worthy of mention, for its treatment here is a clear precursor of Dewey's analysis of the relation between image and idea in logic which appeared in the climatic *Studies in Logical Theory* in 1903.[31] In the lectures below we find, in characteristically practical terms, an extended treatment of the stages of the growth of imagery in the child, and a full description of the genesis of the image as a result of the individual's confrontation with an irritating and hence meaningful problematic situation.

[29] Gordon W. Allport, "Dewey's Individual and Social Psychology," in Schilpp, p. 270.
[30] *Ibid.,* p. 271.
[31] *Op. cit.*

There are three other central points of emphasis in these lectures which can be mentioned briefly. First, growth emerges as a mature concept, reflecting Dewey's complete conversion to the biological context of description. This central concept of growth, of course, was to emerge as the basic concept in his magnum opus, *Democracy and Education*,[32] in 1916. The treatment of discipline is a second point of emphasis. The Deweyan notion of discipline as a subordinate consideration is amply in evidence here. Discipline is not formal, external, or separate. It is related intrinsically to ongoing activities directed toward growth. It is not separate from freedom but inextricably bound up with it. Its meaning is to be found in the reciprocal relation between interest and effort. Finally, the essential features of Dewey's view of moral education are manifest at numerous points. Again, all education is moral. The true meaning of moral experience is found in the way in which ordinary problems are confronted and solved. Hence we see that manual training, which was commonly looked upon as specialized, separate, and morally neutral, should serve as a primary vehicle for moral education in that it would provide the means for unified and responsible activity directly related to realistic social and occupational situations. History and literature, traditional vehicles of moral content in education, on the other hand, are seen as less conducive to providing moral development because of their abstract and indirect character.

Precursors of Future Ideas

We have noted some of the aspects of this work that serve as precursors of future ideas: the treatment of habit and imagery, the focus on growth. There are many others. Dewey's development was, of course, continuous, and it would be dangerous to cite one work such as this as an isolated milestone in the development of his key ideas. However, there is considerable evidence that Dewey used his classroom lectures as a means for working out concepts that would later be elaborated in his published works. Jane Dewey tells us:

> For a number of years Dewey gave during the three winter quarters courses entitled "psychological ethics," "the logic of ethics," and "social ethics." The first of those courses was a further development of the principles set

32 New York: The Macmillan Company, 1916.

forth in his *Study* published in Ann Arbor: it developed moral theory in terms of an interplay of impulses, habits, desires, emotions, and ideas. The material of this course provided the background of *Human Nature and Conduct*, which he published many years later. The course in the "logic of ethics" gave an analysis of the categories of end, standard, principle, and obligation, in terms of distinctive functions of resolution of practical problems arising from a conflict of incompatible desires and purposes.[33]

What we have in the course herein in Philosophy of Education is an obvious attempt to bring these principles, developed in the more abstract courses in philosophy, to bear on the central practical problems of education.

And Dr. W. W. Charters, who was a student of Dewey's at that time, writes:

Since Dr. Dewey did not use notes in his lectures, and always talked as if he was only thinking through his ideas, I am sure he used the hectographed records as the basis for his books. In fact, I recognized the material when I read the books later, and could usually find in my notes, almost verbatim, the paragraphs in his lectures, integrated in the developed ideas in his books.[34]

What we have here, essentially, is the pilot study for the *Democracy and Education* of 1916. Again, Jane Dewey writes:

How We Think and *Democracy and Education*, written after Dewey was at Columbia University, are direct fruits of his Chicago experience. His own work and his contacts with others led to a fusion in them of his educational and philosophical ideas; he expresses, in *Democracy and Education*, the opinion that philosophy itself is "the general theory of all education," taking education in a sense broad enough to include all the factors that serve to shape the disposition, emotional, intellectual, and active, of the individuals who constitute society.[35]

And Dewey himself writes:

Although a book called *Democracy and Education* was for many years that in which my philosophy, such as it is,

---

[33] Jane Dewey, in Schilpp, p. 32.
[34] From a personal letter to the editor, April 10, 1965.
[35] Jane Dewey, in Schilpp, p. 33.

was most fully expounded, I do not know that philosophic critics, as distinct from teachers, have ever had recourse to it. I have wondered whether such facts signified that philosophers in general, although they are themselves usually teachers, have not taken education with sufficient seriousness for it to occur to them that any rational person could actually think it possible that philosophizing should focus about education as the supreme human interest in which, moreover, other problems, cosmological, moral, logical, come to a head. At all events, this handle is offered to any subsequent critic who may wish to lay hold of it.[36]

An analysis of the content of the two works yields striking similarities, for the core of the later work is to be found in these lectures. Not only is the general approach similar, but also specific treatments of the value of certain subjects, of the method of creating interest, of the mode of discipline, are strikingly similar.

However, the differences are real and equally significant. There is a difference in tone and style. The method of the lectures is direct, informal, often anecdotal. Dewey's career was in part that of an academic philosopher and in part that of a social reformer. In the lectures the constant emphasis on reform is most apparent, and it is through this concentration on the deficiencies in contemporary theory and practice that the positive statements of position are formed and grouped. Points are stated and restated, emphasized and re-emphasized, always with apt illustrations culled from current practice. Contemporary theorists are attacked with regularity: Harris, Hall, Bain, Baldwin, and many others.

There is a difference, too, in content. Many of the points made in the lectures seem exaggerated when compared with their treatment in later works. There are various examples, but the treatment of Herbartianism is most illustrative. Dewey's preoccupation with Herbartianism was pronounced, and this is an indication of the extent to which this doctrine, with its formalisms, had taken hold of current educational theory. In his typical fashion, which indeed reflected his own view of learning and change, Dewey used this theory with all of its

[36] "From Absolutism to Experimentalism," in Adams and Montague, pp. 22 f.

appurtenances as a focal point. He used it as a basis for his reconstruction of educational theory, now attacking its apperceptive psychology, now challenging its theory of the formal recitation, now attacking its theory of correlation, then criticizing its theory of the culture epoch. For Dewey saw Herbartianism, particularly as it had become hardened and formalized in the hands of its American interpreters, as a halfway house between a traditional and a truly modern educational theory. This was typical of Dewey's approach. As a focal point for attack he used not the obvious excesses and abuses of uninformed practice, but the most sophisticated doctrines available, and in doing so used them, at each point, as a lever for working out his own ideas. By 1916 Herbartianism is no longer a vital force in educational theory and it receives very little attention in *Democracy and Education*. Here it serves as a vehicle for the generation of those ideas that would supplant it and become the basis for the accepted modern theory of education.

Similarly, there are many other shifts of emphasis. Manual training, which plays such a central role here, later receives much less attention as such. The superficial aspects of manual and vocational work are later de-emphasized, and the more logically central notions of experimental learning take their place. The treatment of imagery, which serves here as a vehicle for Dewey's final rejection of idealism, also becomes de-emphasized and absorbed into a new experimental logic in which the psychological, physical, and the rational are united. On the other hand, some notions which are introduced here are later given greater emphasis and a more central role in Dewey's theory. The treatment of Greek dualism which appears but intermittently here becomes a central focal point in the 1916 work, and a major premise in *Reconstruction in Philosophy*[37] in 1920. The merging of subject matter and method, treated in extended form in the lectures, becomes a central consideration in his later treatments of education, extending to his clarification and reiteration of his position on this issue in *Experience and Education*,[38] in 1938. The treatments of habit, impulse, co-ordination, and growth have already been mentioned.

[37] New York: Henry Holt and Co., 1920.
[38] New York: The Macmillan Company, 1938.

Conclusion

Here, then, we have a work unique in the Dewey canon in both its style and content, at once illustrating the stage of development of a seminal mind coming to maturity, and the process of a mind at work, "as if he was then only thinking through his ideas." The complexity of the ideas, and the complicated and only finally coherent rhetoric apparently served sometimes as more than a challenge to his students. Again Dr. Charters writes:

> One summer quarter (1901) Dewey's course was based on Berkeley, Royce and Hume—a tough course, later the basis for *Studies in Logical Theory*. One reason why it was so difficult for us was that Dewey was still fumbling his way from his earlier Hegelian psychology to his later pragmatism.[39]

There is some irony in the readily apparent contradiction between Dewey's preachment and his practice regarding educational methodology. Mrs. Charters says:

> There was one class, in which a book was used as a text, Jane Addams' *Democracy and Social Ethics*, and Jane Addams was invited to meet the class and we all, for the one and only time, had general class discussion throughout the course.[40]

Another former student, Harold Larrabee, remembers Dewey this way:

> In the classroom, Dewey seemed to possess almost none of these pedagogical essentials. There were none of the recommended "lecture techniques" or histrionic devices of the education courses, to say nothing of today's "battery of visual aids to instruction." His appearance was farmer-like, weather-beaten, and utterly unpretentious. Some of his women students said that they found it hard, occasionally, to repress a desire to straighten up his neckties. He remained seated throughout the hour and seldom seemed to be looking directly at his audience. Often he

39 W. W. Charters, letter, April 10, 1965.
40 *Ibid.*

would turn in his chair and glance sideways, as if half-looking out the window and half-absorbed in his private thoughts. His facial expression was solemn, though it lighted up at times with something like a chuckle, and occasionally his hand would ruffle his shock of hair or tug at his moustache. Questions from the floor were not exactly discouraged, but they were not invited.[41]

And in an attempt to explain Dewey's enormous effect on his students, Larrabee says:

> His students came to recognize that an hour listening to Dewey was an exercise in "man thinking." They saw a well-stocked and original mind, remarkably free from any sort of bias or prejudice, engaged in the patient and honest exploration of "whole situations" in experience with the aid of penetrating distinctions and a full-fledged "theory of inquiry."[42]

These lectures certainly give ample evidence of that quality.

In the intricate meaning of his ideas, in the subtle and inventive attempt to relate them to considerations of central practical import, we have here a wealth of materal for Dewey scholars that should not only shed light on the historical development of his thought, but also clarify many of the facets of his thinking that seemed vague in the context of his formal publications. There is, for example, a striking consistency between the educational theory presented here and the clarification of his mature position in *Experience and Education* in 1938. These lectures should help to shed light on the subtle and rich centers of Dewey's educational thought.

REGINALD D. ARCHAMBAULT

Providence, Rhode Island
September, 1965

---

[41] H. A. Larrabee, "John Dewey as Teacher," *School and Society* (October 10, 1959), LXXXVI, p. 378.
[42] *Ibid.*, p. 380.

LECTURES IN THE

PHILOSOPHY OF EDUCATION

⇶ 1899 ⇷

BY

JOHN DEWEY

SYLLABUS

THE UNIVERSITY OF CHICAGO

PEDAGOGY 1 B 19. PHILOSOPHY OF EDUCATION.

BY JOHN DEWEY.

1898–1899—Winter Quarter.

A. The Nature and Process of Education.

I Its Conditions. (1) An educable being (See *Fiske,* The Meaning of Infancy, in Excursions of an Evolutionist; also, Destiny of Man, pp. 35–76; *Butler,* The Meaning of Education, pp. 3–34); (2) a social standard, or determining habits.

II Informal Education. (1) A process (a) of growth, (b) of adjustment. Possible conflicts. (2) Modes of Informal Education; (a) Stimulation; (b) Imitation (*Baldwin,* Mental Development, 81–91; 263–366; *Harris,* Psychological Foundations of Education, pp. 295–305 and N. E. A. Proceedings, 1895, p. 637; *Royce,* Century, May, '94); (c) Suggestion (*Baldwin,* ch. vi; Pedagogical Seminary, vol. 4, article by *Small; Thomas,* La Suggestion); (d) Influence of Environment; (e) Conscious Communication. (3) Types in Stationary and Progressive Communities.

III Formal Education. (1) Relation to Informal; (2) Education and instruction—place and function of knowledge. (Brunetiere, Education et Instruction); Herbart, Science of Education, chs. i and ii, and Bk. II, ch. iv; Herbart Year Book, Fourth Year, Article by Seth.

IV Resulting Conceptions. Definition, (1) Two Aspects: Individual and Social. (2) One-sided Definitions from this standpoint. (3) Break-down of Individualtic Definitions. (4) Of Sociological. (5) Current Practice a Compromise.

2 Elements in Definition (a) Discipline or Training, (b) Information, (c) Culture; One-sided definitions again. Elements united in idea of Socialized Growth. Ideals of Humanism and Realism, etc.

3 Education as Growth involving Reconstruction; (a) Beginning, (b) Process, (c) Result, (d) Significance from this standpoint of (i) School (ii) Subject matter (iii) Method; (e) Ideal of Reconstruction *vs.* (i) Development of Faculty; Interpretation of Faculties; *vs.* (ii) Preparation.

V The School as a Social Institution.—(1) Its Organization and Administration. (1) Relation to Community Life at Large. (2) Relations to Special Institutions as (a) Family, (b) Church, (c) State and City. Harris, No. Am. Rev., Sept., 1881, and Psychologic Foundations of Education, chs. 31 and 32; Vincent, Social Mind and Education, esp. ch. iv; Rosenkranz, Philosophy of Education, pp. 143–149; Barnes, Child as Social Factor, in Studies in Education; Plato, Republic; Aristotle, Politics, Bk. I—Ward, Dynamic Sociology; Fouillee, Education from National Standpoint; Hinsdale; Studies in Education, Social Factors U.S. Education, p. 313; Meyer, Die Sociale Frage und die Schule; Dewey, Pedagogical Creed; Small, Some Demands of Pedagogy upon Sociology. Monroe's Bibliography, p. 162. (Rosenkranz, Phil. of Ed., Part III, (Historical.) Barnes, Studies in Education, p. 13 and 112 (Historical.)

2 Internal Administration; (a) Significance of Order and Government; Authority; Self-Government; Punishment; (b) The Positive and Negative in the Ethical Resources of the School: General Social Ideals, Motives and Habits *versus* Specialized School Virtues; School and Organized Community Life.

On *Moral Education,* see Hall's Bibliography, 178–183; Harris, St. Louis Reports, '70–'71; Malleson, Early Training of Children; Adler, Moral Instruction of Children; Spencer, Education, ch. III.; Bain, Education as Science, 99–119, and ch. XII.; Dewey, in Herbart Year Book, Third Year; Laurie, Institutes of Education, pp. 219–238; Hall, Pedag. Seminary, Vol. II., pp. 72–89; Herbart, Sc. of Ed., pp. 200–252.

School Discipline: White, School Management, pp. 114 & 190; Wickersham, School Economy, ch. IV.; Baldwin, School

Management; Laurie, The Training of Teachers, p. 309; Rosenkranz, Philosophy of Education, ch. II.; For Inductive Studies, see Barnes' Studies in Education, 26, 71, 110, 149, 190, 212, 228, 254, 270, 332 and 344 and Pedagogical Seminary, vol. iii, p. 235.

B. *Intrinsic Organization of School Life.*

I Content and Form of School Life. Content is Curriculum or Course of Study; Form is Method. (a) Organic Relation to School Life; (b) Organic Relations to Each Other; (c) Organic Relations of Psychical and Social. On Psychology in Reference to Education: see Harris, Report of Com. of Fifteen; Dewey, Ed. Rev. XIII, p. 356; Bain, Ed. as Science, pp. 1–10; Findlay, Ed. Rev., vol. 14, p. 236; Royce, Ed. Rev., vol. I, pp. 15 and 121; Sully, vol. 4, p. 313; Muensterberg, vol. 16, p. 105. See also McLellan and Dewey, Psychology of Number, ch. I.; (d) Relation of Pupil and Teacher—of Interest and Aims—Significance of Information, Discipline and Culture from this Point of View—Utility and Self Development.

II Factors in Problem. (1) Organization involves (a) differentiation, or division of labor; (b) interaction or mutual responsibiilty. (2) It is Organization for Life-Process or Growth—a problem involving order in continuity as well as at any given time—Starting Point and Aims.

III Characteristic Epochs in Growth. (1) Direct Experience —Outgoing, Spontaneous, *i.e.* Unreflective; (2) Consciousness of Means and Ends as distinct—of skill and rules as necessary; (3) Consciousness of Organization itself; (a) Generalization conscious; (b) Specification conscious; (4) Consciousness of Calling or Function in Life.

IV Educational Equivalents. (1) Home and beginning Elementary; (2) Later Elementary, so called Grammar or Intermediate; (3) Secondary; (4) Higher Training for Vocation and Profession; Characteristic Subject Matter.

V Practical Problems Involved. (1) Significance of Grades and Grading—Promotions, etc.; Examinations, etc.; (2) Adjustment of Established Subdivisions to one another, (a) Kindergarten, (b) Intermediate, (c) High School and College, (d) College to University and Professional School; Practices in Various Countries; Line of Movement and Solution; (3) Class Organization and Individual Growth (a) The Tutor *vs.* Class, see Newman, on Idea of University, (b) Uniform *vs.* elective Curriculum, (c) Specialized *vs.* General instructing Force.

Upon *Examinations:* Ed. Rev.; vol. 12, p. 133; vol. 16, 166; Fitch, Lectures on Teaching, ch. 6; Latham, Action of Examinations.

Upon *Gradation:* Harris, Psy. Found. of Education, ch. 36; Jackman, The School Grade a Fiction, Educational Review, vol. XV, p. 456; Prince, Grading and Promotion, Ed. Rev., vol. XV, p. 231; Laurie, Occasional Addresses, p. 1; Packard, School Supervision, ch. X.

Upon "Electives:" G. H. Palmer, The New Education, (College); see also the Andover Review for 1886, articles by Ladd, Garnett, Gilman, Denison and Howison; Pres. Eliot, Educational Reform, p. 125, 273, 303, 375; Hinsdale, Studies in Education, p. 6; Ed. Rev., vol. XV, p. 418; vol. X, p. 12. Hall's Bibliog., p. 204.

On *Promotions:* Atlantic Monthly, March, 1897, Shearer, The Lock-step in the Public Schools; Nat. Ed. Assn., vol. for '98, pp. 422–448; see also vols. for '93 and '95; Harris, in St. Louis Reports for '72–'73; Pickard, School Supervision, ch. XI; Ed. Rev., VII, 516.

On *Class and Individual Instruction;* Parker, Ed. Rev., VI, 342, also 410; Fitzpatrick, Departmental Teaching; Ed. Rev., vol. VII, p. 439; Search, Individual Teaching, Ed. Rev., vol. V, p. 154; see also VII, 305 and 515; Harper, N. E. A. Proceedings for '95, pp. 990–93.

C. *Organization of Subject Matter.*

I Theories of Selection.   1 Application of Previous Principles. (1) Differentiation of Experience leading to efficiency and content in function. (2) The working out of this principle, (a) Standard of Value, (b) Significance of Types of Study —Science and Humanities.

2 Theory of Isolated Values and Their Co-ordination—Curriculum a Composite—Dr. Harris's View.

3 Culture Epoch Theory, (1) Stated, (2) Criticised; True significance of History and Literature.

II Theories of Interaction—"Correlation."

1 Application of Previous Principles; (1) Direct Experience: Communication, Construction, Expression and Inquiry; (2) Evolution into Indirect. Consequent Interrelation (a) Mastery and Relationships of Technique of Communication—so-called form studies; (b) of Construction and expression—Manual Training and Art; (c) of Inquiry— Method in Science and History; (3) Motive and Application the Basis of "Correlation" at this Stage; (4) Specialized

Values in Final Stage; (5) Confirmation from History of Science; (6) Genetic and Static Classifications.

2 Logical Co-ordination—Theory Stated and Criticised; Value in Recognition of Objective Relationships.

3 Herbartian Correlation; Theory Stated and Criticised. *Values in Education* (General). Spencer, Education, ch. i, ii; Butler's Meaning of Education, What Knowledge is of Most Worth; W. H. Payne, Contributions to Science of Education, ch. 3; Bain, Science of Education, ch. 5; Holman, Education, ch. iii; Laurie, Institutes, esp. 211–226; Ed. Rev. vol. i, 105, by Patten, (college); vol. iii, p. 1, by Jenks; ix, p. 323–390 by a number of writers; x, 209 by Baker; Hinsdale, Studies in Education, Dogma of Formal Discipline; Youmans, Culture Demanded by Modern Life, Discipline, pp. 1–56; M. Arnold, Culture and Anarchy.

Curriculum in General. Dewey, in Ed. Rev. vol. xiii, p. 356; Bain, Science of Ed., chs. vi and vii, Sequence, ch. xi, The Renovated Curriculum; Hinsdale, Studies in Ed. Sources of Human Cultivation; Maxwell, Grammar School Curriculum, Ed. Rev., vol. iii, p. 472; Prince, Mass. Board of Education, 1897 and 1898; Hanus, Attempted Improvements in Course of Study, Ed. Rev. xii, p. 435; Eliot, Ed. Reform, p. 151, 253 and 197; Report of Committee of Ten; Dutton, Ed. Rev., XII, 335; Laurie, The Training of Teachers (Primary), 121; (Secondary), 187; Laurie, Occasional Addresses, p. 59 (Secondary); Aber, An Experiment in Education. Beale, *et al*, Work and Play in Girls' Schools; Spencer, Aims and Practice of Teaching; Barnett, Teaching and Organization; all give detailed statements regarding the theory and practice of the course of study in English schools.

Curriculum Herbartian: Rein *et al.*, Theorie und Praxis des Volkschulunterrichts, 8 vols.; Culture Epochs, vol. I, 16–62; Concentration I, 63–87; Formal Steps of Method, I, 88–131; Value of Myths, Tales, etc., I, 132–150: Geometry in Grades, vol. IV, pp. 214–263; VII, 124–168; History, vol. V, 28 ff; Geography, III, 165–187 and VII, 63–97; Science, IV, 143–199 and VII, 98–137 and VIII, 51–118; see also De Garmo, Herbart; Rein, Outlines of Pedagogics, (trans. by Van Liew); Dodd, Introduction to the Herbartian Principles of Teaching; Ufer, Pedagogy of Herbart.

A book entitled Herbart und die Herbartianer contains full bibliography of Continental Herbartian Literature; Culture Epochs, p. 61; Concentration, 61; Formal-stages, 63; Myths, Tales, 64.

Upon Values of Various Subjects in Curriculum; see (besides references under Values in General, Herbartian Curriculum and Correlation), Dr. Harris, St. Louis School Reports for '68 (Three R's), '69, '71 and '72.

Correlation, &c.: See references under Herbartian Curriculum; also Herbart Year Book, Years I and II; Vincent, Social Mind and Ed. Integration of Studies; Parker, Talks on Pedagogics; Fitch, Lectures on Teaching, ch. XV; Harris, Psy. Foundations of Ed., 321–332 and Ed. Rev., vol. XI, p. 322; see also Report of Com. of Fifteen; Lukens, Ed. Rev., X, p. 364, XI, 72; DeGarmo, Ed. Rev., IV, p. 422, and V, 450; McMurry, Ed. Rev., IX, 27; Gilbert, XI, 313; Jackman IX, p. 464 and XI, 72; Hinsdale, X, 152; see also N. E. A. Index Titles: Studies, Correlation of and Isolation of.

Culture Epoch Theory: In addition to Hebartian references, see Herbart Year Book, I and II; Vanderwalker, Ed. Rev. vol. XV, p. 374; Vincent, Social Mind and Ed., ch. XII.

Language. Bain, Science of Education, ch. ix, Mother Tongue, ch. x, classics; Jacobi, Primary Education, ch. iv; Collins, Study of English Literature (college, literature *vs.* philology); also 19th Century, Feb., 1895; Lavisse, Etude et Etudiants (classics), p. 35; Laurie, Training of Teachers (Latin), 213; Hinsdale, Teaching the Language Arts; Mc-Murry, Special Methods in Literature and History (p. 3–45 on myths and tales) and in Reading; Laurie, Lectures on Language Teaching; Farrar, Essays on Liberal Education; Price, Ed. Rev. xi, p. 12., N. Y. Teacher's Monographs, vol. i, No. 3.

Mathematics. Whewell, Thoughts on Study of Mathematics; Sir Wm. Hamilton in Dissertations on Philos. and Literature (reply to Whewell); Bain, Education as Science, p. 288; Cajori, Teaching and History of Math. in the U. S.; Fitch, Lectures on Teaching, ch. xi; McLellan and Dewey, Psychology of Number, Indices of Ed. Rev., '91, '92, '93, '95, Pierce, March, 1898; Harris, Psy. Found. of Education, ch. 37.

History. Hall (ed.), Methods of Teaching History; Adams, J. H. U. Studies, Methods of History Study; Barnes, Studies in Historical Method; Hinsdale, How to Study and Teach History; Kemp, Outline of Method in History; Lorenz, Der modern Geschichtsunterricht; Hinsdale, Studies in Education, p. 206; Fitch, on Teaching, ch. xii; G. Smith, Lectures on the Study of History; Freeman, Methods of Historical Study; Droysen, Principles of History; Salmon, Ed. Review, May, 1891, Sept. 1896, and Feb. '98; Rice, Sept., 1896, also Rice, Outlines of Course in History and Literature.

Art in Education. Bain, Science of Education, ch. 13; Waldstein, Studies of Art in Universities; N. E. A. Proceedings

Index; Harris, Psyc. of Ed., ch. 38; Crane, Relations of Art to Education; Langl, Modern Art Education; American Education in Fine and Industrial Art.

Manual Training. Ham, Manual Training; MacArthur, Education in Relation to Manual Industry; Love, Industrial Education; Stetson, Technical Education; N. E. A. Proceedings, '89, p. 117, and '97, 742; see also Index.

Sciences: Youmans, Culture Demanded by Modern Life; Preyer, Naturforschung und Schule; N. Y. Teachers' Monographs, Vol. I, No. 2; Huxley, Science and Education; Jos. Payne, Lectures on Education, p. 253; Fitch on Teaching, ch. XIV; Jackman, Nature Study, also Ed. Rev., Jan., '93, May, '95, and Oct., '95; Harris, Psych. Found. of Ed., ch. 39.

Geography: Geikie, The Teaching of Geography; McMurry, Special Methods in Geography; Parker, How to Study Geography; Mill, Hints on Geographical Books, (chs. 1 and 2); Laurie, Occasional Addresses, p. 83; Davis, Ed. Rev., May, '92, Jan., '92, March, '94; Redway, in Ed. Rev., Jan., '93, Jan., '94, Nov., '94, Nov., '95; C. A. McMurry, May, '95, Herbart Year Book, Fourth Year; King, Methods and Aids in Geography.

D. *Organization of Method.* SUMMARY AS TO SIGNIFICANCE OF METHOD.

I General Psychology of Method.

1 In direct Stage—(1) Learning by Experience, (a) Organic Circuit; Immediate Attention and Interest; Play; Apperception (b), Implicit Generalization; Habit, the Principle of Organization, (c) Implicit Specializations; Variation in Growth and Use; (2) Consequent Standpoint in Practice; Examples.

2 In Indirect or Reflective Stage; (1) Consciousness of End— Practical; Theoretical—Problem; Control by Problem, Mediate Attention and Interest, Origin and Function of Imagery; Process of Learning one of Direction of Inquiry; (2) Corresponding School Practice; Examples.

II Method in Recitation:

1 Herbartian Formal Steps Stated; Advantages.

2 Criticized; (1) Preparation—Conscious and Unconscious; Real Significance of Consciousness of End—a point, topic, unifying centre; (2) Presentation: Value of Presented Material, Sensations; Objects, Books and Talks; Significance of Particulars; (3) Generalization, Conscious and Unconscious; an Organizing Principle; (4) Application, also an Attitude, not a distinct Step or Function; (5) Types and

Method–Units; Correct Practice, but not in line with Theory.

3 Growth an Organic Process. Dangers of too great formalization. Neglect of the Instinctive, the Habitual, the Motor generally in Herbartianism.

E. *Conclusion and Summary.*

1 Education a Growth—as Reconstruction.

2 The Original and the Acquired. The Individual and the Social. Utility and Culture. The Natural and the Spiritual. The Intellectual and the Ethical. False Dualism in each case. A Unified Conception.

Method in General: McMurry, General Method and Method of the Recitation; DeGarmo, Essentials of Method; Tompkins, Philosophy of Teaching; Adams, Herbartian Psychology Applied to Education; Lange, Apperception; McLellan, Applied Psychology, pp. 167–76, 180–86, and chs. 9 and 10; Harris, Psych. Found. of Education, chs. 4, 22, 28, 30 and 35; Fitch, Art of Questioning.

Interest: Dewey, Interest and Will, Herbart Year Book, Second Supplement; Harris, Ed. Rev., vol. 10, p. 71, and vol. 11, p. 486, and Education, March, '95; McMurry, Ed. Rev., vol. xi, 146; Adams, Herbartian Psych. ch. X; Wilson, Ed. Rev., March, '96; Public School Journal, '95 and '96, articles by DeGarmo, Dr. Harris, Geo. P. Brown and C. A. McMurry.

TOPICS

1 Adjustment of the Parts of educational System to One Another.
2 Grading and Promotions; Class Work and Individuality.
3 Uniform Curriculum and Electives above the Elementary School.
4 Specialized or Departmental Teaching.
5 Preparation of Teachers and the Normal School Problem.
6 Problems of Superintendency.
7 Moral Education, Direct and Indirect, in the School.
8 The Place and Relations of Technical and Professional Education.
9 The Shortening of the Curriculum (involving comparison with French and German Schools).
10 The Enriching of the Curriculum.
11 Correlation, Co-ordination and Concentration of Studies.
12 Culture Epoch Theory.
13 Humanities and Science.
14 History of Educational Practices as Affected by Social Conditions.
15 The Growth of the Curriculum as Affected by Social Conditions.
16 The Conflict of Studies in High School and College.
17 Values of School Subjects.

18 Literature and Language in Elementary Education.
19 Literature and Language in Secondary Education.
20 Literature and Language in Higher Education.
21 History—Educational Value and Methods.
22 Geography—Educational Value and Methods.
23 Mathematics—Educational Value and Methods.
24 The Natural Sciences—Educational Value and Methods.
25 Significance of Play in Education.
26 Significance of Art in Education.
27 Significance of "Manual Training" in Education.
28 Development of Will.
29 The Interpretation of the Pestalozzian Maxims.
30 The Formal Steps of Instruction.
31 Adaptation of Method at Various Stages of Growth.
32 Theories of Classification of Sciences—Spencer, Comte, etc.
33 Problem of Rural Education.
34 Study of Civics, Sociology and Political Economy in Elementary and
   Secondary Education.

In working up special topics the student should consult special
Biographies in Hall and Monroe; also the General Index to Reports
of the N. E. A. and to Barnard's School Journal. He should be familiar with Poole's Index to Periodical Literature, and with the
Yearly Indices (Cumulative) since its issue. The Educational Review should be consulted. The School Review and the proceedings
of the North Central Association are indispensable for topics having to do with secondary and higher education. Upon many topics,
the subject index in the Pedagogical Library is very full. See also
Buisson's Dictionnaire, and Rein's and Schmidt's Encyclopedias.

CALENDAR FOR THE YEAR 1898–9.*

The meetings of the Board of Trustees are held on the second Tuesday of each month.

July 1.	Friday	FOUNDER'S DAY. FIRST TERM of Summer Quarter begins. MATRICULATION and REGISTRATION of incoming students. SUMMER MEETING of the *University* Convocation.
July 2.	Saturday	MATRICULATION and REGISTRATION of incoming students. SUMMER MEETING of the *University* Congregation.*
July 3.	Sunday	THE CONVOCATION SERMON.
July 4.	Monday	INDEPENDENCE DAY; a holiday.
Aug. 11.	Thursday	FIRST TERM of Summer Quarter ends.
Aug. 12.	Friday	SECOND TERM of Summer Quarter begins.
Sept. 14–17.	Wednesday, Thursday, Friday, Saturday	AUTUMN EXAMINATION for admission to the *Junior Colleges.*
Sept. 18	Sunday	BACCALAUREATE SUNDAY.
Sept. 20–22.	Tuesday, Wednesday, Thursday	QUARTERLY EXAMINATIONS.
Sept. 22.	Thursday	SECOND TERM of Summer Quarter ends. LAST DAY for handing in *Theses for the Doctor's Degree*, to be conferred at the *January Convocation.*
Sept. 22–30.		QUARTERLY RECESS.

Jan. 1.	Sunday	NEW YEAR'S DAY; a holiday. FIRST TERM of Winter Quarter begins. THE CONVOCATION SERMON.
Jan. 2.	Monday	MATRICULATION and REGISTRATION of incoming students. WINTER MEETING of the *University* Convocation.
Jan. 3.	Tuesday	WINTER MEETING of the *University* Congregation.* DAY OF PRAYER for Colleges.
Jan. 26.	Thursday	FIRST TERM of Winter Quarter ends.
Feb. 11.	Saturday	
Feb. 12.	Sunday	SECOND TERM of Winter Quarter begins.
Feb. 22.	Wednesday	LINCOLN'S BIRTHDAY; a holiday. WASHINGTON'S BIRTHDAY; a holiday.
Mar. 1.	Wednesday	LAST DAY for receiving applications for fellowships.
Mar. 17, 18, 20, 21.	Friday, Saturday, Monday, Tuesday	SPRING EXAMINATION for admission to the *Junior Colleges.*
Mar. 19.	Sunday	
Mar. 22.	Wednesday	BACCALAUREATE SUNDAY.
Mar. 22–24.	Wednesday, Thursday, Friday	LAST DAY for handing in *Theses for the Doctor's Degree*, to be conferred at the *July Convocation.*
Mar. 24.	Friday	QUARTERLY EXAMINATIONS.
Mar. 25–31.		SECOND TERM of Winter Quarter ends. QUARTERLY RECESS.

Oct. 1.	Saturday	FIRST TERM of Autumn Quarter begins. MATRICULATION and REGISTRATION of incoming students. AUTUMN MEETING of the *University Convocation.*
Oct. 2.	Sunday	THE CONVOCATION SERMON.
Oct. 3.	Monday	AUTUMN MEETING of the *University Congregation.**
Nov. 11.	Friday	FIRST TERM of Autumn Quarter ends.
Nov. 12.	Saturday	SECOND TERM of Autumn Quarter begins.
Nov. 24.	Thursday	THANKSGIVING DAY; a holiday.
Dec. 5–8.	Monday Tuesday Wednesday Thursday	REGISTRATION of resident students for the Winter and Spring Quarters.
Dec. 16, 17, 19, 20.	Friday Saturday Monday Tuesday	WINTER EXAMINATION for admission to the *Junior Colleges.*
Dec. 18.	Sunday	BACCALAUREATE SUNDAY.
Dec. 21–23.	Wednesday Thursday Friday	QUARTERLY EXAMINATIONS.
Dec. 23.	Friday	SECOND TERM of Autumn Quarter ends. LAST DAY for handing in *Theses for the Doctor's Degree,* to be conferred at the *April Convocation.*
Dec. 24–31.		QUARTERLY RECESS.

April 1.	Saturday	FIRST TERM of Spring Quarter begins. MATRICULATION and REGISTRATION of incoming students. SPRING MEETING of the *University Convocation.* ANNUAL ASSIGNMENT of *Fellowships.*
April 2.	Sunday	THE CONVOCATION SERMON.
April 3.	Monday	SPRING MEETING of the *University Congregation.†*
May 12.	Friday	FIRST TERM of Spring Quarter ends.
May 13.	Saturday	SECOND TERM of Spring Quarter begins.
May 30.	Tuesday	MEMORIAL DAY; a holiday.
June 5–8.	Monday Tuesday Wednesday Thursday	REGISTRATION of resident students for the Summer and Autumn Quarters.
June 9.	Friday	JUNIOR COLLEGE DAY.
June 11.	Sunday	ACADEMIC SUNDAY.
June 16, 17, 19, 20.	Friday Saturday Monday Tuesday	SUMMER EXAMINATION for admission to the *Junior Colleges.*
June 18.	Sunday	BACCALAUREATE SUNDAY.
June 21–23.	Wednesday Thursday Friday	QUARTERLY EXAMINATIONS.
June 23.	Friday	SECOND TERM of Spring Quarter ends.
June 24–30.		LAST DAY for handing in *Theses for the Doctor's Degree,* to be conferred at the *October Convocation.* QUARTERLY RECESS.
June 27.	Tuesday	ANNUAL MEETING of the Board of Trustees.
June 30.	Friday	ALUMNI DAY.

* The date of the meeting of the University Congregation is subject to change of one or two days.
† Reprinted from the Annual Register of the University of Chicago, 1899.

ABSTRACTED CONTENTS

c. Suggestion
  (1) Direct suggestion
  (2) Indirect suggestion
  (3) The value of suggestion
      (a) The broadening of stimuli
      (b) The widening of freedom
d. Communication
  (1) An indirect mode of stimulation
  (2) Language as an instrument of communication
  (3) Language as an expansion of experience
  (4) Relation between information and experience

3. Education as an ideal balance
  a. Balance between expression and suggestion
  b. Balance between habit and purposive activity
      (1) Relation to stationary and progressive communities: stationary communities emphasize habit
          (a) Examples: Aztecs, Chinese, Greeks
          (b) Relevance of Plato and Aristotle
      (2) Habits not merely prerequisites to judgment
  c. Balance between individual and society
      (1) Relation to class structure
      (2) Curriculum and class structure
C. Formal education
  1. Relation to informal
      a. Organizing function of formal education
          (1) Simplification of social forces

          (2) Idealization of social forces
          (3) Generalization of social forces
      b. Obstacles to the fulfillment of these functions
          (1) The tendency toward routine. Examples: arithmetic and language
          (2) The isolation of learning from life
          (3) The use of unassimilated knowledge

  2. Education and instruction: the place and function of knowledge
      a. Herbart's view: the equation of education and instruction
      b. Knowledge as an instrument
          (1) Psychological analysis
          (2) Educational corollary
              (a) The isolation of instruction
              (b) Relations to problems of instruction

(3) Information
    (a) Information as knowledge
    (b) The relation of information to discipline
    (c) The criterion for the value of information
(4) Culture
    (a) What is included in culture
    (b) Culture as the adequate functioning of the other elements
    (c) Culture as a sense of values

3. A formal definition of education and its formal elements
  a. Education as reconstruction of experience. Implications
    (1) Educational aims as immediate
    (2) Standards for the beginning and end of education
    (3) All stages of education are of equal importance
    (4) Criteria for selection of content
    (5) Relation between the child and the curriculum
  b. Critique of education as preparation
    (1) The loss of pupil interest
    (2) Passivity of the pupil
    (3) Tendency toward procrastination
    (4) Lack of perspective in the pupil

E. The school as a social institution
  1. Relation to other aspects of community life
  2. Principles of school administration: no specific school virtues
    a. Relations to discipline
    b. Relations to the recitation

II. Intrinsic Organization of School Life

A. Content and form of school life
  1. The logical and psychological principles of organization
    a. The logical—logical principles as incomplete
    b. The psychological
      (1) Importance of the psychological principle
      (2) Relations to social life
      (3) Difference between experience of the adult and the child
      (4) The significance of the social

LECTURE XIV

LECTURE XV

(3) Physical restlessness
(4) Moral awareness
(5) Beginnings of reflection. Images as an example
b. Relations to schoolwork: freedom and discipline

3. The third period—consciousness of organization
   a. Consciousness of the social
   b. Awareness of generalization
   c. Beginning of intellectual and religious interest
4. The fourth period—Consciousness of calling

C. Educational equivalents
   1. The existing system
      a. Unnatural breaks in the system
      b. The isolation of the kindergarten
         (1) Harris's view as typical
         (2) Resulting waste
         (3) Relations to teacher education
         (4) Need for absorbing kindergarten

---

         (5) Froebel's influence
            (a) The tendency to dogmatize
            (b) Overemphasis on geometric forms
            (c) Rigidity of procedure. Examples:
               (i) Literal acceptance of the grammar of occupations
               (ii) Literal acceptance of Froebel's games
      c. The isolation of the primary school—the three R's
   2. Proposed considerations
      a. The early elementary period

         (1) The totality of experience is fundamental
         (2) The transition from informal to formal education
         (3) No differentiation of studies
      b. The later elementary period
         (1) The differentiation of techniques
         (2) Earlier study of the three R's
         (3) Emphasis on instrumental value of subjects
      c. The secondary period
         (1) The differentiation of subject matter
         (2) Logical generalization
         (3) Specialization of habits
         (4) Combination of the two
         (5) The importance of the practical element

(8) No adequate basis for inclusion of other subjects
(9) No provision for direct experience
(10) Arbitrary postponement
(11) No provision for ethical impact of studies
(12) Isolation of studies no psychological necessity
(13) No provision for natural unity

2. The culture epoch theory
   a. General features
   b. Value of the parallelism between the psychological and social
   c. Interpretation of the doctrine of parallelism
      (1) The need for "short cuts"
      (2) No clear basis for emphasis on primitive life
      (3) No standard for determining value of stages
      (4) Present life is the proper standpoint of education
      (5) The importance of relating epochs to the present
      (6) A balance rather than a series of activities needed
      (7) False reasoning from process of child to products of race
         (a) Scheme as based on an aggregate
         (b) Relation between myth and reality
         (c) Myths should be seen in their historical setting
         (d) Breakdown of parallelism in later years
      (8) The child, rather than history, is primary

3. Literature as the center of the curriculum
   a. Literature deals in indirect experience
   b. No substitute for direct experience
   c. Importance of intrinsic connection
   d. Literature presupposes a background
4. History as a basis of correlation
   a. History merely a means of getting at social life
   b. Social life is central
5. Science and nature study as a basis of correlation
   a. Nature itself has no unifying principle
   b. Educationally, nature is inseparable from consciousness

LECTURE XXII

LECTURE XXIII

LECTURE XXIV

b. Instincts and impulses as fundamental powers
c. Primary instincts as roots to action
d. Education as the freeing of instincts
  (1) Contrast between practical and educational value of instincts
  (2) Instincts should serve to increase experience
    (a) Example from use of pugnacity in building character
    (b) Example from use of utilitarian function of manual training
  (3) Freed instincts become social

2. Manual training (direct experience in constructive activities)
  a. Inadequate justifications
    (1) That it is supplementary
    (2) That it is technical
  b. Its value is in its provision for direct experience
  c. Justification for manual training as the proper function of the school
    (1) Division of labor is artificial
    (2) Theory and practice are inseparable
    (3) Direct knowledge of social life is essential
    (4) Manual training represents typical processes of civilization
  d. Its connections with other subjects
    (1) Science
      (a) Knowledge of materials and processes related to scientific development
      (b) An easy introduction to scientific materials. Examples:
        (i) Mathematics

        (ii) Physical and biological sciences
    (2) History
      (a) Knowledge of the growth of inventions and processes
      (b) Affords a recapitulation of the progress of the race

3. History
  a. Educational value in general
    (1) Economic aspects are fundamental
    (2) An understanding of basic forces shaping environment
    (3) Not a materialistic view

(4) The informational point of view

c. Literature in the several periods of instruction

    (1) The elementary period

        (a) Not a distinct study

        (b) No substitute for direct experience

        (c) No special moral appropriateness

        (d) Literature should be a classic embodiment

    (2) The secondary period

        (a) Historical point of view as dominant

        (b) Vehicle for aesthetic analysis

        (c) Vehicle for ethical instruction

    (3) Higher education—specialized study of the literature of subjects

d. Constructive work in literature: the importance of active construction

e. The importance of the image

5. Science

a. Educational value in general—knowledge of the conditions of social life

b. Criticism of alternative interpretations

    (1) The object lesson point of view—provides no basis for motivation

    (2) The animistic point of view

        (a) Prevents economy and continuity of growth

        (b) Neglects aesthetic aspects of nature

c. Science in the several periods of instruction

    (1) The elementary period: geography as the center of science work

        (a) The world as a unifying fact—examples

        (b) A natural basis of correlation

        (c) Combination of analytic and synthetic

    (2) The secondary period

        (a) The classification of the sciences—two points of view

            (i) Comte's hierarchy: from the abstract to the concrete

            (ii) The opposite view

        (b) Appropriate considerations

            (i) Need for prior study of science in elementary school

            (ii) Necessity of relating science and mathematics

            (iii) Both lines must be used simultaneously

4. The psychology of habit
   a. Habit as the organization of impulse
     (1) Repetition as incidental
     (2) Habit as not merely mechanical
   b. Relation of habit and reason. Examples
   c. Habits must be seen in their relations
   d. Habits as a basis for generalization
   e. Deficiencies in the Herbartian theory
     (1) Underestimation of habit
     (2) Underestimation of unconscious elements
5. The psychological relation between means and ends—applications to teaching
6. The importance of problem solving

C. The indirect stage of learning: the image as a vehicle of indirect learning
  1. Images as multifarious
  2. Imagery as a medium for all learning
  3. Imagery and the psychology of thinking
   a. Illustration from geometry
   b. Illustrations from literature, history and geography
  4. Image not merely a copy
  5. Direction of the image is crucial
  6. Imagery as reconstructive
  7. Summary: the four forms of growth of imagery
D. Three modes of generalization
  1. Habit
  2. The use of rule
  3. Conscious formulation of reasons
E. The Herbartian formal steps
  1. Description
  2. Criticism

CONTENTS OF THE LECTURES

A.IV.3   **XII** *A formal definition of education. Discussion of its formal elements.*

A.V.;B.I.   **XIII** *The school as a social institution. The content and form of school life.*

B.I.(a),(b),(c)   **XIV** *Subject matter and method in education: their organic relations.*

B.I.(c),(d)   **XV** *Organic relations of the psychical and social: relations to instruction; psychology and teaching.*

B.III.(1),(2)   *Characteristic epochs in growth: first and second.*

B.III.(2),(3),(4)   **XVI** *Characteristic epochs in growth: second, third, and fourth. Educational equivalents. Elements in the present system.*

B.IV.   **XVII** *The periods of schooling: present practice and proposals.*

B.V.;C.   **XVIII** *Class organization and individual growth. The organization of subject matter.*

C.I.1.,2.   **XIX** *Alternative theories of selection.*

C.I.3.   **XX** *The culture epoch theory.*

C.I.3.   **XXI** *Other bases of correlation.*

C.II.   **XXII** *Positive principles of selection and correlation: basic considerations.*

C.II.   **XXIII** *Psychological aspects of correlation.*

C.II.   **XXIV** *The various types of study—the significance of instincts and impulses.*

C.II.   **XXV** *Manual training (direct experience in constructive activities).*

C.II.   **XXVI** *History.*

C.II.   **XXVII** *History: general pedagogical principles.*

C.II.   **XXVIII** *Literature.*

C.II.   **XXIX** *Science.*

C.II.;D.   **XXX** *The arts. The organization of method.*

D.I.1.   **XXXI** *The psychology of method. The direct stage of learning. Learning and reconstruction.*

D.I.1.   **XXXII** *The psychology of habit.*

D.I.2.;D.II.   **XXXIII** *The indirect stage of learning—the image; Herbart criticized.*

LECTURE I

January 3, 1899

[A.I.: *The conditions of education—individual and social.*]

The purpose of the course is to state general princi-
[I.A.1.a.] ples in philosophic form, but not in empirical detail, with implicit references to practice as working
principles.

There are certain conditions or presuppositions of education: on the one hand individuals physiologically and psychologically capable of education; on the other hand the existence
of social habits and ideals whose application to the individual
constitutes the process of education. The prolongation of the
period of infancy is a fact of great importance. Fiske,[1] first, and
later Butler[2] have emphasized this period as one of dependence
in its relation to society and the individual. In the process of
evolution, when this period became a marked fact, it may be
said to have been the period of transfer from animal to social
life. Out of the necessity for the exercise of care and foresight
on the part of some for the welfare of others, says Fiske, has
grown the sentiment of altruism and family life. Continued
dependence of the child makes family life more than natural
selection. It makes necessary more than a mere temporary relation of the sexes. Habits of foresight and the higher sentiments
have come to center around this more lasting relation. Out of
it have also come, in the struggle for existence, the basis for
great intellectual development, and of social and ethical relations. Infancy is a term to be applied here to the entire period
of dependence. The difference between the child and the young
of lower animal life is very great. A great difference is also

[1 John Fiske, *Excursions of an Evolutionist* (Boston: Houghton Mifflin
Company, 1884), chapter I.]
[2 Nicholas Murray Butler, *The Meaning of Education* (New York: The
Macmillan Company, 1898), chapter I.]

noticeable between the savage and the civilized child. In this fact of infancy lies the possibility of education. In one sense infancy and education are two names for one and the same fact. The young of animals are born with coordinations ready to act on slight stimuli. Their stage of infancy is relatively very short. The child may have more instincts, but they are relatively very undeveloped. Chickens are able to get food by pecking and jumping almost immediately on coming out of the shell as Spalding showed by hooding them.[3] They can do then corresponding acts which children cannot do for months. A child is born with impulses rather than instincts. Impulses are activities once organized as instincts or habits, but which have become disintegrated so that they revive vague tendencies to motor overflow, but not to any well-formed mode of action. These cover a wide range and are developed into habit and ability very slowly. Kicking in an infant is an inheritance of instinct to walk, but it takes months to organize the habit of walking. The young of animals differ from the adults mainly in bulk and strength. The young is simply a reduced copy of the older. The child differs from the adult both in degree of development and bulk. In the animal, reflexes and instincts are at a maximum; in the human, at a minimum.

Comparing the young of savage races with those of the civilized races, the relative precocity of the savage child is very marked, but arrest in development comes correspondingly earlier. This holds generally whenever precocity is found. The general rule is: "Rapidity of growth and arrest of growth are in direct ratio." It is a mistake to fix habits too early. They are then little educable. The street Arab is much keener in his field than the ordinary child, but he reaches mental maturity by seventeen or eighteen and is possessed of little versatility. Precocity should never be pushed, it will take care of itself. Teaching children to make unusual combinations in arithmetic for the sake of show is like teaching tricks to a monkey. Forcing is dangerous. Growth consists essentially in development by the interaction of organs.

[b.]   The essence of education is the continual reforming and reshaping of activities, and this requires plasticity—the ability to reach new and more com-

[3 D. A. Spalding, "Instinct with Original Observations on Young Animals," *Macmillan's Magazine*, 27, 1873, pp. 282–293.]

plex adjustments. It is because of his large number of inherited impulses and instincts, and the delay in their general, final organization, that the educator has time to get in his work. Heredity and environment imply each other. The final form heredity takes is largely determined by environment. It is not possible here to decide the dispute over the inheritance of acquired characteristics. There are, however, certain bearings of the problem worth noting: (1) Too literal or too much transmission would be a detriment, not a help. Too much fixed capital is not best. A convertible capital is more desirable. We do not inherit in an unmodified, fossilized form. Inheritance seems to come to us as an impulse, a tendency, the final shape depending on social influences. (2) With increasing social organization the transmission of ancestral capacities is less and less necessary. It is wrongly assumed that variations would get the better of continuity, unless these were held in check by transmission. It is obvious that this continuity can be better supplied from existing social life. The play of social forces upon one serves to weed out the undesired traits and to preserve the desirable ones. There is, then, on one side, the child with comparatively unformed, immature impulses, and on the other side, a process of selection by social environment which decides what particular habits or results these fall into.

In the physiological nervous structure of the individual, the chief difference between man and animals is found in the greatly increased number of cells in man which have no original function, but whose function is determined by the connection in which they function. These cells are intermediate, and get their final function in some habit. Two thirds of the cortex of the brain has no direct connection with the surface of the body. Only the general outline of the human nervous system is fixed. Education consists in this supplying of the conditions which make impulses work themselves out in one line of habits rather than another—control by supplying and regulating environment.

LECTURE II

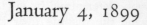

January 4, 1899

[A.I.: *Education as a social function.*]

The educable being is a being who matures slowly,
[I.A.2.a.] thus giving time for the educative influence to operate. The condition of education is a being whose
structure involves a certain amount of plasticity, negatively
and positively; that is, lack of positive organization in certain
directions, and possibility of assuming an organized structure.
The educational process involves the manifestation of these
actions and impulses under certain conditions and the reaction
of the conditions on the impulses. The conditions of the social
environment determine the direction, and fix the value of the
habits. Education implies the existence of social habits which
constitute the standards and ideals for directing and determining the growth of the individual. The habits, customs, existing order and functioning of social institutions fixes the ends
or aims, directly or indirectly, to which the impulses of the
individual are directed. They set the model for organizing the
tendencies of the individual. Impulse is at first unorganized
and becomes organized. It is impossible, in conceiving what
powers of the individual are to be developed, to get beyond
the prevalent social customs. We put content into the powers
of the individual in terms of the existing social order. The content of an educational principle will vary at different times and
with different persons. "The harmonious development of all
the powers of the individual" depends for meaning on the content of social life, and will mean different things to different
people, the meaning being determined by social habit. The
individual is educated as a member of a certain community
and his education will be in relation to the state of society then

and there existing. There is nothing else to be brought to bear upon him or desirable. Social habit determines the standard of education.

[b.] There are two kinds of society, stationary and progressive. Education for membership in these will differ accordingly. In a stationary society reproduction is what is aimed at. It succeeds when it stamps every rising individual with the stereotyped form. In other words, the aim is to bring the individual into harmony with the letter of the fixed social state.

The conception of society as progressive is that it is not fixed but that it must improve upon itself,—originality, independence, will be developed. Conformity with the social type means that he does not conform with the *form* of the type, or in a detailed and fixed way. Progressive society will make room for a great deal more individualism in its education; it will educate him to change. Yet social habit controls. A freed individual, one who practically determines his own career, will be a necessary product of a progressive society. The order of development has not been from a social ideal to an individual one as is often assumed, but from a stationary to a progressive ideal.

[c.] The great value of the history of Greek education is that it puts before us two important transitions: (1) from an informal to a formal system (a developed school); and (2) from the static to the progressive conception of society. In Greek history the conception of education came distinctly to consciousness, and was made the object of examination. Others, as the Chinese and Babylonians, followed their old system as a matter of habit. The Greeks saw the process and made it the object of an examination. Others taught by maxims, precepts, etc., etc.; the Greeks generalized it and attempted to theorize on it. The Greeks theoretically conceived of their society as stationary and yet they set up a final ideal to be attained and then maintained. They conceived society as involving reform. They set up an ideal society or an idealization of their own social habits and so made a conscious transition from the static to the progressive. Others of the older nations conceived that the individual of their society was to be educated, to be prepared for his place in it as it stood.

(See Mahaffy, *Old Greek Education*;[1] Jowett's *Plato*,[2] Index—
"Education"; *Republic* Bks. 5, 6, 7; and *Laws* for Plato's views.
Aristotle's views, *Politics* Bks. IV and V, Welldon's Translation,[3] Book VIII, and others.) The Greeks brought to consciousness the relation of social order to education. They regarded
education as the chief, if not the only fundamentally important instrument of social progress. That led to their conception
of a type of a perfect society, and to devise a plan to forward
the perfecting of that social order. Every polity has a certain
character back of it. Education is the instrument for developing that type of character. Aristotle has at least the conception
of education as a social function. He states that every kind of
government is relative to the character of society back of it,
and that education is the means of determining this society,
and that therefore education is a public function and not private. The Greeks could not think of it in any other way. To
them it was only a social affair. To take pay for teaching was
about the same as selling one's vote or being bribed. This is
seen in Socrates' polemic against the Sophists. Private pay
was a kind of perversion of public trust. One must be interested in what concerns all citizens. The Greek conception of
education was social and even political. There was a Greek
colony in Italy in which public education was actually administered by the state. (See Rosenkranz,[4] last part, for statement
of educational ideals in different states, and the relation they
bear to society.) Education always has been conceived of as
a social function. The social institution which has been charged
with carrying it on has alone been changed—family, church,
state, etc. These have been accredited servants of the state.
But this means only that the state could best execute its purpose through these agencies. Which of these could best be entrusted with this executive duty at any given period must be
determined by the state of society at that time. The process
of reaching the conception of governmental control of education is important.

[1 J. P. Mahaffy, *Old Greek Education* (New York: Harper & Brothers,
1882).]
[2 Plato, *Republic*, edited by B. Jowett and Lewis Campbell (Oxford: The
Clarendon Press, 1894).]
[3 Aristotle, *Politics*, trans. by J. E. C. Welldon (London: Macmillan and
Company, 1883).]
[4 Karl Rosenkranz, *The Philosophy of Education*, trans. by Anna C.
Brackett (New York: D. Appleton and Company, 1886).]

I have tried to clear up two possible misconceptions: (1) that education has progressed from a social to an individual ideal (it has developed from a stationary to a progressive social ideal), and (2) from a private to a public function (it has never been individual or private).

 # LECTURE III

January 5, 1899

[A.II.(1): *Education as adaptation of the individual to the exercise of its own functions.*]

A discussion of the philosophy of the history of edu-
[I.A.2.d.] cation would turn about the point that while education has always been social, the organ or instrument
to carry it on has been changed,—the family, military organization, church, state, etc. The reasons why one of these is taken
rather than another, and the forms which are appropriate to
each one, would give one of the important keys to the interpretation of the history of education. Plato makes no distinction, in principle, between the education which the child gets
in the family life, and the discipline and control which the
adult gets in the city life through the medium of the laws of
the state. He says education is a lifelong, continuous, process.
The teachers are the mother, the tutor, and the laws of the
state. He looks upon the latter as essentially educational in
their function and not merely regulative, adapted to the grown
person just as directions, rebukes, or commands given to the
child in the home are educational.

One reason why social education could be carried on
[(1)] by the family in Greece was the homogeneity of the
Greek people. They were nearly all personally acquainted, all had the same traditions, believed in the same
religion, spoke the same language, and had practically the
same local environment. In such a solidarity of a community,
the family could be trusted to carry out the wishes of the state.
With great heterogeneity, the family education would destroy
homogeneity of society, and produce anarchy; society would
be disintegrated.

The second instrumentality for education was the
[(2)] philosophic schools. The Sophists were the first pro- ✓∠
fessional schoolteachers. Plato and Aristotle opposed
them but started schools of their own which lasted for several
centuries. Out of these grew organized schools of instruction,
not the family, or the church, or government, but a body of
men whose identity consisted in a common philosophic doctrine. In these schools were taught grammar, rhetoric, mathematics, music, and philosophy. This method of education
continued for many years. This was a time of outward political
disintegration. It was marked by the loss of political standards
and customs and by the loss of independence by Greece in
general and of Athens in particular. The clashing of views
introduced heterogeneity into the social state, from which finally emerged modern life. The philosophic schools preserved
the continuity of Greek ideas and Greek values. As long as
Athens was independent, Greek society was homogeneous,
these ideas existed in the form of habits. The shock of clashing
ideas in the loss of political independence abstracted these
ideas and brought them to consciousness, formulated and reflected upon. They had never been formulated till the shock in
the practical life brought about an organization. There was no
occasion for such formulation in homogeneous society. In the
shock of change these ideas, by their intrinsic value and force,
were preserved.

Egyptian or Assyrian history seems to have little interest
or profit for any but the special student. They had the same
breakup as the Greeks, but the Greek ideas had strength and
scope enough to perpetuate themselves. The case was the same
with the Hebrews, except that in the latter case their ideas were
carried over in the form of religion, while the Greeks took the
medium of reflective thought and philosophy. There could have
been no other instrument of education under the historical conditions, except some such organization as these philosophic
schools.

The third institution entrusted with education was
[(3)] the church. Like the philosophic schools, the church
was the center of ideals, moral and spiritual principles, but it was also a practical organized political institution
formed to perpetuate itself. It had a stronger hold on the people

than the philosophic schools could have. To do this it took a wholly different method from that of the philosophic schools. We can trace the passage of education from the philosophic schools to the church. The history of Alexandria shows the steps by which the control of education in subject matter and method passed over from the schools of philosophy to the church. The church fell heir to the intellectual and moral ideas of the schools and by connecting them with religion put them into a form which appealed to the feelings, emotions, and imaginations of many more persons than they could have done if put in the form of philosophy. They appealed to the imaginations and emotions, and not to the intellect alone, and thus had a working hold on the people which philosophy could not have and therefore carried the practical ends of education further than philosophy could have done. The church transmuted them and extended them further than the school could do.

[(4)] The fourth point is the gradual assumption of education by the state, as we understand it. This movement has not taken place in education alone, but has been a part of the whole readjustment of life. The substance and form of education has always been a matter of public and social concern, though not until recently has it found formal expression. The organ or instrument of education has varied with social conditions, and the explanation of the causes of these transfers constitutes the philosophy of the history of education.

[B.1.] The nature or form of the process by which social life lays hold of and develops the immature being, or by which the being, under the influence of social life develops into full membership in that life is a process of adaptation, of interaction, of adjustment of the individual to social conditions. The educational process ends when the individual gains complete adjustment. The more important question is, how is the idea of adjustment to be interpreted or defined?

[a.] The theory of evolution has made familiar the idea of adaptation to a fixed environment. But environment is really not a fixed, hard thing, and adaptation means, therefore, conformity to an ever changing environment. The environment in the process of growth is being adapted just as much as the organism. It is the adaptation of both the organic structure and the environment to the needs of life. The two function together; both are changed. Adaptation consists in using the environment, getting greater control of the environment and modifying it to suit the needs of the organization. Walking, pushing with feet is using the environment to get hold of objects. Every new power of the organism makes the environment more important and more modified. The change from the use of four feet to that of two represents the possibility of a greater use of environment. When an organism gets the free use of its hands as hands, that fact opens up a new environment and makes parts of the old unimportant. Speech, locomotives, electricity, etc., represent changes of environment—adaptation of old environment to new conditions. It is not an adaptation to something which is already there. By means of these the organism gets hold of new elements. It is the adaptation of nature to new uses. The environment is evolving all the time along with the evolution of the organism. The value of the new organs is that they give broader and greater power and control. (Illustration: great American desert.) Adaptation is always dynamic, not static. It is not any predestined, fixed goal to which the individual must be lifted up, or which he must be stamped with. The process of adaptation modifies existing social forms as well as biological environment. It gives the individual the best use of social life, enables him to use it, control it for further growth, for further life. Adaptation does not mean arrest of progress at any fixed point. It is a balance between the resources of society and the powers of the individual, but it is a moving balance. The more society is at the disposal of the individual the more he can change society. Every invention means a better hold of environment, but it complicates that environment and calls for new inventions. The process of adaptation is a process of getting such control of existing social resources as will make them serviceable in an increase of the values of life.

       On the side of the organism, adaptation means the [b.] change in impulsive tendency to definitely organized power. It is the formation of habits, the change of impulses into habits. The same question arises with regard to habit as arose with reference to adaptation to environment. Habit is not a mechanical routine, a fixed thing, a groove. It does mean a certain fixity, a certain definiteness, a certain probability in advance, as to what the organism will do, but no normal habit ever becomes fixed absolutely. It therefore remains rational, capable of application to a variety of new uses. Habit is continually undergoing minor transformations, minor changes. Psychically a bad habit is one which is not capable of change; a good one is susceptible of change. "Habits are good servants but bad masters." Habits are servants when they are capable of change; masters when they are not.

LECTURE IV

January 10, 1899

[A.II.(2)(a),(b): *Modes of interaction between the individual and the environment through stimulus and response: direct stimulation and imitation.*]

[I.B.1.c.] At the last hour the point was made that the educative process is the process of the interaction between the being who is capable of education on one side, and the social conditions in which he finds himself on the other; and that that process is to be conceived as one of adaptation. It was necessary, however, to explain that the term "adaptation" was not to be interpreted in any hard or fixed sense; that it does not mean that the person is adapted to the conditions which exist at any particular time; that that to which the individual is to be adapted is itself in process of change; that it is itself a growing, developing thing, and the adaptation consists in setting up a certain line of growth in the individual which will be congruous to the social lines of activity in which he finds himself, rather than in setting up in him any fixed habits. The idea was that (using biological terms) the organism is adapted, not to the environment, but to the exercise of its own functions. The structure of the organism is modified, but it is not modified to bring it into conformity with any fixed conditions about it. It is modified to make it capable of the exercise of certain modes of action.

On the other side the environment is continually undergoing a similar process of development; the adjustment itself is being made over, so that it too will be a more effective instrument of growth, of development. The standard, in other words, for both organism and environment is found in the process of growth, of development.

The next thing in order will be to apply that general

point of view to a statement of the educative process in its relations to the individual on one side, and society on the other.

Social growth ✓

[*d*.] The idea of adaptation is that in its full sense, its ideal sense, it is equivalent to growth, and those adjustments, those adaptations which take place at any given time which are not in the line of growth really mark arrests of development, they mark actual hindrances or obstacles in the educative process. In other words, it is not enough to know that an adjustment has taken place, we must also know whether that adjustment tends to fix the conditions as they are, or whether it tends to further the process of growth, to free and bring into play our powers or not.

It seemingly was necessary to make this general and technical statement, first because of the frequent use, particularly in the philosophy based on Herbert Spencer,* of adaptation in another sense, as meaning setting up a fixed instead of a moving equilibrium between the organism and its conditions.

This process of interaction between the individual and his environment, or the conditions in which he lives, can be stated from either standpoint, beginning at either end. We can start with the equipment of the individual, his impulses and instincts, and consider their expression in the social conditions under which the child finds himself, and then the reaction of these social conditions in modifying those impulses, in approving of some and disapproving of others, thereby selecting some and tending to organize them into habits, while the others are ignored and gradually die out; or with the process as beginning on the side of conditions and that the reaction or response which proceeds from the child is response to the stimulus from the environment. It makes no difference what line of consideration we follow, provided we are consistent and do not mix up the two; because it is a process of interaction.

[2.] In what I am now to say I will follow the idea of stimulus and response; that is, of stimuli as coming to the child from his surroundings and his adaptation being effected through the reaction which he makes to these stimuli.

[* Dewey is here referring to the philosophy of "Social Darwinism" based on a concept of evolutionary adaptation leading to a fixed state of perfection.]

I will classify the types of stumuli and response under four heads: (1) the direct stimulation and response; (2) the process of imitation; (3) the process of suggestion; (4) that of communication.

[a.] By direct stimulation I mean, obviously enough, the stimuli which the child gets of his various sense organs through contact with the environment about him and the reaction that he makes to these stimuli, stimuli to seeing, hearing, to touching and handling, reaching, and so on. At first sight this class of stimuli might seem to lie outside the consideration of the educative process, on the basis of the principle previously laid down, namely, social growth. The environment there seems to be a purely physical thing, and to be comparatively unchanged from generation to generation. Of course if we take geological eras into account we would find plenty of change, but in human development it is too small a thing to take into account, and it is always a physical and not a social matter. But that overlooks the fact that the account of the process of stimulation as we have it discussed in physiology and psychology is an abstract one. Certain factors of the whole process are selected for analysis. That is correct enough from the standpoint of those particular sciences, but from the standpoint of the educational process as a social thing, from the standpoint of social science, it is necessary to modify that conception of the process of stimulation.

Concretely speaking there is next to no such thing as purely physical stimulation and response. I will not say there is no such thing at all, but it plays a very minor part in the life of anybody. Of course we are stimulated by light, by sound and by contact, but that light and sound and contact is never a matter of concrete fact. The purely physical thing that is treated as being in physiology and psychology the stimulus, always comes to the individual loaded with a certain value, a certain import, which it gets from social conditions. From a strictly physiological standpoint the savage is stimulated in the same way by light that the Greek was, and the Greek in the same way that we are, but as a matter of actual experience, the light stimulus meant one thing to the savage, another thing to the Greek, and still another to us, and what it means is a function of the surrounding social life. The stimuli, even the sense stimuli, come to the individual saturated with certain meanings that are put into them quite unconsciously by other persons. The stimuli are interpreted to the child just about as fast as he gets them, and as they enter into his experience.

[(1)] The stimuli that play much part in our experience are already socialized. While the stimulus is in one sense a purely physical thing, yet it is socialized in the significance that is attached to it in the individual who is affected by it. Take such a simple thing as the weather, stimuli of temperature which come to us from climatic conditions. Abstractly and theoretically they remain practically the same, but in a hunting community one value will be attached to them, in an agricultural community quite another value will be given to them, and in a city community they will come to mean quite another thing. As a matter of fact, most of the systematic observations on climatic conditions, on changes of the sun and stars, the winds, rain, etc., grew up and were made because of a certain industrial necessity. With a pastoral people whose movements depended upon certain winds which were followed by certain rainfalls, there is a motive for attending to these things which have a significance that they would not have for another people. With an agricultural people the necessity of attending to these conditions is enlarged, and so the significance put into them varies. The child lives in a world where these things come to him clothed with the values that they are charged with in the social life of the people about. The child gets very few naked stimuli. Through the kind of reactions he is encouraged to make and to suppress making, through what he sees other people doing in relation to these stimuli, he gets a certain characteristic attitude all the time toward them, he puts in a certain meaning. All these stimuli have a context. As they occur naturally in experience they are never severed from that context, and the practical import of the stimulus varies with this social context.

For that reason it is of course the most potent influence of education, that is the education that goes on outside of the school. Through what people are doing and not doing, as well as through what they are seeing, and the motions they are exhibiting, they are attaching certain meanings to all the things about us, and to all the stimuli that we get from those things, and it is that more than anything else which creates the homogeneity of any given social atmosphere at any time. It is that which makes the difference between the savage and the Greek, between one country and another, between the country and the city. Every contact that the child has from the moment that he is born is interpreted to him through this social context which puts its own characteristic value upon it. He is so steeped in these socialized stimuli before he ever goes to school that all that formal education can do is to work within the limits which are thus practically set up; making improvements and corrections and developments.

[(2)] It is simply a product of abstraction, of adult reflection when we try to separate experiences into two parts, and distinguish between what the child learns from things and from other people. Much of the current opposition in educational discussions proceeds upon the basis that contact with physical forces is one thing, and contact with people and their ideas is quite another thing. As a matter of fact, there is no contact with things excepting through the medium of people. The things themselves are saturated with the particular values which are put into them, not only by what people say about them, but more by what they do about them, and the way that they show that they feel about them and with them. While of course there is a certain convenience in classifying studies as those which have to do with people and those which have to do with things, when this is made anything more than a convenience in arranging experience, a dualism is introduced, a fixed gulf for which there is no justification whatsoever.

If from one standpoint that complicates the educational process (we cannot lay it out in pigeonholes so easily as we otherwise could), yet from another standpoint it simplifies, because it introduces a unity into the whole educational process which would not otherwise be there. The social element becomes the basic and controlling one in any case, in the study of science as much as in the study of history or literature.

[b.] In imitation the point that is implicit in what I have just been saying of the matter of direct stimulus becomes obvious. Imitation is taking the same attitude practically and intellectually toward stimuli that other people do. Imitation is most explicitly a case of the socialization of stimuli. For that reason I shall say no more about that phase of imitation, but rather speak of two other points which are more liable to be overlooked or misinterpreted.

[(1)]   One of these two points is the relation of imitation to the child's own spontaneous activity, his own impulsive and instinctive tendencies. It is sometimes argued as if imitation were not a process of adaptation at all, as if it were not an interaction between the individual and his surroundings, but were purely a one-sided process by which the environment impressed itself on the individual, that all the individual does is to simply copy, barely reproduce what exists about him so that his own personality does not come into play at all. It seems to me that both Tarde[1] and Baldwin,[2] who have made the most of imitation, have practically fallen into this error. They treat imitation as if it were simply a socializing process in bringing the individual into conformity to the things about him, as if it were not also a self-expression, a self-manifestation. So it becomes a problem how imitation is to be reconciled with the display of originality. As a matter of fact it will be found that imitation always starts from some natural impulse or mode of expression on the part of the child himself, and that the child imitates in any given direction only when he is naturally self-active in that direction. There are times when the child is, so to speak, "cold" as regards the imitation of certain things, and there are times when he is "warm." The times when he is warm are the times when he is naturally interested in trying to do that sort of thing. When the child's talking impulse comes into play he is interested in imitating sounds. Before that period he does not imitate at all, and after the height is past he imitates comparatively little. It will be found that any given line of imitation is at its height just when the instinct in that direction is also at its height, and that imitation can do relatively little in the development of the child excepting as the so-called models to imitate are put before him at the time when he is naturally interested in operating in that direction. So that even imitation then, must start by laying hold of the instincts and tendencies that are operative in the child's own nature, not an external process operating simply from the outside.

[1 Jean Gabriel Tarde, *Les Lois de l'Imitation* (Paris: 1890).]
[2 James Mark Baldwin, *Mental Development in the Child and the Race, Methods and Processes* (New York: The Macmillan Company, 1895).]

The other point follows from that. Mr. Baldwin[3] again
[(2)]   speaks as if the child who is imitating has a conscious
model to copy, as if imitation were a matter of taking
the activity of someone else consciously as a model, as if the
child is very often, when he is imitating, conscious of another
person as furnishing him the model for him to follow. It is
simply that, as matter of fact, the other person does something. The child sees it and is interested and that operates as
a suggestion for him to carry out that line of activity himself.
In other words the child is not really trying to copy a model,
he is simply responding to a stimulus. It simply happens that
what other people are doing gives the child more interesting
stimuli than he gets from things, or his more or less chance
contacts with them. But insofar as the thing imitated operates
educationally, I think it operates simply as a suggestion to
which the child responds more or less in his own way. The
child from his own standpoint is not imitating. A third person
looking at the child, seeing the whole thing, says the child
is imitating the adult, but that is not what is going on in the
child's mind. There is through what the other person has done
something interesting to do. It is suggested to him and he acts
upon that as a stimulus. The fact that someone else has done
something and he must do the same thing does not enter into
the child's consciousness. I mention these two points particularly here, not to criticize Mr. Baldwin's theory, but because
of its bearing on education. It shows the place and the limits
of the place of imitation in education. If Mr. Baldwin's theory
were correct, it would be necessary to make the early process
of education an imitative one. Other people are to do things
which serve as models and the child is to repeat in his own
action the actions of those models. But from the other standpoint the most important thing in imitation is, what are the
child's natural tendencies at this time, what are his own spontaneous interests in a given direction?

Then secondly, imitation is to be used, not as giving
[(3)]   the child a fixed copy which he is to follow, to reproduce literally, but simply to give him a help, a further
stimulus or suggestion in that direction. The value of the
model or the copy which the grown person sets is not to serve
as a copy or a model, but rather to help bring the child to the
[3 *Ibid.*]

consciousness of his own powers and of the best way of handling his own powers. Take it in art, in drawing, or in music, in singing, what is the value of a copy, of a standard furnished by an adult? According to the other theory, that would be the most important thing; the adult furnishes the whole thing and the child copies it. But according to this other theory, the child should first have a chance to act on his own impulse, and then the copy or the model should be furnished him in order to help him find better his own interests. The child tries to find a musical note and the teacher says: "That is what you are after." It serves as something outside of the child to which he is to lift himself up, not to conform to as a model, but to indicate to the child what it is that is his own objective, what it is that if he gets it he will have carried out his own wish and desire, his own idea which is immature and vague. So with the picture as a model in drawing. No one would seriously argue that drawing from a copy is the best way of learning to draw. When it is done at all it is simply a concession. Ideally everyone would, I think, recognize that the artistic process reversed that, that it was the expression of some idea which the child had, and the value of the picture furnished by the teacher was simply to help the child to consciousness of his own powers and of the standards that are virtually implicitly contained within his own powers.

LECTURE V

January 11, 1899

[A.II.(2)(c),(d),(e): *Modes of interaction: suggestion and communication.*]

      The third element in the process by which the child
[I.B.2.c.] is socialized is the process of suggestion. Suggestion
is a form of indirect stimulation which accordingly
as it progresses provides for greater freedom and display of
individuality on the part of the individual in the response that
he makes. Suggestion means that an image is the stimulus
rather than any direct presentation. When the child directly
imitates, of course the full stimulus is actually concretely
presented to him as the basis for response, but when the suggestion is made, there need not be, there usually is not, if the
suggestion is made through language, full presentation of a
stimulus to the senses. It is rather left to the child or the person
to interpret for himself what is said. He takes part himself in
the construction of the stimulus, because there is a certain
leeway, a certain mental play on his own part in settling upon
just how he will take the stimulus. Of course imitation blends
gradually into suggestion. The child does not continue literal
imitation for a long time, he generally becomes more or less
plastic in his imitation; he picks out certain features and
neglects others that are presented, and he augments certain
phases, introduces certain variations of his own, and in that
way the imitative process insensibly passes into suggestion
as the imitation becomes more and more indirect and more
and more flexible.

      Injunctions and prohibitions through language are
[(1)] one form, the most direct form, of suggestion. It
perhaps may seem at first as if the demand were
something more than a suggestion, but psychologically it is not,
unless the person is actually enforced, physically compelled

to do the thing which he is commanded to do. All the command can be is a stimulus to the person addressed to carry out a certain line of activity. As a command the suggestion is a very urgent one, it leaves comparatively little to the child's interpretation, or to his selection, choice, as to the manner or the mode of his response. At least the elder generally adds to it the threat or the fact of punishment so that it does come with almost the force of a direct or physical stimulus, and yet it is always, theoretically at least, open to the child to refuse to obey and to stand the punishment.

[(2)] Then suggestions vary from that form to all degrees of indirectness and remoteness. In our usual conception of suggestion, we imply that the child does not respond immediately, but does exercise his own judgment in some respects in the response that he makes. As the suggestions become more and more indirect, and more is left to the child's own mode of response, suggestion passes insensibly into play. Play is simply a case of suggestion at the other end of the pole from direct injunction. The side of the stimulus is there reduced to the minimum and the factor of response is raised to the maximum, while in direct command it is just the reverse. One of the important facts regarding the psychology of suggestion is that things, as well as words or gestures, are, at a certain period of development, suggestions. They always remain so to a certain extent, but at a certain period things have a very pronounced suggestive force. There is a period in the child's development, generally in the second half of the second year, at its maximum at about eighteen months, when every object that the child recognizes is provocative of a certain kind of activity. He either does not recognize the thing at all, or it is to him simply an excitation to do something with it. The hat is a thing to be put on the head, the drawer something to be pulled out, the broom something to brush with, the pencil something to try to make marks with, and so on indefinitely. The child seems for the time being almost in the condition that the adult is when hynotized; the mere presentation of a familiar object seems to suffice to set going a certain motor discharge. The child is preoccupied, or his attention is diverted in some other direction. That illustrates the point made yesterday that stimuli which from one point of view are merely physical, from a concrete point of view are also social. The response is the use which the child has seen some other people make of the thing; he is habituated to a certain thing according to the way in which others treat it, and he treats it in the same way; not in direct imitation, but without the presence of any other person. The thing has consolidated in it the modes of reaction, or the ways of treating it which are customary in the particular social environment in which the child lives. Now there can be no doubt, on psychological principles, that that suggestive force in things remains, that to the adult everything is something more than the bare object; it is also an excitation, a solicitation to some mode of response. Of course the adult does not respond to that solicitation, simply because his activity is so complex and so well organized that these various stimuli practically check each other, they neutralize each other; or still more because there is some one line of continuous activity on which he is engaged which excludes or reduces to a minimum the suggestive and stimulating power of things. But there can be no doubt that a very large part of the informal education is found simply in this soliciting value which comes to reside in all the familiar objects of our surroundings, according to the use to which they are customarily put.

The great value of course of suggestion, on the social [(3)(a)] side, is that it does extend so largely the range of stimuli. The stimuli which can be presented immediately and physically at any given time are comparatively limited in number. Only the things which are about the child can affect him in that way. Imitation is similarly limited in its range. In the strictest sense some person must be there doing something that the child may have a stimulus, but because suggestion is indirect stimulus, the range of stimulation is indefinitely widened. As to suggestion, anything anywhere in space or anywhere in time may be presented to the child in such a way as to influence and modify his action. Of course one of the chief differences between the animal young and the human young is found precisely here; the animal young is of course open to the physical stimulation, also to the stimulation which comes through imitation, but it certainly is open in a very slight degree, if at all, to indirect stimulation. You cannot suggest an idea, an image to the animal and then leave it to the animal to work over that suggestion and respond to it in its own way.

On the other side, suggestion not only indefinitely [b] widens the number and variety of influences which can be brought to bear upon the child, but as already stated, it enlarges his own freedom. That is, more and more is left to the makeup of the child's own individuality, taste, and preference, in determining the exact mode and character of response in suggestion, than in direct stimulation or in imitation. Educationally the principle of suggestion connects itself, of course, with the principle which is sometimes called ideo-motor action. That is, it is practically a recognized principle of contemporary psychology that any idea that finds lodgment in the mind also tends to get a motor discharge, and that therefore, of itself, without the intervention of conscious volition or purpose at all, it comes to modify conduct. The so-called principle of distracted attention, or diverted attention, is simply a case of suggestion, also a case of ideo-motor action, putting another image in the mind of the child which displaces the one previously there and assumes the control of action. There can be no doubt that one of the chief modes of control of conduct is through the instrumentality of suggestion. That is of course particularly true in the child who is plastic, with habits not yet set, but it is true to a certain extent of the individual at all stages of his existence, and while the point here is particularly discussed in connection with informal education, the question comes up whether upon the whole the principle of suggestion is utilized sufficiently even in school education, whether relatively speaking there is not too much reliance in direct teaching upon formulated instruction, and upon the formulation of specific answers to questions, particularly in the recitation, and whether too little is not left to the unconscious and perhaps, for that very reason, deeper-lying working out of suggestion. The average teacher believes he is hired to teach and is not doing his full duty unless he is conveying positive instruction on one side, or else making the child give back to him the conscious positive formulation of what the child has learned on the other side, and yet that marks a wide departure from the way in which the child has been getting knowledge outside of his going to school. There is a process of receiving suggestions which operates in more or less subtle ways in the child's mind, which requires considerable time for their full assimilation, and which then work themselves out with all degrees of quickness, in some children the response to the suggestion showing itself gradually and in transformed modes, and in others showing itself more quickly. The principle of suggestion suggests the idea of the gradual growth in the way both of full assimilation and inter- pretation of the suggestive material, and the elaboration of the response to it, while the idea of instruction as we usually con- sider it involves a very direct presentation and response, which is quite unlike the spontaneous growth process. As someone has said, a good deal of the teaching is the same sort of thing as digging up seeds all the time to see whether they have taken root or not. The child is not given time to have the ideas soak in, become absorbed so that they make their connections in his mind with a number of other ideas. The influence of conscious formulation is, of course, to isolate that particular idea, and the result of that isolation, if premature, means that it cannot ramify out and make its natural connection with other ideas which the child is getting and so cannot have the influence on his conduct and character that it otherwise would.

The other process I spoke of was communication. [d.(1)] That of course is a further extension of suggestion; it is suggestion made still more indirect. When we suggest a thing to another person we at least implicitly express a preference for a certain kind of reaction, response, on his part. We do not insist, if we are wise, that the response shall literally conform to the suggestion made, but we do expect a certain amount of agreement, of relevancy. What I mean by communication is that we simply put a fact, a truth, a state- ment, objectively before another person, and leave it to him entirely to interpret that, to estimate its worth and value, and so to determine completely for himself what kind of a response he will make. Communication, then, may be called a thor- oughly indirect mode of stimulation. Any communicated fact or truth is a stimulus so far as it is appropriated in any way by the mind of the person to whom the statement is made. That would follow from the general principle of ideo-motor action or the principle of the organic connection between the brain and the nerves that move the muscles. But when we simply make known a fact or a principle to another mind, we do not ex- press any preference, any wish, much less any command as to the particular way in which he should look at that truth and in which he shall respond to it. While it is a stimulus, we do not undertake to determine what kind of a stimulus it shall be. So what was just said of suggestion holds to a still greater degree of communication. It extends still more indefinitely the stimulus which can play upon the individual and his possible freedom in choosing the final mode of action.

[(2)]   Most simply stated, language is after all the chief instrument for socializing the stimuli which play upon the individual. Speech, conversation, language, both oral and written, is the medium that removes practically all limitations in theory to the stimuli to which a given individual may be subject. The only limitation is the limitation in the experience and knowledge of those who carry on the language. It is for that reason that language is made such an important instrument in the formal education as well as in the informal; because it does permit the child to travel mentally through all space and in all time, and to have forces and values brought to his attention which would of course utterly escape him on any other basis. So from one point of view it is impossible to estimate too highly the significance of language, both as to its content and form, as a means of instruction. But the principle, like every other principle, cannot be taken at large. It has to be stated with reference to its own proper conditions. There must be a reality of communication, and not merely a form of it. The reality depends not simply upon what one says, but upon what the one to whom the language is addressed already has in his own experiences and habits. Otherwise we might as well be talking to a deaf person. Words may be uttered to an individual with which he is familiar, but there is no real communication unless there is a background of experiences and habits and of tendencies on his part to which the presented facts or truths make some immediate appeal.

[(3)]   Language is valuable insofar as it serves as an interpretation, as an extension, mediation, of the experience which the child already has. It becomes valueless when it is attempted to make it a substitute for some experience on his part. The value of that principle lies in its application. Certainly when a mass of information is crowded upon the child, either by the teacher who is talking or lecturing, or through the use of a book, there is the form of communication, without the reality. Very much of what passes current in the geographical and historical textbooks can be nothing but an attempt to substitute a made-up experience for the first-hand experience of the child. The child has a right to any truth if it will be at once reacted upon and illuminate and broaden his own experience, if he can appropriate it in such a way that it enters into some living interaction with what he already has. There is then a reality of communication, a reality of socializing the child. But certainly the lessons consisting of information that are made up simply to be learned by the child, consist, in the necessity of the case, very largely of things which cannot assume any such vital relation to his own experience.

[(4)] The difference between information and ideas is that information just as information is, relatively at least, second-handed. It is a thing which has been there in someone else's experience, but which is attempted to be transferred from the other's experience into the child's own, so that it is forced upon him from without. Now in spite of the fact that the ideal of the existing education is the attainment of a maximum of information in a variety of subjects, it is still a pyschological fact that that information cannot facilitate growth excepting as it enters into some direct and living relationship to what the child already has. It is a common thing to condemn the process of pouring into the child, of filling him up with novelties, but it is not so easy to get away from the practice as to condemn it in theory. Education is still controlled by the amount of knowledge necessary to make a well-informed person, and the curriculum is largely laid out for the purpose of having the individual attain this information, and actual growth is a secondary consideration. Some of it does catch and stick and work into character and conduct, and so tends to growth, but most of it remains there simply as evidence of the fact that one has had a proper amount of instruction. I do not wish to make a plea for ignorance, but the amount of information that a person requires in existing society is comparatively a small thing. The necessary amount of training, of control of his powers, of judgment, observation, and action, is very great, but any person who has that control can, with the facilities for getting information through the libraries, magazines, and the possibility of utilizing the experiences of other people when desired, get on with a comparatively small amount of actual information. When we give up the encyclopædia or dictionary ideal of education and substitute for it the ideal of growth, and the subordination of information to the stimulating of a positive interaction and development within the child's own experience, it will mean a revolution in the present educational ideals and practices. I mention this here to bring out the fact that while communication is a formal instrument of education, its value depends upon its being balanced up with direct experience, and direct stimulation, direct contact of the child with his own environment at first hand, so that the final problem is how to secure the balance between the more direct stimulation which the child gets through contact of his own powers and adjustment with the expansion and interpretation through the ideas and experiences of others.

LECTURE VI

January 12, 1899

[A.II.(3);A.III.(1): *The ideal balance between habit and intelligent action. The functions of formal education.*]

         I suggested indirectly at the end of the hour yester-
[I.B.3.a.] day that one of the controlling ideals of the informal education ought to be a certain balance or equation between the direct experience of the child, that which he gets through the putting forth of his own powers, the expression of his own impulses, and the contact with his own environment, and the extension and enrichment of that which is got through the suggestions and statements that come from others. The proper place of what is got from others is to interpret what the child gets through his environment for himself, not as a substitute for it, nor mechanically added on to it.

         There is another balance which is involved ideally,
[b.] and that is between the formation of the powers in the direction of the formation of habits, and the value or meaning which is attributed to the habits when formed. The person who has no habits trained, organized, cannot be an efficient agent, he cannot be what is called practical. To be practical means to have certain habits which operate easily and effectively in connection with the conditions of life, and to be defective anywhere in the habits means to be defective on the practical side. But it is also clear that if only the habits are formed, the life of the person will be exceedingly mechanical. It may be in one way an effective social instrument or servant, but it will be a servant in a slavish, servile way, because he is not aware of the meaning of his own activities, because he does not really appreciate himself, what he has to do and why he should do it, so that there is a balance between

the habits, that is, the unconscious part of the mental workings, the machinery of the mind, the instrument of action, and the ends or aims, the conscious values with reference to which these powers should operate. I suggested the other day that the principle of imitation for instance, if overemphasized, if isolated, would give us a somewhat mechanical product. It might give a being who in a way was effective, and who amounted to something in the maintaining of life about him, but the overemphasis of imitation would lead to the formation of habits without conscious awareness of the value of those habits, of their real good, their purpose; and there being no such awareness of their purpose, there would be no freedom in controlling or in modifying those habits.

[(1)] The education in what I called before the stationary or non-progressive communities is clearly one which is based for the most part on the formation of habits. Comparatively little attention is paid to bringing the person to consciousness in his actions, of making him see and feel the reason for doing certain things, their import as measured by the standards of reaching any result, or contributing to any end. For that reason imitation was, as matter of fact, the chief instrument of education in the oriental, non-progressive society. Moreover, great attention was paid in the formation of habits to the ceremonial education (rites and ceremonies), doing particular things in a particular way without any larger reason, which is the most conservative of all things. A person may be brought up in certain ideas and yet always retain a certain amount of power of reaction, but a person who is accustomed from birth to doing the minute details of life in certain very definite specified ways, which are also made ceremonial, and which are regarded as religious duties, is always so thoroughly formed in the given direction that there is no likelihood of any departure whatever from the habits thus formed.

[(a)] In Earl Barnes's *Studies in Education*[1] you will find some accounts of education considered as a social function, particularly among the Aztecs and Chinese, where this point of which I have been speaking is particularly brought out, showing the extent to which conservatism has

[1 Earl Barnes, ed., *Studies in Education* (Stanford: Stanford University Press, 1896–97).]

gone through the training of these minute detailed habits, thus conserving the conditions of society with the minimim of change. Of course the modern ideal is that there should always be a training in intelligence, judgment, reasoning, which shall finally lay hold of the habits and control them, and whenever necessary, modify them; but it still remains a problem how to secure an equation between the training of habit on one side, and the training of intelligence, judgment, reasoning, on the other.

[(b)]   Almost all the problems that have been discussed in education you will find in one form or another in Plato and Aristotle, or in both at times. In Aristotle's *Politics*[2] (Welldon's translation, Book IV, Chap. XV., P. 210) he says that there are three elements in education which are nature, habit, and reason. Nature corresponds to what I term the impulses and instincts, the original equipment of the individual. The basis is always, he says, in nature. Before that, on page 201, he said: "There are some points in which natural disposition is of no value"; there are certain natural qualities which may be shaped in any direction by habit, but there are other qualities which really must be supplied by nature. In speaking of that on page 180, he compares the Greeks with the northern barbarians on one side, and with the peoples of Asia on the other, and he says that the northern barbarians, "while full of spirit, are comparatively deficient in intelligence." By spirit he means natural impulse, initiative, positive force, what you might call will elements. "The nations of Asia, on the other hand, although intellectual, are wanting in spirit, and hence remain in a state of subjection and servitude. But the Greeks partake of both qualities; they are equally spirited and intelligent." Now to come back to page 210, he says the question is: what is the relative place of habit and of reason in the formation of nature into virtuous and social character? He solves the question in this way. The irrational soul is prior to the rational spirit; that is, impulse, will, desire exist in children from the moment of their birth, while judgment, or reason, is in the course of nature not developed in them until they grow older; and so his conclusion is that the first training must be of the habits, but that later on reason must be trained.

[2 Aristotle, *Politics*, trans. by J. E. C. Welldon (London: Macmillan and Company, 1883).]

Now there is probably the first conscious recognition
[(2)]   in the history of conscious thought of these three
factors in education, the natural endowment and
the training that comes through habit on one side and reason on
the other, and the necessity of combining the two. But it is expressly stated that training of the habits precedes that of
reason or judgment. That of course has been the theory on
which education has since proceeded on the whole, that first
habits should be trained in order that afterwards they might
be put to intelligent use. It is a theory which has controlled
up to a recent time. The idea almost always implies, and
often expressly asserts, that the child should first form these
habits in a practically automatic way until thoroughly familiar
with them, that they might afterwards be put to intelligent use.
The child was taught to read mechanically without any attention to the material read. So the child has been taught number,
not on the basis of any use, appealing to his sense of value,
but simply to give him the habit, the ability, to add, subtract,
and so on, and the theoretical justification is that stated by
Aristotle, that the practical part of a person's nature develops
first, and reason, intellect, judgment, is a later development. I
do not intend to discuss that matter here, because it is a question of psychology which takes us far aside from the point
in hand, but it is obvious that no complete balance can be got
on that basis. There must always be a certain amount of break
between the means of life, and the ends and aims of life.
Of course everyone would admit that there is a certain sense
in which reason is a late development (that is, abstract intelligence). The question would be whether through suggestion
and communication it is or is not possible for the child to
parallel from the start the formation of his habits with some
consciousness of their use and of their relations; whether
it is not possible from the outset for him to get a sense of what
he is doing; to find value, not a full sense of value (no one does
that way) but a sufficient sense of the value of what he is
doing, so that the development of the side of intelligence,
of meaning, shall keep pace all the time with the growth of the
power itself, so that the means and ends in the person's
psychical makeup, or the executive side, that which enables
him to be efficient in his environment, and the intellectual
side, that which enables him to direct his powers to ends in-

trinsically worthy, shall be balanced, and keep pace with each
other. I think you will find that almost all the educational problems regarding what we call discipline, and regarding the place
of technique in any subject, the technique of reading, writing,
or language, the technique of mathematics, art; the problems
regarding the place of that, can always be looked at from this
standpoint, as to what is the proper relation between the
habitual element, the training of the actual power, or the
training of the meaning of what is being done.

[c.] There is a third balance which is ideally involved in
this process, which might be stated as the desired
equation between what the individual contributes, or
is capable of contributing to society, and what he receives from
society. It is ideally necessary that the child should be so
trained that on one side he contributes to the possible maximum of the community of which he is a part, but he will be
slavish and mechanical in doing that unless he receives back
from society the value of his work, of his activity; unless he
is participating in the larger values and the larger life of
society itself. It is obvious that insofar as education is a class
education, it violates that principle. Until a comparatively
recent time all education has been a class education; it has
been assumed, either consciously or unconsciously, that upon
the whole there should be one class to work to maintain society,
while there is another class, which by its nature is more of a
leisure class, which has a sense of social values, and so has
lodged in it the power of directing and managing social affairs.

[(1)] Of course this third point is closely connected
with the second. Just because Plato and Aristotle
assumed that habit came first and reason afterward,
they also assumed that there was a fundamental difference in
people; some could not get much beyond the training of habits,
while others could go on to the higher life of leisure and culture, because they were capable of the development of reason
and so their whole political problem came to be practically how
to secure such an adjustment that the leisure class should
direct, really control, the activities of the working class, who
did the things that made it possible for society to go on. Now
while the theory in Anglo-Saxon countries at least, and in most
European countries, has been given up, and education is considered to be of universal concern, there is of course a strong

survival of the class element and ideals in the spirit in which the educational system is carried on. While we are away from it in form, and partly in content, we are not entirely in content. We permit, formally, every person to get a full development, but we do not have the conditions that see that he shall do so actually. It is a possibility, but it is not insured as a certainty, or even as an actuality.

[(2)]   Besides that, there is still very much in the curriculum itself, and in the methods of teaching it, which tends, largely unconsciously, to perpetuate this fundamental class distinction. Everybody is in favor of a liberal education, and of an education in which culture is the leading element; everybody is opposed to specialization. Nonetheless our current education is a highly specialized one, and often the attempts to make it broader are resisted on the ground that we are introducing specialization. I mean the predominant part occupied by the linguistic element in education. One of the first objections most strongly urged against the introduction of manual training has been that that was introducing specialization, and the introduction of science has been resisted on the same ground. It is thought that to put science in is to put something technical and specialized in. The curriculum, by the nature of the case, presents a course of study which appeals more strongly to one sort of persons than another; and so, independently of anyone's conscious choice, certain persons have been selected to go through school, while others, to whom that form of education did not appeal, dropped out. There are some people who are more interested in the practical side, and others are more interested in the intellectual side. The curriculum of the past and present would show that we make more provision for the people whose tastes are in the intellectual, than for those whose tastes are for the executive side of life, and the attempt to introduce studies that represent the other side is resisted on the ground that it makes education utilitarian and even mercenary. Education cannot be common, public in content and spirit as well as in form, unless it makes a balance, a provision for the training of the different kinds of tastes and capacities which are found in different individuals.

I have said these things under the head of informal education, but I have done so because, although perhaps they

belong strictly under the head of formal education, the spirit
that prevails in this informal education will be that which is
carried over into the formal education. The school itself cannot control the practice or ideas of the people. If society is
convinced that there is a dualism here, that intelligence is an
abstract thing, which comes after the development of the
practical powers and is simply built on the practical powers,
of course the school cannot get very far away from that point
of view, but insofar as society as a whole believes that in training a child to act in certain ways it is always possible to train
him to intelligence in acting in those ways, insofar the school
can work on the same hypotheses.

     Going on to the school, or formal education, my first
[C.1.]   and most general point is that, fundamentally speak-
     ing, in principle the school has no other educational
resources than those which exist outside of the school, that
so far as the principle is concerned it is simply a continuation
of the same methods which are operative in the informal education. The sort of material that instructs children or adults outside of school is fundamentally the same sort that has power to
instruct within the school, and the same sort of contacts and
relations in which one is developed out of the school must be
the chief reliances also within the school. From one point of
view that doctrine of continuity must seem to be axiomatic.
We know as matter of fact that the school has been highly
differentiated, and that the break, the gap, the gulf between
the home and neighborhood life of the child and the school
life, has been made, it would seem, almost consciously. But to
those who keep track of current educational literature, there
is hardly any point which is under more general discussion at
present than the question of what is termed the closer relation of school and home, or the correlation of institutions; to
institute a cooperative relationship between the two, instead
of the gap or separation.

     There seems a very practical existing tendency in
[a.]   the direction of the recognition of this principle, that
     fundamentally speaking, the educative process must
be the same within and without the school walls. Of course the
school is not the home; there is a distinct institution there
which must have its own function, and so when we say the
materials and methods are the same it is not that all distinction

must be wiped out or overlooked, but it does mean that the school has for its function the organization in a more conscious and thoroughgoing way of the resources and the methods and materials that are used in the more unconscious and haphazard way outside. If we say that the business of the school, as an institution, is to organize these educative resources, we have a basis for recognizing both the identity and distinction of school life from home and neighborhood life. In calling this natural education unconscious, in calling it informal, we mean that it is not sufficiently organized. Of course there are advantages to that, but there are also disadvantages. The fact that it is not and cannot be completely organized, makes it more subtle, makes it touch the child on a multitude of points where we could not if we set out to do it on the basis of conscious reflection, but while the school could not be a substitute for the home, it has its advantages in the line of organization.

[(1)] There are various aspects of this organizing function of the school which may be named in detail. In the first place it selects or reduces the complexity of the forces operating outside. In the second place it selects in such a way as to purify them, in such a way as to idealize them; and in the third place it endeavors to arrange them so that they shall harmonize, so that they shall be generalized and unified in a way in which they are not in the everyday process of growth.

There comes a time in the development of society when it is too complex to be the most effective or the most healthful instrument for the education of the child. The current life in its complexity is highly specialized in certain directions. There are a great variety of forces and ideas, occupations, going on. In its complexity, society, being upon the whole adapted to the needs of the adult, has gone too far away from the child. In primitive society the education of necessity occupied a larger place because the plane of society was nearer the child. Every advance in education marks to some extent the introduction of a greater gap between the organized plane of society as a whole and the standpoint of the child.

One thing, then, that the school has to do is to bring back the complexity, the high point of development reached by society, to a plane which will come nearer to the child's own interest, where it shall touch him more naturally. This increasing complexity, I think, is chiefly seen in city life where the pressure of

society and the variety of its interests is so great that the child
is likely to be overstimulated and consequently to become disintegrated under the strain that he is put under unconsciously.
It is a common saying that has a large basis of truth back of it,
that the city has to be renewed every third generation from the
country, that the intensity, pressure of city life exhausts itself
and that the new successful persons are always coming in from
the outside. It is also a matter of common knowledge that certain forms of nervous diseases are more common in city than
in country children. That is simply one aspect of the complexity
of civilization and an argument for the reduction and simplification of life.

Another consideration which points equally to the necessity
of simplification is that in this complexity a great many things
would entirely escape the child unless they are purposely simplified so as to reach him. There are some things which affect
him too much, but there are other things which would not affect him at all. The complexity of business life, industrial relationships, is so great that if the child were left simply to
natural education, it would touch him only in a most indirect
way. Simplification is a necessary condition, therefore, of its
being brought to bear on him at all. The first factor in this
formal education, or the organization of the resources that
make for growth, would be that the school pick out those elements from the existing social conditions which are best
adapted to the child in his existing stage of growth, and which
are most necessary to him in order that a fairly conscious, un-
interrupted growth may be set up.

LECTURE VII

January 16, 1899

[A.III.(1): *The functions of formal education: simplification, idealization, and generalization. Obstacles obstructing these functions.*]

[I.C.1.a.] The point of which I spoke at the last hour was the relation of conscious education to the unconscious process. I had been speaking of the fact that the school simplifies and reduces the existing complexity of social forces and aims for purposes of education, that the child being in what we may term an embryotic condition, that is, not having his habits set and fixed, it is necessary that the environment itself should be of such a form as to adapt it to the embryotic being.

[(2)] The second point is that in selecting, the school should select those processes and methods and materials which are typical, and which are the more enduring, permanent. Since something must be eliminated in any case, it follows without argument that that which is eliminated should be the relatively trivial and unimportant and the transitory. In other words the selection should be a process of idealization. By idealization we mean, of course, taking the best state of things at its best, taking whatever in it is most worthy, and which we are therefore most desirous of perpetuating.

[(3)] The third point is that this selection should be such as not only to purify or idealize the existing social conditions, but should also be of a character to bring them to bear in a generalized, in a comprehensive way, upon the child. We are all familiar with what is termed the assimilating function of the public school, the extent to which our schools take children of different nationalities, often speaking, when they come to school, foreign languages, and having different intellectual and moral traditions. The extent in which the school succeeds in welding these children into fairly homogeneous members of the social system is well known.

To illustrate what I mean by the school having the function of presenting a generalized social environment, it must represent what is most likely to be common, what is most likely to affect the lives of all, and which is most likely to be an influence in eliminating what is merely partial and local in the child's own hereditary and home environment, so as to become a member of the larger community, so that he shall understand the social ideals of the whole community, and shall be so interested in them as to make them his working ideals and habits.

One of the reasons for calling our schools public or common schools is precisely because they do and should exercise this generalized social function, the elimination of what is simply provincial, not only in the child's physical surroundings, but in his intellectual and moral surroundings, and extending his horizon so that he becomes a member of the whole of society, and not simply a unit in a class, much less in a particular party or clique. Of course the change from the stationary to the progressive type of society shows itself in a marked way. In this respect stationary society must act of necessity on a comparatively local basis with reference to the narrow social horizon, but in the things which make society progressive it is considered that the general trend is more important than any particular element within the whole. It is the interaction of the various elements playing upon each other in society which keeps the whole moving, which makes it progressive. When you isolate anything, making it simply local, there is no chance to get a leverage upon it to change it, so it becomes of necessity fixed; but when one local idea, or one local prejudice begins to act on another, the result is friction and gradual attrition, and what is comprehensive is likely to come out of the friction and into the movement. On the social side this would constitute then our standards of what the organizing work of the school as a formal mode of education in relation to the informal is: that it should simplify, therefore select, and that selection should be of a character to purify, idealize, to pick out what is best and at its best in its most intense workings, and in its highest forms, and that we should select a sufficient variety of factors to represent all the present elements in the social life, and then should arrange them so that they shall harmonize with each other—so the child shall be educated into membership of a community as a living whole, and not a fixed unit in a local part of that whole.

[b.] Of course the instrument that chiefly marks off formal from informal education is instruction. Before speaking specifically of instruction and its relation to education, I should like to say something first of the obstacles that there are at present in the way of the school performing adequately these three functions which have just been spoken of.

[(1)] In the first place there is a natural tendency for every social institution, like every habit in the individual, to become set in a particular form, and having crystallized, to go on following its own traditions, its own routine in an isolated way, without sufficient regard to the conditions and the workings of other social institutions at that time. There is a tendency for the school to become an isolated institution, for being looked upon as having its own peculiar interests and methods and both those in the school and outside of the school tend to conceive of the school from that special point of view, instead of looking upon it as simply one among a number of social instrumentalities needing to be judged from the standpoint of its interactions, its flexible response to the other institutions. Of course what that means practically is that the school tends through this inertia to perpetuate the habits of an earlier form of society. When these things in the school took shape, there is a strong probability that they did so in relation to the existing social environment; they were once relevant; but the school having become thus segregated they are maintained more or less independently of what is going on in the world at large.

Some of you may have heard the address given by Mrs. Young,* Assistant Superintendent of Schools, in which she

[* The reference is to Ella Flagg Young, who served as supervisor of instruction in Dewey's Laboratory School at the University of Chicago, under Mrs. Alice Chipman Dewey, who was principal. It was she who suggested that it be named the "laboratory school." In 1909 she became Superintendent of Schools in Chicago, the first woman to hold such a post in a large city. In his daughter's biographical sketch, authorized by Dewey, she says, "He [Dewey] regards Mrs. Young as the wisest person in school matters with whom he has come in contact in any way."

spoke of the fact that businessmen who would not think in their occupations of doing anything but keeping up with the present social movement quite commonly thought the school should keep the curriculum of a generation ago, are quite insistent upon going back to the curriculum of the three Rs with which they and their fathers were familiar when they went to school. Such a point of view cannot arise in any way except in thinking that the school is a separate institution set apart once for all, instead of part of the moving life of society. If people once had it in their heads that it is a part of the larger social movement, it would be impossible for them to judge it in any other way than that when other social forces change the school must change too in such a way as to maintain the spirit of unity, a flexible give and take between the school life and the life outside.

Many things in our educational ideals and in actual subject matter taught often tend to reflect earlier social environment, one which has passed away. Arithmetic is one of the most conservative studies, and not more than a century ago our arithmetical textbooks reflected the ways of doing business of two or three centuries before. A great deal of alligation and of compound proportion and of partnership simply represent matters that were once of practical import but which lost all relevancy with change of conditions. Before the formation of the business corporation or the joint stock company in the sixteenth century, large commercial enterprises were undertaken along with the growth of the geographical world. One man, there not being any joint stock company, would say he would put in so much money for a certain length of time, and another would say he would put in so much for a certain length of time. The arithmetical problems thus made practically necessary under those conditions of doing business lasted for at least two hundred years. In the arithmetics of today there are illustrations of the same sort. Percentage and bank discount have no present counterpart, but having got into the books, the publishers think they cannot sell the books if they are left out, and the teachers think there will be less mental discipline.

[Jane M. Dewey, "Biography of John Dewey," in P. A. Schilpp, ed., *The Philosophy of John Dewey* (New York: Tudor Publishing Company, 1939).]

The relative overestimation mentioned before, of the linguistic factor in education, is of course on the same principle. There was a time when Latin was the only language in which philosophy, science, and literature, especially philosophy and science, were written at all. Of course Latin was then an absolutely necessary implement for introduction to all higher culture; it was as necessary as to be able to read anything is today. It was a sign of the difference between an illiterate and an educated person. Then there was a time when the whole form of linguistic education meant more than it does today. In the first place the methods of original discovery and of free discussion and reflection were not elaborated. Knowledge had to be handed down in a traditional form, in the form in which it had been accumulated, or it was likely to get away. Under these circumstances there was a great premium on the books in which the hold of the world on truth was consolidated. There was little intercommunication; travel was almost unknown. There was no communication by mail or telegraph, no cheap printing, no circulation of books and magazines from libraries such as there is today. At the same time the industrial conditions were different. All industries were carried on either in the home or neighborhood. Of course the factory system, the system of manufacture on a large scale through the application of mechanical inventions is, relatively speaking, a recent thing. There were consequently certain factors in the experience of every person which are not found today. Practically speaking every child came into contact with all the typical forms of industry in his own home and neighborhood. The candles that were burned were made in the home, shoes were made in the home or near at hand, clothing was not only made there, but for the most part the yarn was spun and the cloth itself woven in the home; life was largely rural. If you follow out that line of consideration, the child in his informal education came day by day in contact with a range of considerations lying outside the environment of the city child, at least, of today, and even in the country these elements in the natural development through the environment have been very much reduced.

Under these circumstances then, the everyday life gave the child an industrial and motor education, a training of his habits on the side of making and doing things. It was therefore not only possible, but desirable, for the school to concentrate itself

upon the other side, on the side which was so far away, which
came so little into the child's everyday life. Now there has been
a revolution; it is all turned upside down. The thing that was
previously far away, remote, and hard, is now in the air, the
atmosphere. The learning which was once fixed in books is
now, relatively speaking, in circulation. It is no longer solid, it
is fluid and moving about in waves so that the city or suburban
child, except in the foreign districts, can hardly help coming in
contact with it. Moreover, the outside ways of learning to master things are so multiplied that the child tends to form habits
in the direction of the use and mastery of language in a way
that he could not possibly have done one hundred years ago.
On the other side, this practical side which tends to habits of
industry, had not only a practical, but a moral and intellectual
aspect. It enlarged the child's sense of the world about him,
and brought him into contact with the world in very real ways.
The city child today has an intellectual atmosphere about him
at home, where once he had an atmosphere of work—a practical and industrial atmosphere which has now moved away
from the home to factories and shops. Through the natural
tendencies to isolation and to inertia that accompanied that
isolation, it may be questioned whether the school has kept pace
with this change in social life without; whether it has adapted
itself on the positive or negative side sufficiently to this social
transition. The school is in many respects the most conservative of all social institutions, even more than the family itself,
and therefore there is a tendency for it to lag behind and get out
of adjustment to the other organizations of social form.

A word or two of emphasis on one or two points
[(2)]   implied in what I have just said. First, with the development of synthetic method, that is with the development of methods of controlling investigation and controlling
reflection, the intellectual ideal can and must in the long run
change more and more from one of information to one of ability to use the methods of inquiry and verification. When synthetic method is not developed, learning has to be hung on to
by main force; it must be studied, it must be memorized, drilled
into the mind, or it gets away entirely, but with the development of method the individual has in himself the power to
discover and reproduce those facts for himself when needed.
If all the accumulated learning of the world were to be wiped

out of existence through some catastrophe, and yet people retained their hold on the methods of observation, and thinking, and experimentation, it would not be an irreparable loss, we would go to work and make it all over again, indeed there would be some compensating advantages if we could have such a catastrophe. Yet it may be questioned whether the full significance of that point is understood. Science itself is still taught very largely from the standpoint of more information to be learned, instead of having command of the methods for getting the information; in fact science, which marks a change in the whole mental attitude, has been treated as if what were needed was more of the same sort of thing, more or less detailed facts and principles memorized and carried around by sheer mental strength. The methods of the administration of the school, the methods of discipline, I think, might be said to illustrate to some extent the same survival of social habits and ideals which once were necessary because they were part of the entire social structure of the time, and which failed to modify themselves in accordance with the general social movement. I refer to the general development of the individual. While that ideal lends itself to misinterpretation because it is easy to interpret the ideal of individualization in a wrong direction, certainly that general change in our moral ideals which have gone along with the progressive ideals toward democracy leads also to the way in which the child should be treated. While the school is a very different thing from what it was a generation ago, to say nothing of a longer time, it may still be questioned whether the underlying principle involved there has as yet been universally consciously recognized and acted upon.

[(3)] There is a difficulty of precisely the opposite sort with reference to school education in performing those functions spoken of as desirable. Those I have mentioned so far have come from the perpetuation of something outgrown. There is the opposite danger of introducing into the school the details of contemporary life in a technical and unrelated way. There is danger of putting in some things out of contemporary life too fast and in too crude and unassimilated a way. The point that I spoke of a moment ago, about the introduction of science, equally illustrates this. The tendency has been to introduce science into the high school from the same standpoint taught in the university, and in the elementary school from the same standpoint taught in the high school; introduced in its more technical and formulated aspects. The result was, of course, congestion in the school. We are still in a stage of transition and of compromise. To a certain extent we have kept all the older studies, and in order to meet the current conditions we have also introduced into the school, piled on top of these others, a lot more studies. What we call the old education has maintained itself in certain particulars, but it has given way so far as to admit a number of new studies, and so the child in the more progressive schools, is bewildered by the number of studies forced upon him. Asking a little girl in the third grade what she studied, she mentioned three kinds of arithmetic. She had mental arithmetic, model arithmetic, and written arithmetic. There were two kinds of written arithmetic, paper and blackboard. Well everybody knows that it has become a practical problem to prevent the child from being crowded in this way. A large part of the present educational problem has been called the "conflict of studies." A part of this is due to the premature and unrelated introduction of things from contemporary life. The child should have something which corresponds to science from the kindergarten up, but it is a question of working it over into such shape that it presents itself in relation to the child's immediate experience, instead of as a result of specialization which has been reached at the hands of those most expert in the subject. The textbook is written by the scientific man and he wishes to present it in scientific form as well as content, and it is presented in ways incapable of assimilation by the child.

To sum up, the two chief difficulties in the way of the school carrying out the ideals suggested is, on one side, the conservatism that isolates former ideals irrespective of the change going on in life at large, and the tendency to insert in the curriculum the specialized technical results of contemporary civilization, without regard to the redress, the reproduction which that material needs in order to be capable of application to the child.

LECTURE VIII

January 18, 1899

[A.III.(2): *Instruction and education: the place and function of knowledge. Justifications.*]

[I.C.2.] The point that I take up next, the relation of instruction to education, can of course at this point only be discussed in a preliminary way, because a more minute consideration of the principles involved would take us into the question of the whole psychology of method, but since the distinguishing characteristic of the school as a whole, that which makes the chief distinction on the side of method between the informal and the formal education is instruction, it seems desirable at this time to speak of the question of the relation existing between instruction and education.

[a.] The saying is quoted from Herbart that he knew nothing of instruction which was not educative, and he knew of no education excepting through the medium of instruction. As to the first part of the sentence, I suppose no one would raise any questions. Instruction certainly ought to be educative, that is, the teaching and the learning process ought to conduce to growth, and unless it does conduce to development, it would have the form, but not the reality of instruction. The other part of the sentence, that there is no education excepting through the medium of instruction, would either raise difficulties or else it would be largely a question of minutiae of the terminology of definition. Of course education can be defined in such a way as to exclude the informal education entirely from the scope of education, and in that case it would be simple tautology to say that there is no education excepting through the medium of instruction, but unless the term "education" is restricted to make that statement fit, unless it is already defined so as to include the idea of instruction within it, it certainly seems like a forced statement to say that all education proceeds through the medium of instruction, for it is difficult to see how the idea of education can be reduced below the import for the whole process of growth maintained through learning, and certainly there is learning without what we ordinarily term "instruction." There is a process of learning by experience which constitutes the essence of the pre-scholastic education, and which is maintained through life independently of the scholastic education, "learning by experience" being the general term which would include the various processes of direct stimulation, suggestion, and so on. Whenever an intelligent person does something he is pretty sure to learn something from the results of what he does, and unless we broaden the content of the term "instruction" very much, it hardly seems right to say that all education proceeds through the medium of instruction.

More than that, however, there is the question whether within the school itself it is true that all education proceeds through the medium of instruction. The acceptance of that dictum would seem to make of necessity a somewhat abrupt break between the first going to school and the life of the child precedent to the school period. It might be accepted without question that the general movement of the school ought to be in the direction of instruction, and that the time would finally be reached when the greater part of it would be carried on through that medium. But unless there is to be a sudden and abrupt transition, it would seem that the ordinary processes of learning through experience ought to project themselves for a while into the school life and be only gradually outgrown. There ought to be some place in the school system, and a good deal of place in the beginning grades, for what we might call direct modes of experience, where the child does things for the sake of doing them as he does outside of the school, and has his learning through the doing for its own sake; he learns through his own experience. Then the process of instruction ought to be a gradual systematization of these more direct modes of experience, which should occupy the greater part of the earlier school period. That particular phase of the question will come up again when we discuss the philosophy of the school grade, or the various parts of the school system. Instruction certainly involves as a large part of its content, the idea of education through the acquisition of knowledge.

[b.]   The question of the relation between instruction and education would ultimately take this form: Just what is the place and significance of knowledge within experience? Just what is the relation of knowledge to development of character, and to the enrichment of life? As I said at the outset, that cannot be discussed in detail without reference to psychological considerations which will come up better later on. But there is a certain framework of principles which may be propounded at least as a working hypothesis at this stage of the argument. Knowledge is in no case an end in itself but is a means or instrument for the development of character and for the enrichment of the life experience. That of course brings us back to the first part of Herbart's dictum, that there should be no instruction which is not educative in character. The general point of view presented is that knowledge has both its origin, its starting point, and its function, its application, in something outside of itself, in something which is not merely knowledge, and that as knowledge it serves to cover what would otherwise be a certain gap or break within the process of experience, and that consequently, instruction must grow out of, and terminate in, something which is not learning, but which is an activity that is wider and deeper than the process of learning.

[(1)]   Psychologically, the peculiar function to which we give especially the name knowledge, arises out of some difficulty, some obstacle in the process of direct or practical activity, and the special function of knowledge is first to formulate that difficulty as a problem, and then, secondly, by dealing with it as a problem, as an objective difficulty, and not merely as a case of practical friction, find a method for solution, and then thirdly, utilize the method thus intellectually reached by applying it to the practical current of experience, to make that experience itself run smoothly again. In other words, psychologically knowledge has always, if we go back far enough, a practical origin, and a practical use. It should be noted however, that it is not a mere practical bridge or stop gap. Although it has its origin and use in that way, it also serves to enrich the whole further process of experience, to put more value into it than it would otherwise have, quite beyond the over-coming of the practical difficulties. There is always a difference between a mere means which is done away

with when the end is reached, and a means or instrument
which enters effectively into the final result. Knowledge is
a means or instrument of the latter sort. The scaffolding of
the building is in one sense a means to the erection of the building: and so are the hammers and saws and planes that are used,
but they do not enter actively and vitally into the structure of
the building itself. The architect's plan, as well as the material
that is used, are not only means, but they are also part of the
make-up of the final end. They are not of course there as they
were before, but in a transformed condition they enter into the
final result. So with the process of knowledge, it is not a mere
device that we resort to in order to get out of a difficulty, and
then go on acting again freely and smoothly. The whole process
of formulating the problem and solving it, adds an element to
experience of positive value which would not be there otherwise, so that there is more meaning to experience because the
difficulty has arisen, because it has been formulated and solved.

Putting it in terms which are currently used in educational
discussion, knowledge is considered as a means of furthering
experience, of enabling us to overcome or avoid difficulties, to
manage our conduct economically and efficiently. Knowledge
considered as a means of controlling experience, is what is
meant by discipline. But the fact that it does not remain a mere
instrument of control, of direction, of economy in conduct, but
enriches the succedent experience, gives us what is termed
knowledge as a means of culture. While then it is necessary to
recognize the enrichment of experience, the culture effect, and
not limit knowledge to mere instrumentality and device for
the control of action, it still remains that the origin and immediate purpose of knowledge, as knowledge, as information,
as apprehending more facts and comprehending more principles, is a practical one, the control of experience; while it is,
so to speak, a gift of grace that in getting that additional control of experience, we also get the culture effect, or the added
increment of value in experience itself.

The fundamental educational considerations which
[(2)]   would result from this point of view would be, of
course, the necessity within the school of supplying
a motive for the acquisition of knowledge, a motive which is intrinsic and not simply factitious. I mean by that, that when
there is knowledge which it is desirable to have the child ac-

quire, when there are facts or principles which it is desirable for him to learn, the presentation of them should always be such as to make him see, at least feel, the relevancy of the knowledge which he is to acquire, the necessity for it which lies in the process of his own experience. On the other hand there should always be, not merely the possibility, but the necessity for some application of the knowledge, the learning thus gained, back to the better actual control of experience itself. It is of course the ideal which has been especially emphasized in the Herbartian conception of education, that knowledge should not remain inert, that it should enter into the formation of character, that instruction should not end in itself, but that it should educate.

The point that I have been wishing so far to make is that the possibility of having knowledge become something more than the mere accumulation of facts and laws, of becoming actually operative in character and conduct, is dependent on the extent to which that information is evolved out of some need in the child's own experience and to which it receives application to that experience. We may wish, we may hope as much as we please, that instruction will be effective, that is, that it will pass beyond mere learning into the sphere of character and action, but we cannot insure the reality of that excepting as we observe the psychological conditions involved, which to repeat, are the genesis on one side of knowledge out of a practical need, and the function on the other hand of knowledge, with a certain degree of directness in experience itself.

[(a)] Now the isolation of school from life, of which we have spoken before, as a social fact, also reflects itself here as a psychological fact. The tendency is to isolate the learning process, to isolate instruction, and to attend to it by itself; to have the child learn for the sake of learning; to learn what the teacher or adult appreciates, realizes, is necessary for the child, and which the adult knows the child will have to use or apply some time in life, without the corresponding consciousness on the child's part of the need which there is, or of the use of it in his own experience. Of course all the material is ultimately selected on the basis of need, even as it is. We do not attempt to have the child learn anything and everything. We pick out the things which we concede to be relevant to his needs and we pick them out because, being relevant to his needs, they will have application in his life some time. That is merely a formal and logical reference to experience unless there is the counterpart to this consciousness in the child's experience at the time of learning.

Perhaps the point I have in mind might be made clearer in this way. The adult knows that the child needs a certain amount of arithmetic, grammar, reading, writing, geography, and some time will require all these things in order to get the proper control and guidance of his activities, and they are selected. On that principle it is left to luck and chance whether the thing is so integrated into the learner's experience that it ceases to be inert knowledge, and becomes a positive factor. It may or it may not, depending a good deal upon things which lie quite outside the teacher's control. Upon the other basis the consolidated, formulated material of instruction, the lesson would somehow be led up to, out of the normal, direct experience of the child himself. The little child that makes a garden out of doors and has a hoe, rake, and seeds given him, does not have them simply because later on in life he may be an agriculturalist. The child's own direct activity, what he wants to do, the impulses that he already has, create a demand for those things so that when they are supplied they fit in at once, and they not only prepare him for the farming activity later on in life, but the matter of the hoe and rake becomes a controlling factor in his immediate experience.

[(b)] The problem of instruction, if instruction is really to educate, is to secure that sort of relation with every and any subject in the school, that it shall grow out of, be differentiated out of something in the child's own more natural and spontaneous interests, and that shall again lead on consciously into his further direct and ordinary experiences. So far as that is done the school process is organically related to outside life, not simply in the social sense, but also in the psychological sense. So far as that is not done, the school experience becomes a thing in itself; the child learns to live in two spheres of experience, in two worlds, more or less, and he passes at certain times out of one into another, and vice versa. He associates certain kinds of ideas and experiences with one world and the connection they have with his every day life are more or less a matter of chance; they are left largely to luck to express or realize themselves. The story told by the superintendent of the Illinois schools of a child who did not know that the Mississippi river in the geography was the river he saw every day of his life, illustrates the idea of the separation of the process of instruction from the things of ordinary experience. While that is an exaggerated instance, no one would doubt the tendency of the instruction process as material, to become more or less segregated and formulated by itself. At least we have paid more conscious attention to the formulation of this material as matter for lessons, than we have to the correlate questions: How shall we introduce this as an outgrowth of the child's own experience; and how secure the conditions for its actual present use by the child himself? In order to avoid misapprehension, the point made before had better be repeated, that the younger, the more immature the child is, the greater the need for making this connection directly. As the child goes on he forms certain special habits which become a part of his own life; he gets a positive satisfaction in learning for its own sake, as he does in doing other things for their own sake; and learning becomes a kind of doing, a kind of direct doing which carries its own satisfaction or worth in itself. That is, the enlargement of the child's experience is in and through the learning itself. That is true of the secondary, and of the higher education. But there is possibly an undue isolation which makes the learning process a technical one, and not a part of the whole life process, and which makes the material learned simply an accumulation of facts which are true as facts, but which are so unrelated to experience that they cannot possibly fulfill the ideal of influencing character in any way, or becoming transmuted, unless by chance, into conduct. From the psychological side, therefore, as well as from the social side, the first pre-requisite of the school, or of the organized processes of education, is the instituting of proper organic relations between the school experience and activities, and those of every day life.

[(3)]   So far I have assumed that knowledge does psychologically originate and function with reference to the conduct of life. I have assumed that there is no such thing as intellect as a thing in and by itself, but that intellect means rather the concentration of certain capacities upon certain problems for the sake of something lying outside of the intellect itself. There is a hypothetical justification for that assumption, namely, that it is only on that basis that instruction can be made an organic instrument of education that is a factor in the development of character; that is, unless that is true, it is a hopeless ideal to propose to ourselves that all knowledge shall ultimately terminate in character or in conduct. The result thus far, may be stated then hypothetically: If instruction as instruction is to educate, if it is to result in growth all around and terminate in conduct, then knowledge must be treated as something growing out of a common background of experience and in turn find application in that common experience.

[(4)]   But over and above that there are certain strictly psychological considerations which may be briefly mentioned as going to show that the principle has a categorical and not simply a hypothetical truth.

[(a)]   In the first place if we accept the theory of evolution as applying to the principle of intelligence, we must get that result. Considered as to its origin on the theory of evolution, intelligence, that is powers of observing and reflecting, must originate in the same way in which a tooth, claw, eye, or ear originated: namely, as positive gains for the struggle for existence selected because they further the process of existence. If we do not accept the application of the theory of evolution, we can suppose that intelligence was introduced at a certain time, quite foreign to the practical affairs of life. But if we hold to the theory of evolution applied there, then the dawn of intelligence must have been a favorable variation, it must have been selected and perpetuated because of the practical advantage which is given. Everyone would admit that intelligence would be the most powerful of all instruments or devices for getting additional control of the environment. In other words the development of the brain and nervous system is an even more indispensable thing from the practical point of view than is the development of the stomach, lungs, or heart. Of course it is not immediately, because the person must be able to get food and digest it or he cannot live at all, but granted that capacity, then the increase on the side of intelligence means greater ability to control the environment than any other possible variation of the organs could be.

[(b)] This conception of knowledge which we would derive from the biological point of view, is also enforced by child psychology. A comparatively slight observation of children would show that they are not getting information for the sake of the strictly objective attainment itself. The child is an extremely curious being, an investigating being, and he might be said to have the germ of independent intellectual activity from the start, but the child's curiosity shows itself as a practical thing. The child's investigation is of an essentially immediate character, taking hold of things, throwing them, tearing them open to see what noise they will make, doing what he can with the various objects to see what will happen. Because he does it in order to get some new experiences, it is the germ of the intrinsic intellectual power of investigation which certainly does not show itself in the animal. But yet this purely practical use of intelligence, of investigation, long precedes any consciousness of intellectual problems, any consciousness of scientific truth in the abstract.

LECTURE IX

January 19, 1899

[A.IV.1.(1),(2),(3),(4): *(Justifications, continued). A consideration of one-sided definitions of education: the psychological and the social.*]

[I.C.2.b.(4)(c).] I was speaking yesterday at the end of the hour of certain reasons for the position that the function of knowledge originates and at first has reference to practical conditions which arise outside of itself. I mentioned two points, the argument from the biological side and from the side of child psychology. There is a third point, which, if carried out, would involve an extensive course in psychology. It is the connection of both sensations and ideas with the process of attention.

[(1)] Attention is certainly closely connected with interest, and interest in its ultimate analysis would be a practical affair. The conscious sensation normally accompanies the discriminative process in attention. When we talk of sensations apart from attention we really must be thinking of them as physiological processes. The stimulation of the sense organs as a physiological affair is going on all the time, but a sensation as a conscious mental content is always accompanied with a certain discriminative function of attention. It may be laid down as a general law that we discriminate in order to get the adequate stimuli for further operations; that is, we discriminate in order to get the signs or signals, or clues, to some further operation. It is obvious that in the abstract there are an indefinite number of sensations possible, but at any one time the sensations actually experienced, are a very small fraction of the number of sensations that at any given time are theoretically possible. What is the basis for the selection and experiencing of the few as against the many that are left out?

It is simply that we ignore everything that is irrelevant to the activity that we are engaged upon, that does not seem to be appropriate, that does not fit into what we are trying to do. We emphasize whatever is of assistance with reference to the end that we have in view. A man's discriminative ability is always in line with his habits, his calling, with the results that he is customarily aiming at. The sailor has one kind of discriminative ability, that is, he gets sensations which are relevant to his calling; the hunter is conscious very definitely of still other classes of sensations, because they are relevant to what he has to do. A person in any kind of industry will develop a peculiar sensibility in line with his occupation and aims. The scientific man is conscious of distinctions where the common person would get only a blur or a vague idea. Every new experience begins with what is vague, but as time goes on, it clears itself up, distinctions become prominent and certain points become salient, while there is a background of familiar considerations.

It would be found in any of those cases that that [(*ii*)] growing clearing up of what was originally vague and hazy, is through this process of emphasizing, of seizing hold of and dwelling upon whatever considerations are relevant to the ends we have in view, the results we want to get. If we were merely knowing beings, there would be no ground for this selection at all; all possible sensations would be of equal value, and there would be no reason why attentions should not be distributed over the entire field. Attention however means a focusing, a limiting, a defining, a selecting. The only standard we can find for that selection is the end which we wish to reach. Ideas (meaning by ideas the more general considerations as distinct from sensations which relate to particular objects) fall at the other pole of this process. In saying that we define, we discriminate what will serve as stimuli, as clues, as signals. We say we define the means by which we are to reach our end. The idea is of course that which stands for our end; it is that which represents the purpose, the result that we want to get. Because it is a purpose, because it is what we are after, it cannot be presented as a sensation, simply as a representative, an image or idea. As representing the end which we wish to reach, it serves as a standard for the direction of, and is developed into the plan by which action is to be carried out. Sensations and ideas originate as correlative to each other, representing respectively means and ends. We distinguish on the side of the particular assistances or helps to carrying out a course of action, and we unify, concentrate all this variety of elements that we distinguish on the basis of a single end which we have in view. The moment the mind ceases to have an end or aim before it, instead of being attentive, it goes wool-gathering, or it falls into day dreams or revery. Simply going over your own experience will show you that when your mind is most intense, it is because there is a purpose in view which holds all the centrifugal tendencies of the mind together and which centralizes them. The effort in attention is all due to the fact that there is this single end with reference to which you must manipulate the variety of movements. Let the unity go and the mind scatters itself and the whole strain lets up.

We have in the carrying out of that analysis of attention the factors for the consideration of the psychology of method as the interaction between means and ends in the mental activity, between the observational process which discriminates the conditions, the means, on one side, and the ideal, the intellectual process on the other, which determines for us the purposes, the aims. I shall come back to a more detailed discussion of this point when we come to the consideration of method. I mention it here as indicating that sensations and ideas which are admitted by common consent to be the factors in the process of the intellectual life, have this reference in a normal mental operation, this reference to ends, to purposes, so that here we have a further justification of the statement that the intellect does not originally have reference to things which are merely intellectual, that is, at the outset it functions with reference to practical purposes, or the reaching of some kind of results.

The most general point for discussion is simply the
[D.1.a.] summarizing of the previous discussion in a somewhat formal way, with respect to securing a definition of education, and of the various factors which enter into it. It is clear that in the entire preceding discussion we have assumed an individual on one side as a being capable of education, and the social environment, the social influences stimulating him and selecting his various responses on the other. That would of itself suggest that a comprehensive or philosophic conception of education must include within it an individual phase, and a social phase. Or if we use the terms of the sciences which

treat of the individual and of society respectively, it would show the necessity of considering education both from the psychological and the sociological side. It would intimate that a definition that was exclusively psychological or exclusively sociological in character, would be one-sided and partial. It would also suggest that at different times we might be interested more in one phase than the other, so that we might emphasize at one time the psychological definition and at another the sociological definition.

When either of these definitions becomes exclusive,
[*b.*]   when it ignores the other, it becomes one-sided. I am
not going to give you a catalogue of the various definitions of education which have been developed by various writers from time to time. You will find that in many of the general books on pedagogy. If you will go over one of these inventories, or make such a catalogue for yourselves, you will find that they can all be classified in this way: they are either definitions which pick out the psychological or sociological side simply, or have a more or less indefinite mixture of the two, passing apparently insensibly from one element to the other, or an attempt to get a balance of the two factors. Without going over all the sub-varieties, I will simply pick out a typical definition for analysis from the psychological side, and a typical one from the sociological side, and attempt to show that taken by itself it is so one-sided that it is self-contradictory, that if you take either by itself it is thoroughly inconsistent.

The typical psychological definition is that education
[(*1*)(*a*)] is "the harmonious development of the various powers
of the individual." Now certainly education is that, or ought to be that. In other words the definition is not false, but it is inadequate, it does not explain itself, and when it is set up as final and complete, then it becomes self-contradictory. What do we mean by power? What do we mean by development? What do we mean by harmonious? Just exactly what content, significance, shall we put into those various terms? What is the standard for deciding what we mean by power, and by harmonious development? When we ask these questions we see the necessity of reinforcing the definition, or controlling the definition, by reference to social considerations. There are no such things as powers in the abstract. Power is the ability to do something, to accomplish something. It is

capacity in use, in service. It involves therefore, relation to
the environment, to the conditions under which the work is to
be done. If a human being was living in a vacuum it might
perhaps be possible to tell what a power was in itself and by
itself, although we cannot form any conception of what it
would be like under such circumstances. The only criterion
for deciding between capacity and incapacity, between ability,
that is, power, and useless or actually harmful employment
of energy, is to fix our minds on the kinds of things we want
to do. If we know the kind of results we want to get we can
tell what a power is. It is anything which assists us with reference to reaching that end. We must at least unconsciously
put the individual in a social environment before we can tell
whether any trait of his is really a power, or what sort of a thing
it is, because it is only as it operates in that environment that
it can possibly have any significance, can be a capacity.

        The same thing is true of the other terms of the defi-
[(b)]   nition. The idea of harmonious development: what is
        development? Above all what is harmony? There
generally lies at the basis of this definition a conception of the
so-called faculties of the human mind, the faculty of acting,
of observing, and of judging, and the idea of harmony is that
each one of these shall be developed symmetrically with all
the others. But what is your standard when you try to put any
real meaning into that? Just how far are you going to develop
perception, and why stop? How far are you going to develop
memory? and so with all the other faculties. "It is impossible to
solve many of the specific questions which arise in the actual
education of any particular human being" is a good phrase
which is undoubtedly true, but it is a maxim which has been
of positive value because it has helped take away men's minds
from false ideals of education and given them a vague appreciation of the fact that education must be relevant to the
individual. It is not education unless it succeeds in getting a
growth of the individual, but beyond that mere vague reference
to individuality, beyond that importance which is attached to
the growth of individuality, the term can hardly be said to have
any meaning at all. Are you going to train perception or memory indefinitely? What is the principle that checks, that limits?
If you introduce the thought of the social environment you get
at once the necessary limit and the idea that puts meaning

into those terms. You want to give the person enough observation, memory, and so on, to be serviceable, that he may be able to accomplish something in the world in which he lives, but if you leave that out your idea becomes merely a formal mental gymnastic. Because it is formal it throws no light upon educational procedure at all. All this on the basis that there are some things which may be called faculties, per se, in the mind. When we recognize that there are no such faculties, the definition has its meaning evaporate still more when taken by itself. Faculties are really just habits. Of course there is a certain practical sense in which we talk about the faculty of remembering, or judging. It has a practical power. As a habit, it means something. But the moment it is recognized that a habit is formed with reference to a certain function, with reference to a certain kind of work which needs to be done (and what that is we cannot tell except as we consider the environment in which the function is to operate), we recognize that we might as well try to form a physiology or anatomy of the functions and organs of an animal without reference to the conditions of the environment in which the animal gets its food and carries on its activities, as to try to define education simply in terms of the harmonious development of the individual, without relation to the social environment in which the individual is to use them.

The typical definition on the other side is that edu-
[(2)(*a*)] cation is "the process of adjusting the individual to
civilization." That again is true, like the definition from the psychological side, but the quality of its truth is dependent upon interpreting it with reference to individualistic or psychological considerations. It is obvious that if we leave those entirely out, then we get the idea of fixed adaptation, which we have already rejected. Civilization is taken as something already there, hard and fixed, and the education of the individual is simply to conform him to the character and needs of that civilization. It makes education practically an external process applied to the individual from without, in which the individual, in principle at least, is pretty passive, and it subordinates the education of the individual to pre-conceived political and social considerations. It simply says: Make the individual a comfortable and efficient member of society just as it is.

Now the fact that the society or civilization for which
[(b)] the individual is to be educated is a progressive one,
shows the impossibility of putting any meaning into
that definition without reference to the motives, impulses and
capacities of the individual himself. What is adjustment to
existing civilization? How is that adjustment to be got at?
Suppose we do adopt that in all good faith as the standard of
our educational process and set to work to try and pick out the
methods and processes in the school which would really adapt
the individual to existing civilization; what would we do? It
is obvious that civilization is too complex taken in that fixed
way and it is too changeable to throw any light upon the process
itself. By the time the individual was thoroughly adjusted to
civilization as it was when we began educating and adjusting
him, society would have undergone a transition and the individual would not fit. Take it on the industrial side; try to fit
the individual to the economic conditions. Suppose he has
fifteen or twenty years in which to be fitted into the existing
industrial conditions, the modes of doing business. It would
probably be an exaggeration to say that he would be completely
out of adjustment with his surroundings, but he would be far
from being in harmony with them if changes are to occur as
rapidly in the next hundred years as in the last. The application of science to industry, the control of natural forces, light
and electricity, have completely revolutionized the environment of civilization, at least within one hundred years, and
largely within fifty years, and there is no reason to suppose
that the process has reached its limits. What the character of
the changes is to be no one could prophesy. We must either
guess at the future or else take things as they are. Introducing
a mechanical uniformity in the matter of adjustment would
leave the individual very poorly adapted when he came to make
his way for himself.

While we must adjust the individual in a way to
[(c)] civilization, how is it to be done? If we can put the
individual in the way to do his own adjusting, it is
certainly clear that we will be more likely to be successful than
if we try to do it in advance by the educative process. If we
educate the individual with reference to ability, to get the use
of all his own natural capacities, he can be turned loose in
a changing environment with some strong likelihood of his

being able to make his own adjustment to the varying situations in which he finds himself. One of the phases of the industrial problem at present is the existence of large numbers of persons who are absolutely or relatively incompetent. Perhaps there are not many absolutely incompetent, but there are many who are incompetent to do more than one kind of manual work. They have not been adjusted to civilization, and they are the wreckage, the floats of society, they are the burden of society which it has to carry on its back and assume the responsibility of supporting, while they do bungling work or work of a poor grade. The reason that they are social wreckage or failures, or burdens, is simply, at least partly, in the fact that they never have been educated to utilize their own powers; they never have been educated to habits of self-control and self-adjustment, they never have been rendered flexible, capable of using good judgment during their school years, and the result is that they are not adjusted.

To turn the point around the other way, it would [(3)] mean that in a progressive society the safest and surest way of securing the adjustment of the individual to social conditions is by treating him as an individual on the psychological basis and not exclusively on the sociological basis, with the faith that if he can secure this command of his own resources, he will be able to solve his own economic problems as they arise. The same thing is equally true on the more general social and political side. In a changing and democratic society adjustment to the needs of civilization must mean training for direction, for leadership, to a certain extent, and not simply training for fitting into a preconceived niche in a society that is definitely organized, say on a caste basis, or one of fixed classes of any sort. The education of the individual can be carried on for the most part on the basis of simply adjusting to the existing state of things, but in a democratic society with its mobility and with the responsibilities which are put upon every individual for taking an active and not simply a passive part in social affairs, it is obvious that adjustment must mean such a training as will enable him to put all his powers at the disposal of society, that is, assume the responsibilities that come to him as a part ruler, director, of the whole of that society. There again we are most likely to get that sort of adjustment if we simply give the individual

the best development that he, as an individual, is capable of.
We would seem to have got into a see-saw. The psychological
definition throws us over to the social side to get its meaning
decided, and when we are on the social side we must go back
to the psychological side to get any basis. Is there any way
out of that circle? Otherwise we would seem to be in the condition described by the gentleman who said there were two
theories neither of which was true, but each was useful as
counteracting the errors of the other. The question is whether
there is any unified point of view with reference to which we
can understand and interpret both the psychological and the
sociological factors in education.

LECTURE X

January 23, 1899

[A.IV.1.(5);A.IV.2: *The merging of the psychological and social in definition. The elements involved in education.*]

[I.D.1.c.(1).] At the last time the result reached was that the attempt to get an exhaustive and exclusive definition of education under either the individual or social side was not possible, and that the attempt led to self-contradictory results. The result reached however, seemed to leave us rather in the air in one way. Whichever side we started from we seemed to land on the other side without coming really to a point of rest anywhere. That would be a contradiction unless education itself had within it two phases which correspond to each other, which are correlative to each other, one phase of which might be stated in the psychological definition, and the other phase of which might be stated in the sociological definition. Now that is the state of things. The social view of education considered it from the standpoint of its ends, its value measured by the result accomplished, while the psychological view considered it in terms of means or instrumentalities through which it is carried on. That is to say, the social view takes education from the side of its ends, and the psychological from the side of its means. Of course means and ends are correlative to each other; they have no significance except in reference to each other.

[(2)] The lack in each definition taken by itself is that the conception, say of adaptation to civilization, is imperfect because it does not tell us what kind of an adaptation is possible in the nature of the case. It must be of course adaptation of the person educated, it must be an adaptation of him, not of something else, and of him specifically. It moreover must be through this individual himself that the adaptation is to be secured. The adaptation cannot be attained by external influences, it cannot be attained by putting the individual bodily as it were, into a certain place and pushing and crowding him until he stays there. This adaptation must be secured through the instrumentality of calling into play the individual's own powers. When we see the individual as the means, we get full play for the psychological side of education. The same thing is true on the side of the means used, on the side of the individual. Excepting as we get a social view of education we do not see what the individual is for, what his value, significance, is. The importance of also taking the social relations and factors into consideration in the view of education, is that it gives us all the time a standard, something by which to interpret the various factors and phenomena that show themselves in the individual. Of course any fact if it is isolated, if taken by itself, becomes unrelated and therefore meaningless. We have no standard for judging its value. To judge its value is to interpret it. So any fact in the child, being a strictly psychical fact, is valueless, unless we look at it from the standpoint of what it may result in, of what it may lead up to, or else of the conditions out of which it sprang. When we look at it from that standpoint, we give it a social interpretation. That can be made more concrete by reference to investigations in child study.

[(3)] Various investigations have been carried on concerning the child's moral ideas, his ideas about punishment. A number of the studies in Earl Barnes's *Studies in Education*[1] consist in trying to find out what the child's ideas are about just and unjust punishment, or investigations to get what the child's religious ideas are; still another tries to ascertain his capacity for reasoning. It is a one-sided view if we take those results as being necessarily psychological in character. They may be psychological or they may be social or a mixture of both. That is to say, the child's idea of punishment may represent nothing which is in any way intrinsic to himself, but simply a precipitation of the views that he has heard expressed about him, it may be simply an expression of the way in which he has been led already to view the thing. His ideas about religion would not give us any indication of the child's natural ideas, but would represent instruction or

[1 *Ibid.*]

more or less what the child felt he was expected to say. Even
in such a topic as the child's ability to reason, the results also
have to be interpreted from the standpoint of the child's social
surroundings. There is no such thing as ability to reason in the
abstract; it would represent the amount of experience and the
extent to which his attention has been called by others to certain kinds of facts and their bearings, and those are all social
things. Still further, the child's conceptions about punishment
and discipline and about religion, are social, not simply in the
sense that they reflect the child's past social surroundings,
but also in the sense that they are prophetic of certain results
which it is possible or desirable to secure socially. The only
thing that discriminates the results of such study as that
from mere curiosities, mere collections of stories, anecdotes,
is because we assume that they have a certain prophetic significance, that they mean, if not the certainty, at least the
possibility of certain lines of growth in the future. Taken from
that point of view, as to what they may lead up to, what they
indicate, we are judging them more or less from the social
standpoint.

        To apply this more definitely to education, while we
[(4)] must conceive the results, and the ends, the ideals,
        of education, in social terms all the time, yet we must
translate them over, we must interpret them into the child's
existing powers and impulses, and in that way make them
psychological. Adaptation to civilization cannot be simply and
only a future fact. The child is to be adapted to the social relations twenty years from now and he can be so only as he is
now adapting himself to those social relations. We cannot get
a future adaptation excepting out of a certain measure of present adaptation. When we think of it as a present, and not simply a remote thing, for the first time it becomes vital, and we
see the necessity of translating it over into the child's present
tastes, impulses, interests and habits. That would be our formula on this side. The child must learn to conceive, to feel,
to appreciate himself, and to act himself as a social being.
These social values which he is to realize, cannot be anything
outside of himself; they would not be values, and would not
be social. They must become a part of his own character, of his
own ways of looking at things, and of feeling things, and doing
things. Any other adaptation would be an external thing. The

slave is socially adapted, but it is only as long as he has a master, some one who commands and perhaps threatens punishment if he is not obeyed. Any adaptation not got through the instrumentality of the child's own makeup, would be as formal and mechanical as the adaptation of the slave. To bring the child to consciousness of himself in a social way as a social being is a process which definitely recognizes the whole significance of the social function in education, but which also recognizes at every step the psychological factor. The bringing of the child to consciousness is a thing which involves his own individuality, and is possible only in so far as the conditions and laws of his own being are continually observed. To try and bring out the social element without reference to the psychological would simply result in the formation of certain mechanical habits. The person's activities might externally be socialized like those of the slave. There might not be any political or economic master as with the slave, but the person would be controlled simply by the routine habits formed. He would have no sense of the worth of those habits. He would simply be drilled in doing things at certain times and in certain ways. The result would be that the person could not give his whole self to the service of society. He could only give back to society those mechanical ways of acting into which he had been forced. The result would be a stationary society where the individual would not contribute anything, but simply repeat what society already knew and had taught him to do. But the socializing influence of education which works through the medium of the individual, would mean that the individual use his own powers, put everything in himself at the disposal of the community, not merely his power to do habitual things, but his power to invent, to do new things which would be useful for society.

The relation of the two elements comes out very clearly in language. A person in speaking or writing must communicate something to others. There is the social side. Evidently a use of language that did not tell somebody else something, would not be language at all. A person might as well be raving incoherently. On the other side, the use of language which did not express anything in the person's own mind, which did not spring out of some feeling or experience or thought of his own, would be actually insignificant. It might by accident communicate something to somebody else, as the talk of a parrot might, but it would not be intelligent discourse. All language must have the two functions of communication to another, and of expression of one's self, and those two not alternately, or as two different things, but as aspects of the same process. So education must result in socialization; but it must be the individual himself who is socialized, the process of socialization must be carried on at every step by reference to the individual's own powers.

[(5)]   In the report of the Committee of Fifteen on Elementary Education,[2] you will find the social standard for education laid down very definitely. The object of education is laid down to be adaptation to meet the existing civilization, and the view is held expressly there to be exclusive of the psychological definition. The psychological definition of the training of powers is said to be too formal and would simply result in a mental gymnastic. It is not enough simply to train powers, we must train them in a certain way and for a certain purpose, for availability in community life. Then it goes on to say that after the ends have been determined, after the results to be aimed at have been determined, after the subject matter of education has been selected, then psychology may come in to adapt that material most effectively to the child, in order to tell how best to get the child's interest aroused, and how best to lay hold of and assimilate it; that the psychological considerations may then come in on the side of method. There is a recognition of both the psychological and sociological factors, and from one point of view it would seem to be identical with that just stated; the sociological determines the end, the result, the psychological the means, or the way of getting them.

[(6)]   In the view as laid down in the reports of the Committee of Fifteen, the ends and means do not seem to have anything to do with each other. The subject matter is settled and then the psychological, which in itself is purely formal, simply a matter of gymnastic power, comes in to tell how to bring the child and subject matter into more fruitful contact with each other. What I mean involves a more vital relation between means and ends than upon the surface of it at least, is implied in that view. When the child is being

[2 National Education Association, *Report of Committee of Fifteen on Elementary Education* (New York: American Book Company, 1895).]

brought to consciousness of himself as a being of social interests, and being of social ends and purposes, and as one who
is to form social habits, the psychological helps determine what
material is available just as much as it does to determine
what method shall be used to bring him into relation to the
material at a given time, just because the result is made one
which is to be attained in the remote future. Of course there
is a sense in which geography and arithmetic are picked out
and formulated, not from the standpoint of the child, but from
the standpoint of highly developed society. Just so far as that
is done the material is selected, formulated, and arranged on
that basis and then is presented to the child and all the teacher
can do with the psychology is to try to find out how to arouse
the interest of the child in this ready made, externally supplied
material. There is not only this mechanical separation between
the child and his subject matter, between the psychological
factors that are at work and the social material which is to
be appropriated, but the whole educational process itself becomes mechanical because it is assumed that there are two
things there which have nothing intrinsically to do with each
other, and the question is how to take these two things not
intrinsically connected and bring about some kind of connection between them so that the child shall learn. Such a process
as that makes instruction mechanical, it makes method simply
a matter of devices, of external appliances for handling material which has nothing to do with the child's own make-up, or
his natural condition taken from a psychological standpoint.
If we say that the child is to be brought into consciousness of
himself as a social affair, then the standpoint changes. It is
not simply a question of geography or arithmetic which society
has worked out and which the child ought to know but it is
a question of what is geography and arithmetic to the child
now. What sort of geographical material, what sort of arithmetical material is necessary to fully function, to fully operate with what the child already has? There must be a sense
in which the child's own nature demands arithmetic and geography, in which arithmetical and geographical distinctions
are bound up in his present experiences. To free them, to bring
them out to consciousness, is simply to allow the child's own
powers, impulses, and interests to operate more fully. They
are there, but bound up, and because they are bound up the

child cannot use them freely. But certainly the child lives in a geographical world which has a meaning for him as much as for the adult. The child lives in a world mathematically ordered as much as the adult does. The important thing then, if we assume an organic relation instead of an external one, is that the child shall be brought to consciousness of these values and these relations as they are immediately bound up with his life, in such a way that he can utilize them now, that he can make them available at once.

Perhaps the general standpoint will come out more [2.*a*.] clearly if we pass on to the next point, the consideration of the various elements involved in education. Education is defined from the standpoint of four elements; information or utility, discipline or power, interest, and culture. Now the question of the relation of these four elements to each other is not simply a theoretical one, it is a very practical, pressing problem. You will find pretty much every question of the introducing or not introducing a certain study in the curriculum at a certain time either in the elementary school, the high school or college, will be found to turn upon considerations regarding such matters as discipline, information, interest, and culture; and if the views of different persons vary, it is because they have different definitions of these terms, or they have varying conceptions of their relations to each other. The problem on the philosophic side is whether they are four more or less different elements and education is a compromise of these four different elements, or a certain aggregation of them until we have the proper amount of all of them, or whether education is a more unified organic process, of such a sort that really to secure any one of these means to secure all the others. That is, are they comparatively independent things and hence external to each other, or are they intimate parts of one and the same process, so that if you really get one, you must get all the others?

If we look at the four terms it is interesting to note that they naturally fall into pairs. Interest and culture are both terms which seem to refer to the individual which seem to have their origin and their outcome somehow in the individual. A many-sided interest, which Herbart propounded as the goal of the process of education, is certainly something which inheres in the individual; it is certainly an aspect of the attitude of the individual himself. Culture is evidently valuable as an intrinsic expression, an acquisition of the individual himself. Culture seems to be almost identical with that all-round symmetrical development of the individual which is the essence of the psychological definition, and it is interesting to note that historically the conception of culture and the harmonious development of the individual, both came to consciousness in Germany in the last century, as part of the revival of Hellenism by a return to what was regarded as the ideal of Greek life, and to a certain extent to a freeing of the individual himself from the petty and hampered political and economic conditions of the time in Germany.

Discipline and information seem to point externally, just as interest and culture do internally. Information is generally justified in its claims as an educational ideal on the ground of its utility. Of course utility is distinctly a social consideration. It may be regarded as an element in culture, but for the most part information, just as information, is held to be necessary because of its practical influence on life. So of course discipline on one side seems to be something more or less imposed on the individual. It is the training that he undergoes at the hands of others, and its object is greater power, capacity, to do. Interest and culture seem to refer to the being, the individual, to something which he, so to speak, sums up in himself; but discipline, like information, refers to something which one individual must do to another. Discipline seems to look upon the individual as a piece of machinery which must be trained for the particular work which it has to do. It is through discipline that the individual works into a larger whole, smoothly, as a piece of machinery in that whole. That is what we mean by discipline, the discipline of the school, of the army, and of social life, the capacity to fit harmoniously and effectively in the whole of which one is a part. Of these four elements then, which are currently referred to in education, two seem to center in the being himself, while two seem to tend to the relation of the individual beyond himself, to what he has to do in a situation somewhat larger than himself. Again it is interesting to note that so many of our practical educational problems come precisely from the assumption that these various factors are more or less separate from each other, and that therefore our educational practice must be a choice between them, or else an attempt to combine a certain amount of one with a certain amount of the others. One of the burning problems so much discussed within the last few years, might be stated as: interest versus discipline. What shall be our starting point or chief reliance? The so-called new education is supposed to rely upon and appeal to interest as the chief educational instrumentality; the old education was supposed to set up discipline as its ideal and the disciplinary method was to hold the child to certain problems and exact strict obedience and conformity. Not interest, but effort was exacted from him in carrying out the tasks assigned.

Information, that is, utility, and culture, are again two factors which are currently opposed to each other, not so much in the lower education as in the higher. The very conception of a liberal education to many people implies a certain amount of uselessness in what is learned. It was said of a physicist that he lost interest in the X-rays when it became obvious that they were to be used for professional purposes. Utility in education to many people means the professional, the utilitarian element, which is narrower and mercenary in character as compared with the free harmonious self-development which is supposed to come with culture. In other words, we get in this independence of utility and culture the difference between practical and liberal education. The liberal is education proper, and the practical is preparation for a special calling or profession or outside interest.

The formal analysis then of these conceptions and their relation to each other, may throw light on the whole problem, which is really the fundamental problem in the philosophy of education, of what the relation is between means and ends, between the psychological, the individual as the instrumentality, the agency through which the process is carried on, and the socializing of the individual as the result which is to be attained. I will simply make two remarks about discipline and culture respectively, and then go on with the analysis in the next lecture.

Utility is the conception of discipline which opposes it to interest. The twofold assumption is involved: first, that complete power cannot be got excepting when individual interest is excluded; and secondly, that there is such a thing as discipline at large, that there is some such thing as power apart from power to use, apart from power to apply directly and immediately. The moment we abandon those two assumptions that all real discipline is not simply power in general, but specific power, power in application, and that the only way to get attention fully to operating in order to secure discipline is to arouse interest, that moment we see that the conceptions of discipline and interest necessarily involve each other, instead of being opposed.

As regards culture, a culture which is separated from utility reduces itself of necessity to a class conception. It is a sort of extra polish which some people get because they have leisure and opportunities, and good surroundings, but which other people do not get. Culture, instead of being what it is, etymologically, that is, growth like the cultivation of the plant, becomes this extraneous sort of high polish, a distinctive, exclusive, class attribute, which some people get and other people do not. The culture which is severed from utility in other words, must be a selfish thing, part of the satisfaction of which, consists in the fact that other people do not have it, and in the fact that it makes one distinguished, a shining light amid the mass of humanity. If we think of everybody as subjects of culture, if culture is the ideal of everybody's education, it means simply growth, continued growth up to the limit of each individual's capacity, and when you take that ideal of culture, you cannot oppose it to utility; you cannot separate real growth from actual capacity of service, in some direction or other.

LECTURE XI

January 25, 1899

[A.IV.2: *Analysis of the elements of education: interest, discipline, information, and culture.*]

I shall take up today a discussion of the various ele-
[I.D.2.b.] ments which at different times, and by different writers, have been put into a statement of the end or aim
of education, namely, interest, information, discipline, and culture. My purpose is two-fold: first to clear up the actual meaning of each of these terms; but secondly, and chiefly, to show
their relations to each other in a unified conception of the educative process, to show that they are organic factors in the
single process which has previously been described as socializing the individual.

In the first place, *interest*. This has to do with the
[(1)(a)] attitude of the person, the child or adult, to any subject matter whatsoever. It expresses the accessibil-
ity, the openness or hospitality of the person in question, to a
certain range of considerations; or it expresses the natural
outgoing tendency, the intrinsic, spontaneous activity toward
getting hold of and assimilating any kind of experience. The
question of interest, in other words, is the question of the attitude of the person toward any material or subject matter in
experience, whether it is an object, a fact, a truth, a piece of
work to be done, a result to be reached, or whatever. Interest
is no particular thing, it is no particular portion of the mind
or experience; it is just that whole question of the attitude of
the person as a learning and acting being, in his relation to
the material supplied and ends proposed. The etymology of the
term puts us on the right track, the *inter esse*, the connection, inter-action, between the mind on one side, and the material on the other, as determined by the attitude of the mind
itself; that is, by the intrinsic natural connections which there

are at any time between the mind on one side as a learner and doer, and the subject matter as something to be learned, or the acts that are to be done, on the other side. Obviously then, interest is a two-ended conception, because it is a relation. While our emphasis in the idea of interest is upon the individual, is upon psychical considerations, yet interest is always in something, it always has an object to which it attaches itself. There is no such thing as an interest purely self-enclosed, which begins and ends in the person's own mind. It begins there, but the fact that it is an interest means that it is bearing beyond the mind. It is a reaching out, a movement toward something else, either the subject matter, or an act to be done.

[(b)] From that brief analysis, it suggests itself that the place of interest in the whole conception of education is with reference to the starting point of any process. Since the interest is the attitude, as determined by the structure and the spontaneous, intrinsic tendencies, that interest is the initial point, the point of natural departure in any further movement of experience. When I say it is the initial point, I do not mean that it is found simply in the earlier years of school life. It may be found anywhere all along the line, from childhood to adult years, but its significance for educational purposes is that it does mark the actual starting point for a further movement. The attitude is the readiness and tendency to act, to go on to act in a certain way.

[(c)] Interest then can never be by itself a complete statement of the educational goal; an attitude cannot be the end of anything. An attitude has its significance just because it represents a readiness to pass over into action. As a short-hand expression it is well enough to take the Herbartian one of many-sided interest as the goal of education, but that is only because we feel sure, we take it for granted, that if we secure the interest, the attitude then will go on to realize itself. It is not simply just as interest that this is the goal, but simply because given that interest, we have this reasonable assurance that the purposes and the subject matter in which there is interest will be realized. It is a definition then of the educative process from the standpoint of the attitude assumed on the part of the individual concerned, and that attitude is a thing of fundamental importance. Given a right attitude then, barring external obstacles the further desired ends and experiences will follow of themselves. The attitude is not simply a static thing, it is a tendency, it is a motive, a motor power. When I say that the interest is the question of the starting point, I do not mean that it is simply a point that we leave behind, but it is really a starting point that tends to carry the person ahead and away from what he is.

Secondly, *discipline*. Discipline evidently means ca-
[(2)(a)] pacity or ability when we take it as an element in the educational end. It goes without saying that discipline cannot be an end. We do not want discipline for the sake of itself, we want discipline for the sake of something else. Discipline has reference to means, to instrumentality of action. The discipline of the soldier is for the sake of his function, of his ability to perform his duties in war. The discipline which the child should get in school is not a thing for its own sake, it is to aid his training for the sake of the greatest efficiency with reference to certain duties that he has to perform. Discipline has to do with the forming of habits, and no habit just as a habit is an end in itself. When habits become ends they master us and we are enslaved to them; we lose our freedom; we lose our initiative, our power of personal judgment, and simply fall into the rut which the habits have laid out for us. Habits as instruments of action, as powers, to do things which are decided upon by personal choice and measured through personal intelligence, are absolutely indispensable considerations. Discipline, once more then, has reference to the organization of the means of action; it has to do with the organization of the means of controlling and directing our experience.

The disciplined man is the man that knows how and
[(b)]   when and where to do things. His discipline does not tell him what to do, that must come from his sense of values and relationships, but the discipline comes in the effective and economic realization of whatever ends there are in view. Economy, efficiency, thoroughness in the mastery of the instruments of action, whether physical or physiological or mental, are the things that we have in mind, the relations that we have in mind, in the idea of discipline. Of course means and ends ought to go together. Means are means only for the sake of values. As I suggested the other day there is too frequently a tendency to isolate discipline from its concrete reference to aims and consider it as a thing which can exist in the

abstract, and of itself. The child is supposed to get discipline from selecting intricate problems or puzzles in arithmetic, the conditions of which he does not specifically realize at all, which lie outside the range of his experience. Now test it by what has just been said. That is not discipline because it is not an added means, an added resource. It cannot be used, it cannot be concretely applied, I mean under the conditions stated, of being quite beyond the range of the child's capacity to realize the conditions named. He may be very facile, very glib in the technical way of handling these problems, and yet be perfectly helpless in dealing with the special questions of measurement and value in every-day life. This was illustrated by the story told the other day by Mrs. Young* of the incapacity of the children to tell how much cloth it would take for thirty children, the pieces six by seven inches each, while these children were doing with facility examples in the thousands and millions. If discipline does not give power available for use, it cannot be said to give additional control of the factors of experience. It is a simple illustration, but a typical one.

There are continually things defended on the ground
[(c)]   that while they have no special interest to the child,
yet they are necessary for discipline. Now we have here a simple criterion, a simple test for such statements. If they are really means which can be utilized in gaining ends as these ends present themselves, then of course there is discipline, but if the training thus got stands by itself, if it does not lend itself naturally in power of execution, then there is the form but not the reality of discipline. It is simply a mental gymnastic. A child could be got to do very remarkable things with his little fingers if he is disciplined enough in that direction, but what is the value of it after it is got? If it is really an added resource in life which has a certain range of importance, it is justified; if not, not. The same thing is true in the disciplinary material in arithmetic, geography, science, or language. Here, once more, in discipline, we see the two sides—the individual and the social. As a power, as a development of habit, discipline is an individual thing, and falls on the psychological side, but as a power with reference to ends, with reference to accomplishing something, it enters into the social sphere. The moment we raise the question, what is the value of this power,

[* See Lecture VII.]

what is the worth of this habit, then we have got over into the range of social considerations. As long as we are dicussing the process of forming a habit, the best way of getting the training of power, we are on the psychological side.

Thirdly, *information.* Information represents the
[(3)(*a*)] knowledge of the conditions of action, knowledge of the conditions both specific and general, under which the experience is carried on. That is, experience is not a haphazard, chance, lawless thing. Experience has its regular methods, its laws in other words, and because of these laws certain facts present themselves under certain definite conditions; certain facts exist at certain places and certain events take place at certain times. The significance of information is that it makes known to us these conditions. The value of this information is that it enlightens and instructs the interest, the attitude of the individual. A person has any interest you please; he wants to carry it out, to act upon it. It is obvious that his ability to carry out that interest will depend very largely upon the extent to which he can inform, to which he can enlighten and instruct it through consciousness of the conditions, the state of things, the situation which is relevant. If the interest were not a thing which tends to go out into action, information would have nothing to do with it, but since interest tends to carry us into action, and action takes us out into the world, the successful realization of an interest must be measured by its being controlled, weighted down, by the information that is relevant to it.

The same way with the relation of information to dis-
[(*b*)] cipline, to power. We may have our habits beautifully formed, perfectly at command, ready to apply here or there, but when we come to tell when to use them and when not to, and just how to go to work with this power, it becomes a matter of knowledge of the conditions concerned, it becomes a matter of information. The absent minded man is a good example of the workings of a habit or power or certain kind of discipline, uncontrolled by information, that is, by consciousness of the conditions of the actual situation in which he is at the moment. It is a matter, of course, of common notoriety, that a man may be highly disciplined in certain lines of study, in philosophy or mathematics or language, and have a very high training of his powers in those particular directions, and

yet be very wild in his ideas and judgments about business matters, or about political matters. In fact it is commonly believed, whether true or not, that a high degree of development in these directions actually unfits a man for sound judgment in the participation in the every-day affairs of life. It is due to the fact that this special training is not backed up by intimate consciousness of the conditions of the particular case. No amount of general discipline can be a substitute for this positive, concrete awareness of what the actual make-up of the situation is. That is what we mean by saying a person is too theoretical. There has been a separation of the systematic ordering of the thing, the logical relationships involved, from the consciousness of the obvious facts under which those principles must operate.

Of course that not only gives us a standard of the [(c)] relation of information to discipline, but also a criterion for the value of information itself: it is its relevancy to experience, to action, that makes it an element in the statement of the educational process. If you isolate information, if you leave out of it those three words: "conditions of action," then you lose your standard for telling what the real worth and place of information in education is, or is not. Information is evidently an idea which lies on the objective side, on the side of the subject matter, of material, not on the individual or psychological side. But when that really becomes information, when it becomes applicable to interest and to the direction of habits, when it becomes actually available in experience, instead of representing a mere dead accumulation, then it gets its psychological side. Just as discipline led out from the person into the subject matter, so information leads from the subject matter into the conditions of its appropriation, and assimilation, and actual use, on the individual side. It is not information unless it does inform us, unless it does instruct and enlighten us, and the question of its doing that, is not a question of the mere facts; it is a psychological question.

Lastly, then, *culture*. Culture has been defined as a [(4)] knowledge of the best that has been thought, and said, and done in the world's history. That definition cannot have meant simply knowledge of these things just as knowledge; that would be information. A man might accumulate a whole encyclopaedia of information about the best said, thought, and done, and have no more culture than when he started out. Culture must mean a certain transmutation, a certain working over of that material into the whole character of the individual, not merely his moral character, but the whole intellectual outlook and aesthetic temperament. A certain assimilation, then, is necessary.

Of course it would be a pretty difficult task in five [(*a*)] minutes to accurately define "culture," but we can at least inventory some of the things that we include in it. The first is a certain largeness of horizon, of outlook. Culture is opposed to a certain narrow, intense kind of specialization, not necessarily all specialization, but that which grooves a certain channel which confines the person to the limits of his particular calling, or profession. It is opposed to sectarianism in ideas, not merely in religious matters but in all ways of looking at things and judging things. We talk about breadth of culture; we oppose it to anything narrow, petty, and self-included. It involves a certain aliveness, a certain openness, hospitality to new ideas, to modes of experience, ways of feeling that previously have not been within the person's horizon, however broad it is. It involves not merely a capacity for growth, but an actual interest in growth, the active and not merely negative readiness to seek for and utilize new knowledge. It means a certain flexibility in ways of acting. It is opposed to whatever is pedantic. A man of culture will not be a mere martinet, he will not have laid out in advance fixed ways of acting to which he will adhere under all circumstances. It is a mark of culture not to insist too much on the details of a thing, or on a detailed way of doing things. A flexible play of mind so that a person sees around a particular way of doing or seeing a thing to other modes of getting at it, is an element of culture. It is opposed to rigidity, as much as it is opposed to narrowness. If we take those various elements, largeness of horizon, of outlook, it is equivalent to information. Mere bulk of information does not make a man cultured, but the information that extends and enriches his experience, that puts more meaning into it, that saturates his experience all through, is culture. Flexibility in the use of means, flexibility in making plans, in judging things, in arranging matters, is equivalent to discipline, not mere discipline for its own sake, but which actually lives and operates in experience. This aliveness, this openness to growth is the attitude of the person as a thing which is not self enclosed, but which operates, which functions, in experience.

[(b)] In other words, culture is not a distinct fourth element in education. It is simply a name which we give to the adequate functioning, to the vital outgrowth in experience, of the three elements of interest, discipline, and information. A man of culture is of necessity a man who is interested in things, a man who has concern outside of himself, and a person whose interests have not become fixed by his own habits and calling. He is of necessity a person of discipline in that this largeness of outlook and liveliness of interest does not simply make him easy-going and tolerant in the mere sense of putting up with everything, by not caring especially about anything, but combines this freedom of outlook, with this positive, yet flexible attitude towards things. It is opposed to crankiness, but it is equally opposed to the attitude of easy careless indifference to things. A genuine interest must insist upon realizing itself, it must result in action, execution, and so must have discipline in it and with it. Culture then, which aims at a complete functioning of these elements which are taken from various points of view, really means nothing more nor less than the individual who has developed himself, his individuality, intellectually and practically in social directions.

[(c)] As a single phrase, culture is a "sense of values," both as regards ends and means in life. It is a sense of values regarding ends, that is, it does not confuse the trivial and unimportant and unessential with more enduring things; it has a positive hold on the larger and more important values. It is a sense of values as regards means in that it is flexible with the ways, whether intellectual or practical, of realizing, carrying out the ends in question. It is a conception which in reality is equivalent to education itself. To be cultured in that sense, is to be educated, and for that very reason culture, in its reality, and not in its artificial sense, cannot be treated as a class conception; it is an individual conception. It represents the sense which every individual has in his own work of the value and relationships of that work. There may be defects on either side. A man may have his own work, his own particular calling and yet have no realizing sense of its import and relationships, the bearing of it. There we have what we call the mechanical side. A man has become submerged in his own particular calling or routine. The calling, the line of work, of social service, externally considered, may be very small and minute, but if it is pursued in a certain spirit, a sense of its value, the place that it occupies in the whole of life, then it is not small and such a person has genuine culture. Anyone who has been unfortunate in life, uneducated from the standpoint of the school, but who by his instinct and training has a remarkable and extensive sense of the significance of things in their details, and of larger matters as they present themselves, in life, has a right to be called cultured. It is a purely artificial standard which denies genuine culture to those people. A Japanese once said he would like to be told what civilization was, and asked if it meant "building a certain kind of house with a certain kind of a chimney, and wearing a certain cut of clothing, or not." We are apt to judge civilization from that external standpoint, and so we are apt to judge culture by the outer housing of the thing, the outer dress of it, instead of the extensive sense of the elements that enter into experience.

To go backward very briefly, interest gives us the starting point, the attitude which is the dynamic starting point of any educational process. Discipline gives us the arrangement, the order, the method of the course of experience. Information gives us the positive content, the positive body to the thing. And culture represents the process itself with its products, with its results considered with regard to their value.

LECTURE XII

January 26, 1899

[A.IV.3.: *A formal definition of education. Discussion of its formal elements.*]

[I.D.3.] I will summarize the preceding discussion by giving a formal definition of education today, and then proceed to a restatement of more important considerations involved in that definition. I define education as the process of remaking, or reconstituting, experience, so as to give it a more socialized content, through the medium of increase of control of experience. Following simply the formal definition, we have the three elements: (1) the remaking of experience, as a generic conception. For its specific differentia, we have (2) on the side of end or aim, that this reconstruction be such as to give increase of social import, of social value in the experience; (3) on the side of the way or method in which this remaking takes place, that it be such as to bring it more and more under the control of the individual itself.

On the side of content the aim is social; there is where the sociological definition of education comes in. On the side of form, of method, the end is the increase of power in the selection, direction, and adaptation of the elements in experience; this is psychological. The last two statements evidently correspond to what was said yesterday regarding discipline and knowledge, or information respectively. That is, the increased social content or significance is through the medium of the information which takes the child outside of himself into contact with and recognition of the larger whole of which he is a member. The increase of control over experience on the psychological side is simply the disciplinary process.

Now as to the significance of the definition apart from
[a.]   its mere formal statement; first as to the idea of remaking or reconstruction. What is involved in that?
The bearing of that comes out more clearly on the negative
side, that is, in contrast with certain other preconceptions
regarding education. That definition brings the starting point
and the aim of education close together; it unites them organically in the educative process itself. In other words, education,
if it is education, realizes its aim at every point in the process.
The remaking of experience is just as good at one point as it
is at any other. It is not a remaking which is to be finished up
at a certain point, either when the student leaves the grade
school, the high school, or the college, or when he has
finished his profession. The person should be remaking his
experience anywhere and everywhere all along the line, and
in so far as that remaking, that growth of added value and of
added power is got at any point in the career; there education
has reached its end, not its terminus, but it has reached its
goal, its ideal. The fundamental significance of the idea of
reconstruction is the elimination of the idea of preparation as
the essence of an educational process. Education is currently
conceived, if not formally defined, from the standpoint of
preparation. Persons differ among themselves as to what education prepares us for. One would say that it should prepare
us for citizenship. Another would say that is fitness for a living
which is to come in the future, when the person is grown up.
Another says that the attainment of a certain amount of
actual information, and a certain amount of discipline is the
goal of education, that is conceived as a thing which the pupil
is working toward and which is to be secured as the final
result. Another says that it is preparation for fullness of moral
life, for the development of moral character. While those of
course differ theoretically among themselves as to the practical
working out of education, yet they all agree to the fundamental conception that it is a process of getting ready for
something, that it is merely preparatory.

If remaking of experience is both the process and the
[(1)]   aim of education, then the end is an immediate and
present one, one which is capable of direct consideration of being directly acted upon, and of direct realization,
instead of being set off as a mark clear ahead in the future,

toward which the child is to be lured along by making things interesting, or forced along by disciplinary stimuli, or else by a mixture of the two, so much of one and so much of the other. The fitness for life which is got through the educative process is a fitness for the only life we live, the life of every day. The reality of preparation however, instead of being excluded by that conception, is rather involved. A preparation which is just preparation, a process of simply getting ready, is not the best way of getting ready. The best way to get ready for tomorrow, or next year, is to get all there is out of today and this year. The youth that is getting the maximum of life experience possible as he goes along, must, by that very fact, get a genuinely more complete preparation for future experiences and responsibilities than he can get if we simply scant and reduce his present experience on the assumption that if we hold it down within certain definite bounds and limits, we are thereby securing preparation for the future. It is a consideration probably first stated by Froebel[1] that the most adequate realization of the powers and interests involved at any particular period of the child's development, is the best possible preparation for the succeeding periods in his development.

[(2)] The definition furthermore gives a standard for the beginning and the end of the formal process of education. When shall the formal education begin? Whenever the child can begin consciously to share in the remaking of his own experiences. As I said before, the child is learning by his experience all the time. Experience is remaking in him, but it is a growth rather than a remaking, a reconstruction, because the child himself does not consciously participate in it by making certain things his own ends and aims; he does not use one part of his experience consciously to bring it to bear upon another part. The process of reflection has not begun. When the child can begin to reflect, to turn one part of his experience over to see what the bearing is upon another, then he is more conscious, and formal education can begin. Still there must be opportunity in the school for a continuation of direct modes of experience, the forms of play and occupa-

[1 Friedrich Froebel, *The Education of Man,* trans. by W. N. Hailmann (New York: D. Appleton and Company, 1892).]

tions which the child is engaged in out of school. The process that we would call instruction of learning, definite learning, will always be found to be one of participation on the part of the child himself in the growth of his own experience, and he begins to exercise a certain amount of control in deciding what experience shall be his.

It equally gives the criterion for the cessation of the period, not of growth, but of formal education. When the individual is in command of the method of remaking his experience, when he not only can participate in it, but can administer it, he is obviously out of the period of tutelage, he is a full fledged agent on his own account. The period of formal education comes within the time when the child is capable of helping along, of taking a part in the direction of his activities and experiences, but is not capable of assuming the complete responsibility, when he still needs assistance stimuli presented through others in order that his experiences may best be remade.

[(3)]   The second point which perhaps I have already sufficiently emphasized, is that this conception gives equal importance to every stage of the educative process. There are earlier and later stages, but no lower and higher ones. The experience of the child at the age of four and five is just as intrinsically valuable, is just as much life as that which can be got when the person is in the high school or college; it must be looked at from its own intrinsic standpoint. To get adequate education we must look at the experience which the child is capable of at the time, and must educate him for the time being on that basis. Perhaps it would lead to misapprehension if I said we ought to educate him as if there were no later stages at all, but I doubt if the practical evils of acting on such a statement would be as great as acting upon the assumption that the earlier periods of education are simply to supply tools with which the child can build later on in his educational career. Of course we should not really ignore the later periods, because life is continuous, and we get light by considering what comes after, but when you come down to the treatment of the child, the subject matter and methods that he needs, the criterion should be the best experience and the best control of power which the child can get at that particular period.

In the third place the conception also gives a basis
[(4)] for interpreting the meaning of the material of
instruction; that is to say, objects, books, talks by the
teacher, lectures, conversations, recitations, and so on. In
the current image, if not the express definition of education,
it is assumed that there are three things: the child as he is
now; the child as he will be when he is educated and the
work of instruction has borne its fruits; and that there are a
lot of facts and principles in the various school studies and
the various ways of presenting them, which can be brought
to bear on the child. We do not unify in our conception the
three elements of the child as he is, the result to be reached,
and the instrumentalities, the subject matter of instruction
upon which we rely.

In this other view what we may term the subject
[(5)] matter, the material of education, consists simply in
the evolution or bringing to consciousness the facts
which are involved in the child as he is. It is not something
which is formulated without respect to the child and then
brought to bear on him through a teacher, or lecture, or
text book. The material which the child needs and can utilize
at any stage of his existence is somehow bound up with his
experience as it is. But it is simply bound up, it is simply
implicit, it is not definitely conscious to the child, and the
process of education is this process of interpretation, the
process of supplying the conditions and the stimuli which shall
enable the child to see and to appreciate for himself, and therefore to use rationally the things which are in a blind and con-
fused way already in his life. That would of course hold of
every study. The child has already implicitly a certain geographical, mathematical, chemical, physical, linguistic element in his experience. He cannot differentiate it, he cannot
state it by itself, he cannot formulate it, he has no objective
consciousness of it, and for that reason he cannot control it, he
cannot utilize it either intellectually or practically. The starting point then is always to bring the conditions so that there
will be a gradual growth of this particular subject matter in
which we are interested. The first thing we have to do is to
find out what there is in the child's experience already implicit,
which is relevant to what we want to get at, relevant to the
teaching of the geography or arithmetic lesson. The second

thing is to consider what is the best way, conditions, stimuli, etc., to supply, in order that that may be brought out in an effective way. That of course is involved in the idea of education as a remaking of experience. It is not simply an enlargement, an adding on to experience; it is a qualitative reconstruction, transformation, which must grow out of what the child already has in his own experience. The unconscious assumption is too often that we can simply add to the child's experience. He has so much given him, and so much more is to be superimposed on to what he already has. So the text book in physics begins with enumerating all the qualities of matter, impenetrability, extension, and so on. The child learns them and is supposed to have added to his store of knowledge. It is added on from without instead of being a qualitative reconstruction from within. The book on chemistry begins with definitions of atoms and molecules and such like matters of common experience. The child learning those is supposed to be adding to his experience in those directions.

I once heard a teacher say she did not see how science could be taught to little children because they could not understand atoms and molecules. While it is not true that the etymology of education is "to draw out," as it is sometimes said to be, by the process of directing growth, (getting a plant to grow up on a trellis) so far as the idea of drawing out means this qualitative transformation, this evolution, so to speak from within of what is practically implied but not objectively presented, so far the idea is a correct one. The difficulty is that the process of drawing out is often interpreted as a process of drawing something out of the child, instead of out of his experiences. We make a separation between the child and his experiences, and we interpret it that if the teacher is skillful enough he can educe facts and laws out of the child; they are all latent and if you pull the right string they unravel. It is not a question of the child, but of his experiences, which vary with different children. It is a drawing out of an experience so that it becomes more adequate as an instrument of getting further experience that is the kind of drawing out that we want to get. So far as the child is concerned he is not that passive, latent, being that the conception of "drawing out" would seem to indicate that he was. The child at least before he goes to school, is generally running over with activities, and the chief difficulty is to direct them, to put them to some use, yet in reading many of these conceptions of the drawing out of the child we would think him a purely latent bundle of capacities awaiting the inspiration of the teacher to begin to act in any direction. The opposite is the fact. The child has more activity than he knows what to do with, and the problem of the teacher is to balance up the child with the child's experience; I mean by that, to utilize the overflowing, half instinctive, almost purely impulsive tendencies to act, in such a way that they will tell in this general fructification in experience, in this process of construction.

Going back to the negative side, there are practical [b.(1)] evils that grow out of the conception of education as the process of preparation when that is the point of view from which habitually the process of education is considered. There is in the first place loss of interest. The process of getting ready for something which is coming by and by, is not engrossing; it loses its hold on even an adult, and of course one of the essential characteristics of the child is that he demands more immediate fruits of his labor than the adult. It is not possible for him to project any very remote ends. He loses the sense of relationship unless he sees what he is doing and what he is doing it for; it becomes unmotivated. The future not being consciously present to the child, the point is lost by him. There is a reason for his preparation, but unfortunately it is in the teacher's, and not the child's mind, and a reason in the mind of somebody else, is not particularly enlightening. Because the adult sees certain things that are valuable, the assumption is that somehow the child by psychical or moral contagion is going to take the same point of view and realize the values which the adult realizes. From the standpoint of the continual remaking of experience, the ends, and therefore the motive is present to the child himself. He may not see the reason of what he is doing in its fullness, but there is a motive, a point to it.

In the second place, the conception of preparation [(2)] tends to make the child passive. The full stimulus for the preparation for a remote end, cannot be found within the child, just because the end is beyond the child's own conscious realization. The stimuli to keep him moving toward it has to be supplied from without, and that means that the child is forced into a passive and receptive condition. Everybody agrees that education is not the process of pouring into, or filling up, but it is not possible to get away from the practical implication of that point of view simply by saying we do not believe in it. The only way adequately to secure self-activity, as distinct from mere receptivity of what is poured in, is for the child to have some idea of the significance of what he is doing at the time, making it a part of his own experience.

[(3)]   In the third place, procrastination is an inevitable practical result of the theory of preparation. If we are preparing for something one or five years ahead, there is lots of time left, and it is not necessary to be very busy about it today; we will attend to that when the emergency is a little closer at hand. When the child has not a living motive for doing a thing, of course he tends to do the thing that he is more interested in and put off this other thing until a more convenient season, and if he does not do it, it is because of the external pressure that is brought to bear upon him from others.

[(4)]   The fourth point is the lack of perspective, the lack of the sense of the relative values in education. One of the most successful teachers I ever knew said she considered the chief defect on the intellectual side of the present education, to be just this lack of the sense of relative importance with which the average child left school. Facts and principles stood pretty much on the same level, as things to be learned, and the measure of these values was the relative amount of time and effort necessary to master the different facts, objective facts and statements, that had to be learned. The tendency toward that result follows from considering education as preparation. The goal is way off, there is no standard for the present time. The ideal is removed and cannot be specifically applied to what is going on and being learned at the moment. Applicability, use, is the only standard for measuring relative values in anything. The thing that you need most to do a certain thing with, is the most valuable thing. The thing that does not bear upon your point, that is not usable under the existing circumstances, is unessential and trivial. Now if you take out of the child's mind the sense of end, the sense of availability, you have so far as you can deprived him of any capacity to realize for himself the comparative values with which he is dealing, you have tended to eliminate this factor of perspective.

That of course goes with what I said yesterday about the separation of the idea of discipline, of power, from power to use. As long as facts and ideas stand on a dead level in the person's mind, you have no practical training. When a person acts it is a question of relative value. Probability is the guide of life, and there ought to be an instinctive habit of grading things along the scale of relative values.

LECTURE XIII

January 30, 1899

[A.V.;B.I.: *The school as a social institution. The content and form of school life.*]

[I.E.] It follows from what has been previously said that the school is fundamentally to be considered as itself a social institution, or a mode of community life, having its own experiences and its own value, its own justification or reason for being, inherent in itself. That point of view for considering the school is the important one, is the controlling one as regards the consideration of other points, like matters of school discipline and administration, questions of the curriculum and the courses of study, and questions of method.

[1.] The view is opposed to the conception which regards the school as simply place, or as something which has its sphere limited as being simply a means or instrument for purposes and experiences of life which take place outside of the school. The school, in other words, should have an intrinsic meaning to the members of it, both pupils and teachers, as the family life has or as neighborhood life has, or as later on business or professional life would have. Of course that ideal is not realized when the school is regarded simply as the place where one goes to get instruction, to learn special lessons. It is realized in so far as importance is attached to the relations of the human beings, children and teachers, to each other, and it is felt that the increase of life and the meaning of experience that is gained there is the adequate and ultimate justification for the existence of the school.

There is a very striking passage in Cardinal Newman's book

on *The Idea of the University*[1] where he says that if it came to a matter of choice between the university which provides material of instruction, text books, lectures, and so on, and which gives examinations on the basis of which one's knowledge is tested and degrees given, if it came to a choice between that and a university where there was no instruction at all, but simply a number of young men of different but yet liberal tastes in life who meet together and mingle in a social way, he would prefer the latter; that there is more education to be found through the contracts, and adjustments which are made in a gathering of human beings together, than can be got simply by the application to any one individual of the formulated material of instruction.

I have simply given the gist of the passage which in itself is very fervently expressed. That is a point of view which should apply not merely to university education, of which Newman was speaking in particular, but to education throughout. I do not mean by that that it is necessary to separate one over against the other so that we have to make a choice of one or the other, but I do mean that the human element, the social elements and relationships which come in, are after all the important and controlling consideration, and that the questions of so called order and discipline, questions of subject matter of studies, and questions of methods of teaching, are all questions which have to be referred to this as their ultimate standard and criterion. School life in its idea is an organic whole.

[2.] Applying that point of view very briefly to the question of the school administration, order and discipline of the school, it would mean that there are no specific school virtues. You will find sometimes in books of school management certain virtues set up as belonging specifically to the school: punctuality, obedience, and silence. Now in so far as such ideals are merely school virtues, so far as they are not relations and attitudes which are called for in life in general, it seems that the school has been isolated from other things as an organization or as an institution. The child is regarded as a different being in school than when he is out of school.

[1 John Henry Cardinal Newman, *The Idea of a University Defined and Illustrated* (London: B. M. Pickering, 1875).]

[a.]   The standard for what is meant by school order and discipline must be inherent in the school as an institution. These are simply questions of organization of the life which is going on there. In so far as that organization calls for silence, or promptness, or obedience, in so far of course those are virtues, but it is not that they are school virtues and belong to the school as something apart from other things. All discipline in institutions is the question of the most efficient organization for the particular ends in view. We will get one conception if we consider the school as a mode of social life having its own common ends and interests in which all participate, in which all have a cooperative share, and if we consider that the discipline for securing the best organization for common life and relations. We will get a different view if we set up a certain external end like the learning of lessons, or put in a fixed image, a fixed rigid conception of what school order consists in apart from its contributing to the best organization of the community life.

In a list of questions which were made out by the supervisor of the city schools, this query was addressed to teachers: "Do children in school assist each other when there is need of help as freely and as naturally as they do on the school ground"? I do not know whether the question was asked as a rhetorical question for the sake of the irony involved or not, but the impression left on my mind was the utter horror in the mind of the teacher at the suggestion of the thing, because the whole current conception of the work of the school room is such as to make such an idea abhorrent. Children would have to move around more or less, would have to talk to each other more or less, would have to do a number of things in a free easy way, and they would need a free community life in relation to each other, instead of each child sitting in a certain spot until he has learned his lesson and is ready to recite the lesson he has been studying. The very arrangement of the school room, and the number of children to a teacher would make the literal carrying out of the conception involved in that question practically impossible in most schools. The attempt to carry it out would involve an almost complete change of atmosphere, a change of the idea of being controlled by learning and reciting lessons, to the idea of some sort of community life.

One other illustration is found in the conception of
[b.]   the recitation. There we have the same two ideals
again, one of which considers the recitation the place
for testing the thoroughness and accuracy with which certain
lessons have been learned, and of course incidentally, the
correction of any mistakes that have arisen and the better
bringing out of the problems and truths involved so that the
child shall be able to study better afterwards. The other ideal
conceives of the recitation chiefly from the standpoint of the
cooperation, the participation of the children and the teacher
alike in their various experiences, the information gained concerning problems which have come up, and suggestions made.
When the recitation is conducted from the standpoint of testing the knowledge that has been acquired in the study of
some text book, it is clear that the social spirit is not cultivated
and an individualistic spirit must of necessity be cultivated.
It is well known in advance that the teacher knows that lesson;
he has the text book in front of him and has the lesson better
then the children. There is no motive to recite in enlightening
the teacher or anybody else. It becomes simply a competitive
exhibition, it becomes simply a comparative matter, to see who
can recite best upon that particular lesson. It is really difficult
to tell how much of the excessive competition of later life, how
much of the instinctive tendency to rank one's self by the rate
he can get ahead of somebody else is due to the fact that the
recitation is so largely on a distinctly individualistic basis. It
becomes then not merely a philosophical question, but a practical question, as to whether the controlling point of view in
the recitation is to be considered the social one, the class life,
or whether it is the abstract intellectual one of acquisition of
information, and the gaining of better individual discipline.

The point on which I am to speak chiefly today, is the
[II.A.]   relation of the course of study, the curriculum, and
methods in general, to this conception of education
as a mode of community or social life. If we take the conception of reconstruction of experience as the definition of education, it follows that the subject matter of education cannot be
separated from the actual everyday experiences of the persons
being taught. It is their own experience which is to be reconstructed, it is their own powers, impulses and habits which

are to be brought to consciousness. It is not that they are to learn certain facts or truths in an objective way, but they are to become their own personal possessions, they are to become incorporated so that they shall be a natural and normal part of their experience in its growth, in its outreaching. Of course that might be admitted in a general way and yet it would have to be said that the subject matter of the curriculum involves an organization and a formulation which must go far beyond the actual experiences of the child; that the teacher at least must have in mind the subject matter of geography and arithmetic, and of history and literature, reaching clear beyond anything which the child already has in his experience, or which he is capable of having; and that the significance of the text book and of the other froms in which the facts of the various subjects are given to the child is precisely to secure this required formulation from a standpoint so much higher and comprehensive than the crude, one-sided, more or less accidental experience of the child would permit.

Taking then the subject matter from that standpoint, [1.a.] what we ordinarily mean by school studies, the problem at once arises: what is the concrete relation of those studies to the experiences of the children, that is to their actual daily experiences? The problem involved there is virtually a question of whether the organization and formulation of the course of study should be made out on the logical basis, or on the psychological basis. By the logical basis I mean one which surveys the subject matter in its highest stage of development, irrespective of the way in which it came to be what it is. It takes it as a final result, and abstracting that from the process of its growth, the history of its coming to its present state of perfection, simply aims to secure the most perfect arrangement and classification of the facts and truths as they are given. Of course if a fact is a fact, if a principle is true, it ought to be possible to cut it loose from the particular way in which it has been got at. The truth of the principle of gravitation is not dependent upon the process of discovery which Newton went through. The same way with any scientific fact or law. Some individual through particular experiences and with individual failures and successes of his own, worked that out, but after it has been worked out, it can be cut loose from its psychological connection with any particular individual; it stands as a law which is to be coordinated with other similar facts and laws. The logical arrangement is precisely that which does not view a fact in connection with the process of its discovery, but takes it as a fact, and aims at the most complete and orderly systematization of the fact along with other facts. There is no need to dwell upon the fact of the increase of system and order in that kind of objective, logical classification. It is a way that is our ideal in what we call the school studies, the subject matter, the disciplines needed, arithmetic, algebra, geometry, physics, chemistry, history, and so on. We want to get the truths as they are, and then arrange, classify them systematically, with reference to each other. To secure such an arrangement as that, has been upon the whole, the ideal in the preparation of the text books.

It is not possible to ignore, however, even in these logical arrangements, all reference to the process (not necessarily by which they have been previously apprehended) but all reference to the process by which they are to be apprehended in the future. Even the maker of ideal text books on this logical plan would not put exactly the same facts in the same order and system into a text book for the high school as in that for a college. There would be an attempt to pick out the simpler facts which are most easily observed or apprehended with the least degree of maturity. In other words, a certain reference to the process of realizing the truths involved will come in, even if it is only to simplify the matter somewhat, even if it is only what is left out, and the putting in of more illustrations and so on. While it is true as a rule that the high school text book is simply a simplified, reduced edition of the college text book, it is built on the same general plan, and as was suggested the other day, in the effort to put the same features into the elementary school, that point of view, if not prominent, has at least influenced the movement very much. To many it has been simply a question of simplifying the thing still more, picking out more of the difficulties, and making the material introduced of a more obvious and direct character, yet without entailing change in the point of view. However there is such a marked difference between the prevailing interests and powers of children in the grades and in the high school, that the need for some qualitative reconstruction has been much more felt in the attempt to adapt the studies, elementary science, history, and literature, to the grades, than it has to the high school; while upon the whole the assumption is that boys and girls are simply little men and little women, they are simplified, less capable editions of the adults, and consequently should have simplified editions of the subject matters which the adult has succeeded in getting.

        By the psychological formulation of the subject matter
[b.]   ter of the curriculum, I mean a statement, a selection
        and arrangement or classification, not on the basis of the purely objective relationship of the facts and principles to each other, but on the basis of their most natural and most fruitful assimilation in somebody's experience. From a certain point of view we must start on another theory from the standpoint of the adult. Of course the adult does know more than the child, he knows what he knows more accurately and certainly, in a more orderly, related, and systematic way. To throw away the advantage that additional system in experience has given, to ignore that and start from the standpoint of the child would be an absurdity which no sane person would ever dream of indulging in. But while the adult teacher or text book maker gathers his own knowledge together from that standpoint, in the attempt to make it a consistent whole in itself, he must also remember that that represents, from the standpoint of the child, the result to be reached, that it is simply the goal from the standpoint of the pupil, and that nothing is gained by simply trying to present that goal at once to the child as a result, as an end to be reached some time. It gives rather the standpoint from which the child's present experience is to be interpreted; it represents the possibilities which are implied in the child's own experience; it marks the goal to which he may arrive, if from his present starting point he follows a certain path. In that way it enables us, not only to interpret the child as to what he now is, and also as to what he now has, but it enables us to interpret the typical points in the sequence, in the development of the child's own experience.

        In other words, this logical statement of the subject
[(1)] matter from the educational point of view, simply
        states the problem, it does not solve anything at all. To get the most logical arrangement possible of all the topics in geometry would be an important and valuable thing, but it is not such a result that all we have to do is to present that

formulated logical system to a pupil and ask him to repeat in himself the logic involved in that system. It simply presents to us the ideal, the goal for the development of that pupil. In the second place it teaches us that we must look for things in the pupil's own experience, in his own powers, which tend in the direction of that ideal result; that we must study the child in his present environment, until we find the actual concrete things in his experience which we have in this highly elaborated and objective way worked out in our geometry; and that, in the third place, having found out these things, we must see how to utilize them so that they will develop with the least waste and greatest amount of positive movement toward this ideal which we wish to reach. If I may use the term, the scientific or logical subject matter has to be psychologized, it has to be translated over into the terms of the experiences and mental workings of the individual child; and it is only as it is thus translated over, so that it does become a part of his concrete every day experience and is assimilated, that it does really become educative to him.

                   Now as to the relation of this point to the social life,
[(2)]   the reality of geometry, to use the same illustration,
                   even to the adult, is not found in this objective logical formulation. The reality of geometry is not found in the series of abstract demonstrations. The reality is found in the experiences which these formulae make possible. We all know for example that geometry and trigonometry got their actual beginning in the needs of mankind, in the erecting of buildings and surveying of land. The propositions of geometry are nothing but the abstraction and formulation for purposes of greater convenience and control, of just these everyday experiences. In order to avoid argument, I do not say that that statement is true of all possible ramifications in the development of all subjects; but of certainly the great bulk of studies that enter into the education of anybody, excepting the most advanced specialists, that statement is true. People do not read and write and speak because they have grammar, but they have grammar as an abstraction, a formulation of certain actual concrete relationships that are involved in their daily life; and if the grammar has significance, it is because that formulation assists those daily experiences, it brings them under better control, more systematic and therefore more rea-

sonable control. The same thing is true of arithmetic, geography, history, and so on; all the ordinary school studies. Even in these logical aspects, in the way in which the best informed adult mind would formulate that for himself, they are still abstractions, and abstractions out of the actual experience of men and which have been made for the sake of furthering and enriching that experience.

Now putting that point with the other one, it can be
[(3)] said that we get two forms then of concrete, living experience: the experience of the child and the experience of the adult. Then that experience of the adult is abstracted and formulated, classified, and arranged and takes shape in the various sciences, including all organized subject matters under the head of science, any matter so far as it is put into orderly, related, systematic shape. Now that drawing out into these special forms, of what is contained in a vital living way in the experience, gives us these school studies. If there were no children, if there was nobody to be educated, that would be the end of it; the adults would simply arrange these things to meet their own needs. But since there are children to be educated, and since we wish these children to reach this standpoint in their own experience, since we wish them to come to participate in the living experiences of the adult, these formulated abstractions out of the experience of the adult become also instrumentalities which have reference to the child. They are not simply sciences, they are also studies. We call the logical formulation of these things sciences. The result is that they should be again reformulated as studies; they should undergo this process which I call psychologizing; they should be restated, not simply with reference to their accuracy as facts, and their order in relation to principles, but should be restated in the way in which individual minds get hold of and assimilate and appropriate those facts. That means that they are stated from the psychological standpoint. Then these sciences, transformed into studies, become the intermediate terms, growing, on one side, out of the child's present, immediate experience, and growing over all the time, as the child becomes matured, into the experiences of the adult, and therefore capable more and more of themselves being given the logical formulation.

The school study is also an abstraction from social [(4)] experience. The reality of geometry or geography cannot be in a book or any set of books, nor simply inside of somebody's head, as a mere number of ideas. It must be a part of life somewhere, or else it has no meaning. So on one side these studies are picked out, selected out of life, simply representing its formulation in definite ways, and on the other side they have to enter into the social life, that is the natural experience of the child. Taking them from both standpoints, the subject matter of the curriculum is seen to have this social significance. In getting at this in this way, it is necessary to take up the more general aspect before the more concrete. Later on I shall come back to this and attempt to illustrate, by reference to the historical development of the sciences, the extent to which they have been the outgrowth of the social experience of individuals in life.

In discussing the studies from this point of view, I have virtually also covered the question of method. I will simply indicate the point today and go on to its development Wednesday. According to this point of view what we term method is nothing different from the subject matter. Method is simply this psychologizing of the subject matter. Method is simply a taking of the abstract, that is to say the logical science, and restating it, translating it so that it connects with the immediate interests of the child. Method is the subject matter in so far as that subject matter is capable of actual assimilation and incorporation into the experience of the pupil. If method were anything different, it would not be respectable, it would have no dignity. It might be a necessity, but simply an evil necessity. Just because the child has an experience which is intrinsically valuable, and because the problem of method is how to translate our subject matter so that it is capable of assimilation into the child's experience with the least resistance and maximum fruitfulness, it has this tremendous practical significance of being the connecting link which mediates most easily and effectively between the undeveloped forms, the cruder forms of experience, and the richest and most mature forms.

LECTURE XIV

February 1, 1899

[B.I.(a),(b),(c): *Subject matter and method in education: their organic relations.*]

The question of the relation of subject matter and
[*II.A.2.a.*] method in education is fundamentally the same question that appears in philosophy as the problem of the relation of the subject and object, or of the relation of intelligence, mind, to the world. Of course I am not going to discuss that question from the philosophic standpoint here, but it is pertinent to note that the current conception of the relation of method and subject matter, I mean that conception which regards the problem of subject-matter as one simply of scientific knowledge and classification of materials, relegating method to a merely formal psychological matter, is a survival historically of the medieval philosophical dualism. Of course the whole philosophy of the middle ages was dualistic. Mind was considered to be one entity by itself, having its own structure and formal faculties and modes of operation capable of being treated by itself apart from its relations to the environment. The world, on the other hand, was considered as a purely material thing, simply the object, at most, of spirit or intelligence, but not embodying or reflecting intelligence in its own structure. Now the unconscious, the indirect influence of the philosophic system, is almost always greater than the immediate, direct influence. This point of view as carried out in philosophy, became the common point of view for considering a great variety of matters; morals, theology, and education and the views that were congruent to this dualism permeated the whole intellectual life and finally turned up in a very much modified external form, to be sure, in the whole theory, and equally in the whole practice, of education. It finally became

petrified into this more or less hard and fast separation, this way of considering the material, the subject matter, as a thing which could be settled on a purely external, objective, scientific basis; and while method, having to do with the workings of the mind was intrinsically and essentially something quite distinct from the organization and arrangement of the subject matter, it simply happens that mind has these ways of working, and we must take some account of them in order that there may be the easiest and most extensive arrangement of the subject matter. So methods were built up on this external, mechanical basis, had to be external and mechanical because of the dualism. All methods were thus reduced practically to the devices which somehow would tend to bridge the gulf between the mind and the world of facts, principles, that were to be known, or that would break down the hard and fast wall which intrinsically separated the two, simply a way of making it easier for this separate isolated mind to get at the separate isolated subject-matter.

    Now without discussing at all which point of view is [b.(1)] philosophically correct, it is clear that there are a number of influences which in modern times have been altering this whole conception, which tend to break down the dualism as formulated in the middle ages. On the one hand the continuous growth of science has revealed the world, as both in general and in detail a rational thing, a unified, intelligible system, that responds freely and fully to the application and direction of intelligence to it. Before the rise of science it was natural, almost inevitable, to think of the world as something formal, alien to the structure and functions of reason. It was just hard, brutal matter or externality; but with the development of scientific method and the continuous revelation of order, of meaning, of system everywhere, the world gets to be seen and felt more and more as itself an intelligible, rational order, cohering on a spiritual basis. In other words the world has become more and more spiritualized and idealized through the advance of science.

    The development of industry has brought the world [(2)] into much closer connection with human aims, the human purposes and interests in general. As long as industry was a local thing, as long as it was not organized, as long as it was a patchwork affair, not carried on on a large scale, not involving the application of science to nature, the world naturally presented itself as something, if not alien, at least indifferent to human affairs. But now, through the application of scientific method and the consequent control over natural forces, adapting them to human wants, making them serviceable in the satisfaction of human needs, the development of human powers, the whole face of nature is not merely physically transformed, but the feeling, the attitude toward nature changes. It is so much more intimately bound up with the whole question of human welfare and destiny than it used to be. It is less possible to put the question of human destiny into another world, to locate it entirely there, and consider this world as having nothing in particular to do with the essential human interests; it is impossible because nature touches us so closely at every point. The whole labor problem is simply an evidence of the extent to which human interests and considerations and aims have become bound up practically and ethically with things which used to be disposed of as merely material and natural, and as having nothing to do with humanity at all, excepting in an external way. We find in the literature of nature, like poetry, and in landscape painting, an evidence of the growth of the whole aesthetic interest in nature. The development in this line has been very marked and it has given, historically, a tremendous impetus to the conscious community and identity between man and nature.

If we say on one side that through these and other [(3)] influences, nature, the world of objects, has become more and more idealized, fraught with intrinsic rational meaning and ethical and aesthetic value, it is equally true on the other side, that the mind has become more materialized. I mean by that, it seems to be more and more a matter of actual content, dependent upon relations to the world, and less and less a mere bundle of formal powers which exist apart by themselves. The mind is considered less as an isolated entity, and more as an active function which operates in relation to the environment, which has positive intrinsic relations to the world; it is what it is because of its relations to the world, to the material of experience. I will simply mention here from this side, one influence which has operated to change the point of view, namely, the biological element, the evolutionary view, which is fatal to the idea of mind as a purely independent and isolated entity. Its nature, its growth, its development, from the evolutionary point of view, must be studied with reference to its relations to an environment, to the use which the development of various sense organs and various mental powers has had. It loses its purely independent, isolated validity, and to get at its meaning and significance, we have to throw it into the whole larger process which includes the environment, the world, as well as itself. Now the significance of these considerations, is, of course, that there must be a corresponding reconstruction on the educational side. It is obviously out of the question to gradually surrender this dualism unless we find a more intimate, more organic relationship between subject matter and method in education than has previously been conceived. The inference from what has previously been said is that social life gives us the organic unity of the two. Subject matter represents the content, the valuable material of this social life formulated for purposes of application. In what we call school studies, it is formulated for one specific kind of application, namely, application to furthering the growth of the immature into full membership into, and participation in, social life. Method is a statement of the way in which the individual moves most easily and successfully into such participation in social life.

The generic outcome of the present discussion is [c.] that social life is our ultimate educational standard for determining the value of the subject matter taught, and for determining all questions of methods or ways of teaching; only that social life is not to be interpreted simply as a remote or adult social life, but as a present, immediate, living thing. This particular point we will come back to later on when we discuss the value of special studies, and questions of correlation, and so on.

Here I will simply, chiefly to avoid misunderstanding, [(1)] state a little more definitely what is meant by this social life, or by the socializing of experience. It means at least two things, each of which is as important as the other. It does not mean simply that the child is to be fitted to do something socially, that he is to be fitted to be a social servant or agent. It does not mean simply that he is to be directly fitted to help on the general course of social life. It does mean that, but not simply that. That is one side of it, and to take that alone would give us a narrow view of education. The other side is equally important; that is, the social values and relations must be appreciated by the child himself. He must not only contribute to them, but he must share in them, they must become his; and in any ideal education, there will be, I take it, a perfect balance between those two phases, that in which each individual contributes to the social life in some way, fits into it, and helps it on, and that in which the social life contributes itself to him, so that he feels and appreciates its significance as a part of his own life and conduct.

Using two terms in a technical way, we may say that the individual should be not simply an organ of society, but also a member of society. That he should be an organ of society means that he should contribute, that he should be a social servant or agent. That he should be a social member of society means that he must also get back into his own life, for himself, in his own interests and experiences, results, whatever society can possibly contribute to the enrichment of his own life. That is again the conception of culture from a somewhat different point of view. The individual in his activities, in what he does, in the efforts which he puts forth, should feel the full sense and bearing of what he does.

Unless we realize both sides of this, it would be rather
[(2)(*a*)] difficult to justify some studies which at present seem to be of importance in education. Take for instance the study of history. Of course it is not without its value in enabling the individual to contribute intelligently and effectively to the conduct of social life. But for the most part, if it were simply a question of enabling him to contribute better to the social life, the end would be rather remote. Undoubtedly there are certain moral, intellectual and aesthetic lessons which the child could begin to apply at once; but on the whole the significance of history would be on the other side, to give the child an appreciation of himself in social terms. It is not so much that he may contribute better to society, but that social life can contribute more to the enriching of his life. It enables his individual experience to stretch out beyond its temporal and spatial limits and take in these wider phases of social value. Of course indirectly that very enlargement of the child's own immediate experience serves to make him a more valuable social organ, that is, to make it possible for him to

contribute more effectively to the progress of social life. For the most part that is the indirect side. The direct is that the child is not merely a means of social life; he is a part of social life, and so is an end to which society itself is directly responsible.

[(b)] What is said here of history would be true to a very large extent of the study of dead foreign languages, for instance. It would be pretty difficult to trace any direct connection between the study of such a language to present or future social life, but it is not necessary to show such direct connection, if we can show that the study of it serves to enlarge and enrich the child's own experience, the meaning which he attaches to life. When that is done, indirectly, he must be made a more valuable social organ. I mention this mainly to avoid misapprehension, because it is quite possible to interpret this conception of social life as the standard of education in too narrowing and utilitarian and direct a way, overlooking the continual reaction of the whole thing in the enriching of the child's own life as a part of the social life which is to be developed.

[d.(1)] From this conception of the necessary and organic relation between subject matter and method, certain other more practical considerations follow. The text books for the most part have been prepared upon what you might call the objective basis, upon the basis of the statement and classification of facts from the standpoint of their most accurate formulation and greatest logical relationship. Now so far then as these text books afford the material of education, method on the part of the individual instructor is hampered and becomes very largely an effort to undo the work of the text book; that is, it becomes very largely the work of the teacher to so adapt in the recitation all they got from the text book, that it may be translated out of its objective form into psychological terms in the experience of individual children. That must always be true to some extent. No possible book or article could ever, in its formulation, be adequately adapted to the needs of different children; the teacher would always have to come in as a mediator to make the final connections with human nature. But after all it is an important matter that the text book should be written so as to make this final adaptation on the part of the teacher as easy and effective as possible.

The text book should be written more and more on a psychological and less on a logical basis. The realization of that conception is probably rather remote, because naturally, when a man writes a text book he wishes to cover the whole ground and produce a symmetrical, well arranged, full statement from the standpoint of the science under discussion; but the very fullness of the statement, the very logical symmetry of it may actually hinder it in accomplishing its own real work.

I indicated one of the bearings of that in the conversation yesterday; that is, part of this question of adaptation is a question of changing the stress of emphasis. The text book designed for general use must put everything upon the same level. It might be said that the very first law of the working of the mind is that it never puts things on the same level. The very work of nature is selection, emphasis, the picking out of the things that are most important to the individual at the time, and arranging the other things from the standpoint of this factor of greatest interest and importance as the focus. It is impossible for a general text book to make any provision, or even any allowance for that fact in every subject to every individual. There are points of greatest interest and therefore of greatest ease of assimilation, and a lot more shading out in all degrees to what is relatively cold, and the normal working of the mind is to start from the point of the greatest connection with the self and incorporate other elements through ramifications from that.

[(2)]   Another problem which arises from the separation of method and subject matter, is the existing separation or tendency to separation in training on the basis of scholarship and in training with reference to teaching. The average person learns what to teach but it is quite a separate thing learning how to teach; and he learns how to teach quite isolatedly from learning what to teach. There is a marked distinction between college and normal school education, college education being training to what is called scholarship, and training in the normal school consisting rather in getting knowledge of children and methods and devices in treating various subjects in relation to children. It is obvious that that separation is not favorable from another side. It cannot be said from any point of view to be desirable that the person who has the scholarship should spend a long period of apprenticeship simply in working over that material. The person who tries to find how it can best be adapted to other minds never succeeds very well. On the other side, it is not desirable that a person should learn how to teach at the expense of, or without adequate knowledge of what to teach. It does not conduce to the development of the teacher or those being taught. It may be said that the evil is no greater on one side than on the other. It is simply an abnormal separation which perhaps presents the most serious problem existing at present in the training of teachers.

[(3)(a)] There is a third problem which arises and may be spoken of, that is, the relation between the interests of the child on one hand and scholarship, or a knowledge of the subject matter, on the other. In what are termed the "old" and the "new" education, the old education might be said to have thrown the chief emphasis upon scholarship, upon information and discipline. It took essentially the standpoint of the adult, of the goal which the child was finally to reach. The subject matter was marked off into grades. The child, by the time he got through the eighth grade or the high school ought to know so much, and it was more simple and natural to cut up what he must know into portions according to the time he has to learn it in, and give him so much a year. If it is geography, take one continent one year, and another the next, and as Professor Jackman* says, if you only begin geography at the right year and can make it come out at the right year, you will find there are just enough continents to go around. That is the basis upon which the material of the curriculum has been picked out and arranged, putting the easier things first and the more difficult things last, but upon the whole cutting it out in solid chunks of that sort on the basis of the scholarship or information of the adult.

[(b)] Now the new education has the tendency to start from the opposite point of view. It insists that the interests and impulses of the child are to be consulted and that you get your important criteria on that side. It can hardly be said that the present practice is very consistent in either direction. It is a compromise and oscillation between the

[* Wilbur S. Jackman was a Lecturer in Pedagogy at the University of Chicago at this time. He also served, with Dewey, on the Executive Council of the Board of the Herbart Society.]

two. It is obvious that the standpoint of the child's interests, taken by itself, is as one sided as that of the scholarship of the adult, as a basis. Interest is an attitude, it is not a final end or result. It is simply something to be made use of, it is a tool in the child himself which the teacher can operate, instead of having to find tools outside of the child which are externally applied to him. It is the beginning just as the scholarship side represents the end, and while it is harmful to force down the ends, the results, independently of what there is to start with in the child himself, it is equally harmful to take the starting point, the clues, in the child himself, as if they were final, as if they were the result. So at least the tendency in the new education is too frequently to consult the interests of the child instead of making them the leverage to move the child in the direction of the desired end, to regard them almost as standards for telling what shall, or shall not, be done. The result tends to be a humoring of the child, amusing him, pleasing him for the time being, instead of furthering growth. It tends towards the overstimulation of the child, which is distraction.

[(c)]   The only way to avoid the evils at the extremes, is precisely to secure adequate preparation, both on the side of scholarship and in a knowledge of the psychological side of the relations of the material and a knowledge of the probable course of growth in the child, the waves of development of his interests and tastes, and of how not simply to consult the waves of interest as they arise, but how to utilize them so that the child shall be carried over beyond and ahead. To take advantage of the child's interest, to utilize it, is not a thing which is in any way opposed to scholarship; it is just the reverse. No one teaching even little children can have too much knowledge in order to take the best advantage of the child's interest, and excepting as one sees more or less the possible ends and results from the beginning, it is not possible to take advantage of the manifestations as they come up in the child. Instead of being treated as instrumental, if one does not have a definite knowledge of the subject matter under consideration, the whole thing will be inevitably diluted, reduced, degraded to the level of the child's superficial manifestations of interest. The mere interest which the child has is of a more or less specific, transitory kind, in stones, trees, and animals. It is a thing which cannot be adequately utilized excepting by some one who has a very thorough-going and specialized training in those matters. The child's interest may be met without such a knowledge, but in that case there is no probability of any permanent growth of the thing, leading beyond itself and amounting to anything. It is a good thing, for instance, when the child is interested in the color of flowers or of metals, to have the child paint the things. That is one way to take advantage of the interest, but if the thing simply stops there, the child may have some artistic development, but he has no advantage taken of the interest on the scientific side. Or the interest of the child may be taken advantage of to give a language lesson, to read and spell certain words that he would not know otherwise. So far as it goes it is useful, but it cannot be said to develop the child from the standpoint of the scientific interest, it cannot be said to give him a more intelligent attitude toward nature. That can only be done if the person who is doing the teaching has a thorough-going broad knowledge of the whole field and so surveys it that he can see just what facts, at each particular period, the child can get hold of, the facts that he really needs in order to make his own interest valid and permanently valuable to him. We are still in the period of transition and, consequently, of compromise. The so-called new education, in realizing the value of interest has not sufficiently realized the need of advanced and thorough and specialized scholarship, in order that the interest may be really effective in the educational process.

LECTURE XV

February 2, 1899

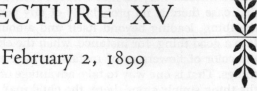

[B.I.(c),(d): *Organic relations of the psychical and social: relations to instruction; psychology and teaching.*

B.III.(1),(2): *Characteristic epochs in growth: first and second.*]

[II.A.2.d.(4)] From what has been said regarding the relation of subject matter and method, it follows that the work of instruction has to be considered from two points of view, or that there is a continual working back and forth, a continual process of translation or mediation over from the standpoint of subject matter, representing the content of social life, to the standpoint of method, representing the existing impulses and capacities of the child. We may start from either end and work toward the other. Different persons may prefer to start from one point and work toward the other, though everybody would have to make the translation both ways more or less; but to some the more natural starting point would be from considering the interests and tendencies of the child as affording opportunities, as presenting occasions for development in certain directions. The instinct, in other words, would be to start the whole matter from the standpoint of the child, and to pick out the subject matter simply as an element in relation to his growth. The natural starting point of others would be a statement of the standpoint of the organization of the subject matter, and then raising the question as to how that was to be most effectively introduced into the life of the child, to become a factor in his growth. Successfully to carry out either way of looking at it would come to the same result as if the beginning had been made from the other side. But since no one person is likely to be completely successful in making such translations, it is of course an advantageous thing that different persons have different tastes and work at it in different ways.

[(*a*)]   In a general way, the supervising and administrative force of any school system would be those who worked from the subject matter over to the child; while the force of class room instructors would be those who started their process of interpretation with the immediate, present children. That is, from one point of view the course of study is laid down, and the connections with society in general, with other social institutions, are made. It is obviously the chief function of the superintendent and supervisory force of any particular educational system not to attend to the details of instruction, but to make just these adaptations in a business way and in the other ways which keep the school system in harmony with the general community life, and to select the course of study on that basis. That point of view becomes isolated from the work of actual instruction; if it is made up as an independent thing, and with the point of view of carrying it over into the life of the child, we get an orderly and logical course of study laid out on paper that does not work in practice as it was supposed to work. The persons whose business it is to go at it through that method must be in contact with the actual work of the class room and be in sympathy with it so as to take into account that side of the matter. So some think no one ought to have anything to do with the system who is not equally capable of teaching classes as well.

[(*b*)]   Now while the teacher, the classroom instructor, is not chiefly concerned with the selection of subject matter but rather takes that as worked out from a different point of view and is mainly occupied with the adaptation of it to the present life of the child, it is equally clear that isolation is not desirable from that point of view either. The classroom teacher should have a broad outlook so as to appreciate the motives which led to the selection of this subject matter at this particular epoch, and how it fits in to what came before and what comes after in the scheme. He must have some sense of its more ultimate value and relations. The isolation that there is often in the present educational system between these two phases of the process, is accordingly very unfortunate. The bulk of the teachers have no legislative power at all, they are not active factors in determining what the course of study shall be. The college faculty generally does organize its own course of study, instead of having to work out one that is imposed upon it from above; the high school faculty also has some determining influence; but on the whole, the curriculum of the elementary schools is laid out by some superior authority somewhere, and the teachers have simply to take as gratefully as possible what the superior authority has provided for them and to attend to inserting it, if possible, into the consciousness of the child. Since education is a vital matter, since it works always from one person to another person, it is obvious that the work of instruction is very much hampered when it is controlled from that point of view. Hence the tendency to organize all teachers, elementary teachers included, into faculties of some sort, into consulting bodies where they have an opportunity to express their own ideas of the best material and proper make up of the course of study, is a very important step in the direction of making the whole educational process more free and flexible. This simply illustrates the point that while it is convenient and desirable to have this division of labor, different persons throwing the emphasis on different points of view, yet the two ends of the process must not become isolated, they must always operate with a flexible, cooperative interaction.

Incidentally, and as a practical matter, the significance of that in raising the standard of the teaching force, and in tending to attract greater ability into the teaching staff, is worth mentioning. Of course you cannot expect, upon the whole, the highest order of ability to go into a work where the main function is simply carrying out instructions which are imposed from above, where there is no chance to legislate, to decide, to have any determining influence in the course of study. Everybody is put on about the same level, the only difference being in their ability to make particular adaptations to the children. The giving of some, if not actually final authority, at least consultative power to the classroom teacher in determining the course of study, would certainly be one of the most important factors that could be got hold of in making a dividing line, in winnowing out those who have no independent interest or initiative with respect to it at all, who simply are mechanically working at something which they do not understand, and with which they cannot really sympathize.

[(5)] I sum up this phase of the discussion by pointing out the various respects in which, on the basis of the principle laid down, psychology may be expected to be helpful to the teacher. I alluded to the various proofs to the effect that psychology cannot be helpful to teachers, but if it is actually helpful to teachers, it shows that there is something the matter with the a priori argument in that direction.

[(a)] In the first place, a psychological interest, if not an extended technical knowledge of psychology, is certainly helpful, enabling the teacher to appreciate the point of view from which the subject matter itself should be approached. Of course psychology can be learned simply as a matter of information like any other subject. In that case it would not be likely to be particularly helpful, but I mean a real understanding of psychology. If one had that, it would certainly be impossible to suppose that the child at different periods of his growth can get hold of material from the same point of view and that all it is necessary to do is to make it easier and less in quantity for children in the lower grades, in order that it may be got hold of.

If the significance of the psychological standpoint is recognized, everyone will see that the kind of interest which is dominant at a certain time, the kind of power which is struggling to find expression, must be the dominant thing in deciding from what point of view the subject matter, whether scientific, literary, historical, or linguistic, should be approached. If we could tell even in a general way what the point of view was with which the child instinctively approached the material and the point of view from which it commended itself, we should have the criterion for selecting the phases of the material which are most likely to be helpful to him. That is to say, we would see that there were certain phases of the subject matter, certain lines of facts and principles, which were most intimately connected with the particular point of view which is dominant at the time. We should get what has been termed in some studies, a circular method in the curriculum, rather than a step ladder method. I mean by the step ladder method that of cutting up the subject matter into so many longitudinal sections.

The Germans currently recognized in history three
[(i)]   distinct points of view from which any or all material
may be gone over; not that there are so many historical facts which are to be divided up, but that you can take any
material and approach it from the biographical and personal
point of view; and then secondly from what might be called
the episodic, or story point of view, the development of certain
lines of interest or certain consecutive movements of certain
forces; and then thirdly, a more analytic study of the forces
at work at any particular time, and the problem of how these
forces conspired to produce the particular results. Without
raising the question as to whether there is any validity in those
three particular points of view, it illustrates what I mean by
the circular mode of experience, based upon some psychological consideration of the dominant interest, at a given period of
mental development.

Mathematics has probably suffered as much as any-
[(ii)]   thing from the attempt at longitudinal arrangement.
In the first place it was assumed that all arithmetic is
simpler and easier than all algebra, and all algebra than
geometry; and then arithmetic is broken up into different things
like fractions, decimals, multiples, percentage, and so on, and
the child is supposed to learn a certain amount of this each
successive year of his period. Looking at the material from a
psychological point of view, it becomes obvious that there are
geometrical propositions which are simpler and lie nearer the
child's experience than a great deal which is in the arithmetic;
and so in algebra there are many problems which are more
easily apprehended than many of the more difficult ones in
arithmetic. It becomes obvious that the separation of ratio,
percentage, and fractions, however much a matter of convenience for scientific purposes, is unpedagogical. The child
can more easily comprehend ratio, fractions and whole numbers when they are presented all at the same time through different conditions, than when they are strung along through a
series of years and treated as if each one was a discovery of a
new topic with new principles.

The second point where psychology can help is in giv-
[(b)]   ing an individual a method by which to interpret the
particular phenomena of child life as they present
themselves. We can have not only a general conception of the

normal course of development with consciousness of the dominant interest and point of view of each, but we can also have
a definite consciousness of the principles which are involved
in all mental working, so that the particular facts of human
nature as they show themselves will mean something instead
of being hard and opaque, or else regarded as accidental curiosities or utterly incomprehensible peculiarities, or even as
they often are, as actual moral perversions. Not a mere knowledge of so much information about psychology, but a personal
appreciation of the factors that are involved in habit, in attention, that are involved in carrying on the process of any
inquiry directed to the solution of any problems, will make
those facts self revealing; while to another person who has not,
either by instruction, or by a more conscious study of the
matter, acquired a knowledge of the principles, these same
things will be so meaningless and so opaque as to set up a wall
that practically cannot be passed, between the teacher and the
child.

[(i)]
                I heard the question propounded one day to a body
         of teachers as to what the kind of difficulty was when
         the child who meant to attend, and who in one sense
was straining all his powers to attend to a lesson, would after
all go over the lesson with simply a feeling of strain and without getting anything out of it. One person present who had been
teaching a great many years, said it seemed to him axiomatic
that there were only three explanations. One was that the
child did not want to attend. That was ruled out by the statement of the problem which supposed that the child strained
all his powers to attend. The other two explanations were that
the child was so thoroughly fatigued that he could not attend,
or else mentally incapacitated. It is obvious that the second
point would have something to do with it, and that some knowledge of the psychology and physiology of fatigue might come
in to enable the teacher to understand that phenomenon. But
when you come to mental incapacity there is evidently an absolute vacuum in that man's mind in regard to psychology: the
failure to analyze that statement, to break it up, to say what
incapacity means in details of the working of the mental machinery. It might mean imbecility, either total or partial, but
that is about the only sense in which the term incapacity could
possibly have any meaning. Anyone who has a psychological

instinct would at once go on to break up such a conception as
that of incapacity, to see whether it was due to lack of relevancy
of the matter; whether the matter was too remote, having no
background, no points of connection with the child's experience; or whether, while it was theoretically in line with the
child's experience, it was not presented in such a way as to suggest to the child the points of connection or questions had not
been asked which would put the child's mind in the receptive
attitude regarding it; or whether the child was without a sense
of any motive, end, or problem involved there. I need not go on
to indicate all the various possible alternatives there might be.

      The same thing is true, not only with intellectual
[(*ii*)] phenomena, but also witth moral phenomena. Our
      natural point of view is eminently practical rather
than psychological. We tend to treat various things as moral
facts and to react to them simply as moral exhibitions of anger,
impatience, impertinence, of vanity, and so on. Now the reaction to them in that way is simply a reaction in bulk. We may
suppress the reaction in that way, we might suppress the outward manifestation of that particular kind, and congratulate
ourselves that we are working reforms in the child's character,
but any successful response on the part of the teacher must
be made by conscious insight into the stimuli, into the conditions which have been actually operative and which have produced that particular phenomenon. In other words, without
some psychological insight, we treat these moral facts, these
facts of conduct, exactly as a physician who would confuse
the symptom with the disease. The facts of anger and impatience are primarily simply symptoms. To find out what
they are symptoms of is to go back into the child's own mental
structure, make up, his sense of the stimuli which act upon
him and the way in which he tends to react upon them. So we
make our response by getting a leverage in some of these influences which operate within the child, instead of simply making a gross, bulk reaction upon him from the outside.

      Of course there are a great many other ways and de-
[(*c*)] tails in which psychology might be available to the
      teacher, but it is sufficient to suggest these two main
heads: first, an awareness of the general concrete process of
growth. Of course that is not going to apply literally to every
individual, but that same thing is equally true of the growth

of plants and of animals. We certainly can be sure that if we know what the general, what the normal process of growth is, we shall be very much more able to deal with the exceptional cases when they do present themselves. The second is the process of the psychological machinery, the conditions and stimuli that are operating in bringing about the phenomena that we actually see. It is not simply a question of having certain faculties, like perception, memory, judgment, attention, and so on, and asking how those particular faculties may be trained. The only value that there is in those classifications is simply to give better insight into particular facts regarding memory and attention, and so on, as they show themselves.

I will postpone the discussion of the topic that is put next in the syllabus until later on; that is, number II at the bottom of page 3: "Factors in Problem." I will postpone it until I come to C on page 5 "Organization of Subject Matter" and I will go on now with the third head: "Characteristic Epochs in Growth" top of page 4.

[B.] I have just been saying that one of the important ways in which the knowledge of psychology is educationally valuable is in giving insight into just this matter of the characteristic epochs or periods of mental development. That of course is the field about which all the various investigations in so-called child study are carried on; at least that is their centering point. Of course we do not know very much about it yet. It has not been studied long enough or in sufficient detail either extrinsically or intrinsically. We can lay down therefore only very general statements. In setting these forth, I shall only give the conclusions. I shall not be able to present to you the data which in my own mind justify these statements.

I have marked off here four different periods. I have left out the period of early infancy because that does not come within the scope of any formal treatment of education. But beginning at the end of the early period of infancy, say the third year, I should say that the first period lasted until about seven years of age. Of course these dates are not a matter of any great importance, they are simply certain rough signboards. The second period extends from the age of seven to adolescence, or better puberty, at twelve or thirteen years of age; while the third period extends to the age of eighteen or twenty.

Now as to the distinguishing psychological character-
[1.] istics of these different epochs, I shall say that the
chief characteristic of the first is the control of experience and of conduct by images which operate through the
immediate interest which they possess. The child, so to speak,
is propelled along with, or through the medium of the images
which are uppermost in his mind, and which are seeking for
manifestation. I have called that in the outline the period of
direct experience; that is, it is outgoing, spontaneous, and unreflective. We could hardly say that the child is propelled from
behind, from merely unconscious instincts, as he is in the
period of early infancy. They are present in his mind as images
and they work themselves out. It could be otherwise stated as
the play period, meaning by play that there is no conscious
distinction between process and product. That is, the child
makes no conscious distinctions between his means and his
ends. He does not control his action on the basis of ends which
are ahead of him, but the end has an immediate present hold
on him, it is its own immediate justification and he acts because of the value which it has for him at the time.

With the outgrowth into the second period (it does
[2.a.] not come with a bound or jump) images begin to
present themselves of more remote considerations,
and the child begins to do things which are not of immediate
interest to him, because he feels, if he does not clearly see, the
reference which those things have to the getting of the end, the
result, which lies somewhat ahead of him. There is a consciousness of means and ends which is distinct, so that the child can
move back and forth from one to the other. If play and work
had not such fixed meanings, we might call this the beginning
of the consciousness of work, not in the sense of drudgery,
of tasks, but in the sense that the child controls, that he regu-
lates what he is now doing, on the basis of something which is
future.

I happened to see one day a number of children all either
six or seven years of age as they played hide and coop together.
It was clearly the first time that a large number of the children had ever played the game. They simply sorted themselves
out into two groups. Some of them were carried away by the
momentum of what they were immediately doing. If they got
started to run for the goal they continued to run quite irre-

spective of whether they would accomplish the purpose of the game better by doing something else or not. Sometimes the child blinded, if he was running, kept on instead of trying to touch the goal. Others tried to adapt their movements to the paricular end in the game. That is a very simple but a very good illustration of what I mean by the two epochs. In one the child's movement is controlled simply by the dominant interest at the time. He does not stop to relate it to some other end, and ask how what he is now doing can best be adapted to bring about the further result.

[(1)] The whole transition from plays into games is very instructive in regard to this change in the whole attitude of the child. By play I mean that the child simply follows the image of the moment, he works it out according to the various suggestions that come up in his own mind or in the mind of someone near, but there is no particular end in view, and there are no rules to regulate the play. The game always has a point. There is always some particular end to be reached and therefore the game as a game has rules which lay down the particular way in which the child must carry it on in order to reach that end. When the child begins to feel dissatisfied with his mere free play and takes an active interest in games, it shows that his whole attitude is undergoing this transformation. He is beginning to look at what he does, not as merely a present thing, but he is looking at it as a means which therefore must be controlled, must be governed by something beyond. A sense of the significance of rules, of definite ways of doing things in order to reach an end, now begins to have some meaning for him. Of course in the early part of this period the end must be very close to the child, it cannot be put very far off, and the rule must be pretty concrete, say do this and that and you will get the other thing.

[(2)] With the consciousness of the distinction of means and ends, or present and future, and their adaptations to each other, the control of one with reference to the other, the child begins to get a consciousness of the significance of skill. As long as there is no consciousness of the difference between means and ends skill has no meaning, and the only thing is to follow the images which are interesting, and work them out to make them more interesting. But when one is conscious of a remote end then he is conscious of differences of the way of reaching it. Doing it in one way will reach a certain result successfully while another way of doing it will prove less so. So the child learns the way of realizing different modes of execution. The question of skill is the best adaptation of means to ends.

LECTURE XVI

February 6, 1899

[B.III.(2),(3),(4): *Characteristic epochs in growth: second, third and fourth. Educational equivalents. Elements in the present system.*]

[II.B.2.a.] The beginning of the second main period of development, as I said the other day, was the dawning consciousness of ends to be reached and therefore of the control, the direction of the immediate activity by the image or thought of the end to be reached. At first, naturally, this end takes a practical form. It is such an end as would be found in playing a game where there were certain rules to follow in order to reach a certain point; or in doing a piece of work of no very great complexity; and of following a story where the whole interest was not simply absorbed in the development of the story, but where part of the interest was reflected interest, that is the mind took the attitude of anticipating and of valuing the details that present themselves with reference to the bearing that they have upon the probable final outcome of the story. Of course that mental attitude is different from the one in which the story is followed simply for the sake of the story—the incidents and happenings as the story goes along.

[(3)] This is, as has been noted by various students, a period of great motor activity and of motor uneasiness or what might be called the motor self-consciousness. The child before this period is physically exceedingly active, but because his means and ends are one, his physical activity, if he is a normal child, is taken possession of almost completely by the image that dominates his mind. It is sometimes said the small child has no power of continued attention, yet one of the most marked characteristics of little children is their absolute absorption or intentness on what they are doing at the moment. There is more likely to be a complete image of the particular process of action than in the older child, because his ends have got more remote, take the form of ideas as something to follow. There is likely to be an immediate superabundance of means, of physical energy, which is not so taken possession of, not administered by the idea as thoroughly as it was in the earlier stage. This physical restlessness, irritation, tendency to senseless activity, is on the whole more marked with the child of six or seven, and often of eight years of age, than it is in the earlier period.

[(4)]   The child also morally gets a start in what would be called willfulness and of conscious selfishness, that he had not had before, and psychologically, very much for the same reason. In being conscious of ends he necessarily distinguishes between himself and other people in a way in which he could not possibly do as long as he was simply dominated by the interests and suggestions of the moment, but when a person is capable of projecting an end, that means that he is projecting himself, marking out his aims and purposes from those of other people, and so the consciousness of the necessity of adjustment between the ends of the individual and those of the other people, or the consciousness of clash, is likely to come in at this time.

[(5)]   There is another trait that seems worth mentioning (I cannot begin to go over the details) and that is the fact that in a little child the image so thoroughly dominates what he is doing that he has no standard, no criterion for judging what he does. This point is perhaps best seen in the spontaneous drawings of children, where absurdities, impossibilities of form, size, perspective, and arrangement of bodies are passed over. The child does not care about that at all, the walls of his houses are transparent because he is more interested in what is inside than in what is outside, and whatever interests him most is drawn big and the things about which he does not care, are drawn small. This is illustrated by the kindergarten child who made the stocking at Christmas time outside the house, because it was too big to get in.

Now as the child becomes conscious of ends, he gets a basis for not only practically controlling his immediate activities, but he gets a basis for valuing them, for getting their relative or comparative worth. How much does it contribute to the realization of the end? It is the beginning of what may be called a reflective attitude, the attitude of turning back, judging, criticising what has been done, not from the standpoint of abstract principles or laws, but from the standpoint of relevancy or irrelevancy with reference to the results that one is after. Because of this fact there is likely also to be a break in the child's experience at this time, unless the child is very fortunate in temperament, or carefully guarded against the environment. As long as the child is not conscious of the relation between means and ends, he gives imagination free play, and the same object will represent a half dozen things in succession, in making pictures. He may have nothing but a blur and yet tell you quite a story of many things going on, that are invisible to the adult. The image is the important thing and anything serves as a clue to embody that to the child. As he grows older and is conscious of the new relationship between these ideas and their embodiment, he begins to see the crudity of his acts and loses the spontaneity of the imagery itself.

Somebody has proposed that a census be taken to show where all the bright children go to, because up to a certain age almost every child seems to have a peculiar individuality which has its own artistic charm. A few years later children seem to be pretty much alike and become commonplace. Part of that is undoubtedly due to just this fact, that with this growing consciousness of the success of various acts, with the impossibility to the child of finding his ideas sufficiently realized through the medium of play, he loses the stimulus to the imaging itself, and he gradually brings his images down somewhere near the level that it is actually possible for him to realize. It becomes a matter of importance then, to see to it that there is some media supplied for the child between his imagery and his powers of execution. His powers of execution can be trained so that he can carry out imagery as far as possible if other means of expression and relation be provided, so that his images which constitute his own particular individuality, can be kept alive. With some children there is the opposite danger. That is, instead of losing the images or having them reduced, degraded to every day ordinary powers of realization, as the split comes in the child becomes fanciful, over-imaginative in his own inner life and carries on his outward occupations very largely irrespective of what is going on inside. Such cases are rarer than the others, but it is not uncommon for children to lead a dual life of this sort. They have certain feelings and ideas which they realize might look ridiculous which they carefully protect and cultivate, and which have a great influence on their character and conduct, although no direct signs of them ever appear.

[b.] These considerations seem to me to give the psychological basis for the general principle of school work at this time: on one hand to utilize and cultivate the child's sense of growing ends as controlling his action and thoughts, and on the other hand to facilitate the interaction between the image side, which stands for ends, and the physical and motor immediate activities through which these images have to find their embodiment; to see to it on one hand that he gets the power of controlling his immediate activities by the consideration of results, and on the other hand that he retain something of his freedom and fullness of power in setting before himself a large range of idealized values and contents which outrun his powers of immediate embodiment, and yet which are kept in some kind of relation to what he is doing. The basis for the introduction of art, literature, and particularly history, in the earlier years of the elementary school, seem to come from this line of psychological considerations. The child seems to take a turn during this period, about the age of eight and a half or nine. The seventh and eighth years might be called working toward practical ends or aims, but there is a physical change of some sort which takes place at about the date mentioned. According to some writers this is probably the time when the brain centers which control the peripheral muscular coordinations ripen, the main muscular activities having to do with the larger trunk and more massive bodily coordinations. There is apparently on the intellectual side the growth of interest and power of getting at details, not merely in action but also of the intellectual elements. A study of the drawings of children seems to show that. He also gets a growing sense of rule, not merely like the rule of a game, but having a certain intellectual element in it, of how an end is best to be reached, such as we have in arithmetic, rules of regular analytic procedure. If this apparent fact should be corroborated by continued investigation, it would indicate that this is the time when the child is ripe for introduction to technique, the technique of reading, drawing, writing, manual training, or whatever the thing may be.

Up to this time he should be getting what skill he can, but merely on an empirical basis. Now he is capable of appreciating more in an analytic way the significance of the proper method of doing things. That does not mean that he is completely ready for it, or that there is any revolutionary change, but simply that that phase of action, the formulated method of doing things, appeals to the child more after that time. To give a possible application, that would indicate the best time to introduce the child to phonic analysis in his reading; he would appreciate the analysis as an actual assistance of a method which he himself could follow in constructing his own results. Up to this time he grasps the thing more as a whole in itself. It is certainly a marked empirical fact that it is during the grades of school life that correspond to these years that the child is supposed to get his mastery of the fundamental methods of study, reading, writing, and arithmetic. Not that he is supposed to learn all the refinements and details, but the child at the end of his fifth grade has learned how to read, if he is ever going to, as a rule; not all the possible words, but he is expected to be able to read. He is supposed also to have mastered all the fundamental operations and rules for conducting them in arithmetic and then be able to go ahead and apply them in certain directions. It is about this time that the great tendency to leave school comes in. At the end of the fifth or sixth grades, they or their parents feel that they have the accomplishments that they came to get, and now can go to work. The grades from four to six seem to be the critical years in school life for the mastery of a rudimentary intellectual technique. They thus grow out of the earlier period where the interest is more in content, in the images and substance for its own sake, and look ahead to the later period, the period of adolescence, where the interest is mainly on the side again of content, and not on the side of the form or technique of handling that content.

The third period is the period of adolescence, but so
[3.] much has been written about that of late that you can
easily consult for yourselves, that I shall only mention what seems to me its chief feature, and that is the sense

of the inclusive, comprehensive wholes with reference to which details and also rules, procedures, generalizations, have to be placed.

[a.] Physiologically this period marks the introduction of the child into full membership in the social whole. He is himself now becoming consciously a part of humanity through sharing in its generic characteristics, and it does not seem to me forced to say that the counterpart of that is found in his whole intellectual and moral life; that he is everywhere coming to consciousness of something larger, more complete, of which he had not previously been conscious; and the necessity of measuring himself and the details of his own experience by placing them in this larger, more organized whole. His interest is in social relations and affairs, in the idealistic, romantic elements in life, and in conduct growing from this same root; while the studies taken up are in a more intellectual direction.

[b.] This is the time when generalization means something on its own account. Before this it was simply known as the rule or method, which is quite different from a generalization as a generalization. Studies that have been made in drawing, history, and arithmetic seem to show that the child at this time feels the need of generalization, for some way of organizing the various details of his experience which before this have been carried on more or less unconsciously, but which are scattered until he gets hold of the principles that help him function in some whole.

[c.] We often hear of the upheaval which takes place at this time, but I think it is easy to exaggerate that upheaval, to make it more revolutionary than it should be. There is no doubt however, that there is a normal reconstruction at that period. If you say it is the time when he becomes conscious of society as society, of God, and of all the more fundamental issues which concern and fill the mind, of restating the various details in relation to the inclusive wholes, we can see why it is a period of not merely quantitative growth, but of large qualitative reconstruction; the point of view is larger and everything has to be looked at from the new point of view. Probably it is the beginning of normal conscious intellectual and religious interests. The child's moral interests up to this time are (would be if they were allowed to take their own course) mainly in the details of conduct. Certain things are right and others wrong. One is good if he does this, and naughty if he does that. That is different from any consciousness of duty or obligation at large, as a controlling motive for action, or any sense of ideals, moral laws, or principles as a basis for conduct. I think it will be generally found that when an attempt is made to appeal to those general moral motives and considerations in the child much before this time, the result is either that the child throws them off as "water from the duck's back" or he tends to be made morbid and morally artificial in this direction; there is psychologically no basis for the purely general principles, like the sense of obligation and of duty in general, as to why they should mean anything in the regulation of life. The tendency has been to isolate the moral from the intellectual and suppose that he has a conscience already made which can be appealed to per se, but I do not think it can be said that the results of that method of looking at the thing among the Puritans were so happy as to commend the method for continued adoption. What psychologically corresponds to the rule is the habit. If the child's moral life can be upon the basis of forming intelligent habits, then you will have a back-ground at this time for reflecting on those habits, for reorganizing them, seeing their relations to each other and to the whole of life; but an appeal before this time is apt to be premature.

[4.]   After this general reconstruction in which the youth measures himself and his world and experience in relation to a larger world, in relation to other courses of conduct and more important issues, comes the time when he has to not merely place himself intellectually and emotionally, but practically; that is, choose an occupation in life. That means of course that he is practically placing himself in relation to the larger whole of society and of the world. There is a division of labor which comes in, and in theory at least, in ideal, he is picking out the line of work which is best suited to his capacity and in which he is capable of rendering greatest service to society. That naturally marks the termination of the period of formal education. That is, the previous period, if it is what we term a liberal, free education, should have given the youth a definite sense of the world, of life, and of his own powers, of his own particular tastes and capacities, so that he really can measure one in relation to the other and make the adjustment. Somehow he is going to connect them, and make the adjustment of himself as a particular individual to the whole of life. It is what constitutes the choice of a profession, and the education, then, should be of the kind which enables him most successfully to complete preparation for this calling or vocation. The vocation in idea, no matter how far we are from it in practice, marks the completed adjustment between the psychological and sociological elements in education. If the individual has not a calling which gives himself full play there is something the matter; if he has not a calling which will give his full value to society, which will give him the opportunity to render to society all the service that he is capable of, there is something the matter. The problem of selecting and preparing for the life-work means that this problem which has been latent through the whole educational process, now comes to a focus and has to be settled.

[C.]   Going over briefly the various phases of the educational system in relation to this very out-lined statement of mental development, you get three or four periods according to how we draw the dividing line. That is, we could say that the first, elementary and general, was up to the period of puberty, the second up to the period of beginning to specialize for a vocation, and then this third period.

[1.]   Now it is obvious that that, prima facie, does not accord with the educational scheme in this country. We have the elementary period broken up into three: the kindergarten, primary, and grammar, or, as it is called in some places, intermediate. Then we have the high school which is the secondary period par excellence, but if we say that that only is the secondary period the question arises of how to dispose of what we call college education. Most educational writers are now agreed that the first two years of college work logically belong to secondary work. Then we have the last two years of college work to which it is very difficult to give any name in particular at all—the period, in most colleges, of elective studies which is justified on the ground of the liberal culture of the education which is neither disciplinary nor professional, but is located in between to help the person strengthen the weak points and make up for the gaps in his previous education. After that we have what would be regarded as the more strictly professional work. Many persons draw the line between graduate work in the universities and professional work, reserving the term "professional" for law, medical, and divinity schools, and would have some other name for specialized work that is done in the graduate schools giving the degree of Ph.D. If you will think of it however, you will find it is hard to get an idea by which you can specifically designate the graduate work in universities. It is difficult to say why pursuing specialized studies in Greek or biology is not as distinctly professional in character as the work done in the law or medical schools.

[a.] Of course it is not a matter of any great importance intrinsically that the classifications and divisions of our school system do not agree with those which we seem to arrive at by a study of epochs of mental development; but in so far as these breaks are real, practical breaks, so far as there is not a continuous systematic organization of the school system, it becomes a very practical matter indeed. On the administrative side the chief problem in the United States at the present time is to secure a better adjustment of the various parts of the educational system to each other; the whole question for instance, of the requirements for entrance to college. That is, the leading question under discussion as regards the relation of the high school and the college is simply a question of adjustment. It becomes recognized that we have barriers that are artificial, and now the chief thing is to do away with them. If you were to go over the particular problems in the high school so far as they are preparatory, and all the problems on the college side of just what to require for admission, it is a question of getting a freer interaction. Any break of this sort means waste and the problem of eliminating waste on the administrative side is the question of breaking down the barrier and getting a single unit, an educational system which will take the child from his fourth until his twenty-first or twenty-second year, or wherever his education should stop.

[b.] To go back to the beginning now, the first isolation is between the kindergarten and the primary school.

Historically it is easy enough to account for this. The kindergarten came into existence after the recognized school had taken form in pretty definite, mechanical shape. The kindergarten movement as instituted by Froebel rested on quite a different conception of the child and what his education should be, and it was no part of the first educational institution. It was carried on through voluntary agencies, philanthropy, charity, and as a private school. The result has been that the kindergarten became isolated and a distinct thing by itself. It is a new idea to many people that the kindergarten is or should be simply a part of the educational system; they are so in the habit of looking at it as a thing by itself, of looking upon the kindergarten child as different from the primary school child, to be treated by different methods.

[(1)] You will find for instance in *The Psychologic Foundations of Education* by Dr. Harris[1] the statement that the kindergarten period corresponds to what he terms the symbolic period of development. It should deal with the child's fancies and imagery, be symbolic in character, while the primary school is what he terms conventional, a very different basis and end and intellectual content, not building upon the child's own imaginative views of things, but simply in acquainting him with the conventional media of human intercommunication, the forms and devices for reading, writing, and arithmetic. Anything that can be got over and above that is so much gain, but the purpose is simply this one of giving the child the mastery of the means, the conventional media of human intercommunication, simply the forms in which knowledge is transmitted from mind to mind. From one point of view this might better be called the symbolic period; it is simply the mastery of certain conventionalities of language.

[(2)] That point of view formulates the existing thought. The kindergarten is regarded as freedom, play, spontaneity, as devoted to the moral development of the child. A definite change is made in the primary school where lessons are learned with a view to mastering these particular modes of language apart from intellectual content and moral content. The child himself does not undergo any such abrupt revolution. The child who leaves the kindergarten at five years and nine months and goes into the primary school at the end of the vacation at six years, has not undergone in his make-up any such complete revolution as he finds in the two environments that are about him. The result must be a great deal of waste and of friction. A lot of things are started in the

[1 William Torrey Harris, *Psychologic Foundations of Education* (New York: D. Appleton and Company, 1898).]

kindergarten that do not lead anywhere; beginnings are made which are not carried out and things are thrust into the child's consciousness for which he has no previous preparation. The kindergarten has been going its own way without any thought what the child is to be after it leaves the kindergarten.

Take simply one point. Preparation for teaching the [(3)] four and five year old child has been absolutely separated from preparation for teaching the child of six and seven years, having special schools for training the kindergarten teacher as well as for teaching the kindergarten child. Unless we do assume that the child is really quite different it would be obvious that anything that prepared the teacher to teach the child of four and five would also prepare him to teach the child of six and seven. There is no more abrupt change at this time than between the ages of seven and eight and ten and eleven.

The doing away with the kindergarten as a specific [(4)] kind of education, different from anything else, and absorbing it, making it an organic part of the whole educational system, is a very pressing problem. It is a problem on both sides. There is equally the problem on the side of the primary school of introducing the informal, the direct immediate experience, the element of play and imagination which would connect it with what is really psychological in the kindergarten movement. There is also the fact that the child of six is much nearer the child of five than the child of seven. Really this period should last up to the age of seven. If there is to be a break from the form of free expression over to learning lessons, the natural time for it would be seven rather than six. Or to put it more strictly, the age of six is really the transitional year in which the child is passing over from the direct immediate forms of experience to the capacity to appreciate ends and regulate his conduct with reference to them, to perform his tasks, not as drudgery but as things to be done.

LECTURE XVII

February 8, 1899

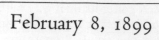

[B.IV.: *The periods of schooling: present practice and proposals.*]

[II.C.1.b.(5)] I mentioned at the last time that when the kindergarten originated it was such a marked departure from the ideals and the methods of education that were current it inevitably, by the very necessity of the situation at the time, was marked off as a distinct institution. The fact moreover that it dealt with children of an age which up to that time had not been generally included within the scope of education, tended in the same direction. There were other points which were inherent in the teaching of Froebel himself, or of his earlier followers who systematized his point of view, which worked in the same direction.

[(a)] In the first place Froebel was very much influenced by the symbolic and romantic philosophy of Schelling with its combination of a sort of mysticism and romantic elements, particularly the symbolic relation of natural things to spiritual things, and while in some respects Froebel got some of his most inspiring ideas through the influence of that movement, the conception of the unity of man and nature, and the unity of men in society, and the unity of childhood itself, the necessity of educating the child as a whole, as a unity, there were other elements which were imported into his educational system almost bodily from the philosophy of Schelling, which looked at impartially and objectively, do not seem to have any particular belonging there, and yet they have got so worked into the system that with one school at least, they are regarded as absolutely an essential part of it. The tendency was to erect what should have been simply a point of view and a spirit in education into a dogma, into a sort of rigid orthodoxy, and having a creed to which positive assent had to be given.

[(b)] Another influence which tended also toward isolation was the great importance that Froebel attached to geometrical forms and considerations. This undoubtedly partly was connected with his symbolic philosophy. He found great spiritual meaning symbolized by these forms in space, but yet there seems to be something in his own mental make up which gave him a particular interest in geometrical forms and their relations to each other. While there was no doubt that the introduction of these various materials in a somewhat systematic way into early education was a good thing, yet the undue relative importance which this mathematical phase had in Froebel's mind, combined with his symbolism, tended to give the kindergarten a peculiar twist at the outset. When he wrote the modern sciences were not especially well developed. I think if they had been Froebel would have made a great deal more use of biology and the observation of plants and animals, and less of mathematics, but this was about the only thing that was definite and positive enough at the time to seem to lend itself to educational purposes.

[(c)] Another thing to which we owe more to his followers than to Froebel himself was the thorough-going systematization that was introduced, the rigid classification of the various gifts and occupations, and the holding to the rigid sequence, appertaining not only to the succession of one gift as regards another, beginning with the three forms of the sphere, cube, and cylinder, but within each game there was a complete and systematic elaboration of the various steps which must be taken with each one.

If you want to see how far this systematization can be carried, if you will turn to a three volume book in the library by Koehler,[1] you will see with what thorough-going Teutonic system this thing was all worked out, and no child was supposed to get a complete education unless all the elaborate formulae were worked through. While very few have gone to this extreme, yet the kindergarten as it has actually obtained, has had a great deal of this sequence worked into the development of the gifts, for which no justification was ever sought or found

[1 August Koehler, *Die Praxis des Kindergartens*, three vols. (Weimar: 1878).]

in the child's nature. It was simply a fact that it had been worked out and it was the orthodox thing to do.

Two teachers in a kindergarten were over-heard conversing one day, and one said it seemed to her you might introduce the cube and cylinder before the child had finished with the sphere. The other teacher was horrified and the only reason given was that it was contrary to Froebel's procedure. In spite of the fact that the kindergarten has stood for play and freedom, there is probably no part of the school system which has been so thoroughly formalized in certain directions as this work of the gifts carried out in a systematic, organized fashion.

[(i)] Then Froebel, looking at society around him, tried to get what might be called the grammar of social occupations; typical modes of industries upon which society depended, and also picking out the typical processes, not merely external, but what might be called the psychological process, involved in these industries, and to have them reproduced in the school in the form of plays, games, and occupations. That seems to me one of the greatest ideas, one of the greatest single strokes of genius that has ever appeared in educational theory—that conception of picking out the typical social processes, finding their typical psychological form and introducing them into the school with little children. But very much the same thing happened as with the materials of the kindergarten. The thing was over systematized and as the kindergarten went from one country to another, there was not sufficient pains taken to adapt the occupations to the new social conditions. There is no eternal sacred reason why a child in Chicago should follow the same occupations that Froebel found useful in a German town sixty or seventy years ago. The whole environment has changed and the point of view has persisted very much the same in which the occupations have been carried on. I think it is due to his successors rather than to Froebel himself.

[ii] There has also been a tendency to take literally what Froebel meant only as a suggestion. In his songs, with the little plays and games accompanying them in the song book, Froebel seems to have simply looked around and gathered together all the little games that he saw mothers play with their children, and he elaborated them somewhat in order to point out to others that there really was a definite intellec-

tual and ethical content in these things. That again seems to me a wonderful piece of insight in education—this taking things which had been regarded as merely trivial, done to pass away the time, worked out by instinct in the case of the mothers, and seeing that they really had a positive significance not really ideas, but an idea back of them; and appreciating that and attempting to point out with the psychology available to Froebel at the time, the various ideas that lay at the back of these various little songs and games. I think there can be no question that to his mind that was only a suggestion. He wanted to show people that these things which they had ignored educationally had germs of great educational significance. I think he would have been horrified if he had thought these things were to be literally followed out, and yet that is what has been the attempt to do.

I do not mention these things for the sake of criticizing the kindergarten theory or practice, in the first place in its most general principle, the attempt to utilize social occupations and the materials of every day life in combination with the play spirit and capacity in the child himself. Froebel seems to have stated the fundamental principle of early education much more thoroughly and successfully than any one had ever done before, and in stating it now one would have to go back to him to be sure he got the full force of his point of view. Various other matters and considerations that are quite extraneous to that fundamental point of view have got imported into the thing and bound up with it in such a way as to reinforce and perpetuate the isolation of the kindergarten as a distinct institution, instead of its being simply the first part of a process of education which is to go on continuously.

[c.] I need not go over the elements which in the primary school tended to isolate that, which tended to separate it and make it a thing by itself. The simple fact that it was devoted practically exclusively to the teaching of the three R's in a pretty mechanical and routine way is about all that need be said. However statistics that have recently been collected both in California and Massachusetts go to show that at present on the average from seventy-five to eighty percent of the first two years of school life of children at six and seven years of age, are still spent simply on the formal lessons in learning to read, write, spell and cipher. So while a beginning has been made from this side as well as from the kindergarten side, in breaking down the isolation and bringing the two into relation with each other, it is obvious that taking the country as a whole, not much more than a bare start has been made.

Approaching the matter now a little more positively, [2.*a*.(*1*)] without so much reference to historical conditions, it may be said that the fundamental idea of this first part of the educational process of the early elementary period, is that of the totality of experience; that is to say that the child is to be introduced into the typical forms and modes of social experience in an undifferentiated way—in a way which, as far as the child's consciousness is concerned, is undifferentiated; and that from the standpoint of the child himself, the standpoint of method, his powers shall be called into play also in an undifferentiated, unanalytic way; that is, so far as possible the child shall act in the educational process as a whole, with his feelings, his purposes, his aims, and not merely with his intellect,—that is as a learner.

This conception of the introduction of the child into the totality of social life was undoubtedly at the basis of Froebel's attempt to make out a grammar of social occupations, and to see to it that the child was brought consecutively, one after another, into contact with representatives of all modes of social life: that is, working out from the occupations and industries of the home, of the family, into those of the neighborhood, the local shops and stores—industries of various forms, and then out into the wider circle of civic and political life, so far as the child was capable of appreciating in his own experience the forces and the forms there.

It is essentially then just the transition from the in- [(2)] formal to the formal education, the whole standpoint being still that of informal education, but from the standpoint of the instructor, pains being taken to see that all sides of social life are reproduced by the child in play form in their typical meaning, instead of his having simply a haphazard connection with this or that form of social life and without much regard as to whether the connection was with a typical form or a more or less depraved or degraded one. What might be called the saturation of all the peculiar materials of instruction, the study of the materials of work, of construction, of

observations upon plants and animals, nature study; the saturation of the art work, the art expression, the singing, the
drawing; the saturation even of the mathematical, geometrical
factors involved in the use of gifts, and so on, in a social medium, social atmosphere, has been the one fundamental idea
of this early period which is bound to persist.

[(3)] Or put negatively, there is no differentiation of studies. The child does not have studies which he pursues,
he simply is given as rich an environment as possible,
rich that is to say in order to be general, and he has suggestions
of ways of reproducing in play, in occupations, this environment; and the whole process is so organized or regulated as to
bring the child successively into contact with the different
phases of it so as to be sure that he touches his environment
all around and gets out what he can from it on each side of his
being.

[b.(1)] The problem, or the dominant principle of the later
elementary period would of course be conditioned by
the fact that it comes from this background. The child
has been systematically brought into contact with a large environment so as to complete his life, and if his own modes of
response have been called into play, to operating with reference
to the materials of this environment, he will have got all that
he can get out of this phase of his education. The next thing
in order is the gradual introduction of differentiation, and simply as I said the other day, giving the child the mastery of the
fundamental technique, or of the tools for maintaining and
communicating experience.

[(2)] This would involve on one side that the instruction
in the three R's be pushed up a year or two, perhaps
two years on the whole, from where it now is. I mean
so far as the main emphasis of attention is concerned, and also
that these studies be introduced as outgrowths from this background of what might be called homogeneous social experience
on the part of the child; that there be a modulation over from
that experience in such a way that he will see what the need
of these various powers is, so that they shall be objectively tools
for the better maintaining of experience, and not simply that,
but also that the child shall realize them as tools for enabling
him to see the social significance.

In other words, the instrumental value of these vari-
[(3)]   ous more formal studies is the first problem, the supply of a motive, instead of introducing them abruptly
just as studies, as things to be learned. There are for instance,
public schools in Chicago now where all the first year at least,
of instruction in reading and writing is given as an assistance
in carrying on the ordinary work of the school. When there
is something else to be done, not a reading lesson to be learned,
the instructions as to what to do or how to do it are written
on the board and the child learns to read, and then in turn to
write himself in order that he may do something else, that the
school life itself may go on easily and successfully. I mention
that simply because otherwise what I said about realizing these
studies as instruments, as tools in the whole of experience,
might seem too vague and general. I do not mean of course that
that is the only way, or whether or not it is the best way to do
it, but it is one illustration of what would be involved in supplying a motive which would gradually differentiate these powers
out of the back-ground of the child's every day experience, and
give him a motive for using them and give them application,
relevancy, to his ordinary experience.

The secondary period is the period distinctly of the
[c.(1)]   differentiation of subject matter. This differentiation
of which I have been speaking as belonging to the
later elementary period is not specially of the different subject
matters from each other. There is no special reason for differentiating history, geography, and special forms of science. The
child's world is very largely one world, and to attempt to break
it up into different things of that sort, one of which would be
labeled "history," another "geography," and another "science"
in the child's mind, would simply introduce artificial relations.
The differentiation of which I have been speaking is the differentiation of the tools, the technique, the ability to read, to
write, to use number, the ability to use tools of certain sorts,
tools of construction and of artistic expression.

Now when the child is fairly in possession of these
[(2)]   tools, then he can in turn utilize them in order to
break up as it were, the unity of his experience under different headings. He can begin to classify, to arrange, and
to systematize, and when he can do that, then studies as dis-

tinct studies will have a meaning to him. Of course that does not mean that they shall be simply and only distinct, but that now there is a certain mental economy in classifying the facts of the physical sciences by themselves, the chemical sciences by themselves, and the biological sciences by themselves, so that the child can get his own generalization in each science and use it in binding together all the special details which are relevant to it.

[(3)] This differentiation of the subject matter involves also a corresponding specialization mentally in the child's own points of view and habits. Through this classification of each topic by itself and the systematic introduction of the child into each of the groups of study, that is in each kind of science, in various modes of linguistic science, of the vernacular and foreign, and in history and literature as distinct subjects, the child has an opportunity to learn what his own particular tastes are. Until he does touch all these subjects, each somewhat specifically by itself, and at the same time taken in connection with others, he does not have an opportunity to find out what his own powers and preferences really are.

[(4)] The completion then of the secondary period would be reached when this differentiation of subject matter had been reached on one side, and when the child had a fair measure or grasp of his own special powers on the other side. He has been specializing his own powers, he has been discriminating in his awareness of his own standpoint and abilities just as he has been in his knowledge of the various subject matters. He should know whether his tastes lie in executive directions, in practical directions, those connected with doing something, or the directing of doing something in certain forms; or whether in the intellectual direction; if intellectual, whether one form of science or another, or history, or whatever it may be.

[(5)] What I said some time ago about the one-sidedness of the existing education comes in here through the lack of the manual, the practical element in the educational system. The youth has little opportunity to measure his abilities in that direction positively at all. He can only measure them negatively, that is, on the rebound. If he does not like to go to school the inference is that his tastes would be in another direction, but that is a crude method of bringing the child to consciousness of what his tastes really are. It is the method of exclusion carried to the extreme; if he does not like one thing, he probably would like something else.

[d.(1)] Then would come the period of higher education when the youth, having become conscious on one side of himself, his particular individualized self, and having had on the other side a general survey of the whole field of knowledge and of action, he can now really specialize.

[(2)] There is a difference between differentiation and specialization, though possibly I have been using the words somewhat interchangeably. By specialization we mean particular devotion to some one of the sectors of the whole circle of experience which has now been mapped out in a general way as to its boundaries and relations; so that we get there a higher education, particularly a training with reference to vocation, with reference to calling in life. As a matter of the philosophy of education, if we are really serious about the question of education, I think we would all have to agree that education was not completed excepting as it did terminate in some special adaptation to some special calling or sphere of service in life. Of course it is clear enough that we are far enough away from that at present, but to be really in earnest would compel us to reach that result.

[(3)] I do not suppose that would mean that every one would go through what we now call the higher education. Some would naturally become aware of their special calling earlier in the educational period and would get the preparation to enable them to carry on successfully some particular callings further down, while other callings would still be of a character to require much more extensive and prolonged preparation in order to pursue them successfully. It would follow that the mechanic ought to have something which would make him more intelligent, more ethical, more cultured in his calling, as well as a doctor or minister or lawyer. But it would not follow that his special educational period would have to be prolonged as much as the one who was preparing himself for medicine or law or certain forms of specialized teaching.

To recapitulate then, we would get three educational
[3.a.]   periods, or sub-dividing the first one, four. In the
early elementary period the main thing is to give the
child varied content, varied experience to arouse all his capacities into action so far as possible, to keep him from being dormant in any particular direction, or to keep him from being
starved in any particular direction, to see that all round nutriment is supplied him and sufficient modes of positive action
given to call him into action in the totality, in the integrity of
his being. In the second period, the later elementary, while this
connection with the environment, supplying him with positive
materials, should be continued, it should be continued in such
a way as to lead him into the mastery of the fundamental tools
of inquiry and communication. It must be at this time, at from
eight to twelve, that the child can get a consciousness of
method; not merely method in reading, writing, and figuring
but method in observation, in simple investigation, method in
the orderly statement of facts and truths known. In the third
period, the secondary education, there should be differentiation of subject matter in what we may call the various studies
of the school, and those should be presented to the child systematically so that he may see each by itself and each in its
relations to the others, so that he gets an encyclopaedic survey
of the field of human learning and attainments, and on the
other side finds out to what he himself is drawn most easily
and successfully. Then comes the period of higher education
where there would be special adaptation of this particular capacity and interest to the subject matter most appropriate to it.

We would have the period from four to twelve as the
[b.]   period of elementary education. Then we would have
two years from the grades, four years from the high
school, and two years from the college in the secondary, which
would be eight years, but it does not seem to me to be over
sanguine to think if the whole system were organized that at
least two years of that would be saved.

Perhaps to avoid misapprehension I ought to say that it may
seem rather extreme to identify the period of higher education
with the period of professional education. Probably few would
agree with me in making that statement, but if the education
previous to that time has been organized, this general survey,

or what we might call now culture purposes, would have been realized before then, by the time the student was eighteen or twenty. Certain studies are introduced now in the higher education simply because the ground has not been covered before, and because they are really part of a liberal education, but another point which seems to me more important is that from this point of view the ideal of professional education would be broadened.

[c.]   The separation of the professional from the liberal is unfortunate on both sides. To keep up that separation means the introduction of a certain element of in-utility into the liberal so that it is now true in the conception of many people that the higher the education the more un-available it is. That seems to me highly undesirable. If the ends, the ideals that are involved in the liberal can be secured and at the same time made relevant to some calling, to some actual service in life, there will be a great gain in ethical content, in the earnestness and seriousness with which the student goes at his work. As long as it is isolated as a thing of culture apart from availability for service, the full ethical motives cannot possibly be there, at least for most people. On the other hand the separation of the professional from the liberal makes it too technical in character; so when I identify the higher with the professional, I should mean a broader conception of professional than, upon the whole, is current at the present time. I do not mean simply the studies which would seem to be purely of direct use; there are also studies of indirect use. Anatomy, chemistry, etc. are of direct use to the doctor, but the whole field of science is indirectly useful and psychology and other studies of a sociological and historical character would be indirectly useful. It is a matter of the point of view rather than of the special studies pursued. The philosophical, historical and sociological studies would still be pursued in the professional medical education, but pursued from that standpoint, looked at from their relationships, indirect, if not direct, with the life work. So a man who is training for business, to be connected with a railroad or lines of commerce, or insurance, would find various things in science, history, and in social science, indirectly, if not directly necessary, and they would still be studied, but from that particular point of view.

For the present we have four breaks; that between
[d.]   the kindergarten and the primary; then the overlapping between the seventh and eighth grades and
the high school work. There is both a break and overlapping
between the later years of the high school and the early years
of the college; and then there are the later years of the college
course which as I said the other day are neither one thing nor
the other, they are neither disciplinary nor yet have any direct
relations to the future work or calling.

LECTURE XVIII

February 9, 1899

[B.V.;C.: *Class organization and individual growth. The organization of subject matter.*]

[II.D.] I covered part of the material that is given under the heading V yesterday. There are two or three points however, of which I wish to speak briefly.

[1.] There is an apparent conflict in the educational system between the requirements of the growth of the individual and the requirements of the social or organized side of the school. Those conflicts can be brought together under three heads. First the conflict between the varying rates of growth of particular individuals and the average movement of the school organization. The social organization of the school requires some kind of grouping, some kind of massing of students. The combination of that requirement with securing the best individual growth becomes then a problem.

[a.] It is practically a question of grading and of promotion from one grade to another, and there can be no doubt that in many schools under the system of transference from class to class but once a year, the best interests of many individual children have been greatly hampered and their whole development restricted. Of course there have been many attempts, more or less successful, to avoid these difficulties, to get a more flexible system of passing from one grade to another, and you will find in the references under "Promotions" a number of the attempts which have been practically made in the schools of introducing greater flexibility in the working machinery of the school. There is still another principle of solution besides that of having sub-divisions within the various classes, and of having semi-yearly or term promotions, those being the commonest ways of introducing flexibility. It has been seen that this more rapid promotion of individual students is not desirable provided more content can be put into the educative material at each stage of the process; that if there can be sufficient variety and relations of material put into each grade, then the children of various capacities and grades of ability, would have the opportunity each to get what he could.

[b.] The difficulty then is not fundamentally one in the graded system itself, but one rather in the paucity of the educative material supplied, and when the curriculum is sufficiently enriched on its substantial side through the introduction of art work, literature, history, and science, the demand for rapid promotion of individuals from grade to grade is greatly lessened, in fact there may be a danger in it all leading to precocity and stimulating premature development along certain lines.

[c.] The problem then is best solved by the introduction of more nutritive material and then allowing each child to assimilate all he can out of what is given, having in reserve a surplus which is at least up to, if not beyond the capacities of the very best members of the class. Or to state it as a principle, it is possible to grade the material to the children as well as to grade the children to the material; and then the mechanical part of the graded system has been due for the most part to an attempt to grade the children to certain rigid preconceived ideas of just what sort of material should be introduced into each grade. Children of very different ages and capacities live together in families and neighborhoods with practically the same gross or total environment, but each child through interacting in his own way selects from it what he personally can utilize. While of course it would not be desirable to introduce into the grades of the school system anything like that homogeneity of a total environment, it would be found that when the attempt was made simply to supply adequate experience to the children instead of simply seeing whether they have learned a given bulk of information or not, that those of quite different range of ability and degrees of technical attainment, could work successfully and even profitably together. There is a positive advantage as well as of course a disadvantage in having children together whose abilities are not exactly on a par; there is more give and take, there is more division of labor.

[2.] The second conflict and problem arises in the adjustment of the fact that the class is a mass, so to speak, to the fact of needs of the individual.

[a.] Probably you are all familiar with the attempts which have been made in this country especially by Superintendent Search,* what we call the Pueblo Plan to make the individual a unit of education instead of a class. There are in the library a few numbers of the periodical which he issued, devoted to individualism in instruction. Aside from his express attempt to carry out an individualistic point of view, the tendency to lose the individual in the mass is an evil that is deplored by almost all educationalists. The problem is one certainly very difficult to solve practically although the limits can be determined with some certainty theoretically. The individual as the ultimate unit of instruction would practically be equivalent to a tutorial idea; it would mean practically the evolution of the school as a social institution and the substitution of tutors for individual children.

While no doubt intellectual acquisition and the gaining of technical discipline would be facilitated, would be more rapid under the tutorial plan, most persons would agree that there were disadvantages which were much greater than the advantages. The intellectual development under such circumstances lacking contact with other minds and the points of view of other minds, would almost certainly be one-sided. More might be learned and there might be a certain gain in immediate power to control the workings of one's intellect, but the intellectual attainment would be more set off by itself, it would be more a thing by itself. There is something which in the reality and in the concreteness of mental growth can come only from the give and take of experience. If the intellect were an isolated machine that could be set going by itself, the tutorial system would be an ideal thing; but since the intellect is simply an abstract in the whole of a person's experience, anything which tends to reduce the social factors that work in the experience would also tend to reduce the genuineness of the intellectual

[* Preston W. Search was Superintendent of Schools in Pueblo, Colorado. Together with William Torrey Harris, he attempted to introduce individualized instruction there. He wrote *An Ideal School* (New York: D. Appleton and Company, 1901), describing his views.]

development. Aside from that, there is a loss in many other ways from this isolated development. There is obviously a loss in ethical development through lack of variety and complexity of social relationships. It is proverbially a dangerous thing to be the only child in a family and the same would be true of the only child in a class; the individual would tend to be the whole thing and the result of an opportunity to monopolize the entire situation is always evil, that is, tends to be.

[b.] On the other hand I suppose no one would defend the large size of most of the existing classes in the schools; no one would consider it an ideal thing that forty or fifty children be working over the same lessons in the same class. To determine, however, just where the line does come, that is, just how many it will take in order to get a variety of points of view, to get a real intellectual and moral division of labor, to get interchange of thought and opinion, and not only the friction of mind, but the contagion of mind with mind, and yet not have so many as to prevent the opportunity for individual initiative and individual expression, it is very hard to tell.

I have heard the existing system defended on the ground that the recitation is essentially a social matter and that the social side of it is more important than the mere matter of intellectual acquisition. Admitting that statement that the social development is always more important than the mere technical accomplishment, it would hardly follow that the more numbers you get the more social spirit there is. There comes a practical limit beyond which increase in numbers simply means that the whole method of conducting the work has to be routine and mechanical in order to do the piece of work in the time allotted. With forty or fifty children in the class which recites from thirty to forty minutes, it is impossible to get the social side developed, it is impossible to allow each member of the class to express his own ideas, and to have any exchange, to have the recitation in any sense a clearing house. It is a physical impossibility to get the thing done in the amount of time there is to do it in; and accordingly the whole stress of the teacher must be simply upon devising some kind of mechanism of the recitation, to try and get around as rapidly as possible and get an answer out of each child to see whether each has studied the lesson or not. That is about as destructive to any real sociality of experience as the tutorial system itself would be. In the first place there is somewhere a limit of numbers, though I do not think we can say where it is, that would give the individual sufficient play on one side and bring the social influences to bear on the other. One other consideration that comes in is that really individualized instruction would not of necessity mean instructing simply one, two, or three children at once. It is not so much a matter ultimately of the quantity of children whose lessons are heard at the same time, as it is providing material which each child can appropriate and having the arrangement such that each child can work from his own peculiar point of view.

[(1)] The bearing of that last remark however would perhaps come out better if we go on to speak of the third conflict, which is between the curriculum, which of necessity has to be adapted to what we might call the average mind, and the peculiar interest and capacities of each individual mind. There is really no such thing as the average mind, the average child or pupil, and yet the course of study, lessons and so on, have to be arranged on the basis of that mythical personage. Now the question that was referred to yesterday, the question of electives, is the question which emerges at just this point. The elective system is an attempt to make provision for the individual point of view, for the special interests and preferences and modes of working of the individual mind. The required curriculum is supposedly the mass curriculum. What I meant a moment ago was that just in the degree in which there is freedom and flexibility introduced into the whole educational system, just in the degree in which provision is made for the securing of experiences and not simply of learning lessons, it becomes possible to combine what is in outward appearance the uniform required curriculum with the reality of individual choice, preference. It is not, after all, so necessary that the individual should follow this or that or the other particular subject matter, as it is that he should have the liberty and opportunity to approach any and every subject matter in such a way as to make his own special personality valid, to get something out of all the subject matters from his own point of view.

The reality of the question is ultimately one of [(2)] method rather than of subjects. If we take it simply as a matter of the subjects and not of the point of view from which the subjects are approached, the tendency is to give the pupil a rigid curriculum, to subject him to it up to a certain point, and after that to give him an equally unrestricted, uncontrolled liberty. Now the liberty of the individual does not mean, I take it, that he can or should determine from the start for himself what subjects he shall or shall not study. It is a purley abstract ideal. The individual does not know, I will not say enough about the subjects to know what he needs, but about himself to know what his interests and capacities are, and therefore freedom of choice in any early stage of the subject, is only a pretence. A person cannot choose unless he has some alternatives in mind, and unless he has some definite rational motive on which he selects one rather than the other. Until the pupil has had a fairly rounded survey of the materials, and until he has measured himself, he has neither of the necessary conditions for real choice. To force upon him then an elective system is to force upon him the mere form without the reality of choice. On the other hand the real individuality, the real liberty of the pupil should, I think, be recognized just as much at the age of six, seven, or eight, as at the age of twenty or twenty-five. There seems to be nothing in logic, psychology, or ethics, which calls for repressing the individual completely up to a certain point and then suddenly to give him complete freedom from all control and direction. The genuine individuality of the pupil is conserved so far as he is given the opportunity to approach the subject matter, which objectively speaking is one and the same for the whole class, from the point of view of his own particular experiences and interests. Now in thus approaching it, it does not mean that the subject matter is entirely subordinated to his individuality, but simply that there shall be some reciprocity, interaction, in order that there may be a real transformation of the subject matter in such a way as to effect a reconstruction in making over the experience of each individual.

My main point then is that while there are various [(3)] devices, practical methods, which are valuable and some of which are very much better than others for facilitating the solution of the various problems in the school, after all the great question is on the one side to enrich the subject matter of the course of study itself, to give definite content, variety, and intrinsic worth, dignity, to the subject matter, so that each mind at each stage shall find enough to stimulate it and to keep it active, and enough to feed it; on the other side the methods should be made sufficiently flexible to allow for the play of personality in the various ways of going at and getting hold of the subject matter. If those two requirements could be adequately met, these other problems which are now so very pressing would become incidental; they would not vanish, but become simply matters of working adjustment instead of questions of deep and vital importance.

[3.]   There is one other question which does not fall in line exactly with those of which I have been speaking, but to which I wish to ask your attention even if it is only to read some of the references given on it. It is the question called "Specialized versus General Instructing Force" or the question which currently goes by the name of Departmental Instruction.

The question of course has already been solved practically for the college and also for the high school. Specialized instruction is not merely the theoretical ideal, but upon the whole the working rule in these two parts of the educational system. There are many high schools where a number of teachers have to teach a little of almost everything, but it is regarded as a necessity of the situation, not as a good principle.

[a.]   In elementary instruction what is termed the all-round teacher has been the ideal, that is, the conception that each grade should have one teacher and one only for all subjects. You will find some of the arguments on both sides stated in the references under the head of "Class and Individual Instruction" but I simply wish to point out here that while undoubtedly the small child is distracted by too great a variety in his environment, while the adjustments of the small child are made largely through the medium of association and personal sympathy rather than upon an intellectual or even a practical basis, and while therefore for the very small child there is much to be said for not bringing him into contact with a variety of teachers, it is difficult and to my mind impossible, to see how the real requirements of intrinsic value and importance of subject matters are to be made, excepting on the basis of what is termed departmental instruction. As long as the curriculum was narrow and formal, as long as it consisted mainly of the three R's, one teacher could teach everything, there was nothing which was beyond the range, up to the range, of any one person of ordinary, average intelligence. The person had rather to lower his intelligence down to the level of the subject taught than to make any strain, but when the curriculum attempts to cover in a symmetrical manner all the phases of experience, it is seemingly a psychological impossibility to have what is termed an all-round instructor. I will not say there are no such persons in the world, but they are not numerous enough to meet the needs of the schools. Persons who are adequately trained as regards scholarship and method in history, art, and in various forms of manual training, and who can see that the child gets them all in a balanced and symmetrical way are rare. The result of such an attempt would be that the child would get an undue emphasis upon one side or another in the phases of greatest interest to the teacher, while others would be slurred over, and owing to the lack of sufficient technical capacity in the teacher, the child would get not merely a shortage in quantity, but false ideas in quality, which is much more important regarding many subjects. The child responds especially to the way in which he sees other people looking at things, he responds unconsciously to the estimates which other people put on things, and also to the degree of skill, of workmanship, of power, command, control over the subject with which the teacher approaches it. That factor of real skill, ability to control, seems to me one of the most indispensable factors in the moral as well as the intellectual development of the child, and I do not see how that end can be adequately reached excepting on the basis of what is called departmental teaching, which I think would be better named expert teaching.

       The very term "departmental" is a question-begging
[b.]   epithet, it implies an undue breaking up of the thing
       into unrelated compartments which have nothing to do with each other. There are other particular administrative reasons which might be given both for and against, in this question. I simply attempted to point out the considerations which seem to me most fundamental. The objections that are made reduce themselves to two. One is that the unity of the

child is interfered with. I have already admitted a certain force in this for the young child, the child of five, six, or seven. For children beyond that age the remark seems purely dogmatic. There may be truth in it, but the thing has never been tried enough to demonstrate the truth of the remark. The other is that the various subjects taught will not be properly correlated with each other if they are taught by experts. Each teacher will unduly magnify his own subject, go at it from an isolated standpoint, and there will not be what is termed correlation. There would be a very serious objection to that sort of teacher as individuals, but unless people are made cranky by becoming expert in a particular line, the argument would not seem to have force. It seems to me a purely dogmatic assumption that you cannot get experts to cooperate with each other, that you cannot get them to look at the subject in the light of the other departments. In other organizations in life there is intellectual division of labor. It is a very fundamental thing. When each person is doing the thing for which he is best fitted there is the best chance of cooperation, of unification and organization. I think that argument tends all in the other direction, that with one teacher to teach a large variety of subjects it is impossible to get really any correlation. The only way to get the reality is to recognize specialization. It is of course the only practical way by which persons of really advanced scholarship can possibly be brought into the sphere of elementary education.

[III.]   This leads me to the next general topic, that under C, page 5, "Organization of Subject Matter." The question which we now come to in other words, is the two-fold question of first, the selection of the various studies and their adaptation; and second the question of how the various selected studies shall be arranged with reference to each other. The first of these questions I have called that of selection; the question of the arrangement of studies with reference to each other, correlation. I will say a few words about correlation first, though logically it comes afterward.

[A.1.]   The present discussion of the question of correlation of studies has been very largely compromised and rendered unnecessary because it has been approached too much with reference to certain problems which happen to be pressing at the present time, and not sufficiently with reference to fundamental principles. It has been treated simply as a question of correlation of studies, instead of part of the larger question of the organization of experience. What I mean is it was found that too many different subjects were being taught in the schools. New subjects were coming in all the time, old subjects were splitting up and there was practically a congestion in the curriculum and a distraction of the child. It became a pressing practical problem to see how these studies could be made to reinforce each other, to help each other out, instead of serving as rivals, as competitors of each other. I do not mean to underestimate the practical importance of that question or of finding a solution for it. The various attempts that have been made to correlate these school subjects more closely to each other have proved of very great service indeed in the whole matter of educational progress. I simply mean that that is not the fundamental problem of correlation. It takes for granted that there are, after all, this whole lot of different subjects to be taught and that the question is simply one of tying them together, better facilitating the transition from one to the other. But back of that assumption lies the whole question of how there comes to be this variety of independent and isolated subjects, and whether there should be such a variety at all or not.

[2.]   Back of the question of correlation lies, in other words, the question of differentiation, the question of selection. The child starts, before he goes to school at least, with a unity of experience, not with a number of different subjects or studies. The fundamental problem then is how this unity of experience has come to be broken up into this number of isolated school studies. Or putting it in the form of a principle, not historically: how shall the proper differentiation of the unified experience in its various important typical phases, be secured? The question of differentiation is fundamental and the question of correlation should come in only after the question of differentiation has been raised and some attempt made to answer it. Correlating arithmetic and science and geography and history and literature implies that you already have the five different things there which need to be correlated with each other. The first question is: where do these five different subjects come from if they have been introduced bodily from without, already cut and dried and distinct? Then in that case the fundamental psychological principle of education has been wild, there has been no growth, no development of experience from the child himself. If on the other hand, these studies have not been introduced in this external manner they must have been arrived at as gradual differentiation out of and within the unity of the child's own experience, and if the latter is the case, the question is: what has been the course, the procedure of that gradual differentiation? That of course is connected with what was said about the various stages of growth; beginning with that of unity, having its various phases, assuming a variety of forms, but without any conscious analysis by the child himself of the different forms of his own experience. It is simply one life which is now directed this way and now that, and then the other, just as at home he does different things yet without any breaks or conscious analysis of what he is doing at one time and another. Then in the second period of education comes the introduction of conscious discrimination, especially on the side of form or method. Our first question then is: On what basis do we get the variety of school studies? What principles do we have for selecting the various studies like science, history, literature, and the various forms of constructive work, and so on?

LECTURE XIX

February 15, 1899

[C.I.1.,2.: *Alternative theories of selection.*]

I will go on now with the theories which have at-
[III.B.]   tempted to give some principle or philosophy for the
various subjects of the curriculum, that have attempted to afford some rational basis and system for the various studies that make up the curriculum, instead of simply
taking them on a purely empirical basis, or just because they
have been put into the curriculum historically.

I begin with the theory of Dr. Harris. I shall follow
[1.]   the statement that he has given in the *Psychologic
Foundations of Education*[1] but you will find the same
point of view in his article in the *Educational Review*[2] which is
referred to in the outline, and very much the same in the Report
of the *Committee of Fifteen*,[3] which of course was written by
him, and also you will find the elements of it all in his reports
while he was Superintendent of Schools in St. Louis.*

The theory is that of the five coordinated groups of
[a.]   study, each one of the groups representing a certain
distinctive and necessary phase of experience, and all
of them taken together covering in type at least, the whole
sphere of experience; so that you have in the five groups of

[1 William Torrey Harris, *Psychologic Foundations of Education* (New
York: D. Appleton and Company, 1898).]
[2 "The Necessity for Five Co-Ordinate Groups of Studies in the Schools,"
Educational Review, XI, April, 1896, pp. 323–334.]
[3 "Report of Subcommittee on the Correlation of Studies in Elementary
Education," in *Report of the Committee of Fifteen on Elementary Edu-
cation* (New York: American Book Company, 1895), pp. 40–99.]
[* Harris was Superintendent of public schools of the city of St. Louis,
May 1868 to May 1880, and was responsible for writing its annual reports. They, of course, reflected his philosophy.]

study an exhaustive division; that is, all the ground is covered, and also each group represents some distinctive phase of experience, that is, does not over-lap or mix up with any of the others.

These five groups are subdivided into two, of which one has to do with nature, "the realm of time and space" in Dr. Harris's words, while the other has to do with the departments or divisions of human life. The region of nature is subdivided into the mathematical sciences and the physical sciences, the sciences of inorganic nature which depend upon mathematics for their method, and the organic sciences. Sometimes he refers to these latter as geography, the science of the earth with the things that grow on the earth, and sometimes he refers to it as biology, but evidently groups within it all the studies which are of a geographical and biological nature.

The three phases of human life, "the three departments or divisions" as he calls them, are language, literature, and history. The basis for this subdivision is apparently psychological in character. History has to do with the record of the unfolding of the human will, primarily. The language studies represent the crystalization or precipitation in outward form of the thought, intellect, of man. That perhaps will be more clearly seen from the reference on page 322: "In the language of a people are revealed the internal logical laws or structural framework of its intellect and the conscious realization of the mind of the race."*

[b.]   There is therefore a background in Dr. Harris's statement of studies, of psychology and logic. "Grammar," he says, "opens to the child his view of the inner workings of the mind of the race, and helps him in so far to a comprehension of his own spiritual self." It takes the logical and psychological workings of the mind from the side of their most objective manifestations, and as you gradually work inwards to the laws and principles that lie back of the structural side of language you arrive at psychology and logic proper. By literature he means literature as an art, and he groups with or about that, the other arts, something at least about painting, sculpture, architecture, and music; but the one form of art best suited for study, is literature. And then on the psy-

[* This reference is to *Psychologic Foundations of Education, op. cit.*]

chological side it is summed up in the statement given on page 340* which relates to the aesthetic phase of mind, feeling, and imagination. The various school studies there are regarded as having really a philosophic basis, each group of studies representing one of the intrinsically important subdivisions of the totality of experience.

It follows therefore, of course, that in each period of the school life, all of these groups should be represented, and that they should be represented in a symmetrical way; that is, that each year of the school life the child should get something in each of the five lines, and get it in a way to be fairly proportionate to what he gets in each of the others.

Now in criticizing that view, it is necessary first, of [c.(1)] course, to recognize the positive element of value in it, the element of truth that it possesses. It does evidently involve an insight into certain philosophic principles which, unconsciously to those who have made out the curriculum, have yet influenced the formation of the curriculum. It is a good thing to recognize that even in our imperfect courses of study there is yet an attempt to represent and present, with a certain degree of symmetry, all the intrinsic factors in human experience. This systematic survey and classification involved in this, and the idea of the necessity of symmetry, that the child shall at all periods of his career, excepting in professional training, have contact with all the phases in a really balanced, symmetrical way, is a very important conception. But as the point of view is worked out, as it is applied, and particularly as it is applied to the justification of the existing course of study, and to the justification of teaching subjects isolatedly from each other even in elementary education, the theory seems to me to have certain serious lacks, of which I will speak.

In the first place, while we see that these groups are [(2)] coordinated, yet there is no real principle of unity given us. The five lines of subjects are virtually taken ready made, and then it is pointed out that one corresponds to the inorganic phase of nature, another to the organic phase of nature, another to the intellectual phase of experience, another to the practical phase of experience, and still another to the aesthetic and imaginative. But a strictly philosophic

[* Dewey here refers to a chart designed by Harris, and printed on p. 340 of *Psychologic Foundations*]

GENERAL COURSE OF STUDY

CLASS OF SCHOOL.	TOPICS RELATING TO NATURE.		TOPICS RELATING TO MAN, OR "THE HUMANITIES."		
	Inorganic.	Organic or cyclic.	Theoretical (intellect).	Practical (will).	Æsthetical (feeling and phantasy).
Elementary school.	Arithmetic. Oral lessons in natural philosophy.	Geography. Oral lessons in natural history.	Grammar. (Reading, writing, parsing, and analyzing.)	History (of United States).	Reading selections from English and American literature. Drawing and vocal music.
Secondary school.	Algebra. Geometry. Plane trigonometry. Natural philosophy. Chemistry.	Physical geography. Astronomy (descriptive). Botany or zoölogy. Physiology.	Latin. Greek. French or German. Mental and moral philosophy.	History (universal). Constitution of the United States.	History of English literature. Shakespeare or some standard author (one or more whole works read). Rhetoricals (declamation and composition). Drawing and vocal music. Study of works of art in painting, sculpture, and architecture.
College course for A. B. degree.	Analytical geometry. Spherical trigonometry. Differential and integral calculus. Physics. Chemistry. Astronomy. (Etc., elective.)	Anatomy and physiology. Botany. Zoölogy. Meteorology. Geology. Ethnology. (Etc., elective.)	Latin. Greek. French or German. Comparative philology. Logic. History of philosophy. Plato or Aristotle. Kant or Hegel.	Philosophy of history. Political economy and sociology. Civil and common law. Constitutional history. Natural theology and philosophy of religion.	Philosophy of art. History of literature. Rhetoric. The great masters compared in some of their greatest works: Homer, Sophocles, Dante, Shakespeare, Goethe, Phidias, Praxiteles, Skopas, Michael Angelo, Raphael, Mozart, Beethoven, etc.

REMARK.—It is understood that many topics named in the above can be replaced by other topics, which have the same psychological rank as studies.

principle ought to show us the unity which exists between the various members of its system, and show us why there are these various members, and what their relation to each other is. Now we do not get any such systematic, unified view.

[(3)] Take the fundamental division between the two groups of studies which have to do with nature, and the three which have to do with human life. Now as an empirical statement there is no serious objection, but as a philosophic statement, it opens at once large questions. What is the basis of this distinction between something which we regard as purely human on one side, and that which we regard as purely natural on the other? Is this distinction simply a distinction, or does it mark a real separation in two kinds of experience? If it is the latter then there is a very marked dualism introduced into the educational system at the outset, and a dualism which has its practical consequences. As matter of fact the life of man is carried on in the world, and the world of nature. It is a very important consideration in determining what history has been and explaining why it has been what it has. How can the geography for instance, get its full meaning, if it is placed wholly on the side of subject matter which deals with nature, while history is put simply on the side of the studies which represent the department of human experience?

[(4)] We get at once, without any regard to the philosophy of the matter there a harmful division from the educational point of view. Geography loses much of its meaning when separated from history, and history loses a good deal of its content, if you isolate it entirely from geography. There are other questions of just the same nature. Even mathematics originally sprang up, not out of the ground, not out of nature, but out of human life and human needs. Arithmetic, geometry, trigonometry, were at first simply, so to speak, implements of agriculture and architecture, they were necessary tools for doing things that had to be done, just as much as plows and harrows were; they sprang exactly out of the same needs of human nature, and while now with the adult and specialist they have arrived at a degree of independence and of objective self existence, that marks simply the outcome of a long period of historical development. Of course the child stands very much nearer the beginning of that progress than he does the end. It is just because we are adults, because we have had the intellectual development, that we are capable of grasping arithmetic or geometry as a distinct subject matter having its own laws and principles. If the child could see it as a distinct and coordinated study, it would not be necessary for him to study it at all. It is because we have mastered these subjects that they have any such distinct place in our minds. To the child they are very much what they were to the primitive man, so far as his own natural and instinctive attitude is concerned; they are either things without much meaning, or else they are ends and appliances in his every day human experience.

[(5)]   The coordination that we get is a rather formal and external coordination. There is no vital, internal principle of unity discovered which accounts for there being just five groups of studies, and which shows how they are related to each other. The course of study is a composition or aggregation, rather than a whole organ of experiences on this basis. While I do not know that it will necessarily follow from this point of view that each study would have to be taken up as an isolated study from the start, various other writings of Dr. Harris show that that is the way that he himself interprets it. He uses his theory of coordination as opposed to what is called correlation, to combining the various studies with each other, and tends to insist that arithmetic shall be taught just as arithmetic, that geography shall be taught just as geography, and that language shall be taught just as language, and so on, and regard what is called correlation (the attempt to bind these studies into more intimate relations with each other) as tending simply to mix things up, and to do away with this principle of the coordinated value of each group by itself.

[(6)]   Now what I have just been saying about arithmetic as an illustration, applies as a matter of principle to this whole idea of so many distinct or separate studies as regards the elementary period of education. It is just because we have been educated, it is because we have gone through the process of instruction, that these subjects present the distinctness and individuality which they do to us. It is simply because we have worked out of the positive, direct unity of our experience, and have got hold of the method of breaking up our experience and for picking out certain parts of it and classifying them together on the basis of their relation to common principles, that the adult, or the older student, say in the latter part of the secondary period, can get the full force of the meaning of distinct studies at all. To introduce them to the child as distinct from the start, is to disorganize and disintegrate, instead of coordinate and connect. In other words this classification of phases of experience is a classification which can be made only by the trained mind. The experience does not come to us, even as adults, split up in that way, there is not one part of experience which is mathematical, another which is geographical, another which is linguistic, another which is historical, and so on. By the reflective intellect they are made distinct for purposes logical and scientific, but until the mind has reached the point where it is logical and scientific, it cannot grasp the force of these distinctions, and to force them on the mind before that period, is to destroy the natural unity of experience without putting anything in the place of it; anything which the child can appreciate.

If you were to take a square mile territory somewhere, there would be nothing in that square mile of land itself to inform you whether it is a mathematical fact, or a botanical or a zoological, or a geological, or a historical fact. That all depends upon your own point of view, upon the interest with which you approach it, upon the end you have in mind. If you look at it one way it will be geological, but if you have other considerations in mind its botanical phase will be the striking thing. If your point of view is still different, the interest will be historical; there has been some battle, there were some scenes of historic interest enacted on the spot and the ground appeals to you from that point of view. What is true of that piece of ground is true of all our experience in its natural and direct forms, that is, before we have reflected upon it and analyzed it synthetically. It comes to us simply as a whole, and while the child's interest may be directed so that he will now apprehend chiefly the mathematical aspect of that experience, or at other times chiefly the literary significance, yet that presupposes that there is at the bottom a piece of direct experience which is a living unity to him, which is a whole which has not been divided and split up, as simply *a* lesson in geography, or *a* lesson in language, or *a* lesson in literature.

[(7)]   It can be laid down as the principle, without exception, that so far as this point of view could be carried out in education, the whole subject matter would become artificial and unreal to the child, incapable of any genuine apprehension by him. He gets the most out of the language lesson when it is not simply a language lesson, but is an enlarging in some definite direction of the whole of his experience. As matter of fact this logical, this adult classification, is very far from possessing any finality. It in turn represents rather a certain stage in the development of science itself than the ultimatum of science. If you take the studies which are being most actively pursued at present in advanced research, I think you will find most of them spelled with a hyphen: it is astrophysics, or chemical-physics, or physiological-psychology, or the chemistry of physiological action; in other words, while it has been necessary evidently in the historical development of sciences to go a good ways in marking off each from the other, the pendulum has already begun to swing in the other direction, and the chief problems arise precisely from the attempt to break down this rigid barrier between the different sciences, and to carry over the point of view which has been considered the monopoly of a particular subject, into other subjects. The most important experimental work in biology is in the application of physical and chemical methods and considerations. If that is so, how are we going to maintain the rigid mark between the inorganic and organic sciences?

In other words, this very positive and neat pigeon-holing, demarcation of various sciences is, in the light of present development, rather artificial and misleading. If so, it would be a mistake to force rigidly upon the child through all the earlier years of his education, subdivisions that he would have to unlearn and get away from in the higher periods of his education. In fact there is probably no one of us who is not suffering today from just this artificial segregation of subjects and topics in the earlier part of his education. Many of our problems which bother us the most are purely factitious; our thinking has got fixed along the lines of these rigid distinctions between the inorganic and organic, between nature and man, between science and culture, between literature and language, and science and art, and a large part of the function of philosophy is to get the mind back again into a fairly fluent and flexible condition. A large part of its problems arise simply from the necessity of doing away with the factitious distinctions which have been built up with so much labor in the earlier periods of instruction.

[(8)] Another line of consideration is one to which Dr. Harris calls attention. He says it might be objected that drawing and manual training, gymnastics, and the like, ought to be taught in every well regulated school, and the question comes up whether they fall within the five groups. His answer is that they do. Drawing, for instance, is partly physical training with a view to skill in the hand and eye, and as such its principle is in physiology, and partly mathematical with a view to the production of geometric form. As relating to the production of form it belongs to geometry and trigonometry. Admitting that it has been disposed of by dismembering it that way and giving various parts of it to three of the five groups, the fact remains that it is by itself a form of direct activity, and that while its principle may be found in physiology as a matter of coordinating the hand and eye, yet certainly the drawing itself is not a matter of physiology, it is not pursued as an exercise in hygiene; and that brings up the fact that there is no place for motor activity at all. You can dispose of it by saying that its rationale belongs to some other subject, but in itself it is not one of these special five.

The same thing is equally true of manual training. Here is the way in which manual training is disposed of: "The rationale is to be found in applied mathematics; hence it does not furnish a new principle different from that found in the first or the second study relating to Nature." That is, the ultimate technique would be found in the application of mathematics. However manual training is not classed with the mathematical group of studies. The fact is overlooked that the chief thing about manual training is that it is a mode of direct activity or experience.

[(9)] That suggests the more fundamental criticism that in the groups of studies that are stated as belonging to what we may regard the indirect, the technical phases of experience and of education, there is no provision made at all for experience in direct, immediate, practical forms.

History is to be studied as a record of the practical actions of man, the exhibition of his will, but there is no provision made for the exercise in any study of the child's own will, of his own particular activities. So in connection with literature, it is not quite clear whether the study about literature is what is meant, though clearly that is the thing that is chiefly in mind, or whether also account is taken of the direct or productive attitude, the constructive or creative attitude on the part of the child himself. Now that criticism seems to be, not one of detail, but a fundamental one, that the fundamental place of the direct, active, productive modes of experience, is not recognized. While the studies themselves are recognized incidentally, the principle which lies at the basis of them is not recognized. There is an attempt made to account for them just by parcelling them up among the other principles, which are really all of them principles having to do with the reflective study of subject matter rather than with the production of anything.

[(10)] Now because of this isolation of studies from each other, and because of this isolation of studies from what I have termed direct or productive experience, there is a very serious defect forced into the elementary and secondary education. Dr. Harris recognizes clearly enough that the ultimate bearing of all the subjects of education must be upon character, upon conduct, or upon the unity of experience. There must somewhere, then, in the whole course of education, provision be made for the recognition of this inter-relation of the various subjects with each other, and also of the bearing which they have upon conduct. That must be postponed, on the basis of this theory, until the period of higher education. "Higher education seeks as its first goal the unity of human education. The best definition of that part of higher education that is found in the college is, that it teaches the unity of human learning. It shows how all the branches form a connected whole, and what each contributes to the explanation of the others." So on this basis it is only those who go to college who ever got a grasp of the unity of experience after all. That would not be so serious a matter if it were not for the further conclusion that it is only the higher education which can "convert the intellectual perceptions into rules of action." The principle of action depends upon the principle of relations, upon the perception of the unity. We look over the whole ground and we see in virtue of the relations which exist here the reasonable course of action is thus and so.

Now just because there is no unity, there are no rela-
[(11)] tions capable of being grasped either in the elementary or secondary education, the ethical import of the studies cannot possibly be brought home at those periods. You will find that on pages 336–37, "Secondary education does not connect in any adequate manner the intellect and the will. It does not convert intellectual perceptions into rules of action. This is left for higher education."[4] It seems to me that of itself is enough to condemn the principle, in so far as it is a legitimate deduction from the principle. Any principle which makes this separation between information and action, between the intellect and the will, must be either false, or else it is a principle which is to be adopted only after we have found that it is the only possible principle. Every one would admit without question that if there was any mode of education which in the earlier stages made it possible for instruction to have an influence on action, to convert intellectual insight into practical attitude, that would be a better system than one which did not make any provision for it. Now since Dr. Harris's only reason for saying that the earlier stages do not do that is that they present the studies in this isolation which will not enable them to see the unity of the thing, the conclusion would be a condemnation of that isolation, provided it is possible to find any way to avoid that isolation.

Dr. Harris, pp. 334–335,[5] has seemed to intimate that
[(12)] it is a psychological necessity of elementary education that it shall deal simply with isolated fragments.

The child has a tolerably quick grasp of isolated things and events, but he has very small power of synthesis. He cannot combine in his little mind things and events so as to perceive whole processes. He cannot perceive the principles and laws underlying the things and events which are brought under his notice. It is a necessary characteristic of primary and elementary education that it must take the world of human learning in fragments, and fail

[4 *Psychologic Foundations, op. cit.*]
[5 *Ibid.*]

to give its pupils an insight into the interrelation of things.

Now of course from one point of view that is perfectly true; the child cannot grasp formulated generalizations or relations, he cannot get a conscious insight into the relation of things, but there is another assumption made which equally fails to meet the true state of the case. It does not follow because the child cannot consciously relate, that everything comes to him in fragments, that he sees simply isolated things and events. Psychologically it is a later act of mind to define, to analyze, to break things up into consciously isolated fragments, just as it is a more mature process consciously to combine. The characteristic thing about the child is that it is unified on the basis of feeling, emotion, instinct and habit, and while that kind of a system is a very different unity from reflective reasoning it is also a different thing from a lot of consciously unrelated events and details. The child takes the standpoint of the whole as much as the reflective adult does, he takes it more, but it is simply that it is another kind of whole, or the whole from another point of view that appeals to him. We put back our own experience in point of view into that of the child, when we talk about the child taking the world of human learning in fragments. He takes it as a whole so far as he takes it at all. The whole is not as big as it might be quantitatively, but qualitatively it is still a whole. It is just as much a fallacy to read back the conscious analysis into the child's development as it is to suppose that he is conscious of synthesis. What he has is a world directly unified so far as it goes, and later on it is analyzed or defined, and which as it is analyzed needs also to be interrelated, to be gathered up into reflective wholes which take the place of the imaginative wholes of early experience. The child would have to be a logic chopper from the start to have it true of him that he sees things as distinct isolated things and events, and then simply later on learns how to gather them together into these totals.

            I would sum up then by saying that the fundamental [(*13*)] error of this point of view is that it deprives the child in the early period of that natural unity which his experience does formally have, breaking it up into isolated, separate studies and lessons, without its being possible to replace it at the early period by that conscious reflective unity which the mind is capable of grasping later on. So the criticism would simply bring us back a little more definitely to our first position that the elementary period is that in which experience is taken so far as possible as a whole, now emphasized in this particular, now in that, and so is enriched on this side and on that side. This work of emphasizing, of bringing out the features in a common experience, should be as symmetrical as possible, but in the elementary period there should always be the feeling of the whole. Geography should be studied simply as emphasizing, defining in the child's own mind, certain features in his surroundings which he has always been conscious of in a vague and unsystematic way. Then there comes the period of conscious differentiation, discrimination, the bringing to consciousness the material concepts and thus giving the basis for the classifying of material into distinct subjects, and then the interrelating of these into a conscious intellectual whole.

LECTURE XX

February 20, 1899

[C.I.3.: *The culture epoch theory.*]

The next topic for discussion is the doctrine that [*III.B.2.*] goes by the name of the Culture Epoch Theory. Of course I do not intend to discuss this theory in all its bearings, but simply in relation to the general topic under discussion, namely, the attempts to find a philosophical basis for the selection and arrangement of the material of the curriculum. The culture epoch theory, so called, has been developed by the Herbartian school in Germany. You will find very full and explicit statements in the first and second books of the Herbartian Society,[1] which are in the library, and you will also find further bibliographical references there, as well as in the published syllabus.

[*a.*] The position of the theory in general is that the child reproduces in his own development the main stages which have been passed through in the development of the race, with the pedagogical inference from that that the products of the various stages of the race development are the most appropriate material for the child in his corresponding stages of development. There are therefore two principles involved. In the statement of the existing parallelism, which of course is not primarily an educational principle at all, is the first point. It has been approached from the philosophical, the biological and from the historical points of view. It is primarily a question of fact, a question for biology and historical sociology to determine. But assuming that the answer of these sciences to the question of parallelism between

[1 *First Yearbook of the National Herbart Society* (Chicago: University of Chicago Press, 1895); *Second Yearbook of the National Herbart Society* (Chicago: University of Chicago Press, 1896).]

individual development in the existing child and the historical development of the race is in the affirmative, the second point is the educational inference that what the race has produced, what it has left behind it, what has had sufficient value to stand the test of time is the most appropiate material for the instruction of the child. As a pedagogical statement therefore, the theory has always made literature the basis of the course of study, because it is particularly in literature that the products of race development at its successive epochs has come down to us. It is a theory then which in its workings first says that we should study the child to find in what phase of development he is; secondly, we should study the historical evolution of humanity to see what the corresponding epoch of the world's development is; and thirdly, having decided these two points, we should find the great classic creations in that period of world development; and then fourthly, present them as the center for the education of the child, and group around and interweave with them the subordinate subjects of instruction, reading, writing, number, even science, and so on.

The theory certainly meets our attempt to meet one of [b.] the fundamental considerations which has already been laid down, that is, the necessity in our educational theory of taking into account both the psychological and the sociological aspects of experience. This theory begins by asserting that there is a parallelism between the two; it asserts that when it says that the child goes through the stages of development which the race has made its way through. It might be said to take as its fundamental working hypothesis the assumption of mutual connection between the psychological or individual phase of growth, and the historical, sociological phase. From the scientific point of view the upholders of the theory of course have found great support for their doctrine from theory of biological evolution, particularly the discoveries along the line of recapitulation, as it is usually termed; for instance, that the young in the embryonic stage show at least traces in their development of various forms of life which have been passed through in the evolutionary progress, that is, even in the human young there are found signs of even fish and bird life at certain stages of development. That is, the ontogenetic development recapitulates the phylogenetic.

[c.] Now in what I am about to say the general position of parallelism will be accepted, and my remarks will be directed rather to indicating the sense in which that doctrine of parallelism should be interpreted, and more particularly, the sense in which it is capable of application when interpreted, to education.

[(1)] In the first place, even in the biological statement the point that has been termed by Mr. Baldwin[2] that of "short cuts" is one of very great importance, not only in itself, but in the educational bearings of the culture epoch theory. Many of the phases of development in the general evolution which have taken a long period and which represent a great deal of struggle and effort, are gone over very rapidly in the individual development. Not only is that the fact but it is a point of economy, a point of increased gain in experience, that they should be passed over, that they should be reduced to very rapid and transitory phases of existence. One of the objects of education is, as Professor Vincent[3] has pointed out in his book, to increase the number and efficiency of short cuts. One of the reasons for educating is that the child shall not have to recapitulate, in too much detail, the various experiences through which the race has had to pass. It is to put him in the shortest possible time upon a level where he may get the benefits of the previous struggle of humanity, without having to share in the actual struggle itself. If therefore, we were to take the culture epoch theory too literally, it would be a decidedly harmful and restrictive doctrine; it would tend to keep the child too long and with too much emphasis, upon periods of civilization which are, relatively speaking, too low, which are not of greatest importance with reference to his permanent interests.

[(2)] While the doctrine of culture epochs has not taken anything like the practical hold in this country that it has in Germany, where it has had a large influence in shaping the curriculum of many of the elementary schools, there are certain phases of elementary instruction in this country which are closely connected with the doctrine, al-

[2 James Mark Baldwin, *Mental Development in the Child and the Race, Methods and Processes* (New York: The Macmillan Company, 1895), pp. 20 f.]
[3 George Edgar Vincent, *The Social Mind and Education* (Chicago: The University of Chicago Press, 1897).]

though it could not be said as a rule that they are a direct outgrowth. The large emphasis on the myths of the primitive peoples, the large part played by material direct from savage life, for example the use which is made of Longfellow's Hiawatha, are instances of what we find. In Germany there is a more systematic attempt to apply the culture epoch theory, in the application of which the early years of the child are supposed to coincide with the more primitive savage development, hunting, fishing, nomadic life, and so on. When the attempt is made to apply the doctrine it becomes a point of practical significance to know the basis for valuing this reference to primitive and savage life in education, to know the limits of the value which is to be placed upon it. Just because the present recourse to that material has been quite indiscriminate, because it has been sized up bodily as so much available material to interest the child with, it seems to me probable that there will be a reaction; the question will come up whether really the savage life and the things connected with primitive life are so important that we can afford to spend two or three of the most plastic years of the child's life with the predominating influence as that which is connected with savage life.

    The question is already asked whether there is not [(3)] a reactive tendency here, whether it is not in some sense arresting the development of the child, and his insight into higher stages of civilization, to keep him so long in the environment of savage life on the ground that that is parallel to the stage through which he is passing. I do not mean to say that there is no value in that material, but simply that there is a necessity for some standard for determining the value. The mere fact that the race has gone through a certain stage of development does not seem to be an adequate basis for inferring that the child not only does go through it, but that we should emphasize or prolong his passing through it. Physiologically we do not try and keep the child in the stage through which he goes in a very rapid and transitory manner, which has its parallel in the earlier stages of animal existence. We simply recognize it as a passing phenomenon. So the question still remains to be answered: does the parallelism between the child and primitive life have anything more than a transitory importance, or shall it be erected into a determining principle for the selection of the material of instruction for a period of two or three years? Perhaps it represents, it might be argued, what either may or should be a short cut in the process of recapitulation, rather than something to be emphasized and brought to consciousness with much emphasis.

            Another fact is that the later stages of development
[(4)] modify the earlier ones. They are not simply super-
            imposed upon the earlier stages, they are not simply added to that in a quantitative way, but the attainment of a higher standpoint in development means some actual organic reconstruction of the earlier stages. We cannot get away from the fact that we live in a civilized period in a civilized environment and that that is not merely something which has come after primitive stages, but is something which has profoundly modified them, which has given them a different significance than they had when they stood by themselves. Now the specific bearings of these two considerations are, to my mind, the following. In the first place the standpoint taken in education must be that of present life; so then, whenever recourse is had to primitive conditions, it must be not for the sake of the latter, but for the sake of throwing light upon the present. If the child is to be interested in the weapons and dress and canoes of the North American Indians, it should not be for the sake of the Indian, or for the sake of the Indian element in child nature. It is giving that more importance than it really possesses. So far as it is utilizable and available, it should be from the standpoint of the higher products of civilization which we have today. The canoe is important in so far as it makes the steam boat of today have more meaning to the child and as it makes him feel the progress that has been made in the meantime.

            That latter statement suggests my second point:
[(5)] that it is not the absorption of the child in the earlier
            epochs, not the saturation with their spirit which is the ideal, but rather that the child get a sense of movement through and away from. If they are studied so that the child works back and forth, comparing and contrasting more primitive forms with the later ones, there is no danger that the child will take the earlier as possessing value; he will see

them as simply phases of historical evolution, and the negative side will be kept in mind as well as the positive side. We may have all due respect for earlier peoples, not simply the Indians, but the Greeks and Romans, but after all we should not care to reproduce their civilization today. We at least imagine that we have made advance, improvement, that we represent a higher intellectual and ethical plane. Anything that prevents the child from seeing that side, the negative side as well as the positive element, is a detriment; he should see the thing in perspective, should feel it in relation to present conditions; so the standpoint taken should not be the literal living through the earlier civilization, but rather living through the element of growth, of progress contained in it. What did this, that or the other form of life have in it which persists as a permanent element in civilization? What conditions were there that had to be met then that still have to be met? And then further, what element or factor did this particular phase of life contribute to the solution of the problem of humanity and enable it to work out further? I do not mean that the child should consciously present these problems to himself, but that the material should be presented in such a way as to keep his mind moving on in the line of progress rather than simply getting arrested in a romantic and highly idealized manner with the features of savage and primitive life.

The third point which suggests itself is that what [(6)] we have, and still more what we should have in the development of the child, is a balance of various activities, rather than a series. The race has had to work through a series, it has had to do one thing at a time, and exaggerate the importance of that one thing while it was doing it. It had to pass through the hunting stage, the nomadic stage, the agricultural stage and so on. In the life of today something corresponding to all these factors of course remains. That is, the hunting stage is not very important in itself but the necessities of the hunting life produced inventions and tools which enabled the people to get out of the hunting stage into something better and more settled, going along toward the domestication of animals, the agricultural life, and so on. That is what I mean by saying that these various elements should be presented to the child in some kind of balanced relation, rather than in the serial form; and that point will be secured if the material is presented in such a way that the child is continually working back and forth between the present and the past, using the past so as to simplify his sense of the forces and factors which are at work at present, and using the present in order to give a standard for valuing the events and modes of life that we find represented in the past.

[(7)] There is another point. The position that has always been taken by the Herbartian school assumes that the products of a given period of development in the past are the appropriate nutriment of the child when he is going through the corresponding stage of development. This reasoning from the process of the child to the products in the race does not seem strictly logical, and it is on the basis of that very doubtful analogy that they assume that literature is the central focus of the material of the curriculum. The logic of the case would seem to call for the statement that we should go from the processes and points of view at work in the present to the similar processes and points of view at work in the past, but we always find the statement made that it is what the race produced at the given period of development which should afford the material of instruction for the child.

For instance, in Rein's scheme* as given on page 99 of the

*Rein's Scheme:

SCHOOL YEAR	MATERIALS OF INSTRUCTION		GENERAL CHARACTER OF EPOCHS
1.......	Folklore and Fairy Tales		
2.......	Robinson Crusoe		
	Sacred	*Profane*	Mythical and Heroic Mind
3.......	Patriarchs and Moses	Thuringian Tales	
4.......	Judges and Kings	Nibelungen Tale	
5.......	Life of Christ	Christianizing and Kaiser period	Mediaeval
6.......	Life of Christ	Kaiser period	State-building Historic Mind
7.......	Paul	Reformation	Social and Political Development
8.......	Luther	Nationalization	Scientific and Philosophic Mind

First Year Book,* we find that the first year of the school life should be taken up with folklore and fairy tales; the second with Robinson Crusoe; the third with the patriarchs and Moses on the side of sacred history and with the Thuringian tales on the side of German history; the fourth with judges and kings on the side of sacred history and with the Nibelungen tales on the German side, and the four years are classified together on the child's side under "Mythical and Heroic Mind."

I think it is obvious that such a statement will not bear any analysis at all. There was never a mind simply mythical or simply heroic, and never a child simply or mainly mythical and heroic. Any one can set out and collect lots of instances of the spontaneous myth-forming by children, personifications of clouds, the sun, the moon, rain, etc., and draw the inference that the child at this stage of his being is essentially a myth-forming person and therefore is in the same kind of emotional atmosphere that the primitive people were when they formed myths.

[(a)] The first fallacy there is seen in the fact that the result is reached by collecting lots of different things from different children and the impression received is very different from what one would get from observing any one child. If the child once a month develops something of this kind, with one hundred children under observation you would get lots of things, but the average child is more interested in the common, everyday things of life than in these imaginative considerations. The imaginative, myth-making and myth-loving child has no counterpart in the average child. If we found him he would be a monstrosity, needing to be turned over to a nerve specialist. I am not denying the importance of this element in early child life, but we often get a very false view of it. The child is interested in every-day things, and if you follow the average plays of the child you will find that they reproduce the every-day life of the people he sees about him. ·

[* The reference here is to a discussion of Wilhelm Rein by S. C. Van Liew, "The Educational Theory of the Culture Epochs," *The First Year Book of the Herbart Society for the Scientific Study of Teaching* (Chicago, 1895). Van Liew traces the development of the principle of culture epochs through the preceding century, and in doing so treats the interpretations of Rein ¹

Another fallacy is that early people produced myths
[(*b*)] because they were highly imaginative. The main
motives I suppose, were scientific and historical
rather than imaginative; of course not scientific in the sense
that they succeeded very well, but they were actually observing natural phenomena, and they were trying to give some kind
of an explanation of the phenomena. They were myths simply
because they were astray for the most part. They had no
faculty at large, called the imaginative faculty, by which they
could turn a crank and produce the myths and tales when they
wished. They simply did the best they could with the things
they saw about them. The actual student of myths knows better
than anybody else (a fact very largely neglected until lately)
that historical causes and events actually played a very large
part in generating the myths. Probably a large part of the
myths which have come down to us were attempts to carry
along important historical events, or at least represented the
gradual fusion of historical happenings with natural events.

Now all that is very interesting and from the histori-
[(*c*)] cal point of view is very valuable, but it does not
represent to my mind an adequate basis for saying
that the material even for one year of the child's life is simply
myths and fairy tales. The child most naturally gets the bearing of these things when he gets them in their historical
setting. If the child is studying Greek life, it is necessary that
he should know how the Greek interpreted his experience.
The myth then gets positive reality. Of course I am not enough
of a Philistine to think that the child should not have stories
as stories, fairy tales or anything else, told him, but to lay
down as a doctrine that they should be the center around
which all the other studies should group themselves for even
a single year of the child's life, is a very different thing. So
with Robinson Crusoe. That is a great story and I do not
mean to speak in disrespect of it, every child ought to read it,
but the thing which gives it its reality and interest is not the
fact that it is a story, but that it embodies certain fundamental
interests and processes; it does recapitulate in a certain way
the seemingly adverse environment, and gives a graphic account of how headway is made in bringing under subordination to himself the forces of his environment. The question
of taking it as the basis for a year's study is simply the ques-

tion of whether the direct, or the indirect mode of approach is better. That story pictures a very fundamental motive with which the child should become acquainted. It represents the history of invention, the development of ingenuity in adaptation of means to ends in meeting the emergencies which nature presents, and getting the better of them. Shall that be got at with the child through the medium of the story, or can he be given an idea of the way in which mankind has actually moved onward; and cannot prehistoric material such as we have worked out in archeology and anthropology be so adapted as to give the child the reality, and then give the story as an imaginative production? There is always, it seems to me, a certain value and guarantee of value in the fact that things have really happened somewhere, rather than to have been simply imaginatively worked out through the medium of a story. The child should always have a direct relationship with the reality of the situation first, and then with its literary idealization; but the purpose of his educative growth is best served when that relationship is maintained.

When you get beyond the first two or three years it [(d)] seems to me all pretense in keeping up the parallelism; it almost entirely vanishes. In the seventh and eighth years the child is introduced to Paul and Luther and on the side of secular history to the period of the Reformation and to the modern formation of German nationality. These are classified under "Scientific and Philosophic Mind." The child has a scientific and philosophic mind and therefore should have Paul, Luther and the study of the Reformation! In another scheme* which is given in the *Second Year Book*,† we have the mythical and heroic epoch extending from infancy to about the eighth year, then from the sixth to the tenth year on the psychical side the development of imagination and memory, and on the historical side the intermediate epoch (which is not very definite), and after the tenth year, we have on the psychical side the logical epoch and on the race side the epoch of freedom, self government, and recognition of the individual. I just mention that as showing that if you are making a curriculum, after you get beyond the mythical epoch, you practically can have anything you please. It is a question of

[* † Footnotes appear at foot of page 210.]

picking out certain historical epochs on one side and certain psychical epochs in the individual on the other and assuming that there is some occult parallelism between the two.

[(8)]   That suggests my final point. The culture epoch theory seems to invert the true method of approach. It starts really from the historical side and then hunts around for corresponding stages in the individual. The proper order of approach would be the opposite. We first should study the child to find out what his own actual development is, or what the stages of growth, the great rhythms in development are, and then having satisfied ourselves, should hunt around for the material that is most appropriate for that period of mental development, and if we do that I believe we will find that it will represent the line of movement which has cooperated with other movements in bringing things to the present condition, rather than a little historical epoch. Just try to identify the Reformation in Germany with any one particular phase of period, year or month, of actual mental development, and you will realize what is the essential absurdity of the position. There is a period when the child is interested in the struggle of the individual for liberty of conscience, thought, and expression, and undoubtedly, when in that period the Reformation is a particular thing to bring to his attention and may be of

*

AGE OF THE INDIVIDUAL RELATIVELY INDICATED.	PSYCHICAL EPOCHS IN THE INDIVIDUAL.	EPOCHS IN RACE DEVELOPMENT.
From infancy to about the eighth year.	The intuitive epoch sense-perception, as the beginning of intellectual culture.	The mythical and heroic epoch.
From the sixth to the tenth year.	The imaginative epoch, development of imagination and memory.	The intermediate epoch.
After the tenth year.	The logical epoch, thinking and reasoning, receiving prominence.	The epoch of freedom, self-government, and recognition of the individual.

[† This refers to an article by Levi Seeley, "Culture Epochs," *Second Year Book of the Herbart Society* (Bloomington, Illinois, 1896), in which the scheme is reproduced.]

help and interest to him. It is not on account of any preconceived parallelism, but simply because the child has a certain interest and mental and moral need, and we use our intelligence and sense to find material which will satisfy that need. In other words, it seems to me that there is a good deal of useless philosophical formulation and systematization used here in order to justify certain things which might be justified easier on more natural principles. We should carefully watch the development of the child and then hunt through literature and history and science and furnish the material that is most appropriate to the child at that stage of development; and that seems to me the element of truth which in a roundabout way has been put into the statement of the culture epoch theory.

LECTURE XXI

February 21, 1899

[C.I.3.: *Other bases of correlation.*]

[III.B.3.] Quite independently of the culture epoch theory the doctrine may be held that literature is the center of the curriculum, the basis of correlation, and so it may be well to say a few words about that point.

[a.] The philosophical objection to that point of view was indicated yesterday in saying that literature represents an indirect mode of experience rather than direct. Literature always presupposes a certain positive, immediate experience, experiences of what might seem an every day, ordinary sort, especially experiences of a social sort. Now the significance of literature is that it gathers together, selects and idealizes, interprets the best that is in this every day social experience. Provided, therefore, one has sufficient contact with the elements of the every day experience, literature is of great importance in giving the culmination, the completion, the finishing touches, both as to content, to substance, and also as to form. But just because literature does represent the culmination of experience, the selection and idealization of what is best, and of highest value, and is embodied in a form which serves to bring out the high quality content, it cannot be a basis. To make it a basis is turning the thing upside down. It is the apex, the highest expression and formulation of conscious experience; and so while any education would be very deficient and defective which did not introduce the pupil to the best possible expression of the highest quality of human experiences, to attempt to start with it would fail to give any adequate provision for securing to the child the actual experiences which do have this perfected and idealized expression in literature. Its significance lies in the fact that it is just this interpretation, this high interpretation of the elements of ordinary experience. Now to make it the basis will not insure that the child has those experiences. We have certainly no right to assume that the child has had already all the requisite experiences and all that remains to do is to give him the most perfect expression and embodiment of them. If that method is followed, education or instruction becomes literary, in the bad sense of literary; that is, substance is sacrificed to form. Certain views, attitudes, views of things, and attitudes toward things, take the place of consciousness of the things themselves, of the substantial realities.

[b.]   There is no substitute for the first hand, direct, personal, immediate elements in experience. The only way to get it is to experience it; and to attempt to supply that, to furnish it through the medium of literature, means that on the one hand there is a vacuum left, and on the other hand that the virtual attempt is made to substitute this direct interpretation made by other minds for one's own personal experience. Literature, when it really interprets something in one's own life experience or environment which brings it to full consciousness, is certainly a most admirable thing; not too much can be said in praise of it; but that literature should be given to the child as containing somehow the realities which he can only really get in some other way, is a very artificial thing, a thing which leads to false perspective, to unreality in the child's own attitude. That is what I meant, for example, in what I said about Robinson Crusoe regarded as a basis for a year's work. It is a backhanded way, at the very best, of getting hold of the realities, the real forces and conditions involved. When those things have been got hold of in a more direct and personal way, then as a dramatic and idealized summing up of the whole situation, it has positive value. What is said of that I think is true of any topic in literature.

[c.]   This necessary artificiality is seen by going over the schemes of correlation, the Herbartian schemes. The connection between number work for example, and the literary subject matter, is almost always of the most external kind. There is not much mental correlation, or correlation of subject matter, involved in connecting the arithmetic lessons with adding, subtracting, and multiplying the twelve tribes of Israel when Old Testament literature is the basis of work; there is not much substantial correlation in adding, subtracting, and multiplying with various needles of the pine tree bough because you happen to have a poetry lesson about the pine tree. When in an American scheme the Virginia colony is the basis of correlation, it seems rather artificial to confine the arithmetic lessons to problems about pounds of tobacco, gallons of molasses, etc. Now I do not say that the child does not get a little more mental connection there, but there is no very intrinsic connection gained. The connection of science is on almost as artificial and external a basis, of necessity, when literature is taken as the fundamental subject matter. Of course it is quite possible that the child who has a high grade poem presented in a literary way will take more interest in the pine tree itself, will feel the need of studying the pine tree in order to understand the imagery of the whole poem. There are many cases where it might be brought in in a fairly natural way, but to subordinate science uniformly to the possibility of correlating it with the study of some literary work, would I think, be to give science a very false position in the child's mind, to give the scientific ideas a false position, and also if it were carried out systematically would be pretty certain to kill the literary quality of the piece of literature itself. It is not always that you can get so easily and naturally from the poem about the pine tree to the study of the pine tree, and where it is not so easy, the child feels in advance that the poem is not a poem, but an excuse for giving him a certain number of science lessons, or something of that sort.

Stating the principle more definitely, literature is a
[d.]   a record, a record of a very high sort, but none the less a record of the struggles and experiences, achievements, of human beings; and it presupposes that background of actual experience, and is presented out of its own proper relation when it is introduced in other ways.

History has also been proposed as the basis for corre-
[4.]   lation. As a matter of fact Herbartians use both, sometimes history and sometimes literary products. In history we are making a little closer approach to
[a.]   the first hand element in experience of actual growth than we are in literature, in fact literature really presupposes history. History is one step further back, but

history is still in a way indirect and backhanded. It is the study of the record of social life, the study of what social life has precipitated, the way it has crystallized itself in the past. It therefore logically presupposes the forces of social life itself, so that logically at least, it is not the basis. Logically the center is found in the social experience itself. Now of course, in coming to understand that social life, a study of its precipitations, of its objective embodiment in character and institutions and events is a very fundamental matter. Social life itself is so complex that if we could not get at it through its objectification, we should not be able to understand it at all, so in bringing the forces and the meaning of social life to consciousness, history, like literature is exceedingly important, and an absolutely indispensable instrument; but it is not because it is history that it has a place. It is something instrumental, a means of getting at the reality of the social forces themselves which are still at work.

In one of his essays somewhere, Emerson in talking
[b.]   about reading and utilizing other people's experiences, asks the question: why should he be reading George Washington's letters when he has so many of his own that he has not answered? The same point holds of history. We would have no business studying something that has happened, if it were really past, dead, and gone. The only justification for it is that it does enlarge and define and enrich our sense of the present. I do not mean by that that we must always be drawing moral lessons from the past to the present, and say because such things have happened such things are likely to happen now, but simply that we have our whole social imagination enlarged, our whole way of looking at social occurrences; we get a method through history for appreciating and understanding the present. Of course it is commonplace to say that the present is the child of the past and therefore we cannot understand the present excepting as we go into the past. I mean a little more than that, something different from that as well, namely, that the very remoteness of the past, the fact that we do not and cannot possibly get it as a whole, but only in certain leading features that have come down to us, presents us with a certain picture of the operations of the social forces which we could not get if we were simply limited in our survey to the present. There is something more important than past or

present; it is the forces which are at work which have made both the past and which are making the present, and which are going on to make the future. The center of gravity of history, as well as literature, is found outside of itself. It is found in social life.

[5.] I do not know that science or nature study has ever been formally presented as a basis for correlation, although the statement is frequently made, was made in this periodical literature concerning correlation, that such is the theory and practice at the Chicago Normal School; but Colonel Parker* and Mr. Jackman† have always claimed that that was not the true state of the case, that they did not take the knowledge of environment as the basis of correlation.

[a.] There is no need of criticizing a view which no one has presented as valid, but in passing I would remark that if one should take that view, the rock on which it would break is that in nature, just as nature, you cannot find any unifying principle. The environment, just as the world of space and time, is centrifugal instead of centripetal. It carries you on indefinitely from one thing to another thing, from one law to another law. Certainly no one yet has succeeded in discovering any intrinsic, essential unity in the world about us. It is the world about us, it is an environment; that is, we always take for granted human life as the center, as that from which the world of nature radiates and expands.

[b.] Independently from the question whether the point of view is justifiable or not, certainly educationally speaking the only adequate basis for unifying knowledge of the world, things and events in space and time, is their relation to human experience, to human welfare. The control of nature has been a great motive after all, to the study of nature, its adaptation to human needs and interests. Now if it should ever be proved philosophically that nature is a thing absolutely independent of consciousness, that it is an absolute thing in itself, it would still hold true that educationally we would have to treat it as if it were not an independent entity,

[* Colonel Francis Wayland Parker. Parker was principal, from 1883–99, of the Cook County Normal School in Chicago. He led a movement to introduce Froebel's principles into elementary education. His chief work was *How to Study Geography* (New York: D. Appleton and Company, 1890).]
[† See Lecture XIV.]

because in the degree that it is regarded as isolated, cut off entirely from considerations of human experiences and growth, it loses any particular meaning and relevancy. It would be an interesting fact for advanced philosophic investigation, but it would not supply material for every day education.

       In Colonel Parker's book, *Talks on Pedagogics*,[1] there [6.]   is still another view presented which does not classify itself exactly with any of those already discussed, and independently of what I am going to say, I would call your attention particularly to Chapters I, II, and XV. Those chapters will at least serve to illustrate what I said earlier in the course about the natural unity of experience and the extent to which the formal education of the school must go back to and develop out of the natural unity of human experience. It is rather hard to formulate the exact teaching of this book, but the thing that is insisted upon on one side, is the study of the spontaneous instincts, tendencies, and interests of the child, in determining the process of education. In fact the basis of concentration is stated to be the child. It is the child who is the center of the concentration process (pp. 380–83). The center of all movement in education is the child, the central law is self effort, and it is the unity of the child then, which he has taken as giving the basis of the unity of the educative process. Now on the other side it is stated that in all the subject matter of education, in all the studies of the curriculum, the unity is found in the idea of law, that there is after all but one thing which we study, one thing which we should study. That one thing is law. It may have a diversity of operations and manifestations, but as on one side there is the unity of the child, so on the other side there is the unity of law, and the consideration of these two unities, in their relation to each other, affords the basis for the whole theory of education.

       Now that statement seems to me to present the problem and the essential terms in the problem, but to still leave open the actual content of the solution of the problem. Its great value is that it does emphasize the central unity, the unity in the being, and the unity in all the variety of things studied, and when the teacher gets distracted by the multiplicity of things

[1 Francis Wayland Parker, *Talks on Pedagogics* (New York: E. L. Kellogg and Company, 1894).]

which present themselves every day, the multiplicity of studies, and so on, that there are these two fundamental unities which determine and control all those details. But even after we have admitted that point of view, the practical questions, as well as the theoretical ones, still thrust themselves upon us: What does this unity of the child call for, and how shall the unity of law in the world of nature and of society be got hold of? How shall the actual facts of the different studies be so organized and arranged with reference to each other that this unity of law shall be brought to consciousness? And so, while we have as I say, in this book, a statement of the essential conditions that have to be taken into account in the problem, we do not have, so far as the general principle is concerned, anything more than a formulation of the problem itself. We do have a statement of the factors, the unity of the child on one side, and the unity of the world on the other.

LECTURE XXII

February 23, 1899

[C.II.: *Positive principles of selection and correlation: basic considerations.*]

At the last three hours we have considered various [III.C.] theories which have been proposed regarding the fundamental principles for the selection and arrangement of the subject matter of the courses of study, and I shall now go back again to the positive principles that had been stated before I took up these criticisms, and restate them somewhat in the light of what has been brought out in the consideration of these other points of view.

The first statement is that the problem of correlation [1.] itself practically disappears when formal education is made sufficiently continuous with the informal. I mean it disappears in the first epoch, in the early elementary period. The child, as he lives his own life in his own environment, has no need of any scheme of correlation in order to tie his various experiences together. Unless he is over-stimulated by too great variety, and too great novelty in his environment, his various experiences are held together unconsciously by the fact that they do all relate to one world, his world, his environment. The child himself, of course, would not state what the unity of that environment is, it would be very difficult analytically to state it, but there are certain conditions, circumstances, peoples, and things with whom the child habitually associates, and with which he habitually comes in contact, and that familiarity with his environment, and especially the strong personal and affectional element in it, his ties with other people, his dependencies upon them, serve to hold the variety of his experiences together into one whole. Putting it on the subjective side, his habits and his prevailing interests serve sufficiently to unify his experiences, although in quality and in time and in space, they may be quite diverse from each other. Now according to what was previously said, that the unity of that experience should be carried over as the background for school work and so become the basis for correlation during this early period, it is simply this background of the every day, familiar, experience of the child. If we avoid the artificial isolation, or if we avoid abrupt solution or continuity, then as I said, the whole problem of correlation practically disappears. It comes in at this period only if we have unduly and suddenly made a gap between the child's school studies, and his home and neighborhood life. If we make that gap then the question does at once arise: How are we to tie together the various school studies? How shall we prevent the child from being distracted, and his natural powers from being disintegrated, relatively, if not absolutely, through the introduction of a number of studies, each representing to the child a distinct and isolated little world by itself?

[2.]   Stating it a little more formally then, the social element in the child's experience, from the objective standpoint, and his predominant habits and interests, from the individual standpoint, furnish the basis for determining the curriculum in the early period. It is not a matter of so much importance just exactly what the subject matter in the early years be, but it is a matter of importance that the criterion for selecting it be recognition of the controlling and fundamental character of the social element. It is not a matter of so much importance, because the world is very wide and the amount, of course, that can actually be covered in instruction is comparatively small, so there is a very large range for choice, and different schools in different places or in different local environments, or even in the same environment, might find it advantageous to select different factors.

[a.(1)]   Two or three large fields within which selection may go on may be specifically mentioned. One of these large fields, particularly for the earlier period, falls within the present kindergarten, in the occupations and daily pursuits and interests, materials and furnishings of the household life. In spite of the fact that these things touch the child so intimately, he comes in contact with them so constantly, he will not be likely to have brought the things and the relations involved to consciousness very much. He will not have defined either the materials or the occupations, the household occupations, which deal with these materials; much less will he have systematized them, arranged them, in any orderly and consecutive way. Now doing these things give sufficient opportunity for play, for manual work, the child's making, reproducing so far as he can these things, reproducing in play form the household pursuits, and making the beginnings of what later on will be science study, and for the gaining of such knowledge as is suitable to him at the time, of the structure and uses of the materials employed and of the appropriate way of using them.

[(2)] Another field that is also thoroughly social in character is that of occupations that are carried on outside the household, the typical occupations of social life; farming, store keeping, mining, quarrying, the railroad and steamboat as modes of transportation, would naturally be adapted to children of a somewhat older age if they were taken up chiefly from the side of what people do, why they do them, and how they live and work in doing them. The field is itself intrinsically social, but it brings in a larger environment, geography as well as geographical elements in their relation to human life; and it brings in the elements of science study in the structures used and their adaptation to these uses. This field gives plenty of material for free expression in art work, and in connection with whatever may be done in manual work. The study can be made on the social basis, not only with reference to occupations, but also with reference to the social subdivisions that are found on the face of the globe, various tribes and peoples, with special reference to the adaptation of environment, people in warm climates, people in cold climates, in different parts of the globe. Of course the geographical and scientific elements are equally involved there, but the emphasis is chiefly on the social side: how people do; how life is carried on; how the processes which the child is familiar with in one form are carried on; and how they change their forms under different circumstances and with a different environment.

Or again there may be a simplified history of specially [(3)] primitive social development. I mean by simplified history, taking it up, not as history, not so much with reference to what actually did happen, as the typical phases that mankind has had to pass through in its progress, a sort of historical sociology, starting with a simplified form of life, that is with the minimum of tools and inventions, the minimum of control over natural forces, and following out the historical evolution of the various occupations which controlled the organization of life in primitive times: the evolution of society through the hunting and nomadic stages into the agricultural stage, with the modes of life and the implements, materials, and processes which were appropriate to each period.

It is a matter of adjustment rather than a principle, which of these, or other lines that might be suggested, should be utilized as affording the bulk of the early curriculum; and if any one of these were taken there would still be great room for the emphasis of certain phases, rather than certain others. I give these as an illustration of what would be meant by emphasizing the social factor as the basis of the curriculum, and introducing the geographical, scientific, and mathematical factors, not strictly speaking in subordination of these, but in the relationship which they actually bear to the maintenance and progress of social life. Of course social life as a medium has everything in it. People live on the earth; there is the geographical element at once. People in living on the earth have to use certain things, they have to be habitually interested and occupied with certain things, and deal with them along the line of certain processes, observing certain relations. To carry out their purposes, to reach their ends, there have to be adjustments involving number and space relations. In the latter facts there is provision made for the introduction of science and mathematics, introduced in sufficient proportion to give the child necessary instruction, but still introduced in their human and social relationships.

The plea which has been recently made, particularly [b.]   from educators of Clark University, that the early science should be introduced on what we might call a poetical and mythical basis, seems to me simply a false interpretation of this principle which I should regard as fundamentally correct, that the science ought to be introduced in its

human relations. There can be no doubt that the early introduction of science has come very far short of meeting the hopes
originally entertained, and that there therefore has been a reaction, due principally to the fact that it was introduced as
formal object study, that is, a simple knowledge of things; and
this demand for the romantic and poetical and mythical atmosphere about science is a reaction from that isolation of it,
treating science as the mere knowledge of external things and
forces. The child is not interested in things that are simply and
obviously external. He must feel them in relation to life. There
is then the legitimate demand that they have a social clothing
and social coloring; but I think any of the three or four lines
that I suggested afford opportunity for giving the scientific
material this human quality, by giving it in its social functions,
in what it does for men in their actual living, without its being
necessary to have recourse to the romantic dressing up. It
seems to me that it will have a doubtful influence upon the
child, and certainly of a sort which later on will call for positive
and rather violent scientific revolutions. If the child is steeped
in it from the romantic and poetic point of view it will be pretty
difficult to make science itself accurate, and pretty difficult to
make the transition to the more objective and strictly scientific
study; but if it is introduced in its social relations, what men
actually do with things, and what processes they actually
utilize in their daily lives, the material at least can be made accurate as far as it goes, and the transition to the strictly scientific and objective study will be a natural and gradual one.

I shall have something to say pretty soon about this same
point with reference to the actual historical evolution of the
sciences, and attempt to show that that is parallel to this point
of view, that men began science, not for the sake of the study
of the objective world, but simply for the sake of finding out
the things which they needed to use, and finding out how to
use the things which they needed to use, and then we may
recognize at least that truth in the culture epoch theory, that
the child naturally begins with the same attitude toward things
and forces with which the race began, and only gradually and
slowly worked over from that point of view to the more strictly
theoretical one. I simply repeat what was suggested the other
day: no matter how poetic and imaginative the mind of primitive man may have been, the attention of primitive man was

chiefly concerned with getting a living; the imaginative part was the luxury of life, and his interest in fire, water, air, stones, plants, and animals, must have been conditioned, not by his imaginative and poetic tendencies, but by the relations which they bore, or which he thought they bore, to his daily life. While the child is relieved from the stress of this economic stimulus (he does not have to support himself), and therefore his point of view has somewhat shifted, yet the basis of his interest is after all, in what people do with these things and with the question of what application of tools or of heat, or water, or whatever was made by them, how they succeeded in utilizing these things in the daily occupations, whether in the home, or neighborhood, or in the larger world which the child can observe.

Summing this up it seems that the standard of value for studies is social; that, as was said the other day, the ultimate material of study is social life; and that the various studies, so called, only represent, after all, abstractions, and inventories, formulated surveys for purposes of greater convenience, of particular phases of the totality of social experience; and that therefore, philosophically, the basis of the curriculum from the objective point of view, that is, the unifying principle, is found in the consideration of social life; that there is where the unity of history, and of literature, and of science, and so on, is really found; and that in the first period the unity is prominent and the problem of correlation remains in the background. The problem is rather one of differentiation, that is, one leading to the recognition of the diverse elements involved rather than in tying together anything already differentiated.

[c.]   This affords a place again for saying a word about the relation of nature and culture or science and the humanities. These two lines would represent on the basis of what already has been said, a certain fundamental division of labor within the consideration of social life. Social life does not go on in the air, in a vacuum, it goes on in the medium of the earth, and because of that fact, any separation between people and things, between nature and culture, between science and the humanities, is an artificial one, and when erected into a working principle of education, is a harmful one. In the later period of course, after differentiation has been introduced, after the student has worked through the various phases and their relation to each other, he may easily specialize on one side or the other, but it is simply a question of the greater stress of interest, in an emphasis on one side of what is one whole. The nature side is the study of materials and processes by which society maintains itself, and through which it gets its leverage for progress. The culture or humanity side is simply the summing up of the values which society has succeeded in getting out of its life, and conserving them for future use. If we were interested in studying the means, the instrumentalities of social life, we would have what we term nature, that is, nature for educational purposes. If we were interested in studying ends, results attained, actually realized through the use of these means, we would have the culture or humanity side; but means and ends apart from each other are meaningless. Means are means because they serve the realization of ends; and ends are such only because they utilize instrumentalities, agencies. We may paraphrase the famous saying of Kant: "Percepts without concepts are blind, and concepts without percepts are empty." The knowledge of nature without knowing what it leads to in human life, is blind, it is dead; relatively speaking, it has lost its value; but a knowledge of humanities, culture, without a knowledge of its foundations, and a knowledge of its positive basis in nature, is superficial and comparatively speaking, empty. It tends all the time to become merely literary, and to lose its sense of vitality, its sense of its rights in the common earth through reference to which all these values have grown up and with reference to which they must be finally applied if they are ever going to have any influence upon action and become a part of conduct.

LECTURE XXIII

February 27, 1899

[C.II.: *Psychological aspects of correlation.*]

I will rearrange somewhat the order of topics as [III.C.3.] stated, and speak today of the more psychological aspects of correlation. Although the topic really trenches on topics that will be taken up later on under the head of "method," having taken up the matter from the standpoint of the content correlation of the studies, it may be well also to say something about the counterpart of this on the mental side.

The Herbartian theory rests on a somewhat peculiar [a.(1)] psychological doctrine. It represents a somewhat extreme form of the doctrine of atomism and of association in psychology, although it differs in its statement from the familiar English presentations of this point of view; but it holds in substance that every idea is a distinct mental entity, psychical entity, and is brought forth by the reaction of the soul to stimuli; and that it represents a certain qualitative form of the soul itself; that when it is once produced it is an existence by itself which has its own dynamic force, striving to come before consciousness, and striving indeed to come to the summit of consciousness. It is the same idea whether it is in consciousness or beneath consciousness. If you were to think of a cork somewhat heavy which now falls below the surface of the water because of the presence of other corks, and partly by its own weight, and now bobs up to the surface and takes its way to the top of a wave, comes to the height of the field of water, you would have a fair metaphor for the Herbartian idea.

Now these various ideas assist and also hinder each [(2)] other. Those which are alike, which are congruent, reinforce each other. One of these coming into consciousness tends to pull its allied forces into consciousness with it, and to crowd out those which are unlike. It becomes then an all-important matter to get the right grouping of congruous ideas, to get fixed and firm associations formed between the important ideas so that they will always help and reinforce each other.

At this point the theory of apperception comes in, and
[(3)] on the strictly psychical side correlation will be a
matter of presenting ideas in such ways that certain firmly knit associations between them will be formed, so that the dynamic power of one, that is, its capacity for coming to the height of consciousness, will be reinforced, and be reinforced by all allied ideas, or those of a congruous character. By first providing the right presentation and then arranging for the proper combinations and interactions between these presentations, it becomes practically possible to do anything you please with the person's consciousness, and indeed with his character. The Herbartian psychology denies any faculty theory; it reduces everything to these ideas and their various actions and reactions on each other. Desire is nothing but the case of one of these ideas striving against some obstacle to reach the focus of consciousness and they become supreme there. So that by multiplying these ideas in the right way, we are not only determining what the content of the person's consciousness shall be, but also what his desires and motives shall be, and thus how he shall act. The Herbartian psychology has taught what was an ideal psychology for the school teacher, it almost makes the pupil plastic like putty or clay in the hands of the teacher, and the teacher, by supplying the right material, calling up the proper ideas and binding them together, can determine in advance as it were, the right development of character and conduct.

The necessity for correlation is very great, because in
[(4)] themselves, these ideas are independent entities, and
while they are tending through their natural points of agreement to form certain alliances, offensive and defensive, with each other, unless their combinations are somehow controlled, they would be very haphazard, dependent upon the way they happen to be associated, and there would be no guarantee to their tending to the right development of character. But the theory of correlation sees that the forces are combined together effectively and then operate for the proper ends.

Now without going into the minute criticism of the
[b.]   matter, it is safe to say that there are two points in
which modern psychology tends to differ very widely
from the Herbartian, and that the difference in these two points
would modify the educational statement quite profoundly.
These two points are undoubtedly at bottom one, but for convenience may be stated as two.

The first point is that comparatively speaking, the
[(1)]   Herbartian psychology overemphasized the intellectual aspect very much, and under-estimated the instinctive, the habitual, and the motor. To be taken account of
in the Herbartian psychology, you have to have one of these
little ideas which is just the same in consciousness that it is
out of consciousness, and the same out of consciousness that
it is in consciousness. There is no provision made for the force
of the primary instincts and habits, which very largely are
formed unconsciously, and which show themselves normally
only in their results. We form habits without knowing clearly
why or how or even just when we form them. We form them
on the basis of our natural instincts and impulses, our spontaneous out-going tendencies, and those lie in our nature way
below any distinct conscious idea or definite mental content.
I do not mean to say that they are formed or operate ever entirely unconsciously. We are generally conscious of the results,
the values which they lead to, but that is very different from
one of these intellectual mental contents or definite ideas. The
natural equipment of the individual, of this motor, outgoing
sort, is not sufficiently taken account of in the Herbartian
theory.

The second point that grows out of that, is that these
[(2)]   motor tendencies, impulses, and habits, have continuity, and therefore supply in themselves a natural and
intrinsic unification of experience and of consciousness, quite
apart from the formal associations that are set up between our
ideas. In so far as any one has a habit formed in any direction,
he already has a correlation which unconsciously takes care
of a great variety of experiences. Experiences that would otherwise be very diverse are instinctively and unconsciously held
together. In neglecting the side of impulse and habit, the
Herbartians have always neglected the natural correlating element in the mind, the natural synthetic element, that which

most unconsciously and effectively binds together what would otherwise be the scattered variety of our experiences in space and time; and having neglected therefore, this natural bond of union, this intrinsic correlating force, they have had to supply the place of it largely on an artificial basis. The correlation of the material of instruction, binding together lessons in arithmetic, geography, history, etc., was worked out because otherwise they would have nothing but disintegration; that is, on the basis of their psychology, the mind, left to itself, would not supply any natural and valuable unities. It had to be supplied through instruction and the way the material of instruction was brought to bear on the mind, hence the vast importance that they have attached to these external correlations of the various facts, ideas, lessons, studies, and so on, with each other. If you once recognize the correlating force of any dominating impulse or interest or habit, its capacity to pick out (as a magnet picks out iron fillings) and to hold to itself anything that is relevant to itself, we do not have to worry so much about the mere formal objective correlation on the side of the subject matter. The chief thing is to get an important impulse or interest actively at work and then it will tend to the correlating for you. Wherever it operates, it will operate to grasp relevant material, to neglect every thing foreign or alien, and to bind, to associate all the material thus grasped into a continuous and harmonious whole.

[c.] By starting from this standpoint then, I simply indicate what some of the types of natural impulses or instincts are, which are intrinsically of themselves aggregating centers, or concentrating foci for the material of instruction.

[(1)] As stated in the syllabus these types are four. They might perhaps better be reduced to three: communication, construction, and expression. That is, the child has a natural instinct or impulse to tell, to relate, and to demand similar telling, statement, from others.

[(a)(i)] Mr. Baldwin[1] has called attention in his writings on the mental development of the child, to the instinctive demand of the child for social confirmation of his

[1 James Mark Baldwin, *Mental Development in the Child and in the Race, Methods and Processes* (New York: The Macmillan Company, 1895).]

own experiences and ideas. The point can hardly be over-emphasized too much: the demand on the part of the small child that other people shall become acquainted with his experiences and that they shall respond to his experiences either with approval or disapproval, or to somehow reinforce or revise the experience of the child that has been communicated to others. This is perhaps at the very root of the social nature of the small child. It certainly is an instinct on the child's part in the sense that it is not a thing which he does for any conscious or elaborate reason, it is an instinct which finds its best expression in language, although not its only one; it fixes the fundamental significance of language, at least in all the early periods of education.

[(ii)]   The books on pedagogy have too commonly defined language from the standpoint of a statement of thought, have emphasized largely its intellectual and even logical aspects, as if the main purpose of the language were to transmit or carry on some intellectual process of thinking. Of course language is primarily a social instrument or medium. It does communicate thought, but it does that simply because thought is one phase, or one part of the child's life and experience. The primary office of language is to communicate or transmit the child himself, in his conscious experience, and to enable the experiences of others to be communicated to the child in such a way that the relations shall be more sympathetic and fuller at all points, and more flexible and freer. It is that social aspect of the use of langauge which should control practically entirely its use in all the earlier periods of instruction. It should always be remembered that one of the chief, perhaps the chief interest of the child is in telling, in communicating himself and his own experiences, and in getting back the response of the experiences of others. That is the fact which should control learning to read, write, and spell, all the forms of language, as well as simple oral speech. It is only later on that the problem of getting the person to use language at all arises, that it becomes a problem. The question of getting adequate expression in speech, both orally and in writing, is one of the chief problems discussed now as regards high school instruction and as regards the teaching of rhetoric etc., in college—how to break down self-consciousness, how to get natural modes of expression, and so on. But if we take the child, the younger child as he comes to school, when he feels that there is any relation of sympathy between him and others, his desire is for a full and fluent communication. It of course needs training, direction, but excepting occasionally, in rare instances, the tendency itself does not need arousing, unless it has been already repressed or checked.

[(b)] Now the instinct for expression cannot be marked off narrowly from that of communication. The two things run into each other and the expression grows out of communication. I have simply used the term "communication" in a somewhat more technical sense to denote matters where the form of communication is of great importance. Undoubtedly part of the interest in a child's drawing a picture is the same that he has in telling a story; it is just another form of language to him, another means of communication; but it has more of the aspect of what I have called expression in it, a way of telling, a mode of telling as distinct from the mere subject matter that is to be told. It is of greater importance in the communication. The child is interested in what he is going to say, in how other people are going to take it and react to it. But in the expression it is more consciously his own emotion or his own thought about things, which he is thus setting forth, and there is not a social demand for the response on the part of others.

[(c)] The interest in construction is the interest in doing things, in making things, effecting rearrangements of material in space and in time. In the early periods the form constructed may be very transitory, nothing but a rearrangement of chairs in the room to make them into a train of cars; but so far as it does involve the rearrangement of material it involves construction, and will tend to go on to the making of things in more fixed forms. Of course construction and expression are very closely related. Every genuine construction is also an expression; it implies an idea which is being worked out through the medium of the material at hand. I simply mark it off from expression in this way: In construction the rearrangement of material, the product, is of more importance, while in the expression, the material is of no value excepting to facilitate the expression, the manifestation or utterance of the feeling or idea that lies behind. The difference would be between a child drawing a picture of a train of cars, and taking his blocks to build and then play with the train of cars. The obvious, overt element comes in more strongly in construction, while idea or feeling comes in more emphatically in expression. I thing practically all of the important activities of the child excepting those which come from his direct bodily appetites, can be summed up under these heads: an interest in communication, that is, in social conversation leading to an exchange and enrichment of experiences; an interest in construction, which brings about a modification, a manipulation of the world of materials, things, forms that the child finds about him, in order to make them subservient, instrumental, to carrying out some idea or thought of his; and the interest in expression, which might be said to be the interest in communicating an idea or feeling through a certain amount of construction, that is, through a certain amount of doing something. The interest of children in pictures, in little stories, and poems, which lie outside the scope of their own immediate experience, would come under what is meant here by expression.

[(d)]   The interest of inquiry is rather an aspect or an outgrowth of each one of these three interests, particularly that of communication. That is, while the child is an inquisitive being from the first, a question-asking being, it is hardly for the sake of what he finds out that he inquires; it is rather that his inquiry is one way of keeping up his interest in communication. If other things to talk about fail, he asks a few more questions and in that way keeps up the feeling of social relationship. The child like to ask questions and find out about things just as he like to tell stories, or call attention to what he has done, or as he likes to play with the objects that he finds around him; it makes simply an enlargement of his experience. Now the primary problem of instruction from this psychological standpoint is how to convert the interest in communication into an interest in inquiry. That is, the moment the child feels the need of following any special method or order in his communication or construction or expression, that moment he has begun really to inquire; there is something now which he must find out, not simply something to talk about, but something that he needs to find out in order to carry on the work in hand better. He cannot express the idea in picture the way he wants to without some assistance, without finding out more about things or the way of representing them. So with his construction; of course in his every day talking there are multitudes of things touched upon of which the child is largely ignorant, which lie outside his grasp, and with reference to which therefore gradual progress may be made in the way of utilizing his spontaneous inquires of a conversational nature so as to give them a more objective, scientific form, so as to carry over his interest in talking about things into an interest in really finding out something about the matters talked about.

[(2)(a)] Now the point, once more, is that in the earlier periods the basis of correlation, the focus of centralization, may be found simply in the natural interests of the child, particularly as they find outlet in these three ways: communication, making things with his hands, and expressing his ideas, musically, or through color, drawing, and so on; but then as inquiry, the interest in finding out really something about things and the ways of doing things, comes to the front; the child passes over gradually into the attitude of mind which should be characteristic of the later elementary period, when he has to find out about the method, the form, the ways of doing things, the ways of arranging material, the ways of getting questions answered, or the ways of finding out answers to the questions. In other words, his interest is transferred to the technique of communication and of construction and of expression, and gradually to the technique of inquiry itself. Numbers, figures, symbols, are of course themselves part of the technique of communication; they have no independent existence; they are simply conveniences to extend communication. The problem is then, that in the interest of the process of communication itself, the child shall be led to take interest in how communication is best carried on, and be made to realize the form of reading and writing and later on of grammar, all of it as a part of the process of communication, and as a necessary part in that it helps communication to extend its range and enrich its content.

[(b)] I think I have already called attention to the fact that in the Report of the Committee of Fifteen[2] it is stated that the larger part of the child's first three years in

[2 National Education Association, *Report of the Committee of Fifteen on Elementary Education* (New York: American Book Company, 1895).]

school must be taken up with learning the conventions, which I have called the technique of human intercourse, communication, and that it is important that the material for this should be material with which the child is already familiar, that the vocabulary should consist of words which refer to things, actions, and qualities, with which the child is already quite familiar, because then his attention is not distracted by having to grasp the new element of experience involved and can therefore give all his attention better to the form. I allude to that at this point to say that as a principle the exact statement would follow, if what is just laid down is correct, that instead of isolating the content of communication and the form, by taking familiar ideas so that the child can simply attend to the way in which they are expressed, the form and content should rather be bound up together as intrinsically as possible, that the child should use the whole, realizing the value of the form in giving him a new content, or in giving him a better hold on an old content, or to enable him to communicate his experience more permanently to others as can be done in writing as compared with oral conversation. There may be times when attention simply to form is given in the way of a game or play, in which the child will simply recognize forms which fit onto ideas which he is familiar with, but as a principle, it would be that the child must realize the modes of communication with reference to the substance of what is communicated, to be getting new ideas with new forms, and new forms along with his ideas.

Through the technique of construction and expression the child's informal work of the early period is transformed into what may be termed manual training and art, by putting construction and expression together. Just as all the language studies in the curriculum grow out of the primitive instinct of the child with regard to talking, making known his experiences and getting back the experiences of others, so all the various forms of manual training and art which are introduced into the school grow out of the simple interest of the child in doing things, making things, and telling things in a way which brings all the feeling, the force which the things have, into his own mind. So again, from the psychological side, the more formal study of history and science would grow out of the child's instinct in inquiry, considered as an outgrowth of communication, history enlarging his social experience, science, his experience of the world about him. The studies themselves will be taken up later on so I pass over that now and simply say that psychologically, the basis of correlation at this point is some felt need on the part of the child for a given fact or truth.

[(c)]   To contrast that again with the Herbartian correlation, say the question of correlating arithmetic: on one theory it is intended to correlate on the side of subject matter. As I suggested the other day, if you were studying in history the colonial times of Virginia, the arithmetic lessons would deal simply with materials in use then; they would be correlated with the history. Now on this other basis all the correlation we need is that the child shall feel the need, have some use for the arithmetical fact or truth. If he feels any demand on his own part, if he has some activity which he sees can be carried on better or further through the use of the numerical relations, then instruction will correlate itself intrinsically in his own mind to the rest of his intellectual attainments and habits. How far it will be desirable to make it on the same subject matter is simply a question of convenience of detail, or the insight of the teacher at the time. The child may get hold of the principle which he needs by its not having any particular relation with the subject matter which he has been studying. If the child already has the need, some motive supplied under certain circumstances, it could be best met perhaps by giving him a lesson in number pure and simple; but the correlation would still effect itself mentally, simply because the need which the child has and the motive for applying the fact constitute the most effective sort of a tie. The basis of the correlation is still found on the practical side. It is not in the direct instinct and impulse and habit as in the earlier period, but it is in the possibility of utilizing the new facts, truths, or ideas, so as to get enlargement of experience in some way or other.

The same way in teaching the technique of reading. If the child has felt the need of an ability to read, it is simply a matter of detail how far the reading lessons should be based upon something else which he has been studying. You get merely external correlation if that is all you get in teaching the reading. There may be external correlation without psychical correlation at all. All the child's reading lessons may be based on literature, history, or science lessons. On the other hand he may be given a separate lesson in reading by itself, and yet if he feels the relation of the power which he gains to the rest of his experience, he has the reality, although not the outward form of correlation. The main thing to secure intrinsic mental correlation, instead of being scattery or unrelated in miscellaneous heaps, is to see to it that the child feels the need for these things, and that he has the ability to apply them. It is the application which nails the correlation down. If any one uses the fact or truth, brings it to bear upon any other fact or truth, then those two things are intrinsically, internally bound together in his own mind; but there may be all the machinery and form of correlation and yet if there is no opportunity for application of the fact or truth, the mental movement toward totality and harmony will be imperfect at best.

LECTURE XXIV

March 2, 1899

[C.II.: *The various types of study—the significance of instincts and impulses.*]

[*III.C.3.d.*] The import of the recent lectures has been to reach in a somewhat roundabout way, the original proposition that the standard of values, the criterion for measuring educational values, is social; or that the unity for organizing both in the way of differentiating and correlating on the side of subject matter the various studies of the curriculum, is social. Or to repeat what was said earlier about the meaning of social, the statement would take this form: The criterion which measures the value of any subject, educationally considered, is the extent to which it contributes to socializing the consciousness, the experience of the child or youth, that socializing having the two aspects previously spoken of: one to render him more efficient as a social contributor or agent, and the other to enrich his own experience by making him appreciate, by making him feel the significance of the social elements and relations involved. The disciplinary value, so called, would ultimately then be the contribution made in a social way of the person educated. How far does it tend to give him the power, practical and intellectual and moral, to further in a more capable way the well being of the society of which he is a member? That would be simply the ultimate statement of disciplinary value. It would need to be translated over into mere details regarding what habits were formed, and what way those habits were used. But the conception which would unify these various details and make up the actual content of the idea of discipline would be that of increased efficiency in the direction of social agency.

The culture value means once more, primarily and fundamentally, this growth of consciousness as regards the social significance, the social meaning of experience. There is no proportion which can be stated between the extent of an act or of an experience, and the meaning which is capable of being crowded into it, or the meaning which it is capable of gathering up and concentrating in itself. An act measured in time terms, that is, by extent, by quantity, may occupy only five minutes or a day or a week, or whatever length of time you please to assign it, and so it may, as a matter of overt fact, cover a very small area of territory, and yet there may be a quality, a meaning to it which will go on indefinitely in space and time. So far as our experience is really organized, so far as it ceases to be a chaotic, fragmentary, unstable thing, just to that extent the meanings, the values of one experience become interchangeable with those of another. I mean by that, they enter into that so far as our lives are really organized. We carry into each new experience some element of value, some slight increment of meaning, or some coloring, some shading of significance out of a large area of our other experiences; and thus it is that subjects that are apparently very remote, the study of remote periods of history, languages of dead people, may, if approached and assimilated in the right way, really serve to socialize the significance of our present experience, to put more related meaning, perspective, horizon, into it, and give a freer and more flexible attitude, as well as a deeper one, to the whole experience. That is what we would mean in general by culture and value of any subject, this deepening of the quality of consciousness and experience, even if there is no quantity change in its space and time area.

            Having said so much in general by way of recapitula-
[D.]   tion, gathering up the earlier and later parts of the
            discussion of the last two weeks, I will go on to speak more specifically of the various types of study which make up the curriculum.

            The most fundamental, primary thing in life is of
[1.a.] course securing that mastery over the environment,
            (that control of forces and things about us) which maintains and carries on life. It is simply the most fundamental thing because without it, control of things and forces about us, there is no life; that must be secured as a precondition to all other values. That struggle for existence (that is,

the struggle for life, for the maintenance and development of life through adaptation of the environment to the needs of the living being), is recognized by modern biology as the animating spring, as the fundamental law of natural growth, natural evolution. Now when we have human consciousness, of course, that struggle does not cease. The attempt to master the environment, to adapt it to purposes, to ends of life, goes on. Through our consciousness of these ends, and through our more definite and more organized, more scientific consciousness of the world, of the medium in which we live, the form of the struggle changes tremendously. Mere physical strength, or mere sense evidence becomes of less importance, and intelligence, that is, a knowledge of ends that are realizable, and of the means by which they are realizable, becomes of tremendously greater importance when the struggle changes from the mere brute physical one, to a more rational, and in one sense, to an orderly one. But after all, the animating spring, and the fundamental law of human growth, as well as that of the animal, must be precisely that effort to maintain and to further, to expand life, through an ever increasing control of the environment.

[b.] Now that fact fixes, it seems to me, not simply the biological, but also the educational significance of the primary instincts and impulses with which human nature is endowed. There is a very strong, one might say absolute presumption, that any instinct or impulse which is now found in the human being is there because at some time or other it has been actually serviceable, it has been a positive help in dealing with the conditions about them, in maintaining and facilitating life. Of course it does not follow that because it has been serviceable it is now serviceable, or will be so in future conditions without any change or modification. There is a contrary presumption, one might say, that because it was originally evolved as a power, as a capacity in relation to different conditions, it will now need modification, it will need redirection, before it will be available. The significance of that presumption is strengthened by the fact that in any case all the equipment that we have got to deal with the conditions that now face us in our present and future environment is constituted by these instincts and impulses, either in their original or in a modified form. It is a question of using them or using nothing at all; they are all the powers, fundamentally, that we have, and hence once more, the radical significance of education as the process by which this primary equipment of impulses and instincts is made available with the least waste, with the greatest economy of time and effort, and with the maximum of return value for the conditions and situations of existing life.

[c.] Now that may seem a rather elaborate introduction to the consideration of the significance of the instincts and impulses, of making and doing, and of the studies that correspond to them in education, but after all I do not think we can get back to the root, to the basis of the significance of the studies that, roughly speaking, are ordinarily grouped under the head of manual training, without going back to the fundamental relation of these primary instincts to action. They are the root, psychologically, of the person. We must, by the necessity of the case, be first of all active, doing beings, and whatever we are in the way of feeling, or as emotional, aesthetic or moral beings, or whatever we are in the way of intellectual beings, must, if we go far enough back, grow out of and be related to this fact, that first of all we are more or less organized capacities for action, that we are primarily instincts and impulses to do, to act, to manipulate, to modify and adapt the conditions in which we find ourselves.

I should like to give an additional reference at this point, not given in the syllabus. In the *Atlantic Monthly*, beginning with the February number, Professor James of Harvard has begun the publication of various talks he has given to teachers on psychology.[1] Aside from the value which anything coming from Professor James would have on such a topic, it is particularly relevant at this point of the discussion, simply because of the fact that the thing which he emphasizes as fundamental is that the psychical being primarily is this equipment of tendencies in the way of motor instincts and impulses, and that this biological standpoint, as we may call it and as he calls it, really must be accepted as a fundamental one even in education.

[1 William James, "Talks to Teachers on Psychology," *Atlantic Monthly*, 83, February, 1899, pp. 155–162. This was the first of a four-part series, concluded as follows: *Atlantic Monthly*, March, 1899, pp. 320–329. *Atlantic Monthly*, April, 1899, pp. 510–517; *Atlantic Monthly*, May, 1899, pp. 617–626.]

There is another fact which so far I have not spoken
[d.(1)] of and which has very great importance from the
educational point of view—a point which at first
sight might seem to vitiate all which has already been said,
namely: that in the race-evolution these instincts and impulses
of an active practical sort have been evolved with reference
to practical stress, with reference to the struggle for existence,
while the first principle that we laid down about education was
that the child is, or should be, free from this struggle for existence. Now it might easily be inferred from that point, that
these instincts and impulses of this sort cannot possibly have
the significance educationally which they have had biolog-
ically. These powers, it may be said, had their origin and use
with reference to the actual stresses, the actual complications,
difficulties, of living. Now since our ideal is that the child
shall be free from these stresses and strains so far as possible,
in order to get a larger and more undisturbed growth, why
should we attach any great importance to this equipment of
practical instincts to make and to do?

Now that consideration is an exceedingly important
[(2)] one although I do not think the inference is the one
which I have hypothetically drawn. We must do
something with them because they are there; we cannot ignore
them. To ignore them would mean that they are not properly
trained and directed and that the factors that we do try to get
hold of we cannot get hold of in the most simple, easy, and
effective way. But the real significance of the point just made
is this, that in the child these instincts and impulses have
assumed the play form. They are there; they make up the natural equipment of the child; they make up his working capital,
the natural urgencies and motives that keep him going mentally and physically; but as just said they have not the same
immediate practical end to serve which they have had in the
race. They have become in a certain sense typical, or symbolic,
or a phrase that would be less likely to misapprehension, "they
have become free," they now can operate simply with reference
to contributing to the development of the child, to the development of personality, of character and conduct, instead of having to operate with reference to meeting the specific utilitarian
and practical ends with reference to which they originally
manifested themselves.

Take one example from Mr. James. He speaks of the large place occupied in the make-up of the average human being by the instinct which he terms "pugnacity," the tendency to fight, and he points out the evolutionary importance of this in a series of people who had to struggle for existence, make their own way against obstacles, so that the assumption of a certain antagonistic attitude, not being discouraged, gathering themselves together to make headway, was to them a very important tendency which required development.[2] It is still here in our make-up.

[(a)]   Now to illustrate the point which I had in mind (I do not mean that Mr. James is responsible for this application), what are you going to do with that instinct or impulse? It is important to recognize that it has been set free from its original practical importance. That is, the child does not have, or should not have, to meet the world alone with only his own resources to fall back upon, he should not have to call his pugnacious instincts into activity for the purpose of getting ahead, but they are there, and having been freed from this practical end makes them more available for educational ends. The problem now is to get hold of that instinct of pugnacity and use it in the development of the child's character in such a way that it will be transformed into a habit of willingness to face obstacles and overcome them; not because he needs to do this for the sake of keeping alive, for the sake of getting bread and butter and getting a living, but on account of the part which it plays in the enrichment of experience itself, this willingness to meet and overcome obstacles, to put forth effort. First the natural and then the spiritual; and the reason that the natural can become spiritualized, can become idealized, that these traits which from one point of view are simply animal, can become working forces in moral and intellectual development, is precisely that they have lost their original, immediate practical significance, that they exist in the child in the play form, that is, having their meaning with reference to their own exercise and not with reference to any ends or aims outside themselves. In the child then, these instincts and impulses have become available simply for the sake of getting increase in experience itself, and simply for the sake of enlargement of power

[2 William James, "Talks to Teachers on Psychology," *Atlantic Monthly*, 83, March, 1899, p. 327.]

in the organization of habit. It is pretty safe to say that the animal did not originally cultivate these dawning capacities for the sake of any aesthetic or moral end. It was simply a case of necessity; do that or die. But through the prolongation of the period of infancy, the period of dependence upon others, being freed from that practical stress, they are usable simply for the increase of experience itself, and that determines the point of view from which they should be treated educationally.

[(b)] Take one simple illustration from actual manual training. One of the chief ideas of the Sloyd system of manual training is that the child shall make useful objects, and as the system was worked out in Sweden a series of exercises were given which among other things resulted in the production of objects actually usable in the homes of the children who made them.* Great stress is laid by that system of manual training upon the fact that objects made should be usable. Now can we measure that simple proposition by the principle just laid down? It seems to me we can. So far as that use, that utility, is an external thing, so far as the child does make the object definitely for the sake of the use which is to be made of the object, so far the right value of the making impulse of the child is being violated and not really taken advantage of educationally. He is being forced into the attitude, forced to take the point of view which he had better not take until he is older, and which he cannot now take without cramping, restricting his own growth. Now if you should argue that the child should make useful things it would not follow, but it might be better for him to make useful things. If the useful thing means more to the child; if it gathers more content into itself; if more imagery clusters about it; if it holds his attention more closely than making useless things, then by all odds he should make useful things, not for the sake of their use, but simply because the knowledge of that fact on his part puts more meaning into those things. If the making of a plaything or toy would call out more of the child's industry, more of his constructive imagination, more of his persistent attention, why, under those circumstances the plaything would be the better object to make. In other words, whether the plaything

[* See, for example: J. D. Walters, "Ways, Means, and Maxims in Manual Training," in National Education Association, *Journal of Proceedings and Addresses,* 1889 (Topeka: Kansas Publishing House, 1889), pp. 621–628.]

or the useful object is to be made, is a question of detail. Which under the circumstances will mean the most to the child, which will get the most value into itself, and so contribute most to the growth of the child's consciousness? About all you can say is that in the early period the doing of the thing for the mere skill, the doing it for exercise, making joints which do not enter into either playthings or useful objects, will not mean as much to him as if he made an actual object that somehow does enter into his real experience. That is a somewhat commonplace, but possibly all the better illustration of what I mean by freeing these instincts which originally had a utilitarian value, a biological value, to make them serviceable simply for growth, growth of consciousness, growth of power, not for the sake of doing things that are really immediately necessary to be done, but for the sake of the growth and the gain in power itself. An over-utilitarian point of view defeats itself. It is not so useful, it is not so practical, because it limits the child to the present instead of enlarging his capital, his equipment for future use. On the other hand, just because useful things are familiar to the child, because they do already play a part in his life, they may have a greater value for him for purposes of growth than mere useless things, or mere exercise things, would present.

           There is one other point which goes with this freeing
[(3)] of the instincts from the practical stress which they
           are under in the race, and that is, in being free they become also more social. That is, the child does things more with reference to the attitude which other people are going to take, and less with immediate practical success: the desire of the child for approval, that is, for recognition, for having his work passed on and confirmed by others; pugnacity in the sense of competitive instincts, rivalry, measuring what one does by others; imitation, not simply about the way of doing things better, but of putting one's self into sympathetic relationships with others. All these are examples of what I mean by the impulse and instinct getting a more social coloring. While we do not know definitely about it, it is at least conceivable that with the animal the social element in what he does is simply a means to greater practical efficiency, or a means to the maintenance of life, so that strictly speaking, there is no ethical element in it at all; but certainly the human being ordinarily

measures what he does, and his capacity to do, more from the unconscious and conscious attitude which others take to what he does, than he does from the standpoint of objective and overt success. It does not make so much difference to the child whether what he does hits the mark externally, as whether it will call out the approbation and encouragement and stimulation of others. That is possible only because the instinct has been freed from its immediate practical significance and so in this way that fact becomes the fundamental for giving greater ethical, spiritual meaning to the expression of these instincts on the part of the child.

LECTURE XXV

March 8, 1899

[C.II.: *Manual training (direct experience in constructive activities).*]

[*III.D.2.a.*] In taking up the educational equivalents of the activities discussed at the last lecture, we were embarrassed at the outset by the fact that there is no good name by which to single out and sum up this educational counterpart. It is obvious that the term "manual training" is altogether too limited in its scope to carry with it all that meant. That term, "manual training," suggests simply one form of education, education either of or through the manual activities, and while that is a valuable part of education, it is quite different from the consideration of a fundamental standpoint and method in all education, and that was what we had in mind the other day. It is not however, merely a matter of the name; it is a matter of fact also that the reasons upon which manual training has been introduced into the schools, the reasons for justifying its introduction, are inadequate and one sided. Of course it is a great deal better to do a good thing and give a poor reason for it than not to do it all, or to do a bad thing and give very good reasons for it, but after all the reasons that have been given indicate that upon the whole, in the past manual training has been conceived in a supplementary and in a technical way.

[(*1*)] By calling it supplementary I mean that it has been introduced simply as one line of study along with others, just annexed, externally attached, to the others, not involving any qualitative change, reconstruction of the other subjects, and not involving any organic connection anywhere along the line. It has simply been that the entire education was of a too bookish character, did not meet the child's whole nature, or the demands of society, and therefore this line of studies was put in and so we have had manual training schools, and manual training courses in school, or at most the introduction of a certain amount of manual work externally added on to the rest of the work. That is very different from realizing the significance of what is involved there as a standpoint of experience itself. It is a very different thing from realizing the part that has been played historically by the practical activities of man, or that can be played by the instincts and impulses in the child, which are the psychological counterpart of these activities in the race.

[(2)] By saying that the reasons given have largely been technical, I mean that one of the main grounds upon which it has been urged is the professional, trade, or utilitarian idea that persons who have had training of this sort were more likely to be capable of earning their living, and not being burdensome to society than those who have not had it. The principle has found embodiment in some of the manual training high schools whose main object is preparation for trades, and the emphasis is thrown from the first upon doing things which will have a certain commercial value or lend themselves easily to purposes of the market. Those who are acquainted with the recent history of manual training know that that was the idea prevailing in this country until the Centennial Exposition when the Russian exhibitions of the technical schools revealed that they were based upon the exercise idea rather than upon the commercial idea, that is, having the students perform certain exercises resulting in the mastery of certain tools and processes, quite independent of any commercial utility in the products themselves. In fact most of the exercises were of such a nature that the products were not final wholes, and so could not, by the necessity of the case, have any practical value. That plan was introduced into the technical schools, and then found its way into the high schools of the country. That did not do away with the utilitarian conception however, it simply meant that on the whole it paid better in the long run to have students go through a certain amount of preparatory work in gaining skill and knowledge, than to put them at once upon the making of articles which could be sold in the market; so that while the immediate utilitarian reference was taken away, still the whole controlling idea was preparation for professional life along these technical lines. Of course it is the business of professional schools (these higher schools) to train engineers, etc., and I am not saying anything against them as a part of the higher education, and it certainly is indirectly, if not directly, a part of the claim which can justly be made by every school system, that it should prepare persons for useful lives, that is, that it should result in the possession of power on their part to earn their own living in an intelligent, orderly and effective way. But that spirit, that factor of the educational process, cannot be emphasized, cannot be exaggerated so as to regard it as the chief or predominating aim of any one group of studies, like the manual training studies, without resulting in the introduction of a somewhat illiberal spirit, and forcing the studies themselves into a one-sided position.

If the manual training work has any generic significance for education, it must be found in its developmental value, in the fact that it means something in the growth of experience and the enrichment of experience, which cannot be obtained in any other way. And so, while the reasons given have done a very good work in making an entering wedge for this line of work in the schools, still perhaps these reasons which are inadequate, are more serviceable under the conditions than better reasons would have been, and these studies when introduced have done more things than was originally expected. But the time would seem to be ripe now for putting the studies on a strictly educational basis, both in practice and in theory, putting them on exactly the same basis as geography, arithmetic, or history, when one asks what is their intrinsic significance in reference to growth, what part do they play, and how do they play it? The phrase "constructive work," which is coming into use especially for this work in elementary training, also expresses one phase or aspect of their value.

      I come back to the statement that we are somewhat
[b.]   embarrassed by the lack of any term that is at once
      comprehensive and definite in connection with this line of interests. We must go back to a somewhat cumbrous phrase of "direct experience" in order to indicate the importance which attaches to this line of work, that is, that they represent the direct, first hand putting forth of instincts, impulses, and powers, in order to get results of value which have

their immediate significance in experience and are pursued therefore, not simply for the sake of learning something else, but for the sake of what there is in them as experiences themselves. Construction is a very important part of that, but it is far from being the whole of it.

[c.(1)] Without respect to the name, I think it may be said that most of the objections that have been urged to this line of study disappear the moment they are defended, not on technical grounds, but on general grounds. As long as they are defended simply on technical grounds, the answer is easy that it is no part of the common schools' work to make seamstresses, mechanics, or cooks. It is the business of the common schools to turn out good citizens, or more generally yet, good men and women. There are other objections which practically all come back to this same one, that is, they all follow from regarding manual training in too technical a way, but which may be briefly mentioned. It is sometimes stated that this phase of experience can be adequately cared for outside of the school, that the child's home and neighborhood life present to him all the materials desirable in this direction, and that it is the business of the school to supplement, to do what the outside life cannot do, to introduce the child to books, and to methods of the intelligent use of books. There may have been a time when that, in a large measure, was true, that is, when it was convenient as a division of labor to have the home life tend mainly to one side of the education of the child and the school to another aspect of the education. There may be still large portions of the country where that is true, particularly in the rural districts, and in places where factory labor has not reached a high point of development; but in the urban districts, which we all know are rapidly gaining at the expense of the others, the statement that this division of labor can be actually attained, is practically totally erroneous. There is a school principal in this city who sent word to one of the superintendents who was interested in the construction work, that that sort of work might be very necessary in the portions of the city where the children were better off, and had no practical education at home; it might be useful to them, but in the poorer parts the children got all that was necessary in that line at home and it was not desirable to duplicate it in the school and he requested the children to bring things made by them outside of the school as an illustration of his point. Articles were brought in large quantities most of which were pieces of clothing. The other person, somewhat skeptical, asked the children where they learned this, and with two exceptions they replied: "At Mission School." The experiment did not reach the conclusion expected. That is one instance, but it is fairly typical of what obtains in city life, and of the great gap already introduced between the theoretical or intellectual, and the practical, active sides of our nature.

[(2)] There is another reason however, which is more fundamental which may be given for questioning the idea of the whole division of labor anywhere. It is suggested by what has been said: it tends to perpetuate the separation between theory and practice, between the intellectual and the active. If all of one sort of work is carried on in one place, and all of the other in another place, that is, one in the home and the other in the school, without any positive and systematic attempt to make the cross relations between the two, it is practically certain that the child does not get the full educational significance of the practical industrial work that he does at home, and that he does not get the full ethical and applied significance of the theoretical work that he does in the school. It might be said that the thing of fundamental importance is that all should get the culture value, that is, the significance for growth, as regards the enrichment of consciousness, out of their every day work. Now persons may get very good training from a practical point of view in work, from very orderly and industrious habits, and become skillful, and yet get no reflex of that in their consciousness; they may get no sense or feeling at all of the values that are engaged in what they are doing. Those things remain almost automatic, largely mechanical, and are carried on because they have to be carried on, or because they have been taught to do those things.

I need not dwell on the other side: that if the school work is confined to the presentation of ideas, the application of those ideas to the life, the consideration of getting the dynamic expression of the principle learned will be very haphazard and inadequate if it is left to what goes on outside of the school. So whatever point of view we look at it from, it will still remain true that both sides, the theoretical and practical, ought to be

presented in the school in order that one may pass easily and
flexibly into the other. Just what I mean in detail by that will
come out better later on. The great majority of people are for
the greater part of their lives actually taken up with the nec-
essaries of living, either directly or indirectly. Now if their
education has not been of a character to bring out the content
involved in those occupations, to bring out the knowledge of
materials and processes and relationships involved, they might
practically as well never had any education so far as the great
bulk of their daily occupations are concerned. I am not speaking now of the highly educated classes—that is, the learned
professions as they are called—but the great bulk of men and
women. Their education under those circumstances has relevancy to the leisure moments of their lives simply, the hours
that they can get off from their work and sit and read, or go
to lectures, or discuss intellectual topics. Their daily occupations remain of necessity narrow and unilluminated by any
penetration into their deeper meanings and relationships just
because everything that has anything to do with that has been
shoved to one side in their education. Now educational systems are conducted, and educational treatises are written by
the people who have had the specialized training, who are not
engaged in the more immediate stress of work to get a living.
All their activities are more or less saturated with intellectual
content by the nature of the case, and there is then this tremendous tendency to overlook the very different conditions
that they are in from what the great mass of mankind are in
who are still engaged in occupations which require, to some
extent, for a great portion of the day, the actual use of their
hands and the actual contact with material things. I said earlier in the course that our education was still highly specialized, and this is what I meant by that statement. It has not
actually as yet taken into account the necessity that the great
bulk of persons should get their education in such a way as
to give more meaning to what they are actually doing from
day to day.

      There are certain other social aspects. The necessity
[(3)] of having sympathy with labor, of doing enough ac-
        tual work with one's hands so as to know what it
means, and appreciate better the lives of those that are thus
engaged, perhaps need only be barely mentioned here. The

growth of the division of labor, the fact that every one is getting further and further from the processes which actually determine and make up the things which they have to do, would however, be called attention to. For all that most of us, at least most so called educated people, know about the nature of things that are all about them, they might as well be produced by the rubbing of Aladdin's lamp, so far as the knowledge, insight, or sympathy they have with the actual work, and with the actual intellectual inventions and activities which lie back of them are concerned. We simply go to the store and get everything ready made. It is simply an exchange of so much money for these products. A few centuries ago these products were staring everybody in the face; they were produced in our grandmother's household, or in shops so close that people could not help knowing about them. The fact that these things are so far away from our daily lives, that we have so little to do with them, is all the more reason why typical processes which sum up, which represent the principles and factors involved, should be presented to us in education. Please note that I say "typical." It is a good thing for mankind as a whole to have got away from such intimate contact with those processes. It makes for leisure, civilization, life. We have these things accumulated in great factories, and we would not want to have to go back to the hand to hand wrestling with these things, but it is important that something which represents the relationships involved, should become known to everybody, because it is on these things, after all, that our lives depend, and there is no use in trying to erect a superstructure of culture upon a foundation of complete ignorance and lack of sympathy to what is fundamental to life itself.

        That suggests the other chief reason for this line of
[(4)] study. The one dwelt on so far has been the psychological one; that is, that this sort of activities represents most easily and naturally the instinctive attitude of the child that is most in line with the sort of activities and interests which make up his every day life, and that these activities lend themselves to development, being carried further in ways that will result in accretions of experience. But the social aspect of the argument is that these activities represent in typical forms the processes which underlie all civilization, the processes by which civilization has been made to be what it is, by

LECTURE XXV 253

which it is maintained, and by which it will be carried further. Socially below all other modes of action and of experience, are the industrial ones, the economic ones, and until they are somehow adequately represented in typical forms in the school, all the other studies are pretty sure to be out of their just social respective.

I will speak very briefly of some of these connections. [d.(1)(a)]First science. Now the genetic motive for science, as I have intimated before, is precisely in relationship to man's economic necessities and occupations. The point of view first most definitely brought to consciousness by Francis Bacon in saying that knowledge was power and insisting upon regular methods of knowing nature about us in order that we may control nature, that point of view I say, thus brought to consciousness by Bacon, has really been the animating force which has kept alive and kept going what would otherwise have been a simple idle curiosity concerning the world about us. Knowledge of the materials, the things involved in practical action, and of the processes, physical and chemical and so on, by which those materials may be best handled in order to bring about the desired results—this knowledge of materials and processes has constituted the historical backbone of scientific development. If we compare the life of man today with its comparative certainty and assurance, its mechanics and tools, its command over all kinds of natural resources, mineral, animal, and vegetable, to say nothing of the command of modes of energy like heat and electricity, if we compare that with the life of savage man, precarious, uncertain, dominated by the environment instead of mastering it, and ask what has made the difference, there is but one answer. This difference is due to science; that is, to increasing knowledge of the environment and of its forces which has enabled us to use them. We cannot use them excepting as we do know them, and when we know them we cannot help using them.

Now as to the counterpart of that point on the edu-
[(b)] cational side, I would say that while of course the literal steps which have been taken by the race in gaining additional knowledge in connection with the practical struggle to control the environment are not to be repeated by the child, it is a great gain that the same motive which was at work, the same connection between theory and practice,

between knowledge and its application that has been at work in the race, should also be active in the child. That is, when this manual training work is introduced in its proper educational relations, it means that the main, the exclusive stress, shall not be simply upon doing certain things and making certain products, but that the doing of these things and the making of these products shall be accompanied at every step with close attention to the materials used, and the knowledge of the processes, not merely as so many practical details, but in the principles and laws involved in them. In other words, this constructive work affords an almost unrivaled opportunity for a natural and easy introduction to scientific materials and principles. Not that they are technically scientific at this period, but that later on, when systematized and arranged in a formulated way, they become scientific.

I will endeavor to illustrate that point somewhat. [(i)] Take mathematics. It is very clear that few of these constructive activities can be carried on without recourse to measurements in some form or other, and without involving practical and intimate acquaintance with solids and surfaces and lines. They involve contact with quantitative ideas and relations, and can be carried on with sureness and success only as those quantitative relations involved are consciously defined and made exact. The knowledge of the space forms and of arithmetic, of number as a mode of defining these space forms, is an indispensable instrument to any successful pursuit of this constructive work. Now if this work is conceived in the technical spirit, the utilitarian spirit, of course the instructors will not utilize this mathematical aspect any more than is immediately necessary. It will be treated as a purely practical tool, it will be subordinated to just getting the result; but if the justification of the work is regarded as strictly educational, and not in any final practical or professional outcome, then the full significance of these mathematical relations will be apprehended, and pains will be taken to see that they are brought adequately to consciousness. They are brought to consciousness on their own account commonly, and not as mere instruments for doing better work with the hands. There has been a good deal of misapprehension as to what was meant by concrete work in arithmetic in the schools. A good many new methods for teaching elementary arithmetic have been conceived on the supposition that all you have to do to make number relations concrete is to introduce things, shoe pegs, or little blocks of wood, or anything that will serve conveniently the purpose of the teacher, and if the number relations are only taught in connection with these things, the relations themselves become concrete. There could be no greater psychological fallacy than that. Concreteness is a matter of relationship to experience, and an idea does not necessarily become more concrete because it is presented with a material object. It is simply a real relationship between the idea and the object. If the idea is embodied in the object, the idea becomes concrete, but if there is no natural relationship between the numerical idea and the material thing, you simply have an external tying of two things together. The bearing of that remark at this point is that the use of numerical and geometrical considerations in connection with doing work, with the reaching of ends, results that one wants to reach, is really concrete. The relationship between the thought and the thing handled is an intrinsic one. It is not a matter of making up stories or imagining fictions regarding the material or forming pure external relations between the numerical relations and the things which are manipulated. The idea comes in as a necessary method in enabling one to deal intelligently with the things at hand, and so is really concrete.

 # LECTURE XXVI

March 9, 1899

[C.II.: *History*.]

I was speaking yesterday of the connection [*III.D.2.d.(1)(b)(ii)*] or correlation between the constructive, manual work, with science work, and had begun with a few general illustrations. Physics comes in wherever of course, the use of tools or mechanical appliances is involved, or wherever there is a question of the application of energy, force, to bring about some definite result. Chemistry comes in wherever there is the application of any physical energy in such a way as to change the quality of the materials used. Carpentry, wood work with tools, is clearly a case where not only numerical and geometrical considerations are involved, but physical and mechanical principles also. Cooking, so far as it is understood at present at all, with the application of forces, particularly of water and heat to various substances to bring about changes in them, evidently involves chemical principles, and an educational conduct of such work, as distinct from a utilitarian one, would involve calling attention to these chemical facts. The facts, the principles, are all there, and it is simply a question of whether they are utilized or not. If the course is conceived as having for its main object to make cooks, or even to make children more helpful at home, the strictly practical side of it, the formation of certain manual habits, would be the important thing; but the moment it is conceived as strictly an educational resource, the whole point of view changes, and it becomes largely, from the intellectual standpoint, experimental work in applied chemistry. On the other side is the connection with physiology, the necessity and significance of the changes in food materials in order to adapt them to more ready and more effective assimilation by the human system.

There is however, in all these studies, the opportunity not only for the study of forces and processes and principles, but also of the empirical, fact side. The varieties of wood which are used in the wood work, the materials which are used in cooking and in sewing, take us back to animal and vegetable life and afford natural centers for curiosity and for inquiry into the facts of the origin and the study of the plants and animals for instance, from which the textile fibers are got—cotton, wool and silk. In the foods, the study of the plants in which the various foods originate, the knowledge of the food capacity or value of the various plants, the food elements, like starch, etc., and how they came to be in the plants and what the significance; all of this gives the possibility for a considerable range of botanical facts. The geographical side is so evident that it need only be mentioned. The question of the origin of all the materials used, where the plants grow, where the animals are found from which various products utilized are obtained, where the trees grow, and also of the various processes by which these materials are made ready for the market, the lines of their distribution and commercial exchange. All those considerations are extremely pertinent and relevant the moment these studies are regarded strictly from the standpoint of their connection with education, of what they contribute to growth of consciousness and experience, and not merely as additional practical devices.

While I shall speak later on of history, I will men-
[(2)(a)] tion here that all this sort of work has its obvious historical side which is of very extreme importance, namely: the knowledge of the growth of inventions, acquaintance with the primitive processes of agriculture and getting the foods, of primitive tools, mechanical devices, of primitive modes of transportation, commercial exchange, and the original way of making cloth, preparing of the various fabrics and fibers, adapting them to the purposes of clothing, carpeting, and so on; and then the history of the gradual progress in the mastery of man over these materials, in using them on a larger and larger scale and more skillfully and economically.

That history is a double history. On one side it is an external social history, the history of industrial society reduced to its simplest elements, and as the industrial phase of society and industrial problems get more and more prominent, it is certain that industrial history is going to play a larger part as compared with the older political and dynastic history, or even with the newer type of history where more attention is paid to general social development. Then this is also a history of the intellectual development of man and thus is connected with the history of science. It gives us the evolution of practical intelligence, the evolution of intelligence as concretely used with reference to the problems of life and of the environment, and the successive steps which have been taken to overcome the difficulties that present themselves, and in securing a continually better adaptation of means to ends, and also an increasing enlargement of the ends themselves.

There is one point which without controversy is desirable: that the child should recapitulate the progress of the race, that he should go back of present conditions where everything seems to be given, almost without the exercise of intelligence, except in making adjustments of detail, should get himself back in his imagination to the primitive condition of man, face to face with brute nature, with almost no resources to fall back upon, and then follow in his constructive imagination the typical steps by which man has seized upon the salient points in the situation, upon the critical problems, and has evolved devices, has made inventions which have served those difficulties, and which have given the practical momentum onward in civilization. That successive statement of these problems, and the successive solutions of them, even if only in imagination connected with such hand work as suffices to make concrete that imagination, is of much more importance than the simple historical knowledge gained. It requires the child to recapitulate in himself the occasions which have made the race think, and makes him appreciate in terms of his own experience, the sort of thinking that had actually to be done, with the motives for it on one side, and the results that were reached by it on the other side.

I will go on now to history in a more general sense, [3.*a*.(*1*)] not simply as more or less directly correlated with the constructive activities, in which sense I have been speaking of it, but regarding its educational value in general. I wish to emphasize however, the point of connection by restating that the fundamental history of man, the backbone of history by the necessity of the case, is the industrial and eco-

nomic aspect. While it is the flower and the fruit of civilization that most naturally attracts us, the development in literature and science and art, and in better social organization, this
is after all simply the flower and fruit. The roots of the historical development go back to the relationship that exists between
man and his natural environment, and the steps which man
has taken to enable him to bring the environment under control, to subjugate it to ends; and the history which throws the
main emphasis upon simply the fruitage cannot be scientific,
because it is dealing all the time with results, and science involves something more than even a very large and intelligent
inventory and survey of results; it involves knowledge on the
causal side, on the force side, on the dynamic side.

      Now when we come back to the force side, to the
[(2)]   motor factors which have made history what it has
      been, we come always in the last analysis to the in-
dustrial side, to the question of how man has got hold of nature
and has manipulated and administered it for the satisfaction
of human needs and for the development of human power. An
intelligent and orderly insight on that side does for the mind
exactly what knowledge of physical forces does on the side
of natural science. It is very interesting and very important to
know the phenomena of nature on the descriptive side: stones,
plants, animals; but after all the largest possible acquaintance
and amassing of knowledge on that side, a descriptive acquaintance, and even of the systematic arrangement of the obvious,
overt facts, is not science. It is only when we can state it with
reference to the forces which are at work, when we see the
rigid facts as the outcome of processes, when we see how they
were made and came to be what they are, and get it over from
terms of products into processes, that our attitude is scientific.
The same is true of history. I do not say that it should be scientific in the same sense, but simply that the mental attitude,
which is the reality of science for educational purposes, must
be the same in the two, the going back from the more obvious,
external facts, to the consideration of forces. Now without
ignoring the great part which political administration, modes
of legal administration, and military organization have had
as determining forces, without denying that they are really
forces, I mean simply that after all, there are other forces still
back of them; that there are the industrial fabrics, the indus-

trial powers of the people, the way in which they lived, which represent considerations which are more fundamental to these other forms of institutional development. They are in reality crystalizations, precipitations of things which go back to the economic aspects.

[(3)] That point of view has been presented by a certain school of historians as a purely materialistic view; a certain school of German writers in particular, who emphasized this point have connected it with the materialistic philosophy—but that is purely a personal reaction, a purely factitious addition. All that really is involved in it is that we get a simpler view of historical development, a view where the forces are reduced to their lowest terms and more easily grasped and presented to the imagination, when we carry it back to the question of the struggle of man with the particular natural forces about him—climatic and geographical conditions—and the way in which he has learned gradually to utilize those things. It is simply that instead of taking things from the standpoint of ends or results, we should take them from the standpoint of the means which have been instrumental in bringing about the ends. It would be folly to deny the existence of the ends, to deny the reality and greater value ultimately of the spiritual products which has finally grown out of this greater control of man over nature.

[b.] On the psychological side, repeating what has been said before, the advantage of emphasizing this aspect of history is that it does appeal to, and utilize, the main lines of the child's immediate interests. The child's interest in government is not intense, his interest in institutions as institutions, is not intense. He may be easily interested in wars and battles, but it is in the sensational aspects, the emotional, or at very best the moral aspects of heroism, etc., which is of interest in the battles. But the child's interest in the way people live, and how and why they lived as they did, what kind of houses they had, what kind of clothes they wore and how they did business—that interest is endless and ceaseless provided monotony is avoided and the material is so presented that the child has his horizon, his consciousness of life expanded. So much then for the point of connection with history. That does not mean that history is to be correlated in the narrow sense with constructive work. It means that the historical development side in the constructive work is to be brought out, and that the similar standpoint is to be utilized wherever possible in the historical work; but it does not mean that all the history taught shall be in any narrow sense directly correlated with this other work.

[c.] Going back to our fundamental standard of value, that is, the social one, the significance of history must be found in what it contributes to an understanding of social life, that is, the socializing of consciousness. This at once fixes the principle that history is studied not for the sake of history, considered as a record of something that has happened.

[(1)] Perhaps to put it in a way that would mean a little more, history must be studied as indirect sociology, not using sociology in a technical sense, but simply as meaning that the real center of interest all the time must be the getting of a better insight into social conditions, modes of social life and social relationships, and a growing consciousness of the forces which determine social structure and which effect social changes. Of course I am not pretending to say that the scientific historian should, or should not, write history from this point of view. I am simply saying that the claim of an educational value for history must be made along the line of its giving a larger insight into, and deeper appreciation of, social forces.

[(2)(a)] Now if the question is asked, why should we get this in this indirect way, in this apparently round-about way, through history, instead of getting it direct, of course, part of the answer is the one which is on everybody's lips now-a-days: namely, that the roots of the present are in the past, and that no one can understand the present unless he understands it as the outcome of what has gone before. As is frequently pointed out now, all the sciences are getting more historical in their method. The whole attitude of science is historical. The doctrine of evolution itself is the application of the historical point of view to the world at large; one might even say that mathematics is becoming more historical. We define circles and triangles from the standpoint of the process of their generation, and not as used to be done, from the standpoint of the final result or fixed form; and so to know what society really is, we have to get it in the process of its making, and that throws us over at once to the historical side. Any other knowledge would be simply descriptive, simply a massing together of the facts preliminary to explaining and understanding them. That point I think, is thoroughly well taken.

[(b)]   To put it a little differently to bring out more the educational side of it, the difficulty with studying society direct, is that it is so complex and so very close to us. That latter point of course is even truer of the child than it is of the adult. Society, that is the social relations which the child has around him, are the child. He cannot tear them loose from himself, nor himself away from them. It requires a highly trained adult to do it with any success, it touches our feelings, interests, at every point, and to get an objective view of the thing is a matter of great difficulty. The historical view, in the first place, simplifies the social study; it reduces it to a number of simpler elements and forces; and in the second place it eliminates this element of too great personal contiguity, of too great personal attachment and interest. What I mean may be indicated by the difficulty which adults have of taking an unbiased view of the tariff and silver questions, things which are involved in the working of social forces at present, and also the difficulty we have of getting an unprejudiced view of the history of our own country. If you consider how far the principle involved goes you will see the immense difficulty there would be for children in getting any very thorough-going idea of society by attempting to study it chiefly in its present organization and working. The thing is too complex, there is no way to break into it. Where shall you begin? What will you pick out, what leave? It is all so bound up together that there is no apparent way of unravelling it at all. It is not only all interwoven in itself, but with us, our expectations, preferences, ways of seeing and feeling things.

[(c)]   The history then, in giving us an indirect and a remote view of social life, first simplifies it and then enables us to look at it through the other end of the telescope, as it were. It literally projects it, it gets it off where we can look at it, see it, insead of simply feeling it in its relation to ourselves. I should like to repeat here what I said the other day in speaking of the culture epoch theory—the great thing is to work back and forth. The ultimate object of history is to

give us a better understanding of the relations of social life,
and therefore we must start from, and wherever possible come
back to, social life as it is about us. Whatever gain is found
in simplification must be applied to the better analysis and
mental survey of existing social life.

[d.] The value of history as a picturesque and dramatic
presentation, while very important, is I think secondary to the considerations just mentioned. It is
picturesque and dramatic in the first place, because it is social,
because it deals with the same kind of forces and aims which
are at work now and which we are trying to realize now. It
could not have the hold on us that it does have unless we felt
that the situations described are in type like those which we
are ourselves experiencing, that it is a matter of accident that
we live now instead of then. It depends upon an underlying
identification of ourselves with what is presented in history
and it is that which gives the picturesque and dramatic significance, while those elements come out more clearly because
of the simplified, reduced view which we get when we take
things historically. The value of primitive history is in simply
reducing everything to its simplest elements; it gives us the
problem of society in its lowest and fewest terms, and therefore
in a way most easily grasped, particularly by the imagination
of the child. The value of the history of our own country, the
strictly educational value, is that it makes the connection with
present social life much more obvious and more intimate, while
at the same time projecting it sufficiently backward so that
we get out of the immediate stress of the situation and can see
it from the more objective view. The value of the history of
other nations, particularly Greece and Rome, is from the exactly opposite standpoint, getting a still more remote view,
getting a view of a society and civilization whose strong points
were very different from ours, and whose weak points were
also very different from ours. In Greece we have an example of
highly aesthetic and artistic civilization on a small scale and
on which we should consider a very slender and inadequate
material basis. The point in making out the curriculum in history would be to maintain a sufficient balance between the two
points of view, that is, the study of what we feel to be somehow our own, and the study of that which we feel rather is for-

eign, is away from us. It would be of course a mistake to emphasize the latter at the expense of the former, but it would also be a mistake to dwell simply on that which is our own at the expense of this more remote view of what on the surface of it is very different from ourselves.

LECTURE XXVII

March 16, 1899

[C.II.: *History: general pedagogical principles.*]

[III.D.3.e.(1)] The general point of view for considering history and its value as presented at the last hour was with regard to insight into the social forces and the processes by which they result in social structure and the social relationships which are carried out to various forms of social structure. On the pedagogical side one of the chief problems that presents itself is to secure the adequate simplification of the material, to reduce the enormous complexity of detail, constituting our actual historical knowledge, in such a way that it would be capable of assimilation, and yet retain its salient points and be true to its essential spirit.

[(a)] A view which has been advocated a great deal in order to secure this simplification, particularly from the standpoint of elementary education, is what might be called the biographical and story view—the fact that history, at least for the elementary period, should be taught mainly in the form of biographies of great historical character heroes and leaders, and through the medium of anecdotes and stories associated with those great characters.

There is another point of view which goes to the opposite extreme which has not commended itself to as many persons, but has been quite thoroughly worked out in certain places. It is that history should center about institutions. In a normal school in Michigan a course has been worked out on that basis. The idea is that by taking the family in various parts of the country, or some other social form, and by having the child become acquainted with it as it existed in different ages and countries, a systematic view of society as a whole can be gradually built up. On the face of it the latter view would seem to

come nearer the standard presented, namely, history taught
from the institutional point of view; but the question presents
itself whether that is not too analytic to recommend itself for
elementary education, however it might be for a later period.

It is obvious that in these two points of view we have
[(*b*)]   fundamentally the same problem which has presented itself so many times before—the individualistic view on one side, and the socialistic on the other. Teaching
history through the medium of biography represents the individualistic side, and through the institutions represents the
social side. However, there is no need to present either standpoint in such an extreme way as to bring it into opposition to
the other. The biographical standpoint may be taken in such
a way as to reduce history to a number of interesting stories
about great men, practically eliminating the element of growth,
of continuity, and development, putting all these men on the
same level practically, and taking them out of the relationship
to their times, teaching simply from the standpoint of the
interest and ethical content attaching to their individual lives.
While that may be done, and perhaps on the whole has been
done to an excessive extent, it is not necessary. These social
leaders are always representatives, each one representing a
center, a focusing of a large number of social conditions and
problems and forces; and so far as elementary education is
concerned, it seems to me that the ideal should be to remain
true to the historical point of view, that is, to that of growth,
of development, by discussing the development quite largely
as typified and summed up, as represented in individual characters. There can be no doubt that the interest in the child
is largely in the individual, particularly in the striking individual, the heroic individual. To present these individuals
however, isolatedly, apart from the social situations which
called them into being, and apart from the work they did in
meeting the particular problems of the time, is practically to
destroy history and leave off simply with story, with interesting incident. But if we let our minds run over Greek or Roman,
English or American history, we can easily call to mind a number of great figures who were literally representative men, and
through a study which is genuinely historical in character we
can start from the interesting incidents of their own lives and

work through those to a recognition and study of the social
relationships of these persons.

However, I do not think it necessary, even in elemen-
[(c)]   tary education to confine the work to great historical
           characters treated as representatives of social move-
ments, social tendencies and developments. Aside from this
instinctive interest of the child in and for marked individuality,
there is an equally strong tendency in the child of nine or ten
to identify himself in a more or less dramatic way with others,
and the conditions, problems of social organization of a simple sort can be made by him through that dramatic use of his
instinctive imagination. I have seen that worked out with considerable success with children of seven and eight years. For
example, starting with simple conditions of life and the formation of the family, which of course appeals naturally to the
child, and the circumstances under which the different families would be held together into a clan or tribe; then the relations under which these various tribes would come into conflict
with each other, quarreling for land, or some incidental feud,
and the way in which that might develop into war or treaties
and within the clan the various emergencies which might arise
calling for legislation; the person who would most naturally
settle the disputes, the building up of typical forms of government, and the final formation of a community or city. All these
are points which are quite capable of realization by the child
when presented through the medium of a certain dramatic
identification with himself, children often representing various
tribes and carrying out in play forms of typical relationships.
There the child is brought into contact directly with the sort
of problems that are continually presenting themselves in social
life and with the various ways of dealing with these problems,
the various kinds of relationships necessary, both external and
internal in order to deal with these situations. There is a particular advantage here in taking fairly primitive society as the
conditions are there reduced to their lowest terms, and present
themselves in a simple way. Moreover, taking them from comparatively primitive life, these things can be made typical without doing violence to historic truth, which of course is an
important consideration. The value of prehistoric study is of
course obviously in the knowledge of forces and conditions be-

cause we know and can know next to nothing about particular leaders or actual events, while it is quite possible to reproduce the larger and more massive steps of social growth as they occur.

[(2)] Another problem which presents itself is the question of the proper amount and relationship of details.

From one point of view it may be said that there is a great deal too much detail taught, and from another, that there is not enough. There is too much detail in the sense of attempting to give practically all the facts, in trying to give a comprehensive view of American history such as is attempted in the average text book on American History. When that is attempted within the limits of the text book, it is obvious that there are a great number of particular persons, battles, campaigns, etc., spoken of. The result of that multiplicity of details is that details of another sort are inevitably crowded out. That is, the circumstances and conditions which really give each one of the points discussed its meaning, which drives it home to one, makes it capable of translation over into living terms, are almost of necessity left out.

In history the pedagogical demand is more and more for typical cases, for representative topics which will be worked out in a great deal of detail, with a great deal of accompanying circumstance. For example, for a child to simply learn what is in the text book about the Puritans and Pilgrims coming to this country and landing in 1620 on Plymouth Rock, leaves the mind with next to nothing, simply a little information. The reason it means something to the average adult is that he knows so much more than what is in the book; he having read more can hang these few things on what he has previously known. If you go over some of those special points of interest, and striking out all the surrounding details simply reduce it to the bare description which is in the text book, you simply have a basis for some thing; you have nothing which means anything vital or important. If the child spends two or three months even on that subject, working out the reason why those people came over, how they lived, and in getting acquainted with the various individuals in such a way that they mean something to him, working out how the town was laid out and how the people managed their affairs, the thing at once becomes a vital whole. It is obvious that you cannot do that and attempt to cover everything from 1492 to 1899 in one year. You must pick out things which are really representative and typical and work them out with a great deal of elaboration.

[(a)] What the important things are will differ with conditions; they will not be the same in all parts of the country. Taking the colonial period, certain settlements in New England, certain settlements in New York, and in some Southern states, say Virginia, are typical; and also some typical case of migration and colonization in the West may be chosen which will probably vary according to the particular locality of the student himself. But four such typical cases worked out with regard to original sources and bringing the children into contact with the personal lives and the family life, what they did from day to day, would not give merely in the end more actual information, but would cultivate more the historical sense and imagination; and it is that historical sense and imagination, that after all, is the main thing. Such work as that could easily ocupy a year with immensely more profit than attempting to cover the textbook, going over the whole period, in a year.

[(b)] I said a moment ago that I thought more information would actually be obtained simply because memory is a matter of association. If things cluster together each point serves to bring up another one, but when you isolate events and facts you must remember by sheer force, learning the things by continual repetition and review. There is very little carrying power in the mind itself, but when the whole thing is worked out it takes care of itself. It is interesting to note here the long things which a child will remember and the short things he will forget. What would be the use do you think of telling a child a part of an interesting story and then to say: "I will tell you more tomorrow, because you cannot remember any more today?" You can tell a child a story an hour long, if it is told interestingly, and the child will remember it definitely and consecutively, simply because it is an organized whole and all the parts belong together, instead of a lot of sections of things and isolated events. I may add that there has been an immense improvement in American histories during the last ten years in this respect.

What would we say then was desirable as the result
[f.(1)]   in history in the elementary period would be the power
to imagine, to sense social relationships, and to have
in mind some of the chief historical embodiments of the working out of these forces, taking something of Greek life, something of Roman life, something of Feudal life, something of
England in modern European history, and a good deal of the
play of these forces and the forms they have taken in our own
country. American history itself can be treated in such a way
as to recapitulate in itself the historical progress of man. The
child should be left with a sense of these historical embodiments of the social forces in such a way as to feel the momen-
tous continuity and progress, although unable philosophically
in any way to define them. But if the child does not get a sense
of momentum, a sense of moving on into a higher state of
things at each stage, a sense of advance, he is losing one of the
most important points in the study of history.

Briefly as to the secondary period. The problems
[(2)]   which present themselves particularly in secondary
period relate to the questions that come up in connection with the ethical and practical value of history, and in
connection with this, along the line of the relation of history
to what is commonly called civics.

If the knowledge of history does not somehow relate
[(a)]   itself to existing problems and conditions, if the
student does not get something out of it which makes
him more intelligent in dealing with current problems of social
life and of politics, he certainly does not get the full benefit of
it, and it is the study of civil government, now generally called
civics, which has been particularly urged of late as a means of
enabling the student to get practical value and application out
of his history. The child in the elementary period is hardly
capable of taking up that phase of the matter with much advantage, but the average youth of fourteen or fifteen is certainly ready to take something of a living interest in current
municipal or national politics, if he is ever going to.

The difficulty is that for the most part the study of
[(b)]   civics has been conducted in the school simply as a
morphological study, a study of courts, county, state
and national, and so on, and it has been assumed that if the
student will only master the constitution of the United States

and of the state, and the local or county government, some
transubstantiation will take place to make him a better citizen
and to enable him to vote more intelligently. He would vote
more intelligently in a way, but the relationship to actual good
citizenship is certainly pretty remote. The individual could use
this sort of knowledge in order to manipulate other people to
his own ends as well as for anything else. There is nothing in
this morphological side which comes very close to his life as a
good citizen. In the first place it seems to me that the standpoint has been inverted. We ought to begin with the study of
social functions, not with the study of governmental forms.
What is it that has to be done? What it is that the community
has to do for its various citizens is the first thing to get in
mind. The question of just how it does it, by what distribution
of power, by what machinery of courts, police, city council
and so on, is a secondary question, and has really no vital
meaning at all until the person has a definite sense of what
the results to be reached are. The moment it is presented in
terms of function, it becomes another matter. What should
the local community do for the individual? What have I a
right to expect the community to do for me, and what has the
community a right to expect from me? Starting from that
functional side the way is paved for the discussion of the
structural side of the thing, the particular methods by which
it has been found expedient to attempt to realize these ends.

       I do not mean to confine the study of history in the
[(c)]   secondary period to civics. I mean to say that this
       seems to me to give the standpoint of interest in his-
tory at this time. In other words the student is now ready for a
more definite study of institutions, starting not so much from
institutions as the purposes they are meant to realize, and then
there is the basis for comparative study, for historical study.
What was the institutional organization of Greece, of Rome,
of feudalism? What has been the struggle of modern times to
secure what kind of institutions, and why? Why do democratic
institutions conserve the public welfare and also individual
freedom more fully than these other institutional forms that
have previously been studied? This comparative institutional
study with reference to the ethical value of the ends reached
would be the point of view for the secondary schools. When I
say ethical, I mean the enlargement of the freedom of the in-

dividual and the sphere of common interests and mutual services. Along with that, naturally, at this secondary period, goes I think, a good deal of the ethical content in a narrower sense. I think this is a period of somewhat intense interest in many youths, in ethical problems, perhaps it is more intense between the ages of fourteen and eighteen than it is in the later years when the formal study of ethics is generally taken up. Of course history continually presents ethical problems as to why people did certain things; whether they should have done them; what the motives were. There is besides the general, the individual aspect of ethics, the study of character, for which no rules can be laid down in advance, but to which it is desirable to have a great deal of incidental attention paid.

In the transition from the secondary period to higher [(3)(a)] education the student would naturally get a philosophical view of history. The narrow technical sense in the category of causation can be used in the physical sciences but can hardly be applied to history. Causation in the larger sense, in the sense of the philosophy of growth, of movement of historical evolution, is the thing in which the strictly historical study should culminate. An adequate insight into history as movement, as growth, would make impossible both of the extreme types of view which we find currently presented in social and political discussions: extreme conservatism and extreme radicalism. The person who has an historical insight could never possibly be either a mere conservative or a mere radical, he has got the habit of looking for growth through certain movements, of certain determining forces, and he can neither suppose that the present is final and that his duties are exhausted in maintaining things as they are, nor can he suppose that there is any revolutionary, violent, sudden change which can possibly be introduced. He would not be blind to things as they are, nor a believer in Utopias or ideal schemes. He would be looking to see how the forces which are at present at work can be redirected, taken advantage of and utilized, so that they can most fully help realize the ends and aims which are implied in all social growth. Existing social conditions can neither be a finality nor a complete mistake. The question is always a question of reform in the literal sense of that word, as re-forming, re-making, the re-adaptation of conditions so that they will better conserve the present elements of individual freedom and social reciprocity.

[(b)] In the higher period distinctively of course, the general point of view is that it is professional, that it is preparation for particular vocations or callings in life. I need only point out the possibility along that line and the value of the possibility. Professionalism in the bad sense in the professional man is certainly largely due to the absence of any historical background and perspective. A man specializing in science ought to get his science along with the historical development of science; if he is going into medicine he ought to know the history of medicine; if he is going into law he ought to know the history of law and so on; and know the history of these things, not as things by themselves, but in connection with the general progress of civilization. The whole history of civilization can be written in terms of the history of theology, of medicine, of law; the whole thing is there, but taken up from a specialized point of view. When the curriculum is organized so that the elementary period takes up its proper material and does its due work with it, giving the training of instinctive imagination and insight into the forces, and a certain amount of positive information in regard to the way these forces are crystallized, and in the secondary period gives an insight into the development of institutions in relation to the fundamental purposes of life, then the ground will be covered leaving room in the higher period for the philosophical view of history, and also for this professional view.

LECTURE XXVIII

March 17, 1899

[C.II.: *Literature.*]

[III.D.4.a.(1)] The general standpoint for conceiving of the value of literature in education has already been spoken of, namely as presenting a record in an adequate form of the more important values realized in social life. It represents the culmination and the crystalization, in other words, of the highest moments of experience.

[(2)] History, just as history, is a process which goes on in time, various phases of which are therefore transitory and perishable. Institutions are formed; social relationships are organized in ways that get a certain abiding value; persons become articulated into the framework of society; and in that way, as active forces, they remain. But from that side simply, they are like habits in the individual, they are powers which are practically very useful, upon which our successes and achivments in life depend, but which, after all, just as habits, have no adequate reflection in consciousness. A glance backward at history will show us that it is the degree with which various peoples have come to consciousness of their own institutions, of their own activities, that become aware of the significance of their lives, of the values bound up in their experiences, that has fixed their place in history much more than the mere objective institutional importance. It would be very hard I think, to justify the relative importance which we apply to Greek civilization as compared with Egyptian, Phoenician, or Assyrian, or Chinese, simply on the basis of the institutions, the social and political life, objectively measured. Taken from that standpoint certainly many of the lives of these other people were carried on on a much larger scale, over longer periods of time, involving the destinies of more human beings, and probably with more political changes, actions and reactions; but what made the Greeks preeminent was that they had the faculty of getting back of that institutional life, of seizing upon its meaning, and then of embodying that meaning in terms of art and literature which made it capable of appealing to other individuals, after all the events just as events, and very much of the institutions, just as institutions, had completely disappeared. Literature from that standpoint might be called social self consciousness. I do not mean that it is the only form of social self consciousness, but it is the form of self consciousness which is most fitted to perpetuate itself, to communicate itself, make itself felt with other peoples and in other times. The close connection between history and literature, their intrinsic relationship, becomes, I think, obvious from this point of view, and it suggests the pedagogical alternatives which present themselves in the teaching of literature.

As distinct from this point of view we have what [b.(1)] might be termed the individual genius point of view, that which regards every great literary or artistic production as the result of inspiration, mysterious and unfathomable inspiration of some individual mind, the tendency of which therefore is to isolate the piece of literature studied from its historical setting and relationship, which is considered to be irrelevant. This school insists upon the eternal worth of literature; it is above time, above history, simply an inspired utterance from one individual to another individual. The falsity of that point of view of course we cannot go into here. I should simply say about it something of the same sort that I said about the similar view in history, that which regards history for the elementary period as the biographical study of great men. There is no need to underestimate the importance of great individuals in giving expression to social situations and ideals, but after all, the content of literature, the truth that there is in it, cannot be, by any possibility, an individualistic thing. The form may be literature, but the substance cannot be literature. The substance must be life, it must be akin to the thoughts and the feelings of the common men of the period, or else it is a simple curiosity, or at least a freak of high culture or polish, but without any permanent and substantial claims to a position in education.

Connected with this as at least a degenerate form of
[(2)]   the individualistic form in literature is the sentimentality which looks at literature simply from the emotional point of view, both as regards the subject matter and
the form, which throws all the emphasis upon the beauties of
thought and imagery and style, and which aims consciously,
not indirectly, but directly, simply at stimulating and arousing,
on the part of the student, the capacity for feeling a particular
kind of reaction in the presence of literary masterpieces. There
is no doubt as to the importance of that feeling, and if one has
it not naturally, of having that capacity aroused; but it is a
question simply of whether the securing of that result is made
the main and conscious aim in the teaching of literature, or
whether the main aim is to get a reproduction and communication of the actual value, content, and have the emotional reaction grow out of this personal reproduction of the thought,
of the life material that is contained in the literary classic.

The rhetorical and pseudo-aesthetic standpoint for
[(3)]   teaching literature may also be mentioned. It consists
in an attempt to state in intellectual terms just what
this sentimental attitude does in emotional terms. It has a large
apparent apparatus of aesthetic terminology and theory, in
virtue of which it attempts to measure the value of different
literary types and the significance of various figures of speech,
the tragic element, the sublime element, etc., and to dissipate
the content of the experience which is contained in the literature in this mere critical apparatus for handling and classifying the literary form. Not that there is not a specific place in
education for the study of literary form as such, or the rhetorical side, but that that is secondary. We lose any significance
for judging of the form, we lose any standard for measuring
the value of the form side, excepting as we have first got a
grasp on the content, and then ask ourselves how that content
can best be expressed and conveyed.

The chronological and informational standpoint of
[(4)]   teaching literature, that which has found expression
in the average text books on English literature and
the somewhat prolonged publishers' catalogues and inventories
of various writers and their works, need hardly be mentioned.
We all at once recognize the insufficiency of the informational
point of view, and the absurdity of teaching from that point of

view is perhaps more evident in literature than anywhere else: the supposition that anyone has anything of literary value by knowing the names of authors and when these authors lived, and the titles of their books, and the years in which they were published. The most that can be said for that idea is that it enables the person to pass himself off as an educated person. In playing the game of authors one is more amusingly reaching the same end. The reference book is of course an exceedingly valuable thing in anybody's library or education but the reference book was never meant for a text book and it has been a common practice to use books whose sole function was as general reference books, as text books in the study of literature proper. Classical dictionaries and various other reference books are valuable as a basis for looking up illustrations of various kinds, but that of course has its place in research work and particular forms of specialized work and when it goes under its own name there is no objection to it. It is simply not education in literature.

Speaking very briefly of the presentation of literary [c.(1)(a)] material in the three stages of education, I should say that in the elementary period the significance of literature is, from the child's standpoint, incidental. I mean by that, that it cannot, from the child's standpoint, very well be made a distinct study. It is simply a medium, a vehicle for conveying others' experiences in an intensified and concentrated form. Now that does not mean that from the teacher's standpoint any less importance should be given to literature, or any less time should be given to it, than at present. It does not reduce the importance of it or the time-claim of it to the minimum by any means, but it simply says that the primary thing is in the reality, the first hand realities of the experiences themselves, and the worth of literature is in making these vivid and in giving them the form which will stay by the child.

From that point of view it is not possible to say too [(b)] much about the value of literature in the elementary period. The child is not yet awakened to the significance of an intellectual formalization. It becomes therefore the problem of how he is to keep a grip on his first hand experiences. How is he to realize them on the side of intellectual or emotional values when he has not the machinery for turning them over into their strictly reflective equivalents? The story, the poem then, which has the imagery and human setting, and that which has fineness of touch in the mode of presentation, supplies us with the medium, with the vehicle, by which we can translate back to the child his own experiences in such a way as to idealize them and give him a vivid and lasting hold on them. Perhaps enough was said a few weeks ago about the danger of substituting literature for first hand experience, instead of making it an interpretation and culminating expression of that experience. When that is done, what the child really gets is, for the most part, the mere sensation, the mere emotional reaction. He simply does not get the idea, the thought; he does not get the imagery, the literary content and value itself. It is very easy to tell stories to children in such a way that the mere sensation, the reaction at the proper time shall become the chief and absorbing thing. Irritating the emotions of children from this point of view comes in, and the element of exaggeration. On entering some school rooms you hear a great big tone of voice which is simply adapted to catch the attention of the child for the moment by the sensation aroused, but not in the least by any permanent value that can remain in his consciousness. This exaggerated teaching of literature becomes simply a method of disintegrating the child. He demands similar excitation in the future. There is an article in the March number of the *Atlantic Monthly* on the kindergarten child after he has left the kindergarten which states the supposed experience of one teacher who had been put through this sort of educational pablum.[1]

[(c)]   Probably enough was also said the other day about the value of the myth and the story, that is the simple story as the basis of instruction in elementary education, when speaking of the Herbartian theories of education. I hope you will read for yourselves what the Herbartians have to say on that point and their assumption that this material is particularly appropriate for moral instruction—"heart stuff," "disposition stuff," as they call it—assuming a certain natural appropriateness or tendency of this kind of material to lend itself to the realization of moral truth in the form which the child is capable of realizing. There is much in the old Socratic dialogues as to whether virtue can be taught which is very

[1 Marion Hamilton Carter, "The Kindergarten Child—After the Kindergarten," *Atlantic Monthly*, 83, March, 1899, pp. 358–366.]

instructive. There is a great difference between teaching virtue and teaching about virtue and much can be taught as virtue through talking about and discussing virtue, and yet there may be next to no effect on character or conduct. There may be no motor reaction or response. That seems to me the fatal error in the assumption of the Herbartian school, that the literary material is the chief and most important medium of instruction in the earlier period. It tends to substitute the form for the content. When I say form I do not mean the disparagement of form. In its right place it is necessary to its adequate embodiment in consciousness. Content without form remains dead and barren, but there must be the content there which the child can get hold of through more direct ways than through stories, and when we get to myths as the main nutriment, the case becomes to my mind still worse. The tendency is then, to exaggerate simply the sensational and emotional at the expense of the real.

[(d)] The actual selection of literary material then for the elementary school, while a difficult matter, is a matter of detail which will depend very much upon the other work that is being done in the school, and upon the particular changing conditions from day to day. There ought to be sufficient variety so that all that is best in the school work can finally be summed up, recapitulated and embodied in as classic literary form as possible. But when I say classic it does not mean that something that already goes by the name of "classic" should be used. Something which the teacher herself invents, if it is a clear, straight-forward and human expression of the thought studied, may be, from the child's standpoint, more classic than something called "classic" but which would not appeal to the child in the same way. I suppose I hardly need say here that in essence the same qualities of style make a thing classic to the child and to the adult: clearness, vividness, forcefulness, and coherency. The peculiar style which has been cultivated by certain writers for the benefit of children is a thing which has no justification excepting as it reveals the ignorance of child nature; I mean the "O" and "Ah" style, and the style that introduces the greatest number of "so's" possible. It also introduces adjectives. If there is anything foreign to the child nature it is this adjective style. The child mind works directly, in a simple straightforward way. The style is being cultivated through the adults who have first sentimentalized the child and then wish to have the child realize himself the same sentiments which the adult has surrounded him with. It is a great cloud of foggy idealism.

In the secondary period of education it seems to me [(2)(*a*)] the historical point of view should become dominant; that is, you can carry out my line of thought by simply referring to what I said yesterday about the teaching of history in the secondary period. Literary classics which have been produced in the different historical epochs should be consciously brought to the attention of children with the part which they played not simply in embodying the ideals of the people of that time, but in conveying those ideals, and making them operative in life since their time. While the students of foreign languages have had an opportunity to work out this conception, it should also become equally available for all. That is, all students in the secondary period should become acquainted with Homer whether they are studying Greek or not, and with Virgil whether they are studying Latin or not, and so on.

In the secondary period also, there is at adolescence [(*b*)]   the awakening of the reflex and distinctly emotional consciousness. There is a basis for aesthetic analysis within certain limits, for conscious attention to the best modes of communicating certain ideas, and of arousing certain emotions, or making a certain conscious distinction between the thought and the form of its expression, and for studying the form as an instrument of the expression and the realization of the thought proper; while before this the child's standpoint has been a naive one, simply interested in the story as a story, in the thing as a whole.

The same reflective consciousness coming up on the [(*c*)]   intellectual side makes literature perhaps the unequal instrument at this time for more specific ethical instruction. Great literary classics do involve ethical problems and attempted ethical solutions which the child, after adolescence, is likely to have an interest in, and while formal instruction in ethics would be too formal or subjective, the literary form of it, being objective, gives the student a chance to work them out in terms that do not lie too close to him, and which are not so apt to be sentimentalized on one hand, or fossilized through excessive formulation on the other side. Any one acquainted with a number of high schools can pick out some where the study of literature is a medium for developing the intellectual content of the child at that time, and presents problems sure to present themselves, and the ways in which they have actually been met at different times.

[(3)]   The growth of the significance of literature in general, getting a catholic and flexible view with an acquaintance of forms of thought and of the expression of thought, would naturally make the transition over to the third period, that of higher education. Here the form of literature study would naturally become specialized. There would be the unspecialized background according to the individual's own taste, things that he had read because he liked them; but literature comes more and more to mean, after this period, the literature of one's particular subject. The chemist talks about the literature of his particular pursuit, and the astronomer about the literature of his profession. The literary man would not recognize them as literature at all but for the specialist, who has the adequate background of culture, I think there is no misnomer in the term of "literature." It is the medium in which the range of important ideas are studied and communicated, and has as much claim to be called literature as have the literary essays and poems to which the average literary man would like to restrict the term.

[d.]   I perhaps ought to mention the constructive work in literature, what passes generally under the head of language lessons, or composition work, or essay work. While the child's power of appreciation will very obviously outrun his own powers of expression and construction, yet the vitality of his own appreciation and interpretations will depend very largely upon the extent to which he himself assumes the attitude of a creator of literature. Excepting as accident or the temperament of the individual guarded us against it, any instruction in literature wholly on the receptive side would be in the end comparatively futile and factitious which has not been balanced by having the pupil from the first put himself in the attitude of being himself an expresser, a creator, trying to put his own emotions and thoughts and images in such shape that they would appeal, with a certain degree of force and vividness, to others. I have heard the value of literature in education defended on the ground that most of us were not creators, that we had to be passive in this sphere, and that it enabled us to get beyond our limitations, in coming in contact with the products of other persons' minds; but I do not believe that the person who does not put himself in the attitude of a producer will ever get into contact with the products of other persons' minds. The best way to build up his own imagery and to key up his own genuine emotional appreciation with respect to the writings of others is to have him actively and positively attempt to build his own nature and bring his own emotions to some sort of articulate expression. Undoubtedly there must be a working back and forth; the individual's own expression must be supplemented and he must be stimulated by being brought into contact with other work produced by others, and that must be an individual stimulus which should spur him on to attempt to better realize and embody his own conception; and this balance should be kept up from beginning to end, first in oral expression and then later on in writing.

[e.]   The chief instrumentality in teaching literature in the secondary period, from the psychological point of view, is the image. I think there is not a point in modern psychology which can be so directly helpful to the teacher as the work that has been done in the study of various forms of imagery, visual and auditory, and so on. If there is a piece of literature, whether descriptive prose or a piece of poetry, which the teacher wishes to have the pupils appreciate and get the force of, there are a number of ways in which it may be done. The form, rhetorical and aesthetic, may be analyzed, the attempt to get at the underlying thought in the abstract and reflective way; or again the dictionary, encyclopaedia and reference book may be brought in and the literature worked out in its historical ramifications; but all of these are indirect, they are circuitous. The way in which the individual mind might appreciate a piece of literature is and must be through the imagery with which he responds to it. To keep the attention at the time then, on the imagery, ask what the image conveyed here is, and the image conveyed there, and in the next passage, and consecutively to build up these images and relate them is to get the only sure guarantee that the student will have an original appreciation and comprehension of the literature. If he can get that, there is the basis for the feeling reaction; if he has not got that, any feelings which he thinks, or says he has, have psychologically no rooting at all, they are purely factitious. If he has that he has the basis for appreciating elements of thought; he can see how the author has gone to work to bring out the significance of this and that in conveying this vivid and comprehensive conception of the whole. To ask a secondary school pupil to give his idea of one of Wordsworth's nature poems is almost sure to bring out some more or less madeup response. The pupil has not the experience nor the reflective power to formulate the idea which he gets from it except in very striking cases. To ask what the image which he gets from it is, and to ask for the consecutive building up of that image on one side, and its elements on the other, and for the feelings which these images naturally call out, is a thing which is within the grasp of any intelligent high school pupil, and is a thing which so far as it goes belongs to the individual himself. It is not something which he thinks that he ought to have. It is not that he feels that he ought to like this piece of literature, but it is a process which so far as it goes, is actually and consecutively gone through with in his own mind.

LECTURE XXIX

March 18, 1899

[C.II.: *Science.*]

[III.D.5.a.]   I have already mentioned the general point of view which controls the value and place of science in education in referring it to the supreme educational standard which we have adopted, namely, the social one. In its application to science that meant that the educational value of science has been in bringing to consciousness a knowledge of the materials by which social life is conditioned, and a knowledge of the processes, the changing of energy and direction of energy through which social life is fundamentally maintained. Put in a simpler form, it means that science is the knowledge of the natural medium or environment in and through which social life exists and advances. The fundamental thing then is the keeping of the study of natural facts and forces in their relation to human life, and as has already been said, that does away with any fundamental dualism such as we often have set up between science on one side and the humanities on the other. Of course at a certain point in the educational development, it would be convenient as a division of labor for some to specialize along one line, which for convenience we would call the humanities, and for others to specialize along another line which we may call that of natural science. But this is simply a case of specialization, of emphasis or stress, just as one person might specialize in political economy, another in chemistry, another in mathematics. The distinction does not mark any fundamental line of cleavage in the curriculum itself. As I have had occasion to say before, the philosophical dualism which we have inherited from the middle ages, has affected our consciousness in general, and our educational theories in a great many more ways than we at first suspected. The drawing of a rigid line between theoretical and practical in education, between the sciences regarded simply as a study of a purely external world, a purely objective and material world, and the culture studies or humanities, regarded as acquaintance with things which have to do simply with man and the higher spiritual affairs of man, is simply a survival and transfer of this general dualistic point of view over into common consciousness, as it has expressed itself in education.

[b.]   The point of view just spoken of in its educational workings out, may be conveniently opposed to two others, one of which I will call the object-lesson point of view, and the other of which the animistic point of view.

[(1)]   The object lesson point of view explains itself. I do not mean however, mere object lessons, but the whole conception which conceives of science as making us acquainted with purely external and objective facts and forces. The object lesson in the narrower sense takes any particular thing or object and proceeds by analysis to draw attention to its qualities of form, structure, and so on. The object lesson point of view in science treats the whole external world, the world of plants, animals, minerals, etc., as if it were simply a more enlarged and important object such as is studied in an object lesson. The whole point of view is analytic and morphological. That is, it is engaged in the analysis of qualities of form and structure, and at the very best, of causal relationship. It is regarded as a great big thing, or collection of things, quite outside of ourselves and our consciousness, but about which it happens to be advisable, and to a certain extent necessary, to gain as much information as possible.

There have been several attempts in the last century to introduce a larger amount of science into education and to carry it back into elementary education. So far as the immediate purposes were concerned, these movements have largely failed. It has changed the point of view somewhat, but none of these movements has accomplished what was hoped and expected at the outset, and the basal reason for that is simply, I think, because this purely objective external point of view has been taken. We need only to take the standpoint of psychology, and the concrete psychology of the child, to be assured in advance that that standpoint must fail. There is no such division in the child's mind, or even probably in the mind of the average common sense adult, any such consciousness of any real line of cleavage between what he would call himself, and the world that he lives in. He does not mix himself up with the world, but he always conceives of himself as living in the world and of the world as the sphere of his activities and interests, and the two sides are woven together at every point. That is particularly true of the child who lives a unified, naive, and objective life. There is no basis of any lasting or intrinsic interest in this object-lesson point of view.

[(2)]   Now the reaction from that point of view has brought about the animistic point of view which may be regarded as the wholesale production of human interests and preferences over into the world of nature, regarding nature itself as animated in a way, simply and only from the human point of view, the poetizing of science for children, or the mythological treatment of science. Now it is obvious that this point of view has attempted to avoid the errors of the purely objective point of view, introducing this unnatural split between the living, experiencing individual and the world in which he lives; but the difficulty with it is that it is simply reaction, and thus at bottom is simply a negative thing. It bases itself on the insufficiency of the opposite principle rather than on any coherent point of view of its own. The subordination of science to literature as in the Herbartian school is one attempt, although by no means an extreme one, of this animistic point of view. There is in it no wholesale carrying over of human feelings into the natural world, but simply the general subordination of it to materials derived from stories and poems. From various sources there has lately come up, particularly in this country, a positive assertion that the world must be approached from the animistic standpoint. You will find that best expressed in the writings of Stanley Hall and some of his pupils at Clark University.*

[* G. Stanley Hall served as President of Clark University from 1888 until 1920, after having been a professor of "psychology and pedagogy" at Johns Hopkins while Dewey was a graduate student there. At Clark he was the leader of the child study movement, using laboratory observations and questionnaires. The results of these researches were published in the journal *Pedagogical Seminary*. It is these writings that Dewey refers to.]

Now the difficulties of that point of view on the
[(a)]   strictly pedagogical side need hardly be insisted upon.

It sets up something which afterwards must be
knocked down, it instills into the child's mind at a certain
point something which later on he must consciously get away
from; he must undergo quite a distinct revolution in his mental
attitude in order to get over to the strictly scientific point of
view at all. It is literally recapitulating, not simply the progress
of the race, but the struggles of the race, and setting up in the
child's own experience the very obstacles and defects which
the race has had to struggle to get away from. The individual
will have to go through that violent wrenching to get away from
this emotional point of view to the critical point of view which
is the very essence of science in its later development. From
the standpoint of economy, continuity of growth, any such dis-
solution, any such reaction and revolution of mental attitude
is to be avoided if possible. Psychologically where the theory
goes astray is in supposing that because the world of nature is
related to man and man's concerns, it is related primarily
through his feelings, his emotions. The major premise may be
granted, that the world in the ordinary consciousness is conceived in its relations to human experience and human concerns, but why should these interests and concerns be treated
as existing chiefly in the medium of feelings and of the images
that attach to those feelings? It is rather our active instincts,
the sphere of our active interests, that bind nature and man
together, than the sphere of the feelings and the emotions.
Here, as in what I was saying yesterday about literature, the
position of the feelings is secondary and reflex. The primary
point of view is that of action and of the impulses and instincts
which lead over into action. Now the working out, of course,
of that point of view educationally, and particularly a statement of the practical difference, depends upon whether we
take the feeling point of view to get the bond of union, or the
active point of view. To state these matters would require considerable time. I simply would refer you for one illustration, to
what I said in speaking of the constructive activities, that is,
the natural approach of the child to material forces through
what he does in a constructive and active way—say cooking
and carpentry work, and so on.

Another radical fallacy in the doctrine is that nature
[(b)]   has no poetic significance until these purely personal
feelings and emotions are inserted into it. Nature has
itself its aesthetic aspects, its beauties of form and color. There
is no idea more poetic to the mind which grasps it than the
whole idea of growth, of life, the mystery of change and of
continual development. Now for a mind to get into a sympathetic and natural attitude, where it realizes, feels and appreciates this continual on-going of natural forces, the continual
evolution, conception, and out-growth of new forms, it is infinitely more poetic and contains within itself the promise and
assurance of a more poetic point of view in the future than
any factitious ascriptions of human feelings and emotions to
plants, animals, stones, sunlight, and so on. For a child really
to realize the beauty of sunlight for instance and the significance of the prismatic colors, is a more poetic fact than to
have the colors of the prism labeled sun fairies for him. As a
matter of fact, it seems to me that the ultimate result of this
is to put in a lot of arbitrary associations between the child's
mind and the actual facts and forces, so that he never realizes
the intrinsic poetic value bound up in the things themselves
when they are approached from the standpoint of their own
beauty and their own living development.

To come back to the more positive statement, the
[c.(1)]   conception which I have set forth would, in a way,
make what we would term geography the center of
science work explicitly during the period of elementary education, and be the background and correlating center of all
the other sciences, even in the secondary period.

The world on which we live is after all the centraliz-
[(a)]   ing and unifying fact. Take mineralogy, the study of
soils, stones, and minerals. It is obviously simply
picking out certain phases, certain parts of the earth as a
whole. Take botany, plants. For a specialist the structure of a
plant has a meaning in itself, but concretely in reality the
plant grows in the earth, it belongs to the earth as a whole,
and it loses something of its meaning when you wrench it
away from where it belongs. The same is equally true of animal
life. The specialist can study zoology as a thing by itself, but
at the outset animals live and move and have their being in
the actual total environment. Some live in the air, some in the

water, some in this climate and others in that. To get it in its
totality we have to get it as a geographical fact, at least in its
geographical setting.

The study of the plant from this point of view works in both
directions. On one hand it works back to the place where the
plant grew to the soil in which it grew. Take the soils around
Chicago here—the lake sand on one side and the plants which
grow in it, and the prairie loam on the other side and the
plants that grow in that. Starting from those plants themselves
the child's mind can be easily carried back to any point, to
glaciers, the ice age, the formation of the great lakes, and the
significance of the western prairies. On the other side it leads
out to the commercial side of geography, the significance of
all these natural forms as determining modes of human intercourse, the production of certain materials, their manufacture
and exchange, which of course are not ultimately matters of
accident, but are determined by questions of geographical
environment, which at least never completely over-ride questions of natural environment.

In the study of the processes of the growth of that plant in
its environment, chemistry at once comes in. If you take the
plant by itself and pull it to pieces you do not get chemistry
any more than mineralogy or geology; you simply have a dead
plant whose parts you can have analyzed and technical labels
put on. But take it in its geographical relations and then how
does it interact with this natural environment? How does it
get its food? What does it do with its waste products? You get
the chemistry of the food materials as they are separated from
the soil, the question of assimilation and the nutrition in the
plant in forms of starch, sugar, and so on. In the consideration
of plant physiology you get questions regarding the breathing
of the plant, and so on. You get the chemistry of the atmosphere, carbon dioxide, the relation between the plant and animal in maintaining the natural equilibrium.

But I need not follow up that line of thought further.
[(b)] My point is that if you take the geographical point
of view you do not have to hunt for correlations, you
have the single concrete whole, the earth of which plants,
animals, water, etc., are all particular parts, and you are led
on from one to the other and the chemical and physical forces
by which they act on each other and so keep up the life of the

whole. In taking the geographical point of view in connection with human life the points would be the way in which the structure of the earth has affected human activity, in the way of hostilities, making separations and isolations which have determined national character, and in the propagation of ideas; on the other side, the reaction of human ideas on nature, the transformation which the face of nature has undergone through human effort in taking advantage of these points of leverage which nature itself has presented to man, so that the sociological aspect continually comes in in the geographical point of view, as well as the more naturalistic aspect.

[(c)]   Observation on this basis never reduces itself to mere analytic observation of structure, form. Observation is always synthetic as well as analytic; it always consists in placing the object studied, whether plant, animal or mineral, in its larger setting, and seeing the part which it plays there. I would like to refer more expressly here to the book by Mrs. Aber entitled *An Experiment in Education*.[1] The whole book, so far as elementary education is concerned, is the best thing ever published, I think; it is all well worth reading. But it is of particular value on the subject of science. She suggests that when a child sees or thinks of a piece of rock, he should see and feel it as a part of the thin crust of the larger whole; it should not be mere stone, a mere isolated object, but an intrinsic, integral part of this world whole. Of course you cannot get the child to do that at the outset, but that should be the ideal with which all study of science in elementary education should be approached, so that every analytic study of the particular points of color, form or structure, should also be accompanied by replacing the analyzed detail, by seeing it in the place which it occupies, the function which it exercises in this larger whole of the ever changing and ever growing earth.

[(2)(a)(i)]   The few remarks that I shall make about science in the secondary period would better be compared with the discussion in philosophy regarding the classification of the sciences. You will find Comte, who attempted one of the first modern classifications

[1 Mary R. Aber, *An Experiment in Education* (New York: Harper and Brothers, 1897). Mrs. Aber conducted experiments in the eighties in private schools in Boston and Engelwood, Illinois, designed to provide children with greater freedom, intrinsic motivation, and realistic projects. See particularly Part III, chapter 1, p. 107.]

of the sciences, classifying them in the progress from the abstract to the concrete, in a sort of step ladder, each lower step in the ladder serving as a standpoint for regarding the next, and the method which gives us the leading conceptions which are to be used in the next science. You will find the account in any of the books of the positive philosophy of Comte, and criticisms of the same in Herbert Spencer. Comte's order is: first mathematics, which gives us the ultimate abstraction of nature. Mathematics as it grows into mechanics affords the standpoint and the basis of physics. Chemistry is still more concrete than physics. That introduces conceptions of function by which we get into biology, and then we come to the most concrete of all the sciences, that which deals with the most complex and detailed and intimate facts, namely, sociology. In that way you get the hierarchy of the sciences. Any conception of the classification of sciences has at once its pedagogical bearings. Take the questions continually coming up in high schools as to the order of the sciences, which in the first year and which in the second, and if you are to accept this scheme you will get one order. The students ought to get a good basis in mathematics and perhaps along with that, physics. Then chemistry, and the study of plants and animals would not be begun until the student had a good grounding in physics and chemistry. That, quite independently of Comte, is the point of view which has been urged for both high schools and colleges. It is the scheme on which many high school curriculums have been worked out.

[ii] You will find others taking the opposite view, saying that you should begin with physiography, physical geography, as the fundamental or first year science, that you should go from that to botany and zoology as your second year sciences, and then the chemistry, and that the last year should be devoted to physics, that you should work from the more concrete sciences to the more abstract.

[(b)] It is obvious that there is a real problem there. Something could be said for both sides. It is true that any scientific, comprehensive view of physics rests on mathematics. If you are going to get any fundamental explanations in chemistry you must fall back on your mathematics and on your physics. If you are going to carry your knowledge of biology back to any causal relations you must get to considerations of chemistry and physics. So there is something to be said for the first arrangement. On the other hand it is the natural pedagogical order to begin with the concrete and work to the abstract. Moreover, because physics is the most mathematical of the sciences, it is urged that it cannot be studied until one has a pretty thorough knowledge of algebra and geometry, and therefore physics must be postponed until the student has mathematics.

[(i)] I do not propose to solve that apparent contradiction in the teaching of secondary science, but simply to make one or two remarks. The first is that the whole problem is now greatly complicated because of the lack of any introduction to science in the elementary period. If the opportunities of elementary education were thoroughly utilized, then in the elementary period the student would have got the reality of what is attempted now in the first year of the high school course in physiography, a knowledge of the interaction of physical energy and of qualitative changes. He would have got his concrete background and would be ready for differentiation, which as a rule he is not ready for in the existing high school, and the claim for physical geography as the basis is for something to give the student a sort of survey of this interaction of physical forces and facts. It cannot adequately be done in one year, although if the student has been led from the beginning of his education into a thorough knowledge of the world as the home of man, one year could probably be spent profitably in reviewing, classifying, and systematizing somewhat, the facts got in a more incidental manner previously.

[(ii)] The second point is that there can be no doubt of the necessity of keeping mathematics and the sciences in as organic relations as possible. That is, there is a very natural correlation. Mathematics should, wherever possible, be held as aids and helps in dealing with questions that present themselves in science, and wherever possible, every advance made in mathematics should be used as a matter of the better comprehension of the facts, particularly of physics.

[(iii)] But the third remark perhaps makes the other two unnecessary. It is that there is no need of adopting either of these plans in any exclusive way. If the student has had his elementary period taken advantage of and can carry two of these lines abreast without getting mixed up, if the student is not acquainted with the main forces in the world in his elementary period, it would be misleading to attempt to carry the physical and the biological sciences parallel with each other. But if he has this knowledge of the earth as a background there would be no danger of confusion. The student could carry the two lines at once, he could easily have some in each school year, possibly every week, and insure the continual working back and forth, using the more fundamental sciences as methods to help explain the more concrete sciences that deal with life, and at the same time get his center of interest in the more abstract ones from the things which are, after all, most interesting and concrete, that is, the things that are clearly and obviously living and growing, and have most intimately to do with human welfare.

Another point which is of fundamental importance [(c)] for the secondary period is that considerations of method, that is of generalization, come more and more to the front.

There are two kinds of generalization, one is the sim- [(i)(a).] ple static formulation reached as the result of comparison and abstraction, by which we simply learn that a certain principle or law is found in a great variety of phenomena. Psychologically such a generalization as that is cut in two in the middle and is rendered inert. The real significance psychologically of the generalization is that it affords a method for the attack upon further subjects. It affords a point of view which helps organize and illumine further material. The chief difficulty in the secondary school period is that the generalization remains so largely nothing but bigger facts; they are more important facts than the knowledge of the details, but so far as the mental attitude is concerned, they are much the same sort of things. They remain simply more comprehensive surveys, they do not get the dynamic quality, they do not become utilized as method, carried over into new fields and used for their assimilation. We think of them as the final goal and ignore the importance of them as starting points, as ways of getting at new facts. Take the law of gravitation. Does it not represent in the ordinary mind an ultimate, final thing? And for that reason it is relatively dead. It is a summary that culminates, it is not a method by which we get at a lot of new material. To the ordinary mind it is simply a summary, it is a great big brute fact. To the student who has got at it experimentally it is a thing to be appealed to in every new experiment and consciously used constructively. But after all, until the spirit of investigation, the work of inquiry, that which is the reality of the laboratory, permeates the whole thing, these generalizations will for the most part remain simply as big statements of ultimate fact, and not as active psychological weapons and instruments.

[(b).] From the psychological standpoint then, the importance of generalization considered as methods to be applied to new fields of fact or to new sciences is the chief thing, and I venture to say one of the reasons why mathematics is not for so many minds what it ought to be is just because it remains so unapplied. If the student goes on far enough in science in college or graduate work he finally sees some applications of his mathematics as methods, but from the lack of correlation in the secondary education mathematics remains a thing by itself, a peculiar lot of symbols, interesting or uninteresting according to individual temperament, but which do not seem to have any vital place in the whole sphere of knowledge.

[(ii)] Two years ago I visited a normal training school in New Haven and found a fourth year class getting a pretty good introduction to calculus. The gentleman at the head of the school had previously been a professor in the Sheffield Scientific School and he said that most of the high school students understood the meaning of it better than his college students had done simply because he introduced them to calculus in connection with their constructive work. They saw the advantage of calculus as a method, that they could do things which they could not do by using ordinary algebra as the method of attack. That is what I mean in speaking of the value of generalization as method. Geometry is taught still as a comprehensive science. A person must demonstrate all the problems in Euclid or else he does not know geometry. From the standpoint of real education, geometrical method is of more importance than to be able to demonstrate the seventeenth proposition of the eighth book, and all the rest of the problems in Euclid. If a student could really get the geometrical method when he needed to demonstrate any proposition he would not have to depend on memory or on working them out by the laborious process which the average person goes through with in his geometry. It would mean something which would be alive, he would have some way of seeing into the thing. This is a matter of the future, although there are schools where a pretty good start has been made, but the first person who succeeds in working out the real correlation of mathematics with science and advanced forms of manual training, will have done more to simplify the problems of secondary education than any other one thing that I can think of.

In the higher period it is only necessary to repeat once [(3)(*a*)] more the general point of view of the specialist. Biology and chemistry have their significance for the physician. For the person going into modern commercial life, into manufacturing on a large scale, mathematics have their significance, and so on. Students who have been taken through the preceding periods can now specialize without any danger of narrowness. It is simply carrying the method standpoint a little further, and having his adequate background there is no danger of his becoming a mere specialist, as there is now in scientific specialization when the broad foundation has not been laid in the elementary education.

The only other thing that need be mentioned in higher [(*b*)] education is the significance of bringing to consciousness the method of science, that is, of realizing the significance of truth and the various forms of truth, and the various methods by which truth is got at, the philosophy of the sciences, particularly the logic of the sciences. That would naturally come in at this higher period to serve as the correlating union just as the concrete earth comes in in the elementary period and just as the application of one science comes in in the secondary period.

LECTURE XXX

March 20, 1899

[C.II.;D.: *The arts. The organization of method.*]

[*III.D.6.*] There remains one group of studies to speak of, namely the arts. In taking them up it is important to discriminate between the psychical and educational reality of the art idea and the forms which conventionally and traditionally go by that name.

[*a.*] The term "fine arts" as ordinarily used is restricted to such things as music, drawing, painting, sculpture, and possibly including literature in some of its highest flights. If we look at it from the psychological side however, art is a term with a very much more extended meaning. It signifies essentially any adequate mode of self expression, any outward act or attitude which conveys with a certain degree of purity and completeness and transparency, the mental state, the ideas and emotions that lie back of it. The reality of art applies to conduct, in other words, as well as to those things which we more technically term the fine arts; just as there are some who get expression through fine art, color, tone in writing, and so on, others would get their most adequate expression in the relations which they would take to other people, in flexible and sympathetic relationships socially, in ways of friendship, and so on, in tact, ease and grace of manner, as conveying the element of personality. Of course moral conduct is from that standpoint another form of art, so far as it is an adequate embodiment of any outward concreting of the personality that lies behind.

[*b.*(1)] Now this extended meaning is essential to take into account from the educational standpoint. Many of the modern aesthetic writers hold that the origin of art is in play. Whether that is so or not, the free play of the child is certainly a mode of art in this larger psychological conception of art. It is an adequate expression of the mental and emotional attitude that is behind. It is so immediate that you can't draw a line between what the child is thinking and doing in genuine play, the doing is such a transparent expression of the psychical reality. The same point applies however, not only to play, but to what the adult might term work, or to the various forms of constructive activity, so far as those are carried on by the child for the sake of the direct interest which he takes and finds in them, that is, as simply ways of externalizing and conveying his dominant thoughts and feelings. So far as the mental attitude and the mental result is concerned, and those are the important things educationally, I do not believe any line could be drawn between what the child is doing when he is engaged in drawing or painting, or modelling in clay, and what he is doing when he is cooking or working with tools in wood, provided in all cases he is doing the things because of the value there is to him in doing them, and not for the sake of any practical or utilitarian result that is to be gained.

        The constructive activity, so far as it is controlled, not [(2)] by some external end which it is deemed necessary to gain, but so far as it is controlled through being an aim to embody adequately or to convey adequately some interesting idea, it is artistic in spirit. That may be generalized by saying that the art form should be the determining principle for all early education. The child who likes numbers, whose mind gets play in perceiving and defining relationships of space and quantity, is doing what for him is an artistic mode of expression, while he may fall far behind in expressing his feelings and ideas through the medium of a pencil in what is termed "drawing," but the thing to look at is this expression, this carrying forth, or realizing of the individual mental attitude. We cannot find any discriminating line by taking the external thing simply, which the child is doing, and say because in one case he is using his pencil to make figures with, he is not artistic, while in the other case because he is using his pencil to draw a dog's head with, he is artistic. It is a question of first having the interesting idea to express, and then secondly, being able to express it with a certain degree of freedom and adequacy. All the rest of it is simply the external mode in which the expression goes on naturally, in that some persons would be deft along one line and other persons along others.

[(3)]   The standpoint may be restated simply by saying that the adult separation between beauty and use has practically no existence for the child. His experiences come to him as totalities. They are either interesting or they are not, but where anything really interests him, takes hold of him as worthwhile, it does connect with his own personality, with his own individuality in such a direct and immediate way that it is simply thrusting in another standpoint to try and set up certain things as merely useful and certain things as merely beautiful. As I said before in speaking of the manual training work, there may be some cases in which future use comes in as an additional element of interest. It is not that the thing is done for the sake of its use, but simply because it has a use it means more to the child. There are other cases undoubtedly where the lack of any external use will be a portion of the value or meaning of the thing. And out of these two classes there comes later on a more conscious and obvious distinction between the useful thing and the beautiful thing, or between what we call the fine arts and the useful arts, the useful arts being devoted to the production of realities which are valued as means to something else, while the fine arts are valued simply and only as recapitulations and expressions, as typical or representative expressions of the simple value of living itself, without having to be put to any outward use. While music may have a value in making soldiers more enduring and courageous, or in making children more quiet and tractable, it is not the fact that it has those uses which make it an art or music. It is music because in and of itself there is a satisfactory expression embodied of thought and feeling. However, I would insist that for the elementary period, and probably for the whole period of adolescence, the distinction is not natural. The child either does or does not do something. He either finds himself, finds worth and significance in what he is doing and experiencing, or he does not. If he does there is no striking illumination in calling it art or considering it from the standpoint of beauty or use. The thing is simply to give the child such variety in the forms of expression, to give him a sufficient number of modes of uttering his own feelings and emotions, so that he gets an all around development, and will have the basis laid for whatever capacity later on may show itself in artistic directions in the more limited and technical sense of that term.

Regarding the arts in that more limited sense, I do not
[(4)]   know that anything need be said which was not said
about literature, which is, in that sense, a form of art,
namely, that it is not its content, but its form which differenti-
ates it from ordinary everyday experiences. The arts are representative, that is, they take the factors, the elements of every
day experience and reproduce or re-present them, but the reproduction is in such forms as let us get at the more transient
elements in these ordinary experiences. The representation is
in such forms as to idealize the everyday experiences. That implies that in education this balance shall be maintained, that
there shall be the adequate background and content to ordinary
and every day experience, and that the art work shall grow out
of them by giving it a heightened intensity and significance,
that is, shall not be externally superimposed on it, or arbitrarily
substituted for it. Continuity between the two is the important
thing in education.

In leaving this subject I may add that personally these
[c.(1)]   remarks have most of their meaning for me because
of the criticism which I have perhaps heard most
often upon the work undertaken in the Elementary School.* It
is that the work is too utilitarian and materialistic, too much
attention is devoted to the manual and industrial side, and that
there is not therefore enough attention to the poetic, imaginative, and spiritual, ideal aspects of children's natures. Hearing
that objection so often has made it necessary for me to reflect
upon the matter more or less, and it seems to me that the objection is one which holds simply because of the attitude into
which the adult has gradually got educated, but that for the
child there are no such dualisms, there are no such separations,
and it is not desirable that they should be reproduced as the
child grows up, in any such fixed form as they exist in the mind
of the adult at present. The only idealism and spiritual value
that after all, amount to very much in life, are those which do
grow out of every day things and occupations, which represent
our growing consciousness of the depth of meaning contained
in these every day things, and which find finally some application in every day life, instead of being set off in a little sphere
by themselves, so that we pass from the things which we call

[* Dewey is here referring to his Laboratory School.]

material to the things which we call spiritual as many people pass from week days to Sundays and back again.

[(2)] The significance of the arts in the secondary education, in detail has not, I think, been sufficiently worked out so that we can make any very definite statements about it. In general it would conform to the general principle laid down, that is, the student should become conscious of his particular form of artistic capacity, of whatever mode or line it is, in which he can most freely and sympathetically embody himself, that he should have sufficient practice in the arts, both in the broader and more technical sense, so as to measure himself, so as to see what he can do or whether he can do anything or not, and thus finally be prepared to specialize in a more intelligent way: on the basis of the broader culture, on the basis of putting more meaning into what he does, finding really an artistic wealth in that instead of going through life as so many of us are apt to do, more or less dwarfed and stunted because we have never had sufficient opportunity to express ourselves along these lines, and whatever capacity we might originally have had has consequently atrophied for the lack of any utterance or any stimulus which would produce expression of itself.

[(3)] So far as higher education is concerned, it would simply indicate that there is a point of view from which the arts may be pursued which makes them an important part of the higher education, as important indeed as are the studies which are embodied in the higher education. There is a standpoint from which music could be taken up and pursued as a genuine and valued subject of the university education, or painting or sculpture, as much as advanced scientific research or linguistic investigation. On one side they have sufficient content in themselves to be proper studies, and on the other side they do mark specialized professions or vocations in life.

[IV.A.I.] I shall go on now to the next main subject, namely that of method. In taking it up I wish to recall briefly two conceptions previously presented. The first is that there is no objective distinction between subject matter and method. The distinction is simply a convenience of treatment. Educational subject matter, to be real subject matter, must be subject matter of experience, and as such, that is, as experience, it involves the process of experiencing, it involves the mental attitude taken toward it, the interest there is in it, the reaction to it, the process of assimilating it. It is a matter of convenience to distinguish between what is experience, and the way, the process, the how of the assimilation. In the discussion of method we simply emphasize this latter aspect, the how of experience, as distinct from its what, although in reality the how and the what always go together.

The other point is that in considering method we have [2.] also to go back to considerations regarding the process of mental development, of growth. Whether the epoch stages of growth as I roughly outlined them in a previous lecture are correct or not, we cannot get any principles regarding method which really amount to very much unless we do get a proper statement of the stages of growth, for experience is not the same at different stages. The attitude taken toward it is not the same, interests are not the same, and accordingly the process of experiencing is not the same. I do not mean that it is absolutely different, but simply that we must take into account the typical attitudes and interests characteristic of various stages of growth.

I mention this point particularly because the Her- [a.] bartian school, in its desire to get a scientific account of method, has insisted upon the unity of method, that there is one essential and intrinsic process of assimilating the presented material, and that accordingly there are certain formal steps of method which the mind always goes through in the same order, and which therefore should be adhered to in all instruction. Now it is certainly a commendable thing to have endeavored to base the theory of instruction upon the discovery of the unity of the mental process. Unless that can be done there can be no scientific pedagogy. It would be at most a collection of various traditions, devices, and convenient things to do. But because there is some kind of unity of mental process, of natural operations and method, it does not follow of necessity that that process shows itself in exactly the same way at all stages of development, and that therefore it gives a formula, or outline of steps which may be followed in recitation. There is undoubtedly unity of vegetable life, there is a unity in the life of any given plant, but we do not on that account ignore the distinction between the seedling and the plant as it is approaching maturity, and the seed bearing plant. We would not say that any definite scheme of structure or mode of treatment of the plant could be rigidly followed at all times because there is a single unity of life process. We would first penetrate to the unity of the life process and then give equal value to the different forms in which it manifests itself at different stages; and the discovery of the different forms would be of as much importance for the scientific botanist as the recognition of the unity. The same holds, I think, with regard to the unity of mental operation.

[b.]　　I shall come back later on to the formal steps, so called, of the Herbartian school. I will simply mention here that as ordinarily given they are as follows: (1) preparation, or calling into activity on the part of the pupil those ideas and interests which will help him in receiving and apperceiving the new facts, or truths, the new lesson in other words; (2) objective presentation, putting before him either in form of actual objects or pictures or conversation, something of the facts or truths to be studied; (3) comparison, seeing the points of likeness and difference between this new material and others of something the same sort, previously studied ;(4) generalization, perception, and formulation of the common elements thus reached through comparison; and (5) application, or using the general principle, the general truth arrived at to help grasp or deal with or explain some new facts not previously studied. Now it is held by them that from the standpoint of psychology and logic the mind must go through those successive steps in the complete assimilation of any subject matter whatsoever. Accordingly the work of instruction is to simplify and systematize and arrange those steps which the mind must go through with so that it will do so with the least friction and with the maximum of clearness and final positive result. I say it is the fundamental thing in the scientific theory of instruction that it should go back to the recognition of some determinate process of mental operation as the basis of its instruction, that it should realize some law or principle. Then learning or gaining experience is not a haphazard chance matter which can be gone at this way just as well as that, but there is a process there which has just as much reality and certainty in its way, as the law of gravitation or any law which is studied in the physical sciences. Taking that standpoint, it is the only thing which justifies any-

thing which could call itself in the most remote degree, the
science or the art of education. It does not follow from that
standpoint of the single process with its own law or principle,
that the mind would go through it at different times in any
such way that it could be set off in these uniform steps, or if
we were agreed that the mind does go through all these steps
in a general way, the thing which is presented at one stage
would differ so much from what is presented at another stage,
that comparatively little is gained by giving them all a common
name.

As the basis then for considering method, I shall call
[3.]   attention to three types of mental attitude: (1) what
was previously called direct experiencing, the practical and so to speak motor attitude; (2) indirect experience,
in which the reflection and observation are utilized upon the
occurrence of some difficulty in order to ultimately further
the direct experience; (3) the attitude of intellectual operation, of observation and generalization, as a specialized attitude, as something which has meaning in and of itself. To
recall what was said before, the first of these attitudes is the
whole of the early elementary period, the second is that of the
later elementary period, while the third is that which comes
to the foreground in the secondary education.

 # LECTURE XXXI

March 21, 1899

[D.I.1.: *The psychology of method. The direct stage of learning. Learning and reconstruction.*]

As has been frequently suggested the term "learning"
[IV.B.] and consequently the term "teaching" or "instruction"
which is its exact correlate, has a two-fold meaning
which I will term the direct and indirect. The direct is that
ordinarily termed learning by or through experience. We do not
set out to learn anything. We set out to do something, but in
the doing there is an enlargement of consciousness, an enlargement of our horizon, a gain of information which comes in
incidentally, or in relation to the active experience itself. It
goes without saying of course, that the child is naturally one
who learns by experience, not because he intends to learn, nor
because he has lessons set him. The psychological basis and
counterpart of that learning by experience may be termed either
the coordination, or organic circuit.*

To indicate a little more definitely what the nature
[1.] of the coordination is, the start, so far as consciousness at least is concerned, is made with some instinct
or with some active impulse. There is an uneasiness or an instinctive tendency to move in some way or other, to turn the
head, the focus of the eyes, to reach with the arms, to handle
with the hands, to balance the whole body or move the body as
a whole, to run or to walk; and this energy corresponds to that
impulse, being discharged through the efferent nerves, the so-
called motor nerves, resulting in muscular movement, in
change of the whole body and possibly in change of things, objects in space. Now that change thus brought about through

[* See Dewey's most important treatment of this material in: "The Reflex
Arc Concept in Psychology," *Psychological Review*, III, July, 1896, pp.
357–370.]

the extension, through the carrying out of the impulse, results in impression, in changes of conscious awareness, of new values, new qualities in things, which of course from the physiological side correspond to the stimuli that come in through the sensory nerves. That impression then is associated, or rather fused, assimilated, with the original instinct or impulse, so that it now has a conscious meaning, value attached to it which it did not have before. Through this return into consciousness of the effects produced, changes brought about by acting on the instinct or impulse, we learn what it means; it is revealed to us in terms of what it will effect, not externally simply, but in changes of feeling which it brings about in our experience. The impulse in being brought to consciousness has been interpreted, has a conscious meaning put into it, but it still retains its outgoing motor tendencies, so that upon appropriate occasion it again discharges in action, and through that action again, new experiences are had, new movements are made, new sensations experienced, which are returned, so to speak to consciousness, and which enlarge our consciousness of the impulse still further, which make it more definitely a consciously valued thing, instead of a blind working tendency.

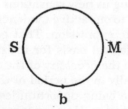

As an illustration, take it on the basis of some physiological stimulus. The impulse operates. Call the half of the circle marked "M" the outgoing or expression side; the point "b" the point so to speak where the impulse strikes the object. Then as soon as that is done, on the Sensory side, marked "S," or the incoming side, the doing reflects itself in sensations, and the circuit is completed. Only now, from now on, the character of the impulse or instinct is changed. It is now modified and also more or less controlled by the results of its previous operation. Take the standard case in the psychologies, the child reaching for the candle flame. In the first place the physiological stimulus on the eye of seeing the light, operates through an instinctive, at least partially instinctive coordination in the brain. It discharges into the channels along the path that goes to the arm centers, and the child goes to the candle flame. As he touches the flame he gets impressions of heat and pain. Now those sensations are not isolated; they do not stand by themselves; they are fused with this previous coordination existing between the stimulus of light, and the next time it is not merely a reaching in response to the stimulus of light. The stimulus is modified into a light, a light-heat-pain stimulus, and that discharges into quite a different path, and calls for a different kind of activity than the mere light stimulus alone would do. The next time the child holds himself still or he moves away.

[2.]   If you will work out a few instances in that line in your mind, you will see that all we learn we learn in that way, having some instinct and finally some habit, getting new sensations and experiences, having those react, modify, reconstruct, and control, and stimulate in a new way the old instinct or habit which is expressed in action and gives birth to new experiences which modify in turn instinct and habit, and so on indefinitely. It is that which makes the continuity of our mental life, this continual expression of our impulses in action, giving us new sensations and ideas, and those being at once related to our active tendencies and directing and changing their future expression. That general point of view gives us the psychological basis for insisting, as I did in the earlier lectures, upon the necessity of the child's taking a practical attitude, especially in the period of the elementary education, that is, of there being opportunities for him to act and to learn through his action. He cannot really learn anything in any other way, and it is simply a question of organizing and enlarging that tendency of the child to act, and to learn through his acting, which gives meaning to the elementary period of education.

[a.]   There are two aspects of this recoordination or reconstruction that takes place, which may be spoken of. As we act we get two types or classes of impressions or sensations, one the so-called muscular sensations (I use this term as a very general one) or those which result from a movement of the body and which tell us about the changes which have taken place in the attitude and movement of the body. The child in reaching his arms gets a sense of reaching things. He does not feel the same as if he kept quiet or as if he moved his leg; but if he feels or sees anything he gets sensations which correspond to the qualities of the object. It is important to note that practically every movement enlarges the sense of the body as the organ of action, and also enlarges our acquaintance with our environment, with the world of things with reference to which we operate.

[b.] If there were time to follow it on, I would try to show how that results in a two-fold modification or reconstruction there: one in the formation of habits, that is the strictly active and motor side, and the other in the consciousness of ideas which tell us what the uses of the habits are, which inform us what sort of results we reach when our habits are put into operation. I cannot go into detail here, I simply suggest that what I mean by habit is not any routine, nor yet even a perfectly well established tendency to action, but simply the expression of any impulse so far as that is in any degree modified or controlled by its own previous manifestations so that there is a continuity established between the past and the present. What we have done has not disappeared, does not remain inert. It determines, it fixes to some extent, our future attitude and future tendencies to action, and that is the root fact in habit, this establishing of a connection between the future activities and the present, through the modification of our tendencies to action by the results of our past experiences. That is purely a practical thing so far as it goes, it is an unconscious thing. It is not left to our thinking or reflection to decide upon this matter. "The burnt child dreads the fire" as in the first place he reached for the bright light. His physiological and psychological structure, so to speak, has been modified so that instead of having to reflect the next time, he will instinctively withdraw or hold back, and consciousness, if it comes in at all, will work in the opposite direction. The habit then, represents the unconscious side of the organization of activity and experience. It is a name for a fact however, that every expression of activity serves in and of itself to some way modify future attitudes and tendencies in action. Now if that were the whole of this process, we simply would become more and more perfect machines all the time. As a machine we would act more economically and successfully. But the action also reflects itself in conscious changes, in new values, in awareness of new qualities, and so the habit, the strictly practical and motor side, is accompanied all the time by a running commentary of sensations and ideas which tell what its value is, a running commentary not only of sensations, but feelings, pleasures, pains, and emotional excitations, of like and dislike, of desire and aversion that go along with the experience.

[c.]   Now this of course is learning by experience in the typical form, and has its special application in the early years of life. It indicates how the child learns to walk, talk, manage his body, and control his sense organs, not only practically, but intellectually, so that he gets something by using them. All that tremendous start which the child gets in the first two or three years of his life, is of course a growth which he will not begin to equal in any other two or three years of his life. There is a good article in the last number of *School and Home Education* by Professor Kirkpatrick on "Learning Voluntary Movements" which is right along this same line.[1] Now the stimuli which set the impulses and instincts into operation are practically provided for in the organism itself in the early stage. The child who lives in anything approaching a normal environment cannot help having the stimuli which will call out these instincts and impulses. They are general in character, not highly specialized and refined; they are common, such as the environment repeatedly presents, and they are very largely taken care of in the physiological structure of the organism itself. In learning to walk one of the stimuli is the contact of the feet with some surface. It is probable that the child begins to walk from the time he is a month old. He is having stimuli and moving his legs in a more or less rhythmical manner. That is the reason why, given anything like a healthy environment, the education of the child takes care of itself during the first two or three years. Education is nothing but the affording of the appropriate stimuli to call forth the activities in the most important direction. Nature itself, personifying nature, furnishes stimuli in the early period. Hence it requires a good deal of ingenuity or extremely unsanitary and pathological conditions really seriously to check the learning of the child in this early period. But now all these

[1 E. A. Kirkpatrick, "Learning Voluntary Movements," *School and Home Education*, XVIII:7, March 1899, pp. 337–344.]

main activities are worked out; walking, talking, and the control of the body, muscles and sense organs, the stimuli become more specialized, they must be more refined, select; they must be adapted more definitely to call forth particular kinds of responses and to avoid other kinds of responses.

[d.]   The work of the school then, or formal education comes in. The education of the school consists in affording proper stimuli, in surrounding the child with conditions which will call forth by preference certain responses and let other impulses and instincts remain comparatively dormant, for some of them finally to die out; and also to furnish the conditions so that when these activities or responses take place, there shall be as real and organized a return wave on the impression side as possible. If the child were to act in a vacuum he would not get any results from his acting. If he acts in a poverty stricken environment, he gets a poor return from his action, although we know children of remarkable instinctive action can get a good deal out of a poor environment. If the environment is disorderly, the return wave in consciousness will be similarly broken-up and disorganized. The child may get many experiences, but they will not integrate themselves and so they will not further development of any great account. This lack of organization may show itself either in space, or in time. It is not enough to have it orderly at the moment when the child is operating, but it must be continuous, there must be some uniformity, some rhythm, some line of organization from day to day so that the experience shall be cumulative, shall build up the child's experience. The problem of instruction then, put in psychological terms, in the elementary period, may be reduced practically to the affording of an environment in which the child acts, which stimulates him adequately with sufficient variety and yet with coherence so that the various stimuli serve to cooperate with each other, and an environment of sufficient content, sufficient wealth of its own, so that when the child acts in it, his return wave of consciousness, his income, his impressions, may be valuable and sufficiently orderly, so that there will be a natural tendency in this return that he gets to integrate itself, to build itself up into habit wholes, or in mental or ideal wholes. The organization of the stimuli to action, in other words, is the psychological statement of the problem of elementary education.

There are two or three points that I want to speak of that differ from some of the ordinary statements.

[3.] First regarding the sensation. Psychologies, and following the psychologies the pedagogies, have been teaching for the last two centuries that knowledge, experience, blends with sensations, and that experience is built up out of these sensations. The statement is not exactly false, but it certainly is not more than a half truth, and a half truth which is very misleading in its pedagogical moral. It is only a half truth because it does not place the sensation, because it does not show how the sensation normally comes in, and how it operates in building up the child's experience. It is because the sensations are connected with and grow out of the active impulses, because they are the register, the thermometer which tells us about the degree, and amount, and kind of expression which the active impulses are having, that they really amount to anything educatively. I am not going to argue that psychologically we never have any sensations that are not the accompaniments of our instincts to action. I am willing to admit for the sake of the argument that we do have them, but they are not the ones which lead to mental growth; they do not organize themselves into our useful habits or into our coherent intellectual make up. Supposing you had to shoot sensations in the child indefinitely and at different angles— sensations of light, sound, etc. If that were all there is to it, the more sensations you subject the child to, the more disintegrated he would become, the more overwhelmed. Instead of being helps to his intellectual growth they would be actual hindrances. It cannot be said that the doctrine has never been acted upon in practice with sufficient sincerity so that much harm has come from it, for still you will go into some kindergarten schools and find children all put on edge by the multiplicity of unrelated sensations which they have had suggested to them. The child is taught color just as color, all kinds of colors, and bright colors; sounds, all kinds of sounds, and so on, and they act as excitations, but they have no use; they do not play any part in the scheme of his activities because they do not lend themselves to any purpose, and the result is physically as well as mentally harmful. What always remains true, if not carried to this point of excessive over-stimulation, is that sensations thus introduced, do not get their organic place in such a child's life. What do such sensations amount to? Sensations should lead to an idea, but when the child is simply stimulated to these externally presented sensations, what natural lines of intrinsic association, integration are afforded him? The whole thing remains external; it does not lend itself to the growth of the child. It is not a mere fact of sensations, or the multiplicity of sensations, but the relevancy of the sensations. The fact that the sensation is an index, a reflector of some activity that is going on, on one side, and on the other side that it serves to reinforce, maintain, or better, direct that activity in the future. Sensations of touch which the child gets, say from the use of his hands in modeling, which he gets from his use of tools in making things, or from his pencil or brush in painting are educative, because they are impressions which on one side tell him what he is doing, give him a sense of his own action, and on the other side they are the necessary means which he must utilize in order to improve his activities, to carry out his ideas better. But such sensations are not brought to consciousness by themselves, they are always communicated with the larger activity of which they are a part and within which they are functioning. To make a sensation conscious by itself is always abnormal, unhealthy. We recognize that that is the case in the matter of taste, that the value of the sensation of taste is really in directing the process of eating intelligently. It is only a glutton and epicure who takes his sensations as things by themselves, and that is an unhealthy thing even from the moral point of view. It is possible to give a child an abnormal appetite for colors and sounds, putting him in the attitude of consciously wanting more excitation. There is no difference between that and the abnormal thirst of the drunkard, and the abnormal appetite of the glutton. It is not that in one way all that is said about the importance of sensation at the beginning of the educative process is not true, but simply that instead of being placed as they should be in the process of action, they have been treated as isolated things in themselves, and thus their proper function has not been brought out.

 # LECTURE XXXII

March 22, 1899

[D.I.1.: *The psychology of habit.*]

[IV.B.4.a.] There are two or three points further of which I wish to speak briefly with reference to habits, for the psychology of the habit is more than anything else the basis for the consideration of method in any of the later phases—that is, the intelligent theory of habit, the theory which sees habit in its relations on one side, to the conditions of its formation, that is, to the impulses which get organized into the habit, and in reference to the use of the habit on the other side, its significance in reaching ends, in reaching valuable results. I mention these two points particularly, because the current theory and the current practice which embodies, even unconsciously to the teacher, this theory, is very apt to fail at both ends, that is, with relation to the dependence of the habit on its spontaneous impulses on one side, and with reference to the necessity of a conscious valuable result being fulfilled by the habit on the other. The current assumption very often is that the habit may be induced practically from stimuli which are pretty external in character. That point of view finds its embodiment in the prevailing conception that habits are formed by repetition, that all you practically have to do is to give some stimulus and you will get a person to do something, and then you have him keep on doing it, you have him repeat it over and over again, until finally it becomes ingrained in his structure, it becomes a habit. That conception even if unconsciously adopted, is really the presupposition of most that is called drill, of what is regarded as intellectual discipline. The point of view is to my mind false and pernicious in its practical bearings. Theoretically speaking it puts the cart

before the horse. Repetition plays some part in the formation
of habit, but it is a strictly subordinate part. It puts the cart
before the horse because it is truer to say that we repeat because we have habits, than that we form habits by repetition.
Its fundamental falsity is in ignoring the fact that the fundamental basis for any habit is the projective outgoing force of
some natural impulse, and that the habit is simply the organization of that impulse, it is losing its more or less blind and
chaotic character, and getting definite shape.

   The moment you take that point of view, the whole
[(*r*)] conception of drill and repetition is put in quite a
   different light. Instead of being regarded as a thing
distinct and carried on by itself, it becomes at the very most
an incidental question. The fundamental question is to call the
impulses into play through their own intrinsic stimuli so that
they will work themselves out along certain channels and
toward certain definite ends instead of spreading themselves
in a diffuse and random way. The mind of the teacher will
not be on repetition, on getting the child to go over the thing
again and again, but simply on finding a natural stimulus to
his impulses, the stimulus which will call the impulses into
play so that they will reach a valuable result. As matter of fact
a large part of the repetition, in the way in which it is actually
carried on, is due to the fact that we do not find the natural
stimulus to the impulse, and the repetition is simply a device
that we have to get up to try and make good our failure to get
at the thing in the right way in the first place. The child who
has no natural stimulus, no motive for realizing that two and
two make four, will have to repeat that proposition over and
over again until it is driven into him from without, in the cold
chisel method; but if the child has a stimulus to realizing the
significance of the proposition, if he has any need for it, if it
fits organically into his experience, he sees it; and while I
would not say that seeing it once he never would forget, it
certainly would do away with most of the repetition; you would
simply have to give him opportunity to use the fact once gained
to refresh its significance. The child does not have to be drilled
into the fact that snow is cold and ice is good to skate on; his
experience is connected with those things, they mean something to him, and if the appropriate stimulus presents itself

with any kind of frequency, anything approaching frequency, the experience, the meaning, the truth of it carries itself along in his mind and becomes the center for the accretion of other experiences. I have seen first rate children drilled in the proposition that two and two made four until they could hardly be otherwise than suspicious of the truth of the proposition. So I say that in general a large amount of the repetition is simply due to the failure to introduce the fact or truth into any kind of intrinsic relation, any kind of natural stimulus and motive in the first place; it does not grow out of any instinctive impulse in the child. It is something inserted from without, and the repetition is the necessary result of that external stimulus.

[(2)] On the other side the great defect in the treatment of habit was indicated in the quotation which I made from Aristotle early in the course, that first the child should be trained in habits and afterwards he should get a rational training, should come to see the meaning of his acts. Of course that goes along with this repetition idea as the essence of habit. The thing is to be made mechanical, the child is to do it over and over again until he has a habit, and then he is supposed to be prepared for seeing the reason for doing it. It is supposed the child has to learn to read before he can read, the mechanical habit of realizing forms, and then he can read intelligently so as to get at something, get some value out of what he is reading. Of course teachers do not suppose that this first preparation should be entirely blind, that the child should not incidentally pick up a few ideas in learning to read, but the reason for learning to read is regarded as absolutely subordinate, and you remember the quotation from the Committee of Ten on the same point. That is what I meant by getting the habit just as a habit, and then afterwards having some reason for the habit. That split between the habit and the reason for the habit, is the most serious error in all education from the psychological point of view, to my mind; it comes out in so many different ways and induces finally such a radical split in our nature. So many habits are instilled into us whose rationale we have not sufficient grip on; and on the other side, we have so many ideas with reference to which we have no habits. It is a split between theory and practice so that practice remains more or less dead, inert, mechanical in character, and the theoretical side remains simply so much objective knowledge or accumulation, without its having any natural and easy effect on our conduct, on what we do.

Now of course when I use the term "reason" here, it [b.] must be understood in a reasonable way. The conception of reasoning with children does not mean arguing with them as it is sometimes interpreted to mean. There is no greater nuisance in the world than a child who has been argued with until he has learned to argue himself. I never saw a child who could be beaten at that game after he had once thoroughly learned it. Neither does it mean that abstract reasons should be presented to him. It is that the child shall see some point or value in what he is doing. Small children get that simply through hinting or suggesting some point which they assimilate and carry over into what they are doing. I mean that they get it mainly through suggestion rather than through a logical reasoning process. Again it means that the impulse and habit shall be carried to the point where it does bring in some return, where it does make a return wave in consciousness so that the child sees and feels that he has gained something, that he has got something by what he has been doing, so that after that the habit, as the means of operation, and the result, as the end reached through this means, are always associated together in his mind. The isolation of the habit, forming it simply from without, and through the medium of repetition, establishes a systematic separation between the means and the end. When the child has learned a habit simply as a thing by itself, as if it were the whole thing by itself, it is no wonder that after that he is lame and inactive and uncertain in his attempts to adapt his habits to ends. Having been originally formed as a mechanical thing, it is not so easy at a given time for him definitely to turn around and begin to use these mechanical things as intelligent instruments freely at his command for working out problems of reaching ends.

To go back to reading as an illustration, the child who has been taught to read mainly as a matter of quick recognition of forms uttered in corresponding sounds would hardly ever get anything more. Even after he does begin to read for the sake of what is in it and there is a simulation of intelligence in his oral reading, he will have the other habit so thoroughly formed that he cannot get the two things into very organic relations to each other. It may seem impressive, but that is probably in imitation of some teacher rather than actually natural expression on his part of the thought which he has grasped.

Arithmetic would give us a more fruitful field for illustration, because it has been taught that it is necessary for the pupil to learn numerical combinations first so that by and by he can put them to some intelligent use. The thing breaks down every time because it takes training in putting this knowledge to use in order to give facility in it. It is a habit in using numerical combinations that is most necessary, and when that habit is not started from the start, the use of numbers will be, relatively speaking, lame and uncertain and blind. It is perfectly astonishing the amount of knowledge of arithmetic a child may have and the little he may know when trying to apply it to practical life, just because they have not been presented to him in relationship to each other.

[c.]   Repetition on one side and scrappiness on the other are what constitutes too much of our education. (I am of course applying this to the primary period.) Scrappiness comes from not seeing things through, from not following an impulse or idea until it has worked itself out, until it has got somewhere and the child can see what it leads up to, what its actual completion is. I was once told by a gentleman, perhaps unduly pessimistic, that his recollection of his school days was starting a lot of things which he never finished, of which he never saw the real bearings and significance. He would get hold of one thought which seemed interesting and when drilled on that he was given some more, and so on. That repetition comes from the failure to place the habit in relation to its starting point; the scrappiness comes from failing to place it with reference to the realization of some outcome. You once in a while find a man too busy to attend to his own business, and a good deal of school teaching is something of the same sort; there is so much ground to be gone over that there is not time to attend to any of it. It is not recognized that to take one idea or one set of ideas and work them out until the child sees them in their relation to each other is infinitely more important for purposes of growth than it is to have him filled up with a great variety and multiplicity of lessons and facts.

　　　　　There are three other points which I wish to mention [d.]　briefly. First, habit is the basis of generalization in early life. Every habit has a certain momentum beyond itself, a projective force. The nature of habit is to be a tendency that controls future experience. It is this projective momentum of any idea which constitutes the reality of generalization for the immature mind; the idea does not remain fixed, but it has a moving, a dynamic force. The child who really has got hold of an idea will begin to use and apply it; it becomes a way in which he sees other things and interprets them, and in that way there is a core of continuity which weaves his various experiences together. That may not be a logical generalization, but it is a psychological generalization, and moreover I should say it was the only basis for conscious logical reflection later on. There was a method of teaching arithmetic in vogue where the teacher was so afraid the child would not understand that he had to do what is called "analysis." That was supposed to make him understand it; but as matter of fact it reduced itself to verbal formulae into which the child inserted the proper numbers at the proper point in the hope that the thing would come out right in the end. The intelligent application in dealing with new problems, giving them this projective force so that they become the medium of controlling future experience, is the only generalization of any value. We deceive ourselves by thinking that the child, because he can repeat certain formulas has learned generalization. The machinery of generalization gets between the child and the idea and conceals the facts. You may insert the most absurd conditions and relations into an arithmetical problem of this kind and the child will go at it as glibly as if the thing were possible. If you do not believe that, try it with any class of children brought up with arithmetical analysis. Ask how long it will take to load five hundred cattle into freight cars if each car holds twenty cattle, and see how many will go to work. The emphasis has been in the wrong place, in not attempting to realize and apply, to deal with the actual conditions presented. If the child gets his habits of orderly work, he will have something, when more mature, to turn back on and formulate into a generalization or relationship.

In connection with the Herbartian theory of apper-
[e.(1)] ception I would also say that the theory underesti-
mates the importance of habit and overestimates the
importance of a conscious idea. We do the larger part of our
apperceiving through the medium of habits than ideas and the
child does the same. The Herbartians insist on the first stage
being that of preparation, when the child consciously reviews
his previous experiences and previous lessons along that subject matter, and gets them into shape to be apperceiving, massing, for apprehending, appropriating new material which is
to be presented. Now that is a great bore to little children. If
they have had an experience which has taken hold of them,
it does not appeal to them to also go over it again and state
it in consciousness. When you come to think of it, it is a stupid
thing after all, to be always doing that, and this continual
preliminary agitation of ideas gets between them and their
objects. When the child comes to a standstill, when he cannot
go ahead, then of course is the time when he has to make his
knowledge and experience conscious. He does have to review
it in order to get a fresh starting point, to see where he is, and
what he already does know that is available. But the natural
standpoint is to use the experiences directly which the child
already has.

I have not time to go over the Herbartian idea, but I
[(2)]   will generalize this criticism and say that the weak
point in general seems to be the under-insistence of
the unconscious element, of the instincts and habits, and the
over-insistence on the intellectual side of conscious ideas. Conscious ideas are extremely important in their place as helps
in dealing with difficulties and conditions when the habit fails.
If the habit does not fail, it is as a rule a waste of time to simply formulate it into conscious ideas. I mean for children of
this period. In the intermediate period of experience the child,
as I said, gets conscious of the difference between means and
ends, or he is capable of presenting ends to himself consciously.
He is therefore conscious of problems, not simply of things
to be done, but ends to be reached, points to be worked out,
and his mental attitude becomes that of adaptation rather
than of direct response to stimulus or to suggestion; that is,
having some problem the question is to go over and reflect
upon his experiences, to review what he already knows, and

pick out the points which are available which bear upon the problem in hand, and to arrange them in order that they will help him solve the problem. At this point then the element of conscious attention to technique, that is to theories or modes of solution, attention to the form of doing a thing instead of the mere doing itself, comes in. The child, having ends which he wishes to reach, must of course now have put at his disposal the most efficient and economical ways of reaching these things, and so analysis comes in. The important point is still to keep this attention to technique, this attention to method, in some relation to the end so that it shall be intelligently worked out and applied, instead of blindly.

This is the period when psychologically, attention, [5.] what the psychologists call voluntary attention, comes to the front and occupies the same position, as in the earlier period, in the formation of habits, was occupied by non-voluntary attention. "Non-voluntary attention" so called, in one sense is no attention at all. It is more than attention. The child who is playing with his ball is not attending to his ball as if it were a goal outside of himself; he is simply playing with it. The artist who is absolutely taken up with his music or painting cannot be said in strict truth to be attending to his music or painting. They are not enough outside of him to give special force to the phrase, "he is attending to it." There is no separation between him and his object. However, my point is not a verbal one. It is simply that when we become conscious of ends more or less remote, and the necessity of selecting and adapting means with reference to the remote ends, our mental attitude is quite different and would be termed "attention" proper. There is now a tension and a moving back and forth; a reaching out of the mind toward some end. The first thing is that there should be an end in consciousness, that there should be a problem of which the child is conscious.

Of course it is quite a different thing to have the teacher conscious of the problem and to have the child conscious of it. We do not really give out problems when we simply give them out. The problem is not really given out until the child conceives it as a problem, until he sees the particular point toward which he must work, until he has an objective in his mind which supplies him with a motive of operation. Now the too frequent custom is that the problem is left to the text book and the teacher, and the pupil is supposed to furnish the solution, and the division of labor is not one that works successfully. Put more specifically, attention of this kind is psychologically an attitude of inquiry. You cannot inquire about a thing until you have some definite point which you wish to reach. When you give out a lesson in geography, latin, or algebra, you do not of necessity induce the inquiring attitude in the mind of the pupil. If it is given to him simply as so much lesson to be learned, it makes no difference how many problems there are objectively involved there. A bright child may more or less instinctively hit upon these salient points and begin to centralize his thinking with reference to them, but the object of instruction is that this work of defining the problems should be assisted, facilitated by the teacher. To exaggerate the statement somewhat to bring out the point: the child ought to recite at his desk, and spend the recitation hour in finding out what the lesson means, in finding out what it is that he must find out, not in learning answers to questions, but in finding out what the questions are. The average recitation is one in which the child is supposed to know by instinct what the questions are, and the recitation hour is spent in trying to find out what the answers are; but not having questions he has no answers; he has at best information which he can repeat from having memorized it.

I might amplify that statement, but the essence of
[6.]   the whole proposition is that the gist of attention is
the attitude of inquiry, and that that attitude implies some conscious end to be reached, some problem, some query which is in the mind, and then the going over of past experience in order to pick out what bears on the point in question, and then in arranging and adapting it. In this process of inquiry there are obviously two sides. One is the analysis, the picking out of material that is available. The mind is put in the attitude of hunting around in experiences and objects and lessons presented, and says to itself: Now how will that do? What help toward solution does this afford? It is the attitude of observation, of discrimination, of mental alertness, of hunting for the answers to the questions that are in mind. On the other side there is the synthesis, the putting together and adapting of the material thus selected to get a solution out of it. I do not mean that the mind first does all its selecting and

then all its relating with reference to a topic in hand, but that there is a constant alternation, first hunting around for something and seizing upon it, and then trying to fit it in to bring it to bear on the end; and the first is the analytic, and the other is the synthetic. The child cannot really then be focused in his attention until he has a definite end in view; he cannot be wide awake excepting as he is hunting around for material that will supply the answer to the question. The intellectually disciplined person then may be defined from this point of view as one who has the habit of formulating problems on one side, seizing upon the salient points about which center the other material, and which if got hold of, give the key to the rest; and then on the other side of attacking intelligently all the available material to fit the facts, statements, and so on, which are relevant to the problem. Any one who has that has mental method of his own: he may not be a walking encyclopaedia, but he knows how to go to work at these things if you give him time, and how to define the problems to himself and work out the stuff that is requisite to answering them. That is the reality to my mind, of intellectual self activity, and when that point is gained all the rest of it, memory, and thinking, and observation are necessarily gained too. Thinking is nothing at bottom but this process of adapting the selected material so as to get it into shape so that it does help solve the problem in hand. I say that the psychology of attention, particularly of attention with reference to the remote end, is the key to the method of instruction in the second period, just as the psychology of habits is in the first period.

 # LECTURE XXXIII

March 24, 1899

[D.I.2; D.II.: *The indirect stage of learning—the image; Herbart criticized.*]

[IV.C.] There is one point further in the psychology of method of which I wish to speak, and that is the nature and use of the image. When we are dealing with direct experience and the modes of it which are appropriate for school use, there is no question of the mental medium or instrumentality through which the learning is carried on. As I said the other day, the learning is in and through the doing itself, is an accompaniment of the acting, being the reflex of the act in consciousness. Now the question comes up: what is the vehicle or instrument of learning in indirect experience, in the learning, in other words, which does not find its complete motivation or its complete satisfaction in the present moment and in the experience of that moment, but which is connected with some future end? The students of Greek philosophy will recall the great difficulty that Plato found with the whole problem of learning. Ignorance seems easy to deal with. If the person is ignorant he is, and that is the end of it. It corresponds to non-being. If a man knows a thing, if he is wise, that too can be easily explained; but learning seems to occupy a midway position, you neither have a thing nor are you entirely without it. If you have it you are not in a condition to learn it, but if you have it not, you do not know how to direct your energies and attention. You remember the intermediate position he gave learning, between wisdom and ignorance, between non-reality and reality, or the intermediate position of the image which in one way is not reality, and yet somehow stands for reality. But now without going into the metaphysical problems which the Greeks found connected with them,

that is, the relation of non-being and being, the psychological
view that Plato struck out, there is one which remains a present
possession, not simply of psychology, but of education. The
image is the vehicle of the process of learning. It is that factor
in our experience which is neither complete ignorance nor yet
complete experience, complete realization. Now the precise
peculiarity of the indirect stage of learning, that is directing
one's attention with reference to problems, is precisely that
we must have some working representative of the fact of the
truth of reality; we must have enough grip on it to have some
basis to start from and to have something to work with; and
that is the image. The image is the means of realization, it is
the medium of building up any experience in such a way that
it will culminate in a final complete and direct experience, or
in a transition from one complete experience or realization to
another complete one; it is the bridge by which we pass from
one experience to another.

    The actual descriptive psychology of imagery was
[1.] however, left in a very backward condition until
    within comparatively recent years, when the studies
begun by Galton and carried on by many investigators have
put at our disposal the great body of facts about the way images are formed, and particularly the type forms of imagery.
Galton's own work was done mainly on the visual "image,"
on the basis of visualization as presenting reality or complete
experiences which were not concretely and actively realized.
But in the technical use of the term "image," it is not of course
confined to the visual mode of presentation, but extends as
well to the auditory, tactual, and muscular or motor forms in
which experiences are presented. On this descriptive side,
however, it may be well to give a word of warning: because psychology analyzes and describes these various types of image,
like the visual and auditory, it is not to be inferred that they
are exclusive of each other or that the child uses only one at
a time, or that the average child would predominantly use one
and ignore the other. The average mental representation, that
is, the usual mental representation of the normal child, would
include as a rule visual, tactual, and motor factors. Adults
are much more apt to be specialized in their imagery because
they have found it more economical in their thinking to select
some one mode, but even with adults I think their specializa-

tion is less exclusive than is often supposed. The same person will use a number of forms, or one type for a certain kind of experiences, and another for another. If there were more time I should like to go into more details on the descriptive side, but the facts are open to anyone in the books on psychology.

[2.]   With reference to instruction, the first thing that it is important to notice is the fact just spoken of, that all learning is carried on through the medium of imagery. If there were a number of different faculties like perceiving, memorizing, imagining, and thinking the theory of instruction from the psychological standpoint would be very complex indeed, and the work of the teacher would be complicated. The teacher would have to ask himself: is this a case of the use of the faculty of perception, and how shall I call this piece of machinery into play, and how pass from one to the other? The necessary result would be that under the stress of classroom work no teacher would have time to pay attention to the psychology of teaching at all; they would not get a lesson taught if they had to go through such a complicated process as that. But the question is one which can be stated in unified terms. It is always simply a question of what images are forming there; how they are formed; what the character or quality of the images are; how they are being ordered with reference to each other. The whole work of instruction can be stated then absolutely in this terminology, the terminology of the formation and movement of images in the pupil's mind; and that fixes the task on the psychological side, of the instructor. It is simply to get the best insight possible into the imagery of the individual mind, meaning by imagery simply the vehicle or medium of mental translation, of mental interpretation, whatever is building up there to stand for the reality to which the lesson has reference, and in which in the pupil's own experience, the lesson must finally culminate if it does become a vital part of his learning, and not a mere memorized possession.

[3.]   Again if I had more time I should like to show how from the psychological side, perception and memorizing and thinking reduce themselves to terms of the formation and movement of imagery. I will however, take thinking very briefly, because the difficulty of making the connection is perhaps most likely to come in there. The difficulty however, arises very largely from the fact that the account usually given of thinking is the logical account rather than the psychological. That is, it is a statement of the results that we get by reasoning, and the way of testing those results, rather than an account of the actual process of the action of the machinery actually going on in any individual's mind when he thinks. You may define reasoning as the process of drawing one truth from two or more other given truths, but that does not throw light on what goes on when the person is engaged in thinking, or how in concrete cases one uses two truths so as to arrive at a third truth. When we ask ourselves the latter question, we simply go back to the question of the movement of images. Thinking, in the technical sense of the term, that is, reasoning, will always be found to begin with two images which are more or less discrepant. You have an image of one fact which seems to be a fact, and an image of another, and the two do not coincide; and the thinking process itself is simply forming associations of other images. On the basis of this rule you find some common image in which the partial ones with which you started are finally reconciled and made harmonious with each other. If you will take in your mind any concrete principle of physics, say some principle in pneumatics, the principle of the pump, I think you will find that even as an adult using freely symbols as you do, your real hold on the principle is dependent very largely on your capacity to translate the principle into a single image or into a series of images. You call up an image of conditions and then an image of something else happening to them, and then imagine a certain result as happening and you will be able to explain intelligently what the principle is. You will find an illustration from physical geography in the movement of tides or ocean currents or winds. The whole point of the reasoning, if it is not merely verbal, will depend on the presence of imagery there. There is imagery and the association of ideas in thinking, in other words, as much as in the ordinary association of ideas. Thinking is nothing psychologically but the association of ideas, that is of images controlled by reference to some end; while in the ordinary association of ideas there is no definite principle of control. One image suggests another, and that another, simply at random and so the play has no value outside of itself, no typical or representative value.

Every high school teacher has been perplexed by finding persons of good mental ability and reasoning powers deficient in geometry. In many cases that will be found to have its basis simply in difficulty of visualization. In geometry the visual imagery is the prominent one, and the pupil who has difficulty in representing to himself in mental terms the form discussed and in seeing the effect of the additional lines of construction which were added, will be in a condition where the whole form of the demonstration will be largely opaque to him, he will not have anything in his own mind which corresponds to them, while another pupil will have a visual image which he will manipulate, and it is really the manipulation of his own imagery that carries the demonstration and memory of the problem.

[a.] Take geometry as a typical case of the application of the psychology of imagery as against the logical account of reasoning. In the logical account it is said that we begin with certain definitions and axioms from which we deductively draw certain conclusions. I will defy anybody to draw any conclusion simply from reflecting on the definition. You can think of the conception of a triangle and you never would know that the sum of its three interior angles is equal to two right angles. So you must begin and do something, you must begin and experiment before you can prove anything. You must use your construction in the relation of new lines, and the only difference between the experimentation carried on in geometry and physics is that the former is on the intellectual side, while the latter involves the actual manipulation of physical things; but the mental attitude is the experimental and constructive one. Now just because the medium in which that is carried on is intellectual, instead of being things, you will see at once the fundamental importance which attaches to the student's having the image, which if he has not, he is in the position of the student going to conduct a chemical experiment but who has neither the requisite metal nor acid. Just so with the pupil who has not the requisite imagery with which he has to operate. The mere figure on the board may be a hindrance instead of a help; I imagine it is to more students than we realize. It is so fixed a thing that it does not lend itself to the proper series of mental manipulations that have to be gone through with.

The significance of the image in literature, geography
[b.]   and history, is perhaps so obvious that we need not
dwell on it. If the person gets anything out of those
subjects, it is obvious that he must get it through his own imagery. That does not mean that it must be visual. It is a surprising thing, surprising psychologically, how small and how
obscure a fragment of an image will finally succeed in carrying a very large load of fairly clear and orderly meaning along
with it. So some persons will do with a very slight fragment of
motor imagery all that someone else could do with a very definite visual image. Of course finally we come to think largely
in symbols, persons whose business it is to think, but the symbol after all, is simply a very reduced and beaten down image.
It is an image with a large part of its character sheared off.
The best illustration I know of is the growth of the alphabet
out of original pictures, and those pictures perhaps a reduction
of gestures. In the Egyptian hieroglyphics you will find this
very clearly marked. Obviously the first stage was the presentation of ideas of ideas through pictures, then as those were
used continuously there was evidently a saving of time by making them more schematic, until they were reduced to the barest
suggestion of the original picture, and in the next stage that
suggestion vanished and we were left with mere symbol. Anyone could trace that as part of the visual complete pictorial
sum. The mental evolution of symbol in anybody's mind is the
same. The original image is too complex to be handled, and
by a process of mental attrition it is worn away and we are left
with a little image which has the power of calling up these
other images when we want to have them do it.

The psychology of literature and science represents two opposite mental movements. The value of literature as literature
is that it requires the continual extension of the imagery. The
point of the literary here is that you should get as large, and
as detailed, and as vivid an image as possible. It works in the
direction of extension, while science works in the direction of
the reduction of the image for the purpose of more convenient
use as tool or instrument in reaching some more remote truth.
Balanced education then, in the secondary period before specialization of vocation comes in, would necessarily demand
work which would call for practice and give habits in the handling of imagery in both directions.

[4.]

Another point is that the image is in no case ever a simple copy of a previous experience. Of course it cannot be. If it were really a copy you could not tell it from the original. We would simply have the old experience over again. To say that it is the image instead of the same experience recurring, means that it involves a certain amount of reconstruction of the old experience. Literally speaking there is no such thing as a purely unmodified recurring of experience, it involves a certain modification, a certain readaptation of the experience previously had. And this is the absurdity of supposing what teachers often suppose, particularly in the elementary period, that only art and literature is the medium for the cultivation of the imagination. The mental realization of any subject matter whatsoever involves cultivating the imagination. You cannot realize it without the use of imagery, and in so far as the experience is not a direct one, the imagination is used in a constructive, at least in a reconstructive way.

[5.]

There has been perhaps more nonsense talked about cultivating the imagination of children than almost anything else. You sometimes have children mentally inert who have to be stimulated and you may have to resort to extreme stimuli to get their imagination into play at all, but those are simply the extreme cases. An average child, brought up in an average intellectual environment, is having his imagination stimulated at every point. The arousing of the image is one thing, but that does not settle anything educationally. The great thing is, how is the image directed? Simply to excite imagery is very likely to lead to over-excitation and to mental disintegration, or as a recent writer has put it, leaving the child in a continual state of suggestibility which approaches a hypnotic condition, so the child is brought up practically to call a thing something which it is not really; now, that is not a matter of the building up of new experiences, but simply consists in transforming real things into unreal things. It is often seriously argued that the more make-believe there is in a thing the greater is the cultivation of the imagination on the part of the child: that he will get more imagination in playing boat and balloon by using cube blocks, or that he gets more cultivation of imagination in playing sweep-a-room than by actually sweeping it, or by playing cook than by actually cooking.

That is a digression about what I was saying that
[6.] literature is supposed to be the only or prominent
means for cultivating the imagination. There are
other factors of the imagination for the cultivation of which
other subjects are adequate, and it is not wise to confuse the
whole subject of imagery with simply the one particular phase
of it which comes out in literature. The image is never a mere
image, but it always involves a working over of previous experience, throwing the emphasis on different phases, making
something stand out that before was blurred. There is no likelihood that anyone would conceive that training the imagination through the medium of these other subjects would
result in simply prosaic or utilitarian habits of mind. The
whole process is genuinely constructive, and so far as the individual himself is concerned, creative, although from the standpoint of other people there may be nothing very new in the
result that he gets. The reason that all imagery must be reconstructive, or is reconstructive, comes out in the fact that it
always represents an adaptation of some previous experience,
regarded as a means to the reaching of some new experience
regarded as an end. You want to do some new thing; you cannot
rely on your habit; in one sense all you can rely on is your past
experiences. But you cannot rely on them just as they were, as
they originally came to you, because what you want to do is a
new thing. There is but one result possible there, that the old
experience be modified, be reconstructed, so that that phase of it
which is serviceable under the new circumstances can be
utilized and the rest dropped out. That adaptation of former
experience to the new conditions is what gives us the image.
The image represents the analysis or the break-up of the former
experience so as to make it available for new relationships;
and then the associative process, the movement of the image,
represents this gradual use of these means to realize the new
end in the adaptation of new conditions.

I will sum up this by saying that in type there are
[7.] four forms of this movement or growth of imagery.
The most direct form is where the image passes at
once over into action, or suggestion passes into play, as with
the child for example. You make some suggestion to the child,
it takes hold of him in the form of image and at once results
in his doing something. There is then the embodiment of the

image in a new end, and we get what is ordinarily called the association of ideas, that is, the process of continuous suggestion of imagery, one image suggesting another image and so on, more or less indefinitely.

The controlled use of this association of ideas constitutes thinking, which in its essence is the use of judgment, thinking things out, using one's ingenuity, one's wits, to solve problems, or to utilize, to select his knowledge and experiences that are relevant, and holding them so as to bring them to bear upon some objective point, and then the use of images reduced to bare symbols.

[D.1.] I wish now to speak of the three modes of generalization in the three different periods of development.

The first I spoke of the other day, the use of the habit, the projective force which any thoroughly realized idea gets, going on to assert itself in, and assimilate to itself, new experiences, what is ordinarily called apperceptions, only regarding them as an active self-assertive process instead of a passive one. Everybody knows that when the little child gets a new idea or new word, he does not wait passively for some strong stimulus to use them. He goes about forcing them upon us, he makes categories of them which he inserts into new experiences until he has them under command. Then he takes some new idea which interests him and goes around projecting that into things and experiences. That is the essence of generalization. It gives the element of identity, the backbone in our experiences.

[2.] In the second stage generalization comes in as the practical method of handling things in order to reach a result. It is neither a habit which instinctively and spontaneously asserts itself, nor a theoretically formed generalization. It is simply that we have found out certain ways in which it is best to do things. It is a rule as distinct from a habit or law. It means that you must take certain material in order to reach a result, and then relate them to each other in a certain sequence. It is that orderly sequence in the selection and arrangement of materials or facts or ideas, which constitutes the essence of generalization at this period. To reach results in arithmetic you must do certain things in a certain way. To appreciate that order in action is to have a generalization which is appropriate at this stage; it is to have method in work.

The third form of generalization, that used in the [3.] secondary period, is that of conscious formulation, having it not simply as practical method, as a sequence of steps, but being able to relate that sequence of steps to the whole process, to the end, in such a way as to see, as to understand why each of these steps is taken. It involves the transformation of the how into the why. Now after what was said the other day about the error in supposing that habit can be separated from reason, you will not think that when I speak of the second stage of the practical method that I mean that there is no *why*, that the child does a thing simply because he is told to. The child knows why, but it is of a practical kind. He appreciates the fact that in doing these he gets a certain result, but he simply does not understand it in its scientific bearings; he could not state it in its objective and final form. The value of the formulated principle in grammar or arithmetic or science is that the person not only knows the why in practical terms and the best way of getting results, but he really can place it, can deduce it, see its necessity and state its necessity with relation to the topic in hand. The purpose of generalization is to give articulation, to give systematization to experience. Generalization is of no value by itself; a person does not really know a thing any better because he understands it in its general form instead of in its particular form, excepting that if he understands it in its general form it becomes a method to him for arranging and harmonizing the great variety of other experiences, so that if the person knows a thing from the center out, he is able to construct it for himself, instead of taking it blindly, and he also is at home under very new conditions. The habit is the instrument which we fall back on and utilize to help us deal with the details of life as they come up, to save us time and strength, to do things quickly with order and system, instead of having to think out everything as new. Now the limit of the habit is the conscious generalization. The use of the habit is in its adaptation to particular cases. We cannot get the maximum use out of habit until we turn it over into a conscious rationale. If we have hold of the principle it makes no difference how different the circumstances are outwardly, we are still able to cope with them. But if we have means only in the form of habit, there is a certain amount of novelty which always grows up if the outward circumstances have changed beyond a given point, or habit is not available. The situation suggests no habit, but if we have it in a rational principle, then as I said no amount of novelty in the circumstances can completely stagger us. That is the advantage of science, of reason, over empiricism, to say nothing of mere routine.

I will speak briefly now of the Herbartian formal [E.1.] steps. I said perhaps enough about preparation the other day. If the child has a habit already formed all the preparation needed is to get the habit active, to give him a stimulus to use that habit. In the later stages, the conscious reflective preparation, the review of previous experiences in relation to the new problem becomes more and more necessary.

Presentation means either presented objects of pictures or suggestions from the teacher, lectures, or statements of the text book, differing in amounts in different periods of the child's life. Material should always be presented, not as something of value in itself, but as material with reference to a problem, or with reference to a question of something to be related which the child already has in his own mind. We do not really go from an abstract to a concrete mode of presentation simply by piling up physical things before the child, simply by showing things to his senses. We may have a thousand things to show him and the instruction may be almost as abstract as if you were simply talking to him. If he has no mental use for those things, no center about which they are to integrate, there is no such contact with his mind as may be called concrete. You will find that fallacy going through all forms of instruction, that by getting things for the child to handle, the subject has been transformed into the concrete.

The third point on which the Herbartians insist is comparison and contrast. In theory they insist that every new material, every idea presented, should be compared or contrasted with resembling facts of the same general nature previously learned. To make a general principle out of that seems to me a superstition. Of course in a great many cases you can give the child a better hold on the particular point in question by comparing or constrasting it with something else. Then by all means compare and contrast; but it is not for the sake of comparison or for any novel thing to come out of it. It is simply a step, a point in getting a better appreciation of what is actually there. There will be cases when you will get a better hold on it by not going off into other fields. Too much comparison and contrast is apt to be confusing. There are salient points which perhaps may profitably be called attention to, but the main point is that comparison is not a step by itself, a process by itself, it is simply an instrument in building up better image of the particular subject being stated. Comparison simply as comparison is an extremely annoying state of mind. But to keep your mind on one particular problem and fact, and then bring in anything else that will help you with that, either by way of likeness or by way of contrast, is a very helpful thing.

The fourth step is generalization. I have said all that needs to be said about that. The fallacy in the orthodox Herbartian theory is supposing that the third form of generalization is the only genuine thing; it is an overlooking of the real skill and practice in generalization when he is forming orderly habits, even if he is not able to consciously state to you all the principles involved.

The fifth point is application. Of course it is a step that needs always to be emphasized. There is so much work which stops short of the application, with simply seeing that the child learns the fact, without making use of it. The only way we can be sure he has learned it is by having him use it. The only criticism I would make on this point is that instead of being the final fifth step, it is really a thing which must be seen to as far as possible at every stage of the discussion; every new idea gained, every new increment of knowledge should be worked out somewhere if possible, in application.

[2.] Regarding the doctrine of the necessary sequence of these five steps as stages of instruction, that seems to me a superstition, making the thing unnecessarily formal. The chief thing is that the pupil should be sure and have some unity of topic or problem in mind as a starting point. Sometimes you may get that best by preparation, sometimes by presenting material without preparation, arousing the pupil's curiosity. According to the Herbartian theory you must not by any possibility present any material until you have gone through the necessary preparation. Generalization should always come after all this preliminary work; you should never make a general statement first. That is a safer doctrine than the other because it is never followed. The text book practically always begins with a generalization and it is safe to say that we should never do that with pupils in the early periods. But with students of maturity there may be great gain in presenting the proposition first. If given as a challenge of his attention you may economize lots of time and mental effort by presenting the generalization first. Without any disrespect to these five formal steps, I think it may be safely stated that a good teacher may always be trusted to use his common sense and vary the order of the particular steps in any degree and to any extent which seems advisable, to begin with application if need be, and end up with stating the question. I wish to say that the formualtion of these steps by the Herbartians has however, been an advantage to the theory of instruction, because it has fixed the attention of teachers upon the necessity of some orderly plan. It arouses the attention to the fact that there is an art in instruction, that it is not a haphazard thing where the teacher can go with a half prepared lesson from the pedagogical side, before children, and trust to luck or the routine habits of teaching to get results. There is really a principle, a theory to it which can be worked out so as to make the recitation an artistic whole.

APPENDIX I

Amplified Bibliography of Works Cited in Syllabus

A.I.(1):

Fiske, John, *Excursions of an Evolutionist* (Boston: Houghton Mifflin Company, 1884), Chapter XII.

Fiske, John, *The Destiny of Man Viewed in the Light of His Origin,* (Boston: Houghton Mifflin Company, 1884), pp. 35–76.

Butler, Nicholas Murray, *The Meaning of Education* (New York: The Macmillan Company, 1898), pp. 3–34.

A.II.(2)(b):

Baldwin, James Mark, *Mental Development in the Child and the Race, Methods and Processes* (New York: Macmillan, 1895), pp. 81–91, 263–366.

Harris, William Torrey, *Psychologic Foundations of Education* (New York: D. Appleton and Company, 1898), pp. 295–305.

National Education Association, *Journal of Proceedings and Addresses,* 1895, "Department of Higher Education," (St. Paul: Pioneer Press Company, 1895), pp. 636–671.

Royce, Josiah, "Imitative Functions and Their Place in Human Nature," *The Century Magazine,* XLVIII, May, 1894, pp. 137–145.

A.II.(2)(c):

Baldwin, James Mark, *Mental Development in the Child and the Race, Methods and Processes* (New York: The Macmillan Company, 1895), Chapter VI.

Small, Maurice H., "The Suggestibility of Children," *Pedagogical Seminary,* IV, 1894, pp. 176–220.

Thomas, P. F., *La Suggestion; son rôle dans l'éducation* (Paris: Alcon, 1895).

A.III.(2):

Brunetière, Ferdinand, *Education et instruction* (Paris: Firmin-Didot et cie, 1895).

Herbart, Johann Friedrich, *The Science of Education,* trans. by Henry M. and Emmie Felkin (Boston: D.C. Heath, and Company, 1893), Book I, Chapters i and ii, Book II, Chapter iv.

Seth, James, "The Relation of Knowledge to Will and Conduct," *Fourth Yearbook of the National Herbart Society* (Chicago: University of Chicago Press, 1898), pp. 7–25.

A.V.1.(2):

Harris, William Torrey, "The Church, The State and the School," *North American Review*, CCXCVIII, September, 1881, pp. 215–227.

Harris, William Torrey, *Psychologic Foundations of Education* (New York: D. Appleton and Company, 1898), Chapters XXXI and XXXII.

Vincent, George Edgar, *The Social Mind and Education* (Chicago: The University of Chicago Press, 1897), esp. Chapter IV.

Rosenkranz, Karl, *The Philosophy of Education*, trans. by Anna C. Brackett (New York: D. Appleton and Company, 1886), Chapter XIII.

Barnes, Earl, "The Child as a Social Factor," in Barnes, Earl, ed., *Studies in Education* (Stanford: Stanford University Press, 1896–97), pp. 355–360.

Plato, *Republic*, edited by B. Jowett and Lewis Campbell (Oxford: The Clarendon Press, 1894).

Aristotle, *Politics*, Book I, trans. by J.E.C. Weldon (London: Macmillan and Company, 1883).

Ward, Lester Frank, *Dynamic Sociology* (New York: D. Appleton and Company, 1883).

Fouillée, Alfred Jules Émile, *Education from a National Standpoint*, trans. by W. J. Greenstreet (London: E. Arnold, 1892).

Hinsdale, Burke Aaron, *Studies in Education* (Chicago: Werner School Book Company, 1896), p. 313.

Meyer, Johannes, *Die Soziale Frage und die Schule* (Gotha: 1888).

Dewey, John, *My Pedagogic Creed*, and Small, Albion Woodbury, *Some Demands of Pedagogy upon Sociology* (New York: E.L. Kellogg and Company, 1897).

Monroe, Will S., *Bibliography of Education* (New York: D. Appleton and Company, 1897), p. 162.

Rosenkranz, Karl, *The Philosophy of Education*, tr. by Anna C. Brackett, (New York: D. Appleton and Company, 1886), Part III.

A.V.1.(2):

Barnes, Earl and Mary S., "Education as Seen in Aztec Records," and "Historical Ideals and Methods of Chinese Education," in Barnes, Earl, ed., *Studies in Education* (Stanford: Stanford University Press, 1896–97), pp. 73–93, 112–118.

A.V.2. Moral Education:

Hall, G. Stanley, and John M. Mansfield, *Bibliography of Edu-*

cation (Boston: **D.C.** Heath and Company, 1886), pp. 178–183.

Harris, William Torrey, "Nature and Importance of Moral Education," in *St. Louis Board of Education Report* for year ending August 1, 1871, pp. 21–37.

Malleson, W., *Notes on the Early Training of Children* (Boston: D.C. Heath and Company, 1887).

Adler, Felix, *Moral Instruction of Children* (New York: D. Appleton and Company, 1892).

Spencer, Herbert, *Education: Intellectual, Moral and Physical* (London: G. Manwaring, 1861), Chapter III.

Bain, Alexander, *Education as a Science* (New York: D. Appleton and Company, 1879), pp. 99–119, Chapter XII.

Dewey, John, "Ethical Principles Underlying Education," *Third Yearbook of the National Herbart Society* (Chicago: University of Chicago Press, 1897), pp. 7–34.

Laurie, Simon Somerville, *Institutes of Education* (New York: The Macmillan Company, 1892), pp. 219–238.

Hall, G. Stanley, "Moral Education and Will-Training," *Pedagogical Seminary*, II, 1892, pp. 72–89.

Herbart, Johann Friedrich, *The Science of Education*, trans. by Henry M. and Emmie Felkin (Boston: D.C. Heath and Company, 1893), pp. 200–252.

A.V.2. School Discipline:

White, Emerson Elbridge, *School Management* (New York: American Book Company, 1893), pp. 114 and 190.

Wickersham, James Pyle, *School Economy* (Philadelphia: J. B. Lippincott and Company, 1864), Chapter IV.

Baldwin, Joseph, *School Management and School Methods* (New York: D. Appleton and Company, 1897).

Laurie, Simon Somerville, *The Training of Teachers* (London: Kegan Paul, Trench and Company, 1882), p. 309.

Rosenkranz, Karl, *The Philosophy of Education*, trans. by Anna C. Brackett (New York: D. Appleton and Company, 1886), Chapter II.

Barnes, Earl ed. *Studies in Education* (Stanford: Stanford University Press, 1896–97), a number of articles on discipline and children's attitudes to punishment: pp. 26–28, 71–72, 110–111, 149–153, 190–193, 213–216, 228–229, 254–258, 270–272, 332–337, 344–351.

Barnes, Earl, "Punishment as Seen by Children," *Pedagogical Seminary*, III, 1893, pp. 235–245.

B.I.:

Harris, William Torrey, "Report of Subcommittee on the Correlation of Studies in Elementary Education," in *Report of*

Committee of Fifteen on Elementary Education (New York: American Book Company, 1895), pp. 40–99.

Dewey, John, "The Psychological Aspect of the School Curriculum," *Educational Review*, XIII, April, 1897, pp. 356–369.

Bain, Alexander, *Education as a Science* (New York: D. Appleton and Company, 1879), pp. 1–10.

Findlay, J. J., "The Scope of the Science of Education," *Educational Review*, XIV, October, 1897, pp. 236–247.

Royce, Josiah, "Is There a Science of Education? (I)," *Educational Review*, I, January, 1891, pp. 15–25.

Royce, Josiah, "Is There a Science of Education? (II)," *Educational Review*, I, February, 1891, pp. 121–132.

Sully, James, "The Service of Psychology to Education," *Educational Review*, IV, November, 1892, pp. 313–327.

Münsterberg, Hugo, "Psychology and Education," *Educational Review*, XVI, September, 1898, pp. 105–132.

McLellan, James Alexander and John Dewey, *The Psychology of Number* (New York: D. Appleton and Company, 1895), Chapter I.

B.V.(3):

Newman, John Henry Cardinal, *The Idea of a University Defined and Illustrated* (London: B.M. Pickering, 1875).

B.V. Examinations:

Seth, James, "The Educational Value of Examinations," *Educational Review*, XII, September, 1896, pp. 133–139.

Paulsen, Friedrich, trans. by Alice Nisbet Parker, "Examinations," *Educational Review*, XVI, September, 1898, pp. 166–176.

Fitch, Sir Joshua Girling, *Lectures on Teaching* (Cambridge, England: The University Press, 1881), Chapter VI.

Latham, Henry, *On the Action of Examinations Considered as a Means of Selection* (Cambridge, England: Deighton, Bell and Company, 1877).

B.V. Gradation:

Harris, William Torrey, *Psychologic Foundations of Education* (New York: D. Appleton and Company, 1898), Chapter XXXVI.

Jackman, Wilbur S. "The School Grade a Fiction," *Educational Review*, XV, May, 1898, pp. 456–473.

Prince, John T., "The Grading and Promotion of Pupils," *Educational Review*, XV, March, 1898, pp. 231–245.

Laurie, Simon Somerville, *Occasional Addresses on Educational Subjects* (Cambridge, England: The University Press, 1888), p. 1.

Pickard, Josiah Little, *School Supervision* (New York: D. Appleton and Company, 1890), Chapter X.

B.V. Electives:
  Palmer, George Herbert, *The New Education* (Boston: Little, Brown and Company, 1887).
  Ladd, George T., "Education New and Old," *Andover Review,* V:25, January, 1886, pp. 1–18.
  Garnett, James M., "The Elective System of the University of Virginia," *Andover Review,* V:27, April, 1886, pp. 359–375.
  Gilman, D.C., "The Group System of College Studies in the Johns Hopkins University," *Andover Review,* V:30, June,, 1886, pp. 565–576.
  Denison, John H., "Individualism in Education," *Andover Review,* V:30, June, 1886, pp. 589–594.
  Howison, G.H., "The Harvard 'New Education,'" *Andover Review,* V:30, June, 1886, pp. 577–589.
  Eliot, Charles William, *Educational Reform* (New York: The Century Company, 1898), Chapters VI, XII, XIII, XVI.
  Hinsdale, Burke Aaron, *Studies in Education* (Chicago: Werner School Book Company, 1896), Chapter V.
  Thurber, Samuel, "Election of Studies in Secondary Schools," *Educational Review,* XV, May, 1898, pp. 417–435.
  Goodwin, Edward J., "Electives in Elementary Schools," *Educational Review,* X, June, 1895, pp. 12–21.
  Hall, G. Stanley, and John M. Mansfield, *Bibliography of Education* (Boston: D. C. Heath and Company, 1886), p. 204.
B.V. Promotions:
  Shearer, William J., "The Lock-step of the Public Schools," *Atlantic Monthly,* 79, June, 1897, pp. 749–757.
  National Education Association, *Journal of Proceedings and Addresses, 1898,* "Department of Superintendence," papers on grading and promotion (Chicago: University of Chicago Press, 1898); pp. 422–448.
  Young, Ella F., "Grading and Classification," National Education Association, *Journal of Proceedings and Addresses, 1893* (New York: J.J. Little and Company, 1895), pp. 83–86.
  "Principal's Round Table," discussing "What Should be Done to Supervise the Work of Individual Students in a Large High School," in National Education Association, *Journal of Proceedings and Addresses, 1896* (Chicago: University of Chicago Press, 1896), pp. 597–604.
  Harris, William Torrey, "Promotion and Classification in the St. Louis Schools," in *St. Louis Board of Education Nineteenth Annual Report* for year ending August 1, 1873, pp. 25–29.
  Pickard, Josiah Little, *School Supervision* (New York: D. Appleton and Company, 1890), Chapter XI.
  Educational Review, Editorial, VII, May, 1894, pp. 516–518.
B.V. Class and Individual Instruction:
  Parker, Francis W., "Departmental Instruction," *Educational*

Review, VI, November, 1893, pp. 342–350.
Educational Review, Editorial, VI, November, 1893, p. 410.
Fitzpatrick, Frank A., "Departmental Teaching in Grammar Schools," *Educational Review*, VII, May, 1894, pp. 439–447.
Search, P. W., "Individual Teaching: The Pueblo Plan," *Educational Review*, VII, February, 1894, pp. 154–170.
Educational Review, Editorial, VII, March, 1894, pp. 305–306.
Educational Review, Editorial, VII, May, 1894, p. 515.
Harper, William R., "Ideals of Educational Work," in National Education Association, *Journal of Proceedings and Addresses, 1895* (St. Paul: Pioneer Press Company, 1895), pp. 987–998; pp. 990, ❬2, through 993 concern individualism.

C.II.3. Values in Education:
Spencer, Herbert, *Education: Intellectual, Moral and Physical* (London: G. Manwaring, 1861), Chapters I and II.
Butler, Nicholas Murray, *The Meaning of Education* (New York: The Macmillan Company, 1898), pp. 37–66.
Payne, William Harold, *Contributions to the Science of Education* (New York: Harper and Brothers, 1886), Chapter 3.
Bain, Alexander, *Education as a Science* (New York: D. Appleton and Company, 1879), Chapter V.
Holman, Henry, *Education* (London: Isbister and Company, 1896), Chapter III.
Laurie, Simon Somerville, *Institutes of Education* (New York: The Macmillan Company, 1892), pp. 211–226.
Patten, Simon N., "The Educational Value of College Studies," "*Educational Review*, I, February, 1891, pp. 105–120.
Jenks, Jeremiah W., "A Critique of Educational Values," *Educational Review*, III, January, 1892, pp. 1–21.
Hanus, Paul H., "Educational Aims and Educational Values," *Educational Review*, IX, April, 1895, pp. 323–334.
Goodwin, William W., "Educational Value of the Ancient Classics," *Educational Review*, IX, April, 1895, pp. 335–342.
Norton, Charles Eliot, "The Educational Value of the History of the Fine Arts," *Educational Review*, IX, April, 1895, pp. 343–348.
Hill, Frank A., "The Educational Value of Mathematics," *Educational Review*, IX, April, 1895, pp. 349–358.
Thompson, Anna Boynton, "The Educational Value of History," *Educational Review*, IX, April, 1895, pp. 359–367.
Woodhull, John F., "The Educational Value of Natural Science," *Educational Review*, IX, April, 1895, pp. 368–376.
Browne, George H., "The Educational Value of English," *Educational Review*, IX, April, 1895, pp. 377–384.
Schilling, Hugo K., "The Educational Value of Modern Languages," *Educational Review*, IX, April, 1895, pp. 385–390.

Baker, James H., "Educational Values," *Educational Review,* X, October, 1895, pp. 209–217.

Hinsdale, Burke Aaron, *Studies in Education* (Chicago: Werner School Book Company, 1896), pp. 44–61.

Youmans, Edward Livingston, *The Culture Demanded by Modern Life* (New York: D. Appleton and Company, 1867), pp. 1–56.

Arnold, Matthew, *Culture and Anarchy* (London: Smith, Elder and Company, 1875).

C.II.3. Curriculum in General:

Dewey, John, "The Psychological Aspect of the School Curriculum," *Educational Review,* XIII, April, 1897, pp. 356–369.

Bain, Alexander, *Education as a Science* (New York: D. Appleton and Company, 1879), Chapters VI, VII, XI.

Hinsdale, Burke, Aaron, *Studies in Education* (Chicago: Werner School Book Company, 1896), pp. 13–43.

Maxwell, William H., "The Grammar School Curriculum," *Educational Review,* III, May, 1892, pp. 472–485.

Report of John T. Prince, Agent of the Board of Education, Sixty-First Annual Report of the Board of Education, 1896–97 (Boston: Wright and Potter, 1898), pp. 275–314. Sixty-Second Annual Report, 1897–98, pp. 267–283.

Hanus, Paul H., "Attempted Improvements in the Course of Study," *Educational Review,* XII, December, 1896, pp. 435–452.

Eliot, Charles William, *Educational Reform* (New York: The Century Company, 1898), Chapters VII, IX, XI.

National Education Association, *Report of the Committee of Ten on Secondary School Studies* (New York: American Book Company, 1894).

Dutton, Samuel T., "The Relation of Education to Vocation," *Educational Review,* XII, November, 1896, pp. 335–346.

Laurie, Simon Somerville, *The Training of Teachers* (London: Kegan Paul, Trench and Company, 1882), pp. 121, 187.

Laurie, Simon Somerville, *Occasional Addresses on Educational Subjects* (Cambridge, England: The University Press, 1888), p. 59.

Aber, Mary Rose, *An Experiment in Education* (New York: Harper and Brothers, 1897).

Beale, Dorothea, *et al., Work and Play in Girls' Schools* (London: Longmans, Green and Company, 1898).

Spencer, Frederic, *Chapters on the Aims and Practices of Teaching* (Cambridge, England: The University Press, 1897).

Barnett, Percy Arthur, *Teaching and Organization* (London: Longmans, Green and Company, 1897).

C.II.3. Curriculum Herbartian:

Rein, Wilhelm, *Theorie und Praxis des Volksschul unterrichts nach Herbartischen Grundsatzen* (Leipzig, Dresden: 1885).

DeGarmo, Charles, *Herbart and the Herbartians* (New York: Charles Scribner's Sons, 1896).

Rein, Wilhelm, *Outlines of Pedagogics*, trans. by C. C. and Ida J. Van Liew (Syracuse, New York: C. W. Bardeen, 1893).

Dodd, Catherine Isabel, *Introduction to the Herbartian Principles of Teaching* (London: S. Sonneschein and Company, 1898). Ufer, Christine, *Introduction to the Pedagogy of Herbart*, trans. by J. C. Zinser (Boston: D.C. Heath and Company, 1894).

Herbart und die Herbartianer (Langensalza: H. Beyer & Sohne, 1897).

Harris, William Torrey, "Course of Study," in *St. Louis Board of Education Report* for year ending August 1, 1869, pp. 95–116.

Harris, William Torrey, "Art Instruction," pp. 103–108, "German-English Instruction," pp. 110–113, "Grammar as Intellectual Culture Study," pp. 144–145, "Mental vs. Written Arithmetic," pp. 144–148, in *St. Louis Board of Education Report* for year ending August 1, 1872.

C.II.3. Correlation:

McMurry, Lida Brown, "Correlation of Studies with the Interests of the Child for the First and Second School Years," *First Yearbook of the National Herbart Society* (Chicago: University of Chicago Press, 1895), pp. 115–133.

White, Emerson E., "Isolation and Unification as Bases of Courses of Study," *Second Yearbook of the National Herbart Society* (Chicago: University of Chicago Press, 1896), pp. 7–17.

Vincent, George Edgar, "Integration of Studies," *The Social Mind and Education* (Chicago: The University of Chicago Press, 1897).

Parker, Francis Wayland, *Talks on Pedagogics* (New York: E.L. Kellogg and Company, 1894).

Fitch, Sir Joshua Girling, *Lectures on Teaching* (Cambridge, England: The University Press, 1881), Chapter XV.

Harris, William Torrey, *Psychologic Foundations of Education* (New York: D. Appleton and Company, 1898), pp. 321–332.

Harris, William Torrey, "The Necessity for Five Co-Ordinate Groups of Studies in the Schools," *Educational Review*, XI, April, 1896, pp. 323–334.

Harris, William Torrey, "Report of Subcommittee on the Correlation of Studies in Elementary Education," in *Report of Committee of Fifteen on Elementary Education* (New York: American Book Company, 1895), pp. 40–99.

Lukens, Herman T., "The Correlation of Studies," *Educational Review*, X, November, 1895, pp. 364–383.

Jackman, Wilbur S., "Mr. Lukens on the Correlation of

Studies," *Educational Review*, XI, January, 1896, pp. 72–74.
DeGarmo, Charles, "German Contributions to the Co-ordination of Studies," *Educational Review*, IV, December, 1892, pp. 422–437.
DeGarmo, Charles, "A Working Basis for the Correlation of Studies," *Educational Review*, V, May, 1893, pp. 451–466.
McMurry, Frank M., "Concentration," *Educational Review*, IX, January, 1895, pp. 27–37.
Gilbert, Charles B., "Practical Correlations of Studies," *Educational Review*, XI, April, 1896, pp. 313–322.
Jackman, Wilbur S., "Correlation of Science and History," *Educational Review*, IX, May, 1895, pp. 464–471.
Jackman, Wilbur S. "Mr. Lukens on the Correlation of Studies," *Educational Review*, XI, January, 1896, pp. 72–74.
Hinsdale, Burke Aaron, "The Laws of Mental Congruence and Energy Applied to Some Pedagogical Problems," *Educational Review*, X, September, 1895, pp. 152–171.
National Education Association Index Titles: Studies, Correlation of and Isolation of.

C.II.3. Culture Epoch Theory:
The First and Second Yearbooks of the National Herbart Society (Chicago: University of Chicago Press, 1895 and 1896) deal for the most part with the Culture Epoch Theory.
Vanderwalker, Nina C., "The Culture-Epoch Theory from an Anthropological Standpoint," *Educational Review*, XV, April, 1898, pp. 374–391.
Vincent, George Edgar, *The Social Mind and Education* (Chicago: The University of Chicago Press, 1897), Chapter XII.

C.II.3. Language:
Bain, Alexander, *Education as a Science* (New York: D. Appleton and Company, 1879), Chapters IX and X.
Jacobi, Mary Putnam, *Physiological Notes on Primary Education* (New York: G.P. Putnam's Sons, 1889), Chapter IV.
Collins, John Churton, *The Study of English Literature* (London: Macmillan and Company, 1891).
Collins, J. Churton, "Language Versus Literature at Oxford," *Nineteenth Century*, 37, February, 1895, pp. 290–303.
Lavisse, Ernest, *Études et étudiants* (Paris: A. Colin et cie, 1890), p. 35.
Laurie, Simon Somerville, *The Training of Teachers* (London: Kegan Paul, Trench and Company, 1882), p. 213.
Hinsdale, Burke Aaron, *Teaching the Language Arts* (New York: D. Appleton and Company, 1897).
McMurry, Charles Alexander, *Special Method for Literature and History in the Common Schools* (Bloomington, Illinois: Public School Publishing Company, 1893), pp. 3–45.

McMurry, Charles Alexander, *Special Method in Reading* (Bloomington, Illinois: Public School Publishing Company, 1894).

Laurie, Simon Somerville, *Lectures of Language and Linguistic Method in the School* (Cambridge, England: The University Press, 1890).

Farrar, Frederic William, ed., *Essays on a Liberal Education* (London: Macmillan and Company, 1867).

Price, Thomas R., "Language and Literature," *Educational Review*, XI, January, 1896, pp. 12–28.

New York Teachers' Monographs, I:3, November, 1898.

C.II.3. Mathematics:

Whewell, William, *On the Principles of English University Education, Including Thoughts on the Study of Mathematics* (London, James Parker & Co., 1838).

Hamilton, Sir William, *Discussions on Philosophy and Literature, Education and University Reform* (London: Longman, Brown, Green and Longmans, 1852).

Bain, Alexander, *Education as a Science* (New York: D. Appleton and Company, 1879), p. 288.

Cajori, Florian, *The Teaching and History of Mathematics in the United States* (Washington, D.C.: Government Printing Office, 1890).

Fitch, Sir Joshua Girling, *Lectures on Teaching* (Cambridge, England: The University Press, 1881), Chapter XI.

McLellan, James Alexander and John Dewey, *The Psychology of Number* (New York: D. Appleton and Company, 1895).

Indices of *Educational Review* for 1891, 92, 93, 95.

Peirce, Charles S., "The Logic of Mathematics in Relation to Education," *Educational Review*, XV, March, 1898, pp. 209–216.

Harris, William Torrey, *Psychologic Foundations of Education* (New York: D. Appleton and Company, 1898), Chapter XXXVII.

C.II.3. History:

Hall, G. Stanley, ed., *Methods of Teaching History* (Boston: D. C. Heath and Co., 1883).

Adams, Herbert B., *Methods of Historical Study* (Johns Hopkins University Studies), (Baltimore: 1884).

Barnes, Mrs. Mary Downing, *Studies in Historical Method* (Boston: D. C. Heath and Company, 1896).

Hinsdale, Burke Aaron, *How to Study and Teach History* (New York: D. Appleton and Company, 1894).

Kemp, Ellwood Wadsworth, *An Outline of Method in History* (Terre Haute, Indiana: The Inland Publishing Company, 1896).

Lorenz, Karl, *Der Moderne Gesehichtsunterricht* (München: M. Kellerer, 1897).

Hinsdale, Burke Aaron, *Studies in Education* (Chicago: Werner School Book Company, 1896), p. 206.

Fitch, Sir Joshua Girling, *Lectures on Teaching* (Cambridge, England: The University Press, 1881), Chapter XII.

Smith, Goldwin, *Lectures on the Study of History* (Oxford and London: J. H. & J. Parker, 1861).

Freeman, Edward Augustus, *The Methods of Historical Study* (London: Macmillan and Company, 1886).

Droysen, Johann Gustav, *Outline of the Principles of History*, trans. by Benjamin Andrews, (Boston: Ginn and Company, 1893).

Salmon, Lucy M., "History in Elementary Schools," *Educational Review*, I, May, 1891, pp. 438–452.

Salmon, Lucy M., "Unity in College Entrance History," *Educational Review*, XII, September, 1896, pp. 151–168.

Salmon, Lucy M., "History in the German Gymnasia," *Educational Review*, XV, February, 1898, pp. 167–182.

Rice, Emily J., "History in the Common Schools," *Educational Review*, XII, September, 1896, pp. 169–179.

Rice, Emily J., *Course of Study in History and Literature* (Chicago: F. Flanagan, 1898).

C.II.3. Art in Education:

Bain, Alexander, *Education as a Science* (New York: D. Appleton and Company, 1879), Chapter XIII.

Waldstein, later Walston, Sir Charles, *The Study of Art in Universities* (London: Osgood and Company, 1896).

Index to Volumes of Proceedings: National Teachers' Association from 1857 to 1870, and the National Education Association from 1871 to 1897 (Chicago: University of Chicago Press, 1897).

Harris, William T., *Psychologic Foundations of Education* (New York: D. Appleton and Company, 1898), Chapter XXXVIII.

Crane, Walter, *Relations of Art to Education and Social Life* (London: Leek Press, 1893).

Langl, Josef, *Modern Art Education*, trans. by S. R. Koehler (Boston: L. Prang and Company, 1875).

Clarke, Isaac Edwards, *Art and Industry. Education in the Industrial and Fine Arts in the United States* (Washington, D.C.: Government Printing Office, 1885).

C.II.3. Manual Training:

Ham, Charles Henry, *Manual Training* (London: Blackie and Son, 1896).

MacArthur, Arthur, *Education in its Relation to Manual Industry* (New York, D. Appleton and Company, 1884).

Love, Samuel Gurley, *Industrial Education* (New York and Cincinnati: E. L. Kellogg and Company, 1887).

Stetson, Charles B., *Technical Education* (Boston: Osgood, 1876).

National Education Association, *Journal of Proceedings and Addresses, 1889*, pp. 617–661, "Department of Industrial Education" (Topeka: Kansas Publishing House, 1899).

Sisson, Edward O., "Mental Results from Manual Training," in National Education Association, *Journal of Proceedings and Addresses, 1897* (Chicago: University of Chicago Press, 1897), pp. 742–747.

C.II.3. Sciences:

Youmans, Edward Livingston, *The Culture Demanded by Modern Life* (New York: D. Appleton and Company, 1867).

Preyer, William, *Naturforschung und schule* (Stuttgart: W. Spemann, 1887).

New York Teachers' Monographs, I:2, June, 1898.

Huxley, Thomas Henry, *Science and Education* (New York: D. Appleton and Company, 1896).

Payne, Joseph, ed., *Lectures on the Science and Art of Education* (Boston: Small, 1884), p. 253.

Fitch, Sir Joshua Girling, *Lectures on Teaching* (Cambridge, England: The University Press, 1881), Chapter XIV.

Wilbur S. Jackman published a number of articles and books concerning the topic of nature study. Several of his books are: *Nature Study for the Common Schools* (New York: Henry Holt, 1892); *Nature Study Record* (Chicago: Werner, 1896); *Nature Study and Related Subjects* (Chicago: Werner, 1895).

Jackman, Wilbur S., "Relation of Arithmetic to Elementary Science," *Educational Review*, V, January, 1893, pp. 35–51.

Jackman, Wilbur S., "Representative Expression in Nature-study," *Educational Review*, X, October, 1895, pp. 248–261.

Jackman, Wilbur S., "Correlation of Science and History," *Educational Review*, IX, May, 1895, pp. 464–471.

Harris, William Torrey, *Psychologic Foundations of Education* (New York: D. Appleton and Company, 1898), Chapter XXXIX.

C.II.3. Geography:

Geike, Sir Archibald, *The Teaching of Geography* (London: Macmillan and Company, 1887).

McMurry, Charles Alexander, *Special Method in Geography* (Bloomington, Illinois: Public School Publishing Company, 1895).

Parker, Francis Wayland, *How to Study Geography* (New York: D. Appleton and Company, 1890).

Mill, Hugh Robert, *Hints to Teachers and Students on the Choice of Geographical Books for Reference and Reading*,

(London and New York: Longmans, Green and Company, 1897), Chapters I and II.

Laurie, Simon Somerville, *Occasional Addresses on Educational Subjects* (Cambridge, England: The University Press, 1888), p. 83.

Davis, William M., "The Teaching of Geography," *Educational Review*, III, May, 1892, pp. 417–426.

Davis, William M., "The Teaching of Geography II," *Educational Review*, IV, June, 1892, pp. 6–15.

Davis, William M., "Governmental Maps in Schools," *Educational Review*, VII, March, 1894, pp. 232–239.

Redway, Jacques W., "Textbooks of Geography," *Educational Review*, V, January, 1893, pp. 153–162.

Redway, Jacques, "The Status of Geography Teaching," *Educational Review*, VIII, January, 1894, pp. 33–41.

Redway, Jacques, "Some Applications of Physiography in History," *Educational Review*, VIII, November, 1894, pp. 374–381.

Redway, Jacques W., "What is Physiography?" *Educational Review*, X, November, 1895, pp. 352–363.

McMurry, Charles Alexander, "Geography as a School Subject," *Educational Review*, IX, May, 1895, pp. 448–463.

McMurry, Charles Alexander, "A Course of Study in Geography for the Grades of the Common School," *Supplement to the Fourth Yearbook of the National Herbart Society* (Chicago: University of Chicago Press, 1899), pp. 121–173.

King, Charles Francis, *Methods and Aids in Geography* (Boston: Lee and Shepard, 1889).

E.2. Method in General:

McMurry, Charles Alexander, *The Elements of the General Method: Based on the Principles of Herbart* (Bloomington, Illinois: Public School Publishing Company, 1892).

McMurry, Charles Alexander, *How to Conduct the Recitation* (New York: E.L. Kellogg and Company, 1895).

DeGarmo, Charles, *The Essentials of Method* (Boston: D. C. Heath and Company, 1889).

Tompkins, Arnold, *The Philosophy of Teaching* (Boston: Ginn and Company, 1894).

Adams, Sir John, *The Herbartian Psychology Applied to Education* (Boston: D. C. Heath and Company, 1897).

Lange, Karl, *Apperception: A Monograph on Psychology and Pedagogy*, trans. by the Herbart Club, ed. by Charles DeGarmo, (Boston: D. C. Heath and Company, 1894).

McClellan, James A., *Applied Psychology* (Boston: Educational Publishing Company, 1889), pp. 167–176, 180–186; Chapters IX and X.

Harris, William Torrey, *Psychologic Foundations of Education*

(New York: D. Appleton and Company, 1898), Chapters IV, XXII, XXVIII, XXX, XXXV.

Fitch, Sir Joshua Girling, *The Art of Questioning, and the Art of Securing Attention in a Sunday School Class* (London: Sunday School Union, 1859).

E.2. Interest:

Dewey, John, "Interest in Relation to Training of the Will," *Second Supplement to the First Yearbook of the National Herbart Society* (Chicago: University of Chicago Press, 1895), pp. 5–39.

Harris, William Torrey, "Herbart's Doctrine of Interest," *Educational Review*, X, June, 1895, pp. 71–80.

Harris, William Torrey, "Professor John Dewey's Doctrine of Interest as Related to Will," *Educational Review*, XI, May, 1896, pp. 486–493.

McMurry, Frank M., "Interest: Some Objections to It," *Educational Review*, XI, February, 1896, pp. 146–156.

Adams, Sir John, *The Herbartian Psychology Applied to Education* (Boston: D. C. Heath and Company, 1897), Chapter X.

Wilson, W. E., "The Doctrine of Interest," *Educational Review*, XI, March, 1896, pp. 254–263.

Harris, William Torrey, "Transcendental Freedom," *Public School Journal*, XV, 1885, pp. 59–63.

Brown, George P., "Educative Interests," *Public School Journal*, XV, 1885, pp. 306–308.

McMurry, Charles A., "Correlation of Studies," *Public School Journal*, XV, 1885, pp. 186–188.

APPENDIX II

Selected Bibliography
of Contemporaneous Writings by Dewey Relevant to the Lectures

Arranged Chronologically

McLellan, James A., and John Dewey, *Applied Psychology* (Boston: Educational Publishing Company, 1889). [First major psychological treatise on education.]

McLellan, James A., and John Dewey, *The Psychology of Number and Its Applications to Methods of Teaching Arithmetic* (New York: D. Appleton and Company, 1895). [Basic principles of psychology as applied to education.]

"Plan of Organization of the University Primary School," 1895, unpublished (Archives, University of Chicago).

"Interest as Related to Will," National Herbart Society, *Second Supplement to the Herbart Year Book for 1895* (Bloomington, Illinois, 1896), pp. 209–255. [A plea for active, intrinsic interest.]

"The Reflex Arc Concept in Psychology," *University of Chicago Contributions to Philosophy*, I, 1896, pp. 39–52. [An article of central importance in the development of Dewey's thought. His criticism of the reflex arc principle and his proposals for a new theory of co-ordination represent a climactic point in the growth of his ideas.]

"Pedagogy as a University Discipline," *University Record*, I, 18 and 25 September 1896, pp. 353–355, 361–363. [Deals with Dewey's view of pedagogy and its basis in scientific theory.]

"Interpretation of the Culture-Epoch Theory," *Second Yearbook of the National Herbart Society* (Bloomington, Illinois, 1896), pp. 89–95. [Criticisms of the naïveté and oversimplification in certain aspects of the Herbartian theory.]

"A Pedagogical Experiment," *Kindergarten Magazine*, VIII, June, 1896, pp. 739–41. [The first published article on the Laboratory School, describing its basic features and its rationale.]

"The University School," *University Record*, I, 6 November 1896, pp. 417–419. [A statement of the rationale for the Laboratory School, with particular emphasis on the analogy between the laboratory in pedagogy and that in basic science.]

"The Interpretation Side of Child-Study," *Transactions of the Illinois Society for Child-Study*, II, July, 1897, pp. 17–27. [A call for the investigation of the child as a social being.]

"Criticisms, Wise and Otherwise, on Modern Child-Study," in National Education Association, *Journal of Proceedings and Addresses, 1897* (Chicago: University of Chicago Press, 1897), pp. 867–868. [Attack on the sentimentality of the Child-Study Movement in its embracing of all children's interests as valuable.]

"Ethical Principles Underlying Education," *Third Yearbook of the National Herbart Society* (Chicago, 1897), pp. 7–34. [The relation between method and subject matter, the individual and the social, and the intellectual and the moral.]

My Pedagogic Creed (New York: E. L. Kellogg and Company, 1897). [The most basic and succinct statement of Dewey's views on education, including a definition of the term.]

"The Psychology of Effort," *Philosophical Review*, VI, January, 1897, pp. 43–56. [The relation between desire and discipline.]

"Review of James Mark Baldwin, *Social and Ethical Interpretations in Mental Development*," *New World*, VII, July, 1898, pp. 398–409; discussion of this review by Baldwin, *Ibid.*, November, 1898, pp. 621–628; reply by Dewey, *Ibid.*, pp. 629–630; same title, but another review, *New World*, VII, September, 1898, pp. 504–522. [A discussion relevant to his treatment of Baldwin in these lectures.]

"The Primary Education Fetich," *Forum*, XXV, May, 1898, pp. 315–328. [An attack on the "correct" approach to the teaching of the three R's.]

"Review of William Torrey Harris, *Psychologic Foundations of Education*," *Educational Review*, XVI, June, 1898, pp. 1–14. [A view of Harris's book as fundamentally traditional, especially in its tendency to designate separate psychological categories and their counterparts in institutions.]

"Play and Imagination in Relation to Early Education," *School Journal*, LVIII, 27 May 1899, p. 589. [A statement supplementary to that in the lectures on these topics.]

"Principles of Mental Development as Illustrated in Early Infancy," *Transactions of the Illinois Society for Child-Study*, IV, October, 1899, pp. 65–83. [Direct application of his views on the reflex arc to the psychology of education.]

"Three Years of the University Elementary School," Chapter IV of the first edition of *School and Society* (Chicago: University of Chicago Press, 1899). [A report on the first three years.]

The Elementary School Record (Chicago: University of Chicago Press, 1900), February-December. [Seven articles by Dewey describing the Laboratory School in detail, dealing with separate subjects and their treatment.]

"Are the Schools Doing What the People Want Them to Do?" *Educational Review*, XXI, May, 1901, pp. 459–474. [A notable attack on traditional education.]

"The Place of Manual Training in the Elementary Course of Study," *Manual Training Magazine*, II, July, 1901, pp. 193–199. [A clear exposition of Dewey's views on manual training as a liberal study, and a further clarification of his views on the culture epoch theory.]

The Child and the Curriculum (Chicago: University of Chicago Press, 1902). [One of the key statements of Dewey's view of education, emphasizing the relation between method and subject matter.]

The Educational Situation (Chicago: University of Chicago Press, 1902). [An explicit statement on secondary education and its subject matter.]

"Interpretation of Savage Mind," *Psychological Review*, IX, May, 1902, pp. 217–230. [Dewey's interpretation of the place of myth in education, together with a criticism of the correspondence theory of the culture epoch.]

"The University of Chicago School of Education," Editorial in *Elementary School Teacher*, III, November, 1902, pp. 200–203. [A statement of the aim and purpose of the new administrative unit.]

Studies in Logical Theory (Chicago: University of Chicago Press, 1903). [The mature statement of Dewey's views on the relation between psychology and logic.]

"Review of Katharine Elizabeth Dopp, *The Place of Industries in Elementary Education*," *Elementary School Teacher*, III, June, 1903, pp. 727–728. [Statement of Dewey's conception of the broadly educative, as opposed to the narrowly utilitarian function of manual training.]

"The Relation of Theory to Practice in Education," in National Society for the Scientific Study of Education, *Third Yearbook*, 1904, Part I, pp. 9–30. [A most basic statement of pragmatic principles, given, significantly, in Dewey's last year at Chicago.]

APPENDIX III

Selected Bibliography
of Writings about Dewey During His Years at Chicago

Baker, Melvin Charles, *Foundations of John Dewey's Educational Theory* (New York: King's Crown Press, Columbia University, 1955). [Discusses systematically Dewey's early educational ideas as they relate to basic philosophical considerations.]

Cremin, Lawrence A., *The Transformation of the School: Progressivism in American Education, 1876–1957* (New York: Alfred A. Knopf, 1962). [The definitive history of the Progressive Education Movement.]

Dewey, Jane M., "Biography of John Dewey," in P. A. Schilpp, ed., The *Philosophy of John Dewey* (New York: Tudor Publishing Company, 1939). [In a footnote to this work Miss Dewey wrote, "This biography was written by the daughter of its subject from material which he furnished. In the emphasis on varied influences and in the philosophical portions it may be regarded as an autobiography, but its subject is not responsible for the form nor for all the details."]

Eastman, George, *John Dewey on Education: The Formative Years,* unpublished doctoral dissertation, Harvard University Graduate School of Education, 1963. [A detailed analysis of Dewey's work in educational theory and practice while at the University of Chicago.]

Feuer, Lewis Samuel, "John Dewey and the Back-to-the-People Movement in American Thought," *Journal of the History of Ideas,* XX, October–December, 1959, pp. 545–568. [A discussion of Dewey's social ideas.]

Ginger, Ray, *Altgeld's America. The Lincoln Ideal versus Changing Realities* (New York: Funk & Wagnalls Company, 1958). [Discussion of Dewey's political theory.]

Goodspeed, Thomas W., *A History of the University of Chicago* (Chicago: University of Chicago Press, 1916).

Greene, Maxine, "Dewey and American Education, 1894–1920,"

School and Society, LXXXVII, 10 October 1959, pp. 381–386. [A valuable discussion of the Chicago years.]

Heidbreder, Edna, *Seven Psychologies* (New York: Appleton-Century-Crofts, 1933). [Chapter VI: "Functionalism and the University of Chicago," pp. 201–233, deals with the development of the new "functional" psychology which Dewey was developing during his years there.]

Larrabee, Harold Atkins, "John Dewey as Teacher," *School and Society,* LXXXVI, 10 October 1959, pp. 378–381. [An interesting discussion of Dewey's own pedagogy.]

McCaul, Robert L., "Dewey and the University of Chicago," I. July, 1894–March, 1902, *School and Society* (LXXXIX, 25 March 1961, pp. 152–157); II. April, 1902–May, 1903 (*Ibid.,* 8 April 1961, pp. 179–183); III. September, 1903–June, 1904 (*Ibid.,* 22 April 1961, pp. 202–206). [An invaluable description of academic politics. Many quotations from Dewey's letters.]

McCaul, Robert L., "Dewey's Chicago," *School Review,* LXVII, Summer, 1959, pp. 258–280. [Describes the city and its relation to the University in general and the education of teachers in particular.]

Mayhew, Katherine Camp, and Anna Camp Edwards, *The Dewey School: The Laboratory School of the University of Chicago 1896–1903* (New York: D. Appleton-Century Company, 1936). [A full, detailed and invaluable account of the Laboratory School and its underlying theory.]

Mead, George H., "The Philosophies of Royce, James, and Dewey in Their American Setting," *International Journal of Ethics* XL, January 1930, pp. 211–231. [An exposition of Dewey's views by an influential social psychologist who was Dewey's colleague in the Department of Philosophy in 1899.]

Parker, Franklin, "A Golden Age in American Education: Chicago in the 1890's," *School and Society,* 89, 25 March 1951, pp. 146–152.

White, Morton G., *The Origin of Dewey's Instrumentalism* (Columbia Studies in Philosophy, 4) (New York: Columbia University Press, 1943). [Discusses the basic philosophy developed by Dewey in his early career.]

Wirth, Arthur G., "John Dewey's Design for American Education: An Analysis of Aspects of His Work at the University of Chicago, 1894–1904," *History of Education Quarterly,* IV, pp. 83–106.

APPENDIX IV

THE ANNUAL REGISTER

IB. THE DEPARTMENT OF PEDAGOGY.

OFFICERS OF INSTRUCTION.

JOHN DEWEY, PH.D., *Head Professor of Philosophy.*
JULIA E. BUCKLEY, PH.D., *Associate Professor of Pedagogy.*
CHARLES H. THURBER, A.M., *Associate Professor of Pedagogy.*
WILBUR SAMUEL JACKMAN, A.B., *Lecturer in Pedagogy.*
MRS. ELLA FLAGG YOUNG, *Lecturer in Pedagogy.*

H. H. KINGSLEY, A. B., *Superintendent of Public Schools, Evanston, Ill.* (Summer Quarter '98).
CHARLES ALEXANDER McMURRY, PH.D., *Lecturer on Pedagogy* (Summer Quarter '98).
FRANK ADDISON MANNY, A.M., *Supervisor of Public Schools, Indianapolis, Ind.* (Summer Quarter '98).

In the University Elementary School.

GEORGIA BACON, S.B., *Principal.*
KATHERINE B. CAMP, S.B., *Director of Science and Domestic Economy.*
KATHERINE ANDREWS, A.B., *Science.*
ALTHEA HARMER, *Domestic Economy.*
IDA M. FURNISS, *Gymnastic Director.*
MAY TAYLOR, *Music.**
LORELY A. ASHLEMANN, *French.*
F. W. SMEDLEY, PH.B., *Manual Training.*

INTRODUCTORY.

It is the primary aim of the Department to train competent specialists for the broad and scientific treatment of educational problems. The

* Deceased.

courses provided for this end fall in the main under three heads: (1)
Courses in psychology and related work; (2) Courses in educational
theory; (3) Courses in the best methods of teaching the various branches.
Only courses of the second class are separately printed here. Courses
under (1) and (3) will be found under their respective departments.

It is believed that any profitable study of educational theory and
method presupposes a thorough grounding in psychological principles;
that a scientific treatment of educational problems demands as a pre-
requisite a familiarity with the methods and results of the modern study
of the development of intelligence; that an appreciation of the ultimate
ends of education requires that discipline in the estimate of values and
ideals which is afforded by ethics; and that a broad outlook is best gained
by an acquaintance with the history of human thought. It is expected,
therefore, that the courses in educational theory will be preceded by the
three Introductory Courses of the Department of Philosophy and that
advanced work in this department will be accompanied by further work
in the lines indicated above. In this connection attention is also called to
the related courses in biology, physiology, neurology and social science.

It is further believed that the theory of education, like that of logic,
has often suffered from failure to keep in touch with the actual research
of advancing science. The successful investigator and teacher of language or natural science should be capable of affording much positive
assistance regarding the methods of teaching those subjects, because of
the close relation existing between material and method, a point often ignored in a purely abstract pedagogy. Arrangements are, therefore, made
with other departments to offer courses in which special emphasis is laid
on the methodology of their respective subjects. In addition to this provision for instruction in the best methods for advanced work, an opportunity for scientific study of the organization of a well-balanced curriculum in the earlier grades is afforded by the organization of primary
instruction in a school already undertaken under the auspices of the
department. The main purpose of the school is to afford an opportunity
for testing and developing proper methods, and to gradually build up an
organized curriculum, in which history and science shall play large parts
from the beginning. Special attention is paid to the questions of correlation, and the proper place of manual training in primary education.

The facilities for observation in the primary school connected with the
Department of Pedagogy give opportunity for careful scientific observation and investigation. Opportunity for more extended observation will
also be afforded in secondary schools.

The department has a library well equipped with both books and current publications. A Museum is also forming. The leading educational
journals are on file.

COURSES OF INSTRUCTION

I. JUNIOR COLLEGE COURSES

40A, 41A. Household Art and
Science in Elementary Education.—This work is divided into
two parts. Five hours a week
will be given afternoons to

M = Minor course = a single course for six weeks. DM = Double Minor course = a
double course (two hours daily) for six weeks. Mj = Major course = a single course for
twelve weeks. DMj = Double Major course = a double course for twelve weeks.

technical work in cooking, sewing, etc., with a view to its use in school. In connection with this actual training, there will be discussion of the educational aims and methods of such work, especially as embodied in the scheme of graded household work undertaken in the school conducted by the department—this covering at present the first six grades. As this work is planned for strictly educational aims, its consideration involves attention to its connections with industrial and physical geography, number-work, simple chemical and physical facts involved, and nature study. This last includes not only study of raw-materials and products, but some observation of plants and animals from which foods, fabrics, etc., are derived.

The other side is implied in the above. It consists in observing the domestic work of the school, assisting in the same, observing related applications in history, geography, and science work. This will occupy about six hours a week—two hours counting for one of credit.

Autumn and Winter Quarters, '98–9; 4:00–6:00.

MISS HARMER.

(The Elementary School Building, 5412 Ellis av.)

40B, 41B.—The same as above, but occupying less time. It includes the afternoon technical work, but much less actual observation, and assisting forenoon.

2Mj. Autumn and Winter Quarters, '98–9.

MISS HARMER.

NOTE.—This class, being of a normal character, will be limited in numbers. In case more should apply than could be profitably accommodated, choice will be made from those whose past experience

II. SENIOR COLLEGE COURSES

1. Educational   Psychology.— This course will take up a number of psychological topics, such as attention and interest; habit, imagery, the training of the emotions and will; observation and reasoning power, and discuss them with especial reference to the methods of instruction and the subjects of the curriculum. In the latter connection psychology of language, number, manual construction and art will receive special attention.

M.   First Term, Summer Quarter, '98; 2:00.

DR. MOORE.

Mj.   Spring Quarter, '99; 2:00.

DR. MOORE.

NOTE.—This course in Spring Quarter will be accepted as substitute for Course 1 under IA: Department of Philosophy.

2. Method   in   Instruction.— Omitting the field of method in education in general, this course will take up the question of method in the arrangement of material for the recitation, and the conduct of the latter. Discussion will center about the formal steps of the Herbartians and will endeavor on the basis of elementary psychology and logic to apply principles regarding the normal movement of the mind to the problem of securing the maximum efficiency in instructing and learning.

M.   First Term, Summer Quarter, '98; 8:30.

HEAD PROFESSOR DEWEY.

and future plans make them most available. On this account it is desirable to communicate as early as possible, either by letter or in a personal interview, with Miss Harmer. Address, care department of Pedagogy. Attention is also called to Courses 42, 43, 44 in Sociology.

3. Special Methods.—A discussion of the selection and adaptation of materials in geography, history, literature and nature study in elementary instruction. The course will involve not only a discussion of principle, but presentation of suitable material.

M. First Term, Summer Quarter, '98; 11:00.

DR. C. A. McMURRY.

4. History of Education.—No attempt will be made in the direction of an exhaustive treatment. Typical phases will be selected with particular reference to the bearing they have had on the development of educational theory and practice.

M. First Term, Summer Quarter, '98; 12:00.

DR. C. A. McMURRY.

6. General Pedagogy.—Pedagogical principles developed along the line of physiological psychology.

Mj. Autumn Quarter, '98; 12:00.

ASSOCIATE PROFESSOR BULKLEY.

7. Principles of Education.

Mj. Winter Quarter, '99; 12:00.

ASSOCIATE PROFESSOR BULKLEY.

8. Great Educational Reformers. —Rousseau, Pestalozzi, Herbart.

Mj. Spring Quarter, '98; 12:00.

ASSOCIATE PROFESSOR BULKLEY.

29. Psychology Applied to Teaching.—Based upon actual observation in the public schools, reading and lectures. A consideration of the demand made by the developing mind at different stages of growth, as indicated by interest, and a study of the natural interrelations of the various subjects. Two hours a week school visitation, with written reports upon the same required.

Mj. Autumn Quarter, '98; Tues. and Fri., 4:00–6:00.

MR. W. S. JACKMAN.

30. Practical Pedagogy.—Preparation of lesson plans, school visitation, reading and lectures. Students are required to prepare and submit for criticism actual lesson plans embodying a rational correlation of subject-matter as determined by the natural interest of the mind at different stages of its development. School visitation with written reports two hours a week. (This course presupposes the work of the preceding quarter.)

Mj. Winter Quarter, '99; Tues. and Fri., 4:00–6:00.

MR. JACKMAN.

31. Evolution and History of Methods.—Reading, lectures, and school visitation. Relation of method to the individual and the school. Method as modified and determined by the relation of the school to the home and to the changing conditions of society. School visitation and written reports upon the same two hours a week. (This course presupposes the work of Courses 29 and 30.)

Mj. Spring Quarter, '99; Tues. and Fri., 4:00–6:00.

MR. JACKMAN.

32. A Study of the Parts of School Systems.—Kindergarten, Elementary, Secondary, etc.

Mj. Autumn Quarter, '98; Mon. and Thurs., 4:00–6:00.

MRS. YOUNG.

33. Positive and Negative Factors in Education.—Existing tendencies and influences which help and obstruct school work. This includes a study of normal and abnormal conditions as found in the child in the school system and in the social environment as related to education.

Mj. Winter Quarter, '99; Mon. and Thurs., 4:00–6:00.
MRS. YOUNG.

34. Fundamental Principles underlying Nineteenth Century Theories of Education.

Mj. Spring Quarter, '99; Mon. and Thurs., 4:00–6:00.
MRS. YOUNG.

III. GRADUATE COURSES

NOTE.—Course 5 is open to Senior College Students who have had sufficient preliminary training in psychology.

5. Genetic Study of Educational Theories.

Mj. Summer Quarter, '98; 12:00.
ASSOCIATE PROFESSOR BULKLEY.

NOTE.—This work in Pedagogy will be conducted along two lines: a) theoretical and historical, b) conferences upon practical questions conducted with the aid of reports on local school conditions, theses, and discussions.

10. General Related View of Modern German Pedagogy.—Educators from the Renaissance are each studied according to the following plan: (1) Biographical events with their special significance for later theory and practice. (2) The distinctive contribution of each individual to systematic Pedagogy. (3) Grouping or classification according to distinctive features into schools. (4) General survey in continuous subjects such as: (a) curriculum; (b) principles generally accepted; (c) theory of knowledge; (d) relation of pedagogic thought to the philosophy and psychology of the period; (e) development in ethical standards.

2Mj. Autumn and Winter Quarters.
ASSOCIATE PROFESSOR BULKLEY.
[Not to be given in '98–9.]

12. Seminar: Herbart.—His pedagogical principles will be related to his psychology and metaphysics.

Mj. Summer Quarter, '98; Thurs., 3:00–5:00.
ASSOCIATE PROFESSOR BULKLEY.

13. Seminar: Pestalozzi.—This will offer for more advanced students a consideration of the philosophic and social problems of the period covered by Pestalozzi's life and of the services he rendered to modern systematic pedagogy.

Mj. Autumn Quarter, '98; Tues., 4:00–6:00.
ASSOCIATE PROFESSOR BULKLEY.

14. Seminar: Froebel.—With present practical applications.

Mj. Winter Quarter, '99.
ASSOCIATE PROFESSOR BULKLEY.

15. Seminar: Spencer.—Herbert Spencer's *Education* with portions of the *Psychology* and *Data of Ethics*.

Mj. Spring Quarter, '98; Thurs., 3:00–5:00.
ASSOCIATE PROFESSOR BULKLEY.

16. Seminar: Comenius.—With present practical applications.

Mj. Winter Quarter.
ASSOCIATE PROFESSOR BULKLEY.
[Not to be given in '98–9.]

19. The Philosophy of Education. —This will discuss the end, nature, materials, and method of education. Under the topic of end, the various historic ideals will be discussed (humanistic, utilitarian, disciplinary, etc.) and their relations to one another on the basis of philosophic principles shown. Its nature will involve a discussion of the relation of education to social life on one side, and to the development of the individual on the other. The question of materials is that of the content of the curriculum and the educational values of the various studies, the criterion used being social. Method involves a discussion of the psychology of the process of learning, its relation to the subject-matter of the curriculum, the significance of construction and expression, of perception, image, and attention. The course will discuss general principles rather than details.

Mj. Winter Quarter, '99; 2:00.
HEAD PROFESSOR DEWEY.

23, 24, 25. Problems in Secondary Education.
3Mj. Autumn, Winter and Spring Quarters, '98–9; 4:00.
ASSOCIATE PROFESSOR THURBER.

27a. The School as an Organization.—Under this head will be taken up the internal and more mechanical aspects of school management and supervision.
First Half of First Term, Summer Quarter, '98; 3:00.
SUPERINTENDENT KINGSLEY.

27b. The School in its Relations to Society.—Under this head will be treated matters of school organization and administration in relation to community life, and the more distinctly pedagogical problems that arise with reference to selection and adaptation of subject-matter to social needs.
First Half of First Term, Summer Quarter, '98; 4:00.
SUPERINTENDENT KINGSLEY.

NOTE.—This work will continue for the first three weeks of the Summer Quarter. The student who completes both sections will receive credit for a Minor. Either may be taken separately, however, and in that case a Minor's credit may be made up by taking one of the courses 28a, 28b that follow in the next three weeks.

28a. Special Problems in School Administration. A discussion of practical questions arising in school administration and supervision. Especial attention will be paid to methods of dealing with children.
Second Half of First Term, Summer Quarter; '98; 3:00.
MR. MANNY.

28b. Social Aspects of the Curriculum.—This course will discuss some of the chief subjects of the curriculum from the standpoint of the social conditions of their origin and historical development and the place occupied by them at present in preparation for social life.
Second Half of First Term, Summer Quarter, '98; 4:00.
MR. MANNY.

NOTE.—These two courses are given for the last three weeks of the First Term, that is, from July 21 to August 12. Taken together they constitute a Minor; or they may be combined with the courses conducted by Superintendent Kingsley during the first three weeks; see 27a and 27b. 27a and 28a thus make a continuous course, and also 27b and 28b.

Related Courses in other Departments.

IV. HISTORY.

26. Teachers' Course in the History of Rome.
DM. First Term, Summer Quarter, '99; 11:00 and 12:00.
PROFESSOR GOODSPEED.

80. Teachers' Course in American History.
DM. First Term, Summer Quarter, '98; 11:00 and 12:00.
ASSISTANT PROFESSOR SPARKS.

VI. SOCIOLOGY AND ANTHROPOLOGY.

95. A Method of Applying Sociological Pedagogy to the Teaching of Economics in Secondary Schools.
M. First Term, Summer Quarter, '98; 12:00.
HENRY W. THURSTON.

98. The Social Mind and Education.
Mj. Spring Quarter, '99; 3:00.
ASSISTANT PROFESSOR VINCENT.

XII. THE LATIN LANGUAGE AND LITERATURE.

7. Cicero's *Letters.*
Mj. Spring Quarter, '99; 8:30.
PROFESSOR ABBOTT.

14. Cicero's *Letters.*
Mj. Summer Quarter, '98; 11:00.
PROFESSOR ABBOTT.

38B. Teachers' Training Course.
Mj. Autumn Quarter, '98; 11:00.
HEAD PROFESSOR HALE.

38C. Teachers' Training Course.
Mj. Summer Quarter, '98; 12.00.

First Term: Syntax of the Verb.
PROFESSOR WALKER.
Second Term: Virgil's *Æneid.*
MR. RAND.

XIV. GERMANIC LANGUAGES AND LITERATURES.

14A. Deutsche Aufsätze und Stilübungen.
DM. First Term, Summer Quarter, '98; 9:30 and 2.00.
Mj. Winter Quarter, '99; 11:00.
ASSOCIATE PROFESSOR CUTTING.

XV. ENGLISH LANGUAGE AND LITERATURE, AND RHETORIC.

12. The Teaching of Rhetoric and and English Composition in Schools and Colleges.
M. First Term, Summer Quarter, '98; 2:00.
Mj. Autumn Quarter, '98; 2:00.
ASSISTANT PROFESSOR HERRICK.

XVII. MATHEMATICS.

30. Conferences on Mathematical Pedagogy.
M. First Term, Summer Quarter; 4:00.
ASSISTANT PROFESSOR YOUNG.

XXI. GEOLOGY.

1a. Physiography.
M. First Term, Summer Quarter, '98; 2:00.
MR. GOODE.

1b. Field and Laboratory Course.
M. First Term, Summer Quarter, '98; afternoons.
PROFESSOR SALISBURY and MR. GOODE.

APPENDIX V

A MEMORANDUM BY PROFESSOR JOHN DEWEY TO
PRESIDENT WILLIAM RAINEY HARPER OF THE
UNIVERSITY OF CHICAGO ENTITLED "PLAN
FOR ORANGIZATION OF WORK IN A
FULLY EQUIPPED DEPARTMENT
OF PEDAGOGY"
January 6, 1897*

The various lines of work which are naturally included within the scope of a University Department of Pedagogy may be reduced to a few main heads. We have:

1. What may be termed for convenience, Educational Physics and Physiology, dealing with the whole plant of educational work and the adaptation of that to the physical being and welfare of the pupils.

2. Educational Sociology which concerns itself with the organization and administration of the educational system, both in relation to other social conditions and institutions and in its own external mechanism and workings.

3. Educational Psychology which deals with all matters appertaining to the adaptation of the school resources and the subject matter of the curriculum to the child. Its problem is how, out of the plant and school system described above, to get the maximum of result from the standpoint of the individual pupils.

4. We have the subject matter of general pedagogy occupying itself with the theorical considerations regarding the nature, ends and aims of educational work and the intellectual organization of curriculum and methods corresponding thereto.

5. Educational History dealing both with the systems which have actually obtained at various times and in various countries, and also with the development of the theory of education as such.

I   Educational Physics and Physiology.

1. School buildings and grounds; city and country; heating, lighting, ventilation, and plumbing; laboratories; school fur-

* Unpublished. The memorandum is preserved in the Archives of the University of Chicago.

nishings, desks, blackboards, etc.; school decoration and aesthetics; all this to be inclusive from the Kindergarten to the University. Besides giving courses, the person in charge of this work would be responsible for the collection of plans, drawings, photographs, etc., from all available sources. Summaries should be given in original investigation along these lines, the construction of proper plans, etc. The work should look ultimately to co-operation with school boards in furnishing information upon these points, copies of plans, etc.

2. School Hygiene. The adaptation of the matters mentioned above to the health of children, including the investigation of the normal and abnormal conditions of the sense of the muscular system in relation to the physical conditions of school work. The nervous and other diseases of children so far as they act and react upon the work of education, should be included, as also the theory of physical exercise and culture in relation to health. The person in charge of such a course ought to be, if not a physician, one who has had a thorough training in physiology and is in close contact with physicians. The seminar work would involve an examination of the actual school buildings from the standpoint of all their sanitary arrangements. On the practical side there would be such cooperation as occasion might suggest with the City Board of Health and with physicians and others interested. Through the museum and library there should also be formed here a sort of bureau of information to which those engaged in actual school administration might apply.

II Educational Sociology.

1. Systems of education in their relation to political, economic, religious and intellectual conditions of society, involving such things as a comparative study of the various European systems in their special adaptation to their surroundings and a study of the various types of the systems found in this country, in their adaptation to their local environments. It would also involve a study of industrial, technical and professional education from the same standpoint.

2. Internal School Organization and Management. This would include a study of the business side; the raising and expenditure of money for school purposes and the proper divisions of labor involved there. It would take up the functions of school boards: the Superintendent, Supervisors, Principals, etc., and their relations to each other. The question of the methods of preparing teachers for their work and so on, would come under survey also. In fact all the problems which have to deal with the actual administration of the school system. The advanced work would consist in an actual examination of systems of Chicago and other cities near enough to be personally investigated with a view of discovering both the methods actually pursued, the defects and the suggesting of remedies.

III   Educational Psychology.

1. Child study, both on the side of its methods and the undertaking of actual work, should receive attention.

2. Course or courses should be given in Psychology as applied to instruction. The question of methods in relation to the learning process of the mind.

IV   General Pedagogy.   This is the head which receives most attention, and in some cases, exclusive attention, in the existing status of Pedagogy in colleges. It deals with the philosophy of education as such and the question of educational aims and means. Beside this general work it should include a more special and detailed study of the school curriculum; of the studies actually pursued in the schools, of their respective values and relations to each other; also a study of the various sub-divisions of the educational system, elementary, secondary, and higher, from the standpoint of their curriculum and their methods.

V   Education History.

1. The history of educational systems as actually organized, for example, the Chinese, Greek, Roman, Medieval; the history of the development of the modern common school system; the history of the development of the curriculum. This is the historical counterpart of what is treated theoretically in III.

2. The history of the theoretical discussion of educational matters. The study of educational classics from Plato down. The study of the epochs of educational reform and the writings which influenced them; the relation of educational thought to philosophical, ethical and religious thought; a consideration of educational theories in their relation to the general culture and intellectual atmosphere of the times.

The above takes up the work of the department from the standpoint of its logical sub-division. From another point of view it may be said that at least four courses should be given as undergraduate courses. These four are general in character and to be taken by those interested in education, apart from specialization along any particular line.

1. The history of educational doctrine.

2. Educational psychology on its theoretical side.

3. Child study.

4. A synoptic view of school organization; the resources of the school; their administration; the chief contemporary problems in educational administration.

In the above nothing has been said about work in the actual training of teachers as it is assumed that for the most part, at least at the outset, the whole stress must be thrown upon the culture side rather than upon the professional. There are two phases, however, of training work whose comparatively speedy inauguration is worthy of consideration.

I. When the Manual Training School is definitely annexed to the University, and its location changed so as to be sufficiently in close contact with University work, it would be highly desirable to have it include a special course for training teachers in the direction of manual training. The introduction of this line of work in the public schools is hindered now more by the lack of properly trained teachers than by any other one thing, as public opinion in general is now decidedly in favor of it. The New York Training School for teachers is the only college of rank now making a specialty of this matter.

III. We have already begun to have applications for teachers who are trained in the methods in use in our University Primary School. As soon as means are sufficient to give us a good supervising principal (a thing very much needed in itself) we should aim at securing a person who should be able to take oversight of and give direction and criticism to a number of assistants who should, at the same time, be taking theoretical work in the University. Such a move would be economical in more ways than one as it would enable us to derive a revenue from our assistants instead of having to pay anything for their services.   R. S.

John Dewey

INDEX OF NAMES
REFERRED TO IN THE TEXT

JOHN DEWEY, *who was born in 1859 and died in 1952, was one of the most outstanding world philosophers.* HUMAN NATURE AND CONDUCT; JOHN DEWEY ON EDUCATION; *and* INTELLIGENCE IN THE MODERN WORLD, *a comprehensive selection from his lifework, are available in The Modern Library.*

REGINALD D. ARCHAMBAULT *attended Brown, Wesleyan and Harvard, where he received his doctorate in the Philosophy of Education. He has taught the philosophy of education at Wesleyan, Grinnell and Brown, where he is now Associate Director of the Master of Arts in Teaching Program. Professor Archambault has written widely on education and on John Dewey in particular. He is the editor of* PHILOSOPHICAL ANALYSIS AND EDUCATION; DEWEY ON EDUCATION: APPRAISALS; *and the definitive collection of Dewey's work in educational theory,* JOHN DEWEY ON EDUCATION, *in The Modern Library.*